Anne Sexton

A Self-Portrait in Letters

By Anne Sexton:

To Bedlam and Part Way Back   1960
All My Pretty Ones   1962
Live or Die   1966
Love Poems   1969
Transformations   1971
The Book of Folly   1972
The Death Notebooks   1974
The Awful Rowing Toward God   1975
45 Mercy Street   1976

Anne Sexton

A Self-Portrait in Letters

Edited by
Linda Gray Sexton and Lois Ames

Illustrated with Photographs

Houghton Mifflin Company
Boston New York London

The editors are grateful to Maxine Kumin, Stanley Kunitz, Robert Lowell, and Suzanne Rioff for permission to print excerpts from letters by each of them.

Poems from ALL MY PRETTY ONES (copyright © 1961, 1962 by Anne Sexton), LIVE OR DIE (copyright © 1966 by Anne Sexton), and TO BEDLAM AND PART WAY BACK (copyright © 1960 by Anne Sexton) are reprinted by permission of Houghton Mifflin Company. "The Reading" is reprinted by permission of the CHRISTIAN SCIENCE MONITOR.

Library of Congress Cataloging-in-Publication Data
Sexton, Anne.
   Anne Sexton: a self-portrait in letters.
   Includes index.
   1. Sexton, Anne — Correspondence. 2. Poets,
American — 20th century — Correspondence.
I. Sexton, Linda Gray, 1953–   II. Ames, Lois.
PS3537.E915Z53 1977 816'.5'4 77-21355
ISBN 0-395-63118-1 ISBN 0-395-62880-6 (pbk.)

Printed in the United States of America

AGM 10 9 8 7 6 5 4 3 2 1

FOR ANNE —

*and for those who have lived with her words,
in thanks for the joy and wisdom she brought
to so many*

Acknowledgments

We are grateful for the generosity of those who shared their time, material, advice, or recollections of Anne Sexton: Bruce Berlind, Elizabeth Bishop, Julie Joslyn Brown, Michael Dennis Browne, Alfred C. Cancelleri, Bev Chaney, Anne Clarke, Robert Clawson, Carol Dine, Stella Easland, Elizabeth Fuller, Arthur Furst, Charles Ghigna, Linda Glick, Dorianne Goetz, Donald Hall, Wynn Handman, David Harris, Joyce Hartman, Anthony Hecht, Anne Hussey, Barbara Kane, Galway Kinnell, Carolyn Kizer, Stanley Kunitz, Maryel Locke, Deborah London, Robert Lowell, Craig Lucas, the Rev. Arthur MacGillivray (S.J.), J. D. McClatchy, Charles Maryan, Rollie McKenna, Nolan Miller, Frederick Morgan, Rose Fillmore Morgan, Joan Nemser, Louise Noble, Joan Norris, Tillie Olsen, Joseph Parisi, Brooke Peirce, Eugenia Plunkett, Ted Polumbaum, A. Poulin, Jr., Joan Reischauer, Suzanne Rioff, Ellin Sarot, Marian Seldes, Alice Smith, W. D. Snodgrass, Jon Stallworthy, George Starbuck, Belinda Straight, Mark Strand, Brian Sweeney, Nancy Talbott, Blanche Harvey Taylor, Deborah Trustman, Tom Victor, Randall Warner, Ruth Whitman, and C. K. Williams.

We are especially indebted to Dr. Howard Gotlieb, director of the Boston University Library Special Collections. The staff of Special Collections was both cheerful and indispensable: Paul Guay, Margaret Goostray, Douglas MacDonald, Charles Niles, Carolyn Sadler, and Vita Widershien.

In addition, there are special people to whom we owe a deep and outstanding debt:

Alfred Muller Sexton II who generously opened his heart to the past.

Wilhelmine Sexton Morse who gave a mother's gift.

Joyce Ladd Sexton for her buoyant spirit. Her mother would be proud.

Louise and Loring Conant for food, warm talk, and a fire on the hearth.

Maxine Kumin, keeper of the gate for seventeen years.

Anne Clarke who gave laughter, wisdom, and encouragement.

Claire S. Degener and Sterling Lord who saw the book whole from its inception.

Haskell Kassler and Larry Levinson, whose wit and skill guided us past legal morasses.

Richard McAdoo, whose solid presence urged us on.

Gail Stewart, our copy editor, who has the eye of a hawk and a sharp green pencil.

Kathleen and Paul Walker for their good humor and steadying hands.

Dr. Stanley King, for he built a bridge across the dark.

Polly Williams Zarella and her smile. She was with us from the beginning, exercising a copy editor's eye as she graciously performed each mundane chore.

Linda Gray Sexton thanks John Freund for the long hours he has spent on her part of this book. For patience, for support, for the silence of love.

Lois Ames thanks her children, Liz and Adam, for whom Anne was a special friend: they have given me the gift of time and kept courage on our doorstep.

Above all, for his courage, perception, and friendship, we thank our editor, Jonathan Galassi.

L.G.S.
L.A.

Foreword

In 1987, I received with sadness the news that *Anne Sexton: A Self-Portrait in Letters* was to go out of print. My regret stemmed not only from the fact that I had worked hard on *Self-Portrait*, my first book, during the tumultuous time immediately following my mother's death, but also from my belief that the book gave the best of my mother to her reading public. The letters capture the spirit of her humor, her wit, her abundance; in revealing the heart's flow of her life through these letters, I had also begun to shape the course of my own life and writing career. Thus, *Self-Portrait* was important to us both. To know that the book would no longer be available felt as if my mother — and my connection to her — was dying once again.

Anne Sexton made me her literary executor on my twenty-first birthday; many uncomfortable decisions and tasks fell to me after she killed herself a few months later, in October of 1974. When I was first approached by Houghton Mifflin to edit a volume of her letters, shortly after her suicide, I jumped at the chance. I was in my senior year at Harvard as an English literature major and had no idea of how to proceed next. Before me I could see only the vast sea of Mother's work and the job of taking care of it. Quickly I began to rely on several key people: Cindy Degener and Sterling Lord, Mother's agents; Jonathan Galassi, Mother's editor at Houghton Mifflin; and Lois Ames, one of Mother's best friends, and the person who was to help guide me through the process of organizing the book. All of us conceived of *Self-Portrait* as a treasure map to Anne Sexton's life for a period in which no biography, or biographical material, would be publicly available for years to come.

Though initially excited by the project, I soon realized that I had had no concept of what it entailed. I spent months working from nine to five, five days a week, in the Boston University library, sorting and reading through all the correspondence Mother had placed there on temporary loan. The special collections library at B.U. was a glass cubicle where the staff could watch those who perused the collections. Under their scrutiny I opened box after box of staggeringly personal material — diaries, journals, notes to Mother's psychiatrist, the correspondence of a lifetime from someone who kept literally everything, including high school scrapbooks and grammar school report cards. I struggled to conceal my reactions as I worked my way through my mother's life, hiding my face in the file folders to seek privacy where there was no privacy to be had.

I spent more hours and many more months working with the files of correspondence and manuscript left in her house at the time of her death. The process was lonely and painful beyond description. I had often been my mother's confidante for secrets inappropriate for a daughter's ears, but this was worse, an invasion of the darkest recesses of the soul. I read of her childhood and the scorched emotions — her perception of having been unloved, unwanted, defective — that haunted her throughout her days. I read of my own childhood, of a mother — my mother — who was incapable of mothering and capable of abuse, crippled by her illness, her immaturity, her own emptiness. I read of her infidelities to my father, to our family. I read of her elation and desperation, her vibrant hates and loves, her burgeoning sense of self. I read of her poetry, slowly raising its voice to lift her beyond herself. I cried. Through her words she resurrected herself; she was all too real. There had been little innocence left for me. Now there was none.

Then came organizing the letters, making selections, editing them, and writing introductions to establish chronology and fill in detail. By the time *Self-Portrait* was in galleys, I no longer saw my mother as my mother; she belonged to the world, as unreal to me, as mythic, as an actress on the stage.

Perhaps putting *Self-Portrait* into galleys and then out into the world was what enabled and motivated me at last to pull the box that held my mother's ashes from its resting place at the top of my father's closet and take it to the cemetery to arrange for burial. I was more than ready to let her go — perhaps, by now, even eager. The day we were scheduled to go to the family plot was sunny, a late summer morning in New England. The year was 1977, three years after Mother's death. My sister and I, my father and his mother, all looked at one another with anxiety. We stood on that grassy knoll alone, except for the plain cardboard box, which, placed by some cemetery official on the ground in front of us and wrapped in brown paper, assumed the weight of the body. It had taken both time and grief to force us to this spot; once there, we did not know what to do. Mother waited in her box; the small hole in the earth waited to receive her. Who would take her there? There was no funeral director to lead us, no minister to fill up the silence with the comfort of words.

That day was a metaphor, a recapitulation, of all the simple steps we had been trying to take ever since her suicide. More than anything else, I longed for freedom, for release, for forward motion. I picked up all that physically remained of my mother. My sister moved to my side, and together we put the box down into the small dark hole in the earth. Joining hands, we began to cry. For my family, a measure of emotional closure on my mother's tortured life had been achieved. It had taken us three years, but she had at last been buried — laid, as they say, to rest. I ought to have known better.

Anne Sexton: A Self-Portrait in Letters was published that autumn to wide acclaim. I spent some time on a publicity tour, giving both interviews and readings from the book. Over and over I read the letter most widely requested, the one written to "the forty-year-old Linda," which closes this volume. All of this took an inevitable toll: my own identity began to falter under the pressure of maintaining my mother's. Gradually I began to refuse requests to read from either the poetry or the letters, acknowledging at last that I had to create a distinction between my life and hers. To establish the necessary distance, I undertook two separate searches, both of which freed me from some of my responsibility to her life and work.

The first of these was to find an appropriate biographer — specifically, someone who had not known Anne Sexton and who could be as objective as possible. The second was to find an appropriate university library and settle her papers, letters, manuscripts, and worksheets into a permanent archive. These tasks proved to be just about as easy to accomplish as editing *Self-Portrait* had been.

Before her suicide at age forty-five, my mother had prepared carefully, making her wishes about nearly everything explicit. She instructed me that her papers, manuscripts, and correspondence were to be placed as a whole in a worthy university library, even though it might be more lucrative to sell off individual items. Once I had located a library interested in the collection, I faced the problem of creating an inventory of all the letters, manuscripts, journals, and paraphernalia, as well as deciding which books from her personal library were to go. This not inconsiderable project took months more of my full attention. When finally assembled, all the material filled more than forty large storage cartons, each hand-packed, waterproofed, and sealed by my husband and me. In loads of five we carted them to the local post office, where they were weighed, measured, and summarily rejected. It appeared we had used the wrong sort of tape for boxes that were to be heavily insured. Eventually we tried three kinds of tape, all of which the post office rejected; only a desperate display of tears right before noon closing on a Saturday at last convinced the postmistress to accept my precious burden.

When I sent the Anne Sexton archives to the Harry Ransom Humanities Research Center at the University of Texas — home to a bounty of important modern poetry collections — I included Mother's typewriter, a pair of her reading glasses, many of the books in her library, a few used checkbook registers, her letter opener, some knickknacks from her desk. She had not instructed me to do this, but I knew the library would most likely set up exhibits of her work, and these personal items would enrich the collection. Much of this was hard to part with.

No decision was quite as difficult as deciding the fate of certain items that were going to be painful for family members, or that could hurt others still living. I had excluded them from *Self-Portrait*, but there remained the question of what, ultimately, to do with them. This difficulty I reconciled by plac-

ing them at Texas under the proviso that they be "restricted"
— accessible to no one except scholars I approved, until well
after the year 2000. In this part of the archives I placed love letters
to and from my mother, private papers regarding my parents'
divorce, and poetry she did not wish to be published, from the
early stage of her career. Later I decided to allow Diane
Middlebrook to use these materials as a source for a literary
biography, which was quite different from making them available by publishing them verbatim.

The one part of the collection — and it was of major importance — that did not go into *Self-Portrait* or the archives at the
University of Texas was the correspondence between my mother
and the poet James Wright. My mother and Wright had engaged
in a fair amount of passion via post for several years before they
began an actual love affair, and these letters contained many long
critiques of the poetry both were writing at the time. The letters would have been a cornerstone of both *Self-Portrait* and the
archives, and in an addendum to her will, my mother had directed me to find them in the home of a close friend. Though
the friend did have a suitcase full of erotic letters to and from
another man, dating from the period following my parents' divorce — and these did go into the restricted collection — the
Wright letters were not among them. I could not understand how
these letters, which my mother had entrusted so specifically to
a close friend, could have disappeared. I searched for them for
the next ten years, asking other friends and colleagues of my
mother's, tracking false leads, and exploring her house from top
to bottom. I have never found them.

In 1980, in the midst of writing *Rituals*, my first novel, which
dealt with a young woman's attempt to repress her sorrow over
her mother's death, I asked Diane Middlebrook, a professor at
Stanford University who had written about Anne Sexton's poetry with impressive skill and insight, to be my mother's biographer. And so it came to be that I no longer carried the weight
of Mother's life — her secrets, her passions, her history — alone.
There was relief in this new companionship, and to my pleasure, Diane found herself relying heavily on *Self-Portrait* for both
chronology and clarification; the book was a visual footprint of
Anne Sexton's life. As Diane wrote to me in 1987, "It's a good

thing (for me) that it was you who sorted the letters and journals and had already lifted a lot of rocks with some creepy things
under them."

During this time two separate evolutions began to take place.
I continued my primary work as a novelist, writing *Mirror
Images* (1985) to give vent to my feelings — in fictional disguise
— about what it was like to be too closely intertwined with a
strong, dependent mother; at the same time, my never-ending
tasks as literary executor grew more complicated. I answered
fan letters from those grateful for both the poetry and especially
Self-Portrait; I managed Anne Sexton's estate and made decisions about when the poetry could be reprinted, which dramatic
productions to support, when to publish a *Collected Poems* and
a *Selected Poems;* I also aided Diane, behind the scenes. This
aid included the decision that proved to be highly controversial
years later: I allowed her to listen to and quote from tape recordings of my mother's psychiatric sessions, even though, to
be responsible, I too had to study the transcripts of those taped
sessions — a job I would have been delighted to avoid. Meanwhile, I had two sons, learned how difficult it is to be a good
parent, and forgave my mother a great deal. I wrote my third
novel, *Points of Light,* from a mother's, rather than a daughter's,
point of view.

When it became clear that *Self-Portrait* was to go out of print,
Diane and I shared our distress and resolved that the biography
must be finished and available as soon as possible, because
without *Self-Portrait,* no chronology of the life would be available at all. We could not foresee that it would take another five
years for the biography to be in the bookstores and that there
would be repeated and frustrating requests from scholars and
fans alike to reprint the letters.

One episode in my mother's life especially perturbed me
throughout the process of working on *Self-Portrait* and then later,
as I watched Diane Middlebrook develop her material. My sense
of agitation increased as the publication date for the biography
approached: now I had to confront this ugly subject with the
perspective of an additional ten years.

I had known about my mother's affair with her second psy-
chotherapist long before beginning the research for *Self-Por-*

trait. My outrage did not awaken, however, until I read the love letters and poetry between the two of them, and until I learned that she (and my father) had paid for each and every therapy session, despite the fact that the couch in this particular doctor's office was not being used for analysis. Later, on reading the foreword to the biography, written by Martin Orne, my mother's first major psychiatrist, I realized that this unethical breach of the analytic contract might have contributed to the downward spiral that led to my mother's death.

I had gone out of my way to protect this doctor while editing *Self-Portrait* by creating a pseudonym for him. Diane also concealed his identity in *Anne Sexton: A Biography*. (I used the name Samuel Deitz, while Diane chose Ollie Zweizung: Ollie after an infamous Oliver of the eighties, and Zweizung meaning "two-tongued" in German.) At the time I protected him, I believed that his relationship with my mother was germane to any complete study of her life, but that his name was not. As I read Martin Orne's foreword, I wondered who had been served by such protection. I had been angry about this affair for years, about what it had done to the relationship between my parents, and about the pain it had caused my father. For the first time I realized that the primary disservice was to my mother, and that her suicide might be linked to it. Since then, I have been troubled by feeling that I should make a formal complaint about this therapist, so there can be no possibility that he will repeat this conduct with another patient. The masquerade continues in this edition of *Self-Portrait*.

When *Self-Portrait* first went to press, there were other, more worthy people who requested protection. Anne Wilder, one of my mother's good friends and confidantes, had insisted that her name be changed. When she read the galley proofs in 1977, she was furious that though she had been given a pseudonym, other factors that she felt might identify her had been left intact. Only a lengthy, soothing phone call late at night prevented her from threatening last-minute action against the estate. Ironically, by the time Diane described the Wilder-Sexton friendship in the biography, Anne Wilder had found the courage to allow her real name to be used and also to make clear the erotic as well as the platonic nature of their relationship. Despite this revelation, Anne

Wilder remains Anne Clarke in this volume of *Self-Portrait*, since I felt the book should be reprinted as it was originally. I salute her fortitude, in memoriam.

I am too far away today to go back to that cemetery hillside in Massachusetts where my mother is buried. Yet I would like to return there now, maybe just for an hour, to put my hand on the face of the granite marker and remember the woman who happened to be my mother but who was first and foremost a *poet*. It comes as a shock to realize that I have nearly arrived at that point in my life of which my mother spoke when she addressed her letter to me as "the forty-year-old Linda." That was in 1969; she herself had just turned forty, and as usual, she was thinking of her own death. "Talk to my poems," she reminded me, "and talk to your heart — I'm in both: if you need me."

In her poems, in my heart, in the heart of all those she touched with her life and work. And yes, with great joy, once again in her letters.

L.G.S.
October 29, 1991

Contents

Illustrations

Prologue

Young

1928–1957

A thousand doors ago
when I was a lonely kid
in a big house with four
garages and it was summer
as long as I could remember,
I lay on the lawn at night,
clover wrinkling under me,
the wise stars bedding over me,
my mother's window a funnel
of yellow heat running out,
my father's window, half shut,
an eye where sleepers pass,
and the boards of the house
were smooth and white as wax
and probably a million leaves
sailed on their strange stalks
as the crickets ticked together
and I, in my brand new body,
which was not a woman's yet,
told the stars my questions
and thought God could really see
the heat and the painted light,
elbows, knees, dreams, goodnight.

"Young"
from ALL MY PRETTY ONES

Anne Sexton smiles out of childhood snapshots and portraits, but even so, her large green eyes convey the pain she would later put into words. When she grew older, she described herself as "a girl who was meant to be a boy, the unwanted third daughter"; her memories were of a childhood studded with physical and mental abuse. Yet her older sister Blanche saw Anne as a "much-loved child, over-indulged — the center of attention." Whatever the reality, an early sense of rejection was to haunt Anne throughout her life and shaped much of her poetry.

She was born Anne Gray Harvey on November 9, 1928, in Newton, Massachusetts, to a family which had thrived in New England since the 1600s. Having begun as middle-class merchants and farmers after their emigration from Britain, her ancestors had attained wealth and prominence by the early 1800s: Nelson Dingley, Anne's maternal great-uncle, was speaker of the Maine House of Representatives and governor of Maine; her maternal grandfather, Arthur Gray Staples, served as editor-in-chief of the *Lewiston Evening Journal*, one of Maine's largest newspapers, and published several books of his own essays.

Mary Gray Staples Harvey, Anne's mother, was born in 1902 in Auburn, Maine. She aspired to a literary career, attending Wellesley College, but her plans were cut short when she married Ralph Churchill Harvey in 1922. Born in 1900 to an upper-middle-class family in Chelsea, Massachusetts, he was a self-confident, handsome young businessman. His father was president of the Wellesley National Bank. Ralph Harvey attempted to enlist during World War I, but the army sent him home when they discovered he was only sixteen. After finishing high school, he began in the woolen business as sample boy, the lowest possible position. However, as the business boomed with wartime manufacture of uniforms and blankets, he rapidly advanced, soon becoming a road salesman. Shortly thereafter his sizable commissions enabled him to take on a partner and establish a business of his own. By the late 1930s, the R. C. Harvey Company was among the most respected woolen firms in Boston, and the onset of World War II capped its growth and development.

In 1923, a year after their marriage, the Harveys' first child, Jane, was born; Blanche followed in 1925 and Anne in 1928. The family first lived in Cambridge, moving later to Wellesley and then Weston. Anne's happy memories centered on Squirrel Island, near Boothbay Harbor, Maine, where the Dingley, Staples, and Harvey clan summered in seven large five-story "cottages." Built atop the shoreline granite with the wind at their back, these summer mansions were anchored into the rock by huge chains. The family lived skin to skin with the sea. From Arthur Gray Staples' study in the "Aerie" the only view that met the eye was one rolling wave after another. Here on the island they built a library and organized their own literary magazine, *Squirrelana*.

The Harvey residence in Weston was equally spacious. The new house glinted with huge windows and a long terraced green lawn spread from the corner of the fourth garage down to the very edge of the street. Its four stories were complete with maids', cook's, and butler's quarters. Here Anne grew up.

Despite her remembered unhappiness, there were moments of joy which she later tried to recreate for her own children. On Christmas, the Harvey children would wake at five in the morning and run to the bedroom window searching for Santa's sleigh. Overhead Anne's great-aunts jingled long strings of sleighbells and stomped through the attic in oversize galoshes, pretending to be reindeer. Her father, in his Abercrombie and Fitch Santa Claus suit, white mohair glued to his eyebrows and chin, stormed through the darkened house booming, "Ho, ho, ho, Merry Christmas!" The children raced through the early morning cold into the brightly lit living room, where aunts, uncles, cousins, and servants gathered around a huge balsam tree sparkling with candles and ornaments. Later, after the opening of presents, came Christmas dinner: silver platters heaped with cold lobster and shrimp were followed by rare roast beef, turkey, and floating island pudding. To end the day, the large family, strong in its traditions, held hands in a swaying circle and sang its own Christmas song like a hymn: "Christmas bells, Christmas trees / Christmas music on the breeze / Merry, Merry Christmas everywhere / Cheerily it ringeth through the air."

But Christmas never lasted long enough. Anne was a demanding child. She felt safest on home territory, and insisted that friends come to her house to play. "It was hard to be Anne's friend," Blanche recalls, "all of her followers were of the slave variety." Even at this early age, she created her own dramatic works and cast herself in the starring roles. Often a source of family irritation, she was forever leaping from room to room with one purpose in mind — to be noticed. Her parents threw up their hands at Anne's pranks. As she whirled through the house like a small dervish, the maid despaired of keeping her clean or tidy; the hems in her dresses mysteriously unraveled five minutes after she put them on. Constantly defying adult authority, she ate cake in her bedroom, threw rotten apples at the ceiling, and rummaged through Blanche's dresser drawers in secret. Once she kidnapped one of her more docile friends and hid her in the bedroom closet overnight until a distraught mother telephoned in search of her lost child. Years later, Anne would describe tearing up Jane's birthday five-dollar bill in a fit of jealousy; on this occasion Ralph Harvey punished her with his riding crop.

Her recollections often centered on pain and physical humiliation. "Cripples and Other Stories" [LD] was explicit about her sense of shame and the conflicting messages she received from mother and father:

> *Disgusted, mother put me*
> *on the potty. She was good at this.*
> *My father was fat on scotch.*
> *It leaked from every orifice.*
>
> *Oh the enemas of childhood,*
> *reeking of outhouses and shame!*
> *Yet you rock me in your arms*
> *and whisper my nickname.*

What Anne could not share with her parents or sisters, she discussed with her "Nana." A spinster and retired newspaper editor, Anna Ladd Dingley had visited the Harveys throughout Anne's childhood, and she became the gentle confidante of her great-niece's early years. Anna and her namesake talked together and napped together under the blue blanket embroidered with Anna Ladd's initials. This close friendship ended when "Nana" lapsed into senility and was carried by ambulance to a nursing home. Anne found the loss devastating.

At school she was beset with further problems. Anne's description of her early education is typically deprecatory: "I went to Wellesley public schools, then to private schools, then back to public. By the third grade my parents were told to give up on me. I'd never learn anything." When she reached fifth grade, the school insisted that she repeat the year and she did. But the loss of familiar schoolmates left her feeling more isolated and unappreciated.

At one point, her teachers and the school authorities urged Anne's parents to get psychiatric treatment for her. When the Harveys indicated their reluctance to embark upon such a threatening course, the school warned them that Anne might experience emotional problems later in life. Mary and Ralph Harvey decided to wait.

In adolescence, Anne's disobedience developed into open rebellion. Constantly seeking love and approval, she turned to her girlfriends for support and to her many boyfriends for adoration. Determined to be a seductress, she practiced kissing — using her full-length mirror as a model. With an arm encircling the bedroom door, she took her own reflection into a deep and passionate embrace. In snapshots taken between 1940 and 1948 a beautiful young girl poses in fashionable and even provocative clothing; Anne's flare for the dramatic had by now become a carefully cultivated style. Friends report that she dominated the dancing assemblies and cotillions: "The boys flocked to her like moths to a flame and the rest of us were left standing." With the other girls dressed in demure tulle, Anne blazed across the dance floor in form-fitting red satin.

Her scrapbooks are filled with literally hundreds of letters from love-struck boys; the pages bulge with pressed orchids and dance cards. It is indicative of her early sense of self that even then she carefully saved her memorabilia. Yet this popular girl would later describe herself to her children as an awkward, ugly teenager: "The boys called me Old Bag of Bones because I was so skinny."

She had little patience for studying; a precocious, headstrong adolescent, she passed the time in math class by writing flirtatious notes to boys. Her classmates remember her as happy, vivacious, and popular, but underneath, she later claimed, lurked exquisite pain which found an outlet in her role as the class rogue, one who laughingly braved all authority. Although her carelessness and lack of attention were the qualities most often mentioned by her various teachers, many of her report cards remarked on her verbal ability and intellectual agility as well.

Very few of her letters survive from this period, but one, probably never sent, is revealing. At sixteen, Anne and her sister had spent a summer on a dude ranch in the West. As always there were boys to entice. But for once Anne met her match: a young man as ruthless in affairs of the heart as she was. However, she accomplished revenge in this undated letter.

Dear Torgie,

I promised you last night that I would write you just what I was thinking. I had not intended to do this; however, I felt so sorry for you that decided you better have the truth.

[several words missing here] not love me in the slightest;

JUNIOR - SENIOR HIGH SCHOOL, WELLESLEY

Name.... *Harvey, Anne L.* .... H. R. No. *307*

Teacher.... *J. Roy Newton* .... Grade. *10*

Subject.... *American Literature* .... Period. *1*

Marking Period	1	2	3	4	Yr's. Mark	SENIOR HIGH CREDITS
Achievement	C	B	B	C	C	5
Effort	F	G	G	G		

SEE OTHER SIDE FOR EXPLANATION OF THE MARKS

A Description of the Student's Work Habits

HOMEWORK

my

1	2	3	4	
✓	✓	✓	✓	Thorough, prompt preparation.
				Assignments sometimes late.
				Preparation seriously neglected.

WRITTEN WORK

			✓	Legible and well organized.
	✓	✓		Legible but not well organized.
✓				Careless; untidy. *to some extent, shows improvement*

TEST RESULTS

	✓	✓		Consistently high.
✓			✓	Uneven; usually fair.
				Habitually low.

PARTICIPATION IN CLASS

✓	✓		✓	Worthwhile contribution to discussions.
		✓		Passive listening; occasional contributions.
				Irrelevant remarks.

USE OF TIME

✓				Efficient direction of own work.
	✓	✓	✓	Effective response to direction and criticism.
				Time wasted; directions not followed.

ATTENTION IN CLASS

✓	✓			Alert response to direction and discussion.
		✓	✓	Occasional inattentiveness.
				Marked lack of concentration.

CONDUCT

✓			✓	Self-control well developed.
	✓			Correction occasionally required.
				Correction frequently required.

See other side

however, upon thinking it over, I wouldn't marry you even if you had $100,000,000.

Undoubtedly, Torgie, your dislike for me has now reached great heights. I have proved so little and yet a great deal in this so-called play. I started it in order to prove my abilities as an actress. Perhaps at the same time I have proved to you that someone with mercenary intentions will invariably receive the same treatment. I hope that in the future you will change your philosophy, expressed by "No one or nothing stands in the way of the mighty Torginson and what he wants." You think you are a gentleman with your effect of polished clothes and mannerisms, but a true gentleman is one that has a kind and humble heart. You may wonder at my saying this for my actions have not displayed me in a very flattering light. But you do not know me, Torgie, except to realize I have a perverse enough character to be able to show your true inferiority — in retrospect to sincere people. It is too bad, Torgie, that you know the price of everything and the value of nothing. At any rate, there have been a lot of laughs and it has been great fun co-starring with you in our little play, "There are all Kinds of People" — What you are you will find.

> *Chalk it off to experience, Torgie*
> *Anne $ Harvey*

In the autumn of 1945 Anne's parents sent her to Rogers Hall, a boarding school in Lowell, Massachusetts, with moderate academic standards. She smoked in the bathrooms and constantly went off campus without permission. Again her grades suffered as she composed letters to boyfriends, whom she did not hesitate to play against each other. One of her favorite tricks was to write passionate love letters to several different young men, and then intentionally mix up the envelopes. In a letter fragment to an unidentified admirer, she managed to encourage and cool his ardor simultaneously.

P.S. I have just reread this letter — it doesn't seem complete — It isn't — it tells you why & how I wrote my last letter — Now I will tell you my thoughts as of now — I am a wreck mentally — the whole thing haunts me — vivid pictures of many moments of our weekend return. Last night "Night and

Day" played on the radio and a dull ache seemed to descend on me. I do not feel any differently toward you than our last night at the Martinique. Except that I realize we cannot be so serious — it is a mistake when we are both so young. But I do want to see you again — and again and again — I am humbly asking you to accept me on such a basis — and trying to tell you how wrong I feel about my last letter — In it I not only over exaggerated but told you of things that could happen (But haven't!)

I cannot impress upon you what great heights of importance your answer to this has reached. Believe me — this is wholly sincere — I don't care about the effect — but just an answer.

— If this seems rather incoherent it is due to the *very* late hour — (3:30 A.M.) —

Anne

At Rogers Hall she began to write poetry. The themes were love and loss, loneliness and despair, and even then there was a disquietude over her own death. She experimented with form, writing cinquains, terza rima, sonnets, and free verse. Persistently reworking each poem, draft after draft, she showed that while she might pay no attention in math class, when interested she could spend considerable time on the smallest details. She published several of these poems in *Splinters,* the Rogers Hall yearbook.

ON THE DUNES

If there is any life when death is over,
These tawny beaches will know of me.
I shall come back, as constant and as changeful
As the unchanging, many-colored sea.
If life was small, if it had made me scornful,
Forgive me; I shall straighten like a flame
In the great calm of death, and if you want me
Stand on the seaward dunes and call my name.

SO

I search within
And more I know
That strange I am
The more I grow —

$$\left(\begin{array}{l}\textit{If I should wince}\\\textit{Or beg to try}\\\textit{To overlook}\\\textit{Then I would lie}\end{array}\right)$$

Now I am sure
That habit's mode
Has turned me off
the righteous road.

Though when I lie
I lie in soul —
An actor's heart
I live my role

If I be false
then I be true
To recognize
the falseness, too.

CINQUAINS

Evil
Beware!
It lurks so near,
Green serpent of fiery breath,
That distorts men's souls, warps minds, 'tis
Jealousy.

Soft Promise
Gently —
The breeze lingers there,
Whispering promise of green life,
Approaching spring, radiant bloom, nascent
As hope.

Mother's Cry
Hear me,
O pounding surf!
Lash on, you bitter wave. Glisten,
Whitecrest, for thy briny deep holds
My son!

So

I search within
And more I know
That stranger I am
The more I grow –
(I If I should ...
 Only to try
To overlook
When I would lie)

Now I am sure
That beliefs made
Has turned me off
The right was road.

For though when I lie
I lie in soul –
An actors heart
I live my role

If I be false
When I be true
To recognize
the falseness, too .

SPIRIT'S HOUSE

From naked stones of agony
I build a house for me;
as a mason all alone
I will raise it stone by stone,
And every stone where I have bled
Will show a sign of dusty red.
I have not gone away in vain,
For I have good of all my pain;
My spirit's quiet house will be
Built of naked stones I trod
On roads where I lost sight
                of God.

In a heated encounter shortly thereafter, her mother, who also wrote poems, accused her of plagiarism, and Anne quickly gave up poetry. The bitterness and sense of defeat she experienced at her mother's accusation never quite left her. Nor did her need to please her father. When in adolescence Anne developed an acute case of acne, she sometimes returned home from boarding school to see the dermatologist. On one of her visits, Ralph Harvey left the family dinner table, saying that the sight of her took his appetite away.

But her years at Rogers Hall gave her confidence. She directed and acted in plays. She started at center on the basketball team and her ability to win the opening tip earned her the nickname "Frog Legs Harvey." In the class yearbook she listed her life's ambition as taking care of children, and her classmates predicted that after graduation she would publish a book entitled *Advice to the Lovelorn in Poetry Form.* She was famous for midnight love notes and her favorite saying was recorded as "I have a letter to compose." In the spring vacation of March 1947, Anne sent the following telegram to her boarding school roommate, Mary Jane Filer: PLANS HAVE CHANGED HAVE FALLEN IN LOVE WITH NED. DIAMOND DUE THIS SUMMER HOPE YOU ARE HAPPY. LOVE ANNE. The caption under her graduation portrait taken that same spring reads, "Hail to Thee Blythe Spirit."

In the fall she entered The Garland School, which was housed in a brownstone mansion on Commonwealth Avenue in Boston. There, girls from upper-middle-class families chewed gum and exchanged gossip behind the notebooks in which they took sporadic directions for maintaining well-supervised households. In later years she would refer to Garland as "a finishing school," often remarking that the only thing she learned there was how to make a perfect white sauce. Most of her days and evenings were spent in planning dates with boys scattered at various colleges throughout New England. Decidedly, for Anne, Garland was a holding pattern before marriage.

Her two sisters had already married in grand style. By spring 1948 Anne was notifying friends that she was engaged to a young man from Wellesley. Then began arrangements for an elaborate wedding similar to Jane's and Blanche's. But in July, at the Longwood Cricket Club, she was introduced to Alfred Muller Sexton II. The handsome young man with the engaging grin was nicknamed Kayo. He had just completed his freshman year at Colgate University and wanted to be a doctor.

Soon Kayo invited Anne home to meet his family in Chestnut Hill. Wilhelmine and George Sexton were strict, serious, and loving parents; they had raised him and his sister Joan to be reserved and well-mannered, and they expected their son to bring home young ladies of similar bearing. But the Harveys used their money to live ostentatiously; at just seventeen Anne had enjoyed the envy of her crowd with her own car, a shining black convertible. She did not conduct herself as a lady should. She smoked. She was too racy, too boy-crazy, too wild — and she was engaged to someone else. During this first meeting with Kayo's parents, Anne wore too much bright red lipstick and stained Mrs. Sexton's best linen napkins a gaudy crimson.

In less than three weeks Anne and Kayo found themselves madly in love, and for once Anne confided in her mother. Mary Gray had watched her daughter break hearts and engagements, but Kayo was a person of substance. She gave her endorsement: "He will take care of you."

Late in the evening of August 14, 1948, Kayo dropped from his second-story bedroom window, picked up Anne in her convertible, and began the long drive to North Carolina, where the legal marriage age was only eighteen. Anne had left the following letter for her parents with a note on its envelope: "To be put on table at breakfast time."

Dearest Momie and Daddie —

I don't know how to begin this letter — So I'll jump right in and take my chances. I am eloping with Kayo. By the time you read this you will have another son-in-law. I know that you like him — that everyone of my friends and relatives, who have met him, like him. And I love him. There would be no reason for you to oppose this marriage. Kayo is a fine person, responsible and kind. He can support me, he comes from very fine people. There can be nothing wrong in my choice.

Please do not think that I am trying to put something over on you. I know that many people think elopement is the wrong way to get married. But I've gone through getting engaged and preparing for a big wedding. I sort of feel as though I don't want to do that again. You have married two of your daughters in the grandest of style — I am the third and last. I hope I am not disappointing you in the way I choose to get married. But I know that you will be happier about this marriage than the one I planned previously, despite how I am doing it. And I want you to be pleased. I love you both so very dearly.

Please don't think that I am unappreciative of all the wonderful things you have done for me. No daughter could have had more done for her than I have had. No one could say that I have eloped because you wouldn't let me marry him. You would let me make my own choice. And I have. I am so happy that you like him too — soon you will love him, I know. I feel terrible leaving my beautiful new room and gorgeous new home. When I sat at the dinner table last night I looked at you both and thought how kind and sweet and loyal you were. I love you both and you are so cute. Daddy in a good mood and mother in a good mood. "I am lucky" I thought. But everyone needs their own home and their own life. Daddy has Mother and Mother has Daddy. And now that I've found the man I want for all my life, to be the Daddy of my children, I just couldn't seem to face the whole thing again. Please believe me — I would never do this if I thought you didn't like Kayo. But you do — and will even more. Actually I'm saving you time and trouble and expense. Isn't it Mr. Neeves who thought it was wonderful when some of his children eloped. Try to think of it that way. Think of how lucky I am to be marrying Kayo. I only hope that I will make as good a wife as he will a husband.

Don't think we are doing this on the spur of the moment — I've thought about marrying Kayo for some time. About a week ago we decided that we would do it this way. I know it seems selfish but we don't mean to hurt you. We are being

married in a little church and the only thing that will be
wrong is that you won't be there. This is a great shock to you
now, we know — but soon it will seem good to you — you
will see what a fine choice I have made. At first we will
probably have a hard time of it financially but we can make
up for it in an abundance of love. Kayo can support me I
know —

Oh please forgive me and understand — I want to be married and have a family. I love Kayo — and we both can't see
waiting while he finishes college. I guess he will work for his
father — that isn't planned so don't mention it to the Sextons.

When you get this we will be married — please give us your
blessing — please don't stop loving me — We love you —
Soon you will be proud of me of us. We are going to have a
happy marriage and lots of beautiful grandchildren for you.
You will be proud.

We will be back a week from Monday — We will be very
scared to face you — so please don't be too mad or hurt. We
don't want to hurt you. I have a sneaking feeling the Sextons
are going to be the maddest as they wanted Kayo to finish college. But he doesn't want to — he wants to marry me. I
know you don't care if I go to Garland and that I won't let you
down that way.

We are going somewhere very nice for our honeymoon —
and will be back for I have a dentist appointment. I will miss
the first day of them — but will be all set for Tuesday morning. It really is sort of funny to come back from your honeymoon to go to the dentist — Daddy, that will make a good
story — oh please think of it that way. Be happy for me and
realize that I feel as I leave tonight that I have your consent.
[. . .]

I love you!

Anne

They arrived in the small town of Sunbury on August 16, 1948,
located a justice of the peace, and were married. The hasty departure
hadn't allowed much time for packing. A wedding snapshot shows
Kayo without a belt, struggling to hold his trousers up, and Anne in a
lacy blue dress with heavy black shoes.

After the brief service they drove to Virginia Beach, Virginia, and honeymooned at the Cavalier Hotel. They sent telegrams to both sets of in-laws.

[*To Ralph Churchill Harvey*]

MARRIED IN METHODIST CHURCH SUNBURY NORTH CAROLINA AT 5:30 MONDAY AFTERNOON. STAYING AT CAVALIER HOTEL WE HAD SWEETEST POSSIBLE WEDDING AND HONEYMOON SITE SEEMS MORE THAN IDEAL. WE LOVE YOU

ANNE AND KAYO

The Sextons threw theirs away in anger, but the one to the Harveys was carefully preserved. Anne's parents wired their congratulations and she responded ecstatically.

[*To Ralph and Mary Harvey*]

[*Virginia Beach
August 1948*]

Dear Sweet Dad and Little Mother —
Just a note of thanks — Everything is so perfect now. Knowing that you and the Sextons still love us and are standing by us makes such a difference. We have been getting millions of telegrams from everyone — You, Nana, Blanche — Kayo's Aunt and Uncle and a phone call from the Sextons last night.
Our wedding took place in the cutest little white church just before sunset. The minister was a young man and he delivered the service in a most straightforward and succinct manner. It really seemed more truly religious than I should think a large wedding should. He gave us a little talk about the seriousness of marriage and he seemed to really like us. The three witnesses he got for us were friends of his. A woman of 40 years and her son and daughter. (about 23 I would say) They were very refined and most hospitable. We got the minister and then went to their house. They got all dressed up for the wedding and picked me flowers from their garden. He told us this was the best hotel in Virginia Beach.

THE CAVALIER
VIRGINIA BEACH, VIRGINIA

Dear Sweet Darling Little Mother –

Just a note of thanks – Everything is
so perfect now. Knowing that you and the
Sisters still love us and are standing
by us makes such a difference. We
have been getting millions of Telegrams from
everyone – You, Mama, Blanche – Kayo's
Aunt and Uncle and a phone call from
the Sisters last night.

We will be home Monday
afternoon or night. Kayo joins
me in saying we thank you and
love you very much.

Love from
your youngest
Anne

P.S. I'm so happy!!!

They certainly knew what they were talking about — it is divine. At any rate after the service they threw rice at us and they had put "just married" signs all over the car. It was so sweet and wonderful that we were both crying as we drove away — the sky was all pink and it seemed like we were pretty lucky people. We are! We are! You are so understanding and wonderful.

This place is like a dream — But I'm afraid we are too much in love to pay much attention to the luxury around us. It seems to me, Mother, that you once told me people hardly ever enjoyed their honeymoon. Well it certainly doesn't hold true for us!!!! This is far more wonderful than I thought anything could be! I am married to the sweetest, kindest and most loving man in the world. I love him very very much — 20 times more than I did when I told him I would marry him. I am such a lucky girl — to have the sweetest husband and the sweetest parents in the whole wide world.

We will be home Monday afternoon or night. Kayo joins me in saying we thank you and love you very much.

> *Love from your youngest*
> *Anne*

P.S. I'm so happy!!!

After a week in Virginia Beach, the newlyweds returned to Weston. Their first concern was the dentist appointment Anne had mentioned in her elopement letter: she had 101 cavities. While the dentist drilled and packed her teeth, Kayo sat on the floor of the office, holding her hand while she cried.

Now came decisions over their future. The Sextons insisted that their son complete his education, and in spite of a wish to be independent, the couple decided to move to Hamilton, New York, so that Kayo could begin his sophomore year at Colgate.

They rented rooms on a dairy farm, where their neighbors were twenty head of cattle; Anne washed the farmer's overalls as part of the rent. She experimented with cooking and took pride in being married on visits to Kayo's fraternity. She wrote weekly letters home to her parents; Kayo corrected her spelling and grammar. In one she confided her heart's desire: an electric Mixmaster.

[*Scott Farm,
Utica Road, Hamilton, New York*]
Nov. 2nd [*1948*] 7:30 P.M.

Dear Mother and Dad,
  I thought it was about time for me to sit myself down and
write you a letter. I have been MONSTROUSLY busy cooking,
washing (and what a wash I had when I got back) cleaning,
giving parties that don't happen, and etc. etc. Doing all my
little wifely duties. [. . .]
  Thank you, Mother, for the advice about the party. The
ideas were all good but we finally decided we would give a
hay ride. We got Reg to fix up his hay wagon and he taught
Kayo how to run the tractor. I was most surprised to find that
you never had a hay ride with horses pulling the wagon —
that is not keeping up with the machine age. (Reg says). Personally I am all for the old fashioned horse pulled wagon. But
we settled for the tractor. All was prepared and everyone was
most enthusiastic about the plan for the evening. Then the
rains came. So no hay ride. We finally ended up at the fraternity house. The weekend proved a great success. All of
Kayo's Brothers (as they call them) are very nice. I have never
met such a friendly group of people in my life. They all act as
hosts from the minute you come into "The House" until you
leave. They leave no stone unturned to see that you have a
good time. And I did. I might remark that the weekend did
not prove as wild as the one I witnessed at Bowdoin! Of
course there was plenty of drinking and necking going on —
But nothing was as fast as Bowdoin. (please pass the tid-bit on
to Brad). I was looking at my very best, if I do say so myself.
Friday I gave myself a very nice sun burn with the aid of my
sun lamp. Therefore Friday night I was a pleasant pink —
Saturday I ranged from a lobster red to a rather ruddy brown. I
did not sleep at all on Friday night — I was really burned.
Right now my face is a mass of peel — but it was worth it.
My complexion was very complimentary all of the weekend
— and I didn't even wear any powder. Saturday night I wore
my chartreuse satin dress. Mother you must remember that

dress. You didn't used to quite approve of it. But it fit the occasion and I figured that now I was married I might wear it. Kayo looked more handsome than ever. He just came home and read my last sentence. So now I have a beaming husband at my side.

Daddy, Alfred (as you call him — and by the way why not Al if you don't like "Kayo"???) received your very newsy letter and check. Both of which received a large welcome from the two Sextons.

I am glad to hear that you are going to New York for a shopping tour. I really can't think of any extensive list at all. My heart's desire is an electric "mix master" (with the orange juice squeezer on top) like the one we have at Pembroke Rd. Also I could use a double blanket cover. I have plenty of clothes, as you know. I would also like some very nice perfume — just like the kind I use of Mother's. And some cologne. That is all.

Kayo is now reading over my letter and making jokes about all the misspelled words. He is going to edit this letter so that you will find it more readable. I just don't have time to think about spelling.

Kayo's work seems to be coming along very well. He has been having hourly exams and the results are proving very satisfying to both of us.

My cooking has taken a slight turn for the better. This morning we had coffee cake with our breakfast. We both thought it was delicious and it was. Tonight I made pineapple muffins — they are muffins with little bits of chopped up pineapple in them and they were also very edible. In fact I get two gold stars for today. I made an apple pie last week that was not so successful. In the first place the recipe was for an eight inch pie and then I found that I only had a ten inch pie plate. This caused me to stretch the pastry out and as a result the filling was too meager. But a first attempt isn't expected to be too wonderful so I do not feel disheartened. Rather I feel very encouraged after my good results of today. Also the food budget is arranging itself better. I have found which markets offer the cheapest goods with highest quality.

My teeth are just fine and the gold is becoming increasingly shiny. I am glad that the worst of my dentistry is over and I can start to chew like a normal being once more.

That is all the news of the moment. Tell Brad that Colby lost to Bowdoin — Jean Vandenburg writes that Dick Bowker (speaking of Colby) wrecked his brand new car and it will cost him 789 dollars to get it fixed so he is selling it for junk. So much for Colby. Thank God it's Colgate.

Well — that's all for now.

Very Much Love

from your youngest
Anne

P.S. The electric blanket works like a miracle!!! We love it.

By Thanksgiving of 1948, Kayo could no longer tolerate their financial dependence on his parents and decided to leave college and get a job. They moved back to Massachusetts, where Anne's father found him a job as sample boy in another woolen firm. Anne took a position as salesclerk at the Hathaway House bookshop in Wellesley, supplementing Kayo's income with her weekly paycheck. The young couple stayed with each set of parents for several months and then rented an apartment in Cochituate, not far from Weston. With romantic nostalgia, they later recreated for their children the years in an apartment so tiny that Anne had to back out of the kitchen before she could turn around. She claimed that they often dined on a single slice of bologna apiece — but rejoiced in the fact that they were making it on their own.

Having proved himself after two years, Kayo accepted a second invitation to join his father-in-law's firm. But his rise in the business was to be delayed, for in the summer of 1950 the Korean War erupted. Like so many others of his age, Kayo avoided the draft by joining the Naval Reserves; he was sent to Baltimore, Maryland, in November for training in navigation. Anne accompanied him there, but returned home when he shipped out on the aircraft carrier *Boxer* in May 1951.

At home, Anne lived with the Sextons, but frequently moved back and forth between their house and her parents'. She modeled for the Hart Agency, a Boston firm where her sister-in-law Joan was also employed. Wilhelmine Sexton spent hours ironing costume changes and chauffeuring the two young women into Boston with the back seat of the car full of petticoats and lace gowns.

Anne's new family now began to notice disturbing elements in her personality. Her moods shifted at lightning speed — alternating between deep depression and extraordinary excitement within a few minutes. Once, when asked to go to the store for milk while her mother-in-law prepared supper, Anne refused to go. She threw herself on the floor, drumming her heels and fists and raising her voice in rage.

Meanwhile, Kayo was on the Sea of Japan, exchanging tender letters with his wife. When the *Boxer* was damaged in combat and returned to San Francisco for repair, Anne drove cross-country to join Kayo, stopping en route in Reno to try her luck at the slot machines — a vice she continued to cultivate through the years.

In San Francisco they lived in a small walk-up apartment overlooking a burning garbage dump. Here they conceived their first child. Kayo was shipped out again to the battle area on the Sea of Japan and in Korea. Anne returned to her parents' home in Weston to await the birth of her baby.

In July 1953, Kayo returned from Korea, but had to wait for his naval discharge in San Francisco. Anne went into labor with her mother by her side at the Newton-Wellesley Hospital, her own birthplace. Kayo phoned every half hour from the bar where he anxiously marked time. At 11:48 P.M., July 21, 1953, Linda Gray was born.

Motherhood was overwhelming. Anne had found childbirth horrifying and later avoided discussing it. The continuous, irksome work of caring for an infant depressed her, and the baby cried incessantly, or so it seemed. Supervision by four capable grandparents added to Anne's feelings of helplessness and inadequacy; living at the Sextons', she resented her mother-in-law's help and advice on the daily routine.

In August, Anne and Kayo moved to a small red-brick house in Newton Lower Falls, a middle-class suburb of Boston. Anne fought bouts of depression and over the next two years was intermittently hospitalized at Westwood Lodge in Westwood, Massachusetts, for attempted suicide. Kayo's mother took charge of Linda.

In July 1954, when Linda was not yet a year old, Anne's "Nana" died at the Woodside Hospital in Wellesley, where advanced arteriosclerosis had confined her for eight months. Anna Ladd Dingley was eighty-six years old. Her death was a blow from which Anne never really recovered.

The next summer, on August 4, 1955, at 7:48 P.M., Joyce Ladd Sexton was born. Anne was unprepared for the responsibility of another infant, an inquisitive two-year-old, a household, and a husband; at twenty-seven, she felt she was drowning. One day, when she found Linda neatly stuffing her own excrement into a toy truck for the second day in a row, Anne picked her up and hurled her across the room. (Years later she was to describe the incident in "Red Roses"

[45].) Her anger and concomitant depression deepened. Despair seized her. Again the family hospitalized her. Linda was sent to Grandmother Harvey and Joy to Grandmother Sexton, while Anne tried to pull the pieces together with the help of a wise and elderly woman psychiatrist.

The next several months were a series of nightmares for everyone. Kayo was bewildered and grieving; he wanted his wife back, just as she had been before. Anne continued to search for a new identity while living in the structured routine of a mental hospital. Separated from both parents, neither child could put down roots. The Harveys and the Sextons reviewed the circumstances daily, alternating between rage and understanding. Anne returned from the hospital, and four months later, Linda came home to stay. But Joy, still an infant, remained with Grandmother Sexton for the first three years of her life, and ceased to recognize Anne as her mother.

Always, life with Anne was a roller coaster. Her husband and children could never be certain what direction her mood might take. Often she was loving, exuberant, exhilarating to live with, but her suicidal depressions and violent expressions of fear and rage were frightening and confusing.

Kayo had managed to advance to the position of road salesman. Like his father-in-law before him, he began to travel through the Midwest, persuading wool merchants to buy his samples. Anne found his absences depressing. As she struggled with the daily routine, she began working with another psychiatrist. Dr. Sidney Martin, a man close to her own age, was able to tolerate her fugue states and midnight telephone calls.

In 1957, she wrote a letter to Kayo while he was at a hotel on one of his business trips to Chicago. The letter, the only one surviving from this period, attempts to convey the depth of her psychic struggles, and her need to love and be loved. With the letter she sent one of the first poems she had written since school days.

[*To Alfred Sexton*]

> [*40 Clearwater Road,*
> *Newton Lower Falls,*
> *Massachusetts*
> *March 13, 1957*]

My Darling,
    I miss you! I adore you all over the page and all over the lonely house ... Your dear sweet face haunts the kitchen and

in the bedroom I see the still made bed, and I know the quick void and loss of you [. . .]

Kayo, I think I am beginning, and I do mean just beginning, to find myself — you realize that I MUST find my own self and be something or someone, not necessarily in any concrete manner, but in a personal manner — However, I am growing, and I am doing it alone — perhaps you feel excluded in this but it can only happen alone . . . I feel the growth in one sharp way — I feel myself beginning to love you instead of just need you. I don't think I have ever loved anyone in my life, not really — just needed them, wanted them to love me to possess me — to become such a part of someone that I could lose my frightened self . . . Now, I am learning — very slowly, with lots of backing and filling, but still learning . . . I find myself occasionally loving you not because I need you, or want your love, and feel in love — but rather an objective welling within my heart that comes from the sometimes whole person . . . whatever it is, I give it to you with no strings attached — You, my dear Kayo, I love.

In a way, it is like starting all over again — what we have had was good, but do you remember how I was always dissatisfied — I hope to reach the stage where I can stop begging for more and find myself giving regardless of what I get . . .

Do not resent my growth, darling, because it is bringing me closer to you in a more delicate way — closer because I want to be yours and not because you are my only refuge . . . In a way you will always be my only refuge — I am so half an orange without you —

Linda is a pixie — she had five friends romping in the playroom yesterday . . . "I had a fun time. We played ghost and witch and we fighted and everything" — thus goes the child's report on a three year old existence. — How fleeting it is — and how nievly (sp ha) special. [. . .]

I am not depressed, except for the reality factor of no Kayo with a wispy wisp to love and tickle — [. . .]

The doves are cooing in the pine tree and spring will come — will come — will come.

You will come home, too — and I can't wait . . .

Kayo! your wife is proud of you — thank God for such as
you in this world —

Last time you were in Chicago for the weekend I received a
letter all about the undulating figures of the women and they
slunk by your table — all the twos and twos while you were
one . . . Put on blinders, Boots, I cannot bear to think of MY
PETE waving stiff in the air for any other than me — I love
Kayo and Boots and Peter —

Anne

Traveler's Wife

Although I lie pressed close to your warm side,
I know you find me vacant and preoccupied.
If my thoughts could find one safe walled home
Then I would let them out to strut and roam.
I would, indeed pour me out for you to see,
a wanton soul, somehow delicate and free.
But instead I have a cup of pain to drink,
or I might weed out an old pain to think.
Perhaps old wounds have an easy sorrow,
easier than knowing you leave me tomorrow.
The mind twists and turns within the choice
of some sagging pain, or your departing voice.
In the last hour I've tried images and things,
and even illusion breaks its filament wings
on the raw skin of all I wouldn't know
about the waiting dawn when you smile and go.
You must not find, in quick surprise,
one startled ache within my vacant eyes.

Chapter I

The Business of Words

December 1957–September 1959

"The great theme is not Romeo and Juliet . . . The great theme we all share is that of becoming ourselves, of overcoming our father and mother, of assuming our identities somehow."

—from Anne's early introduction for "The Double Image" [TB], used during readings of her poetry

In December 1956, Anne had seen the program "How to Write a Sonnet" on Educational Television. Curiosity overcame her fears of rejection and she telephoned her mother, the only person she knew who had written poetry, to ask "What is an image?" Shortly after Christmas she showed her toughest critic her first sonnet of the decade.

Dr. Sidney Martin also encouraged Anne. He recognized that her therapy progressed as she began to discover and appreciate her talents. As if to compensate for all her earlier years of scholastic laziness, she worked hard to learn about both poetic form and herself. She found that emotions she couldn't deal with in therapy appeared increasingly in her poetry worksheets. Spending hours listening to the tape recordings of her psychiatric sessions, and days rewriting her worksheets, she slowly pulled poetry from the dark core of her sickness.

In September of 1957, believing that she needed a teacher, Anne enrolled in a poetry seminar taught by the poet John Holmes at the Boston Center for Adult Education. Here she met Maxine Kumin, who would be her staunch friend and constant companion in poetry for the next seventeen years. Maxine, a Radcliffe graduate, possessed a technical expertise and an analytic detachment that balanced Anne's mercurial brilliance.

As the years went by, Anne and Maxine often communicated daily, by letter if separated by oceans, otherwise by telephone. They supervised each other's poetry and prose, "workshopping" line by line for hours. They discussed husbands, friends, loves, and enemies; they worried and exulted over their children and their publications, borrowed each other's clothes, and criticized each other's readings.

If anyone else viewed Anne's writing as therapy or a hobby, she did not. Very quickly she established a working routine in a corner of the already crowded dining room. Piled high with worksheets and books, her desk constantly overflowed onto the dining room table; she wrote in every spare minute she could steal from childtending and housewifely duties. To make extra money for baby sitters, she began to sell Beauty Counselor cosmetics door-to-door.

By Christmas Day 1957, Anne could present her mother with a sheaf of poems she had written and rewritten over the previous year. She began publishing on a modest scale in *The Herald Tribune, The Fiddlehead,* and *The Compass Review.* On July 28, 1958, "The Reading" appeared in the *Christian Science Monitor.*

THE READING

This poet could speak,
There was no doubt about it.
The top professor nodded
To the next professor and he
Agreed with the other teacher,
Who wasn't exactly a professor at all.
There were plenty of poets,
Delaying their briefcase
To touch these honored words.
They envied his reading
And the ones with books
Approved and smiled
At the lesser poets who
Moved unsurely, but knew,
Of course, what they heard
Was a notable thing.

This is the manner of charm:
After the clapping they bundled out,
Not testing their fingers
On his climate of rhymes.
Not thinking how sound crumbles,
That even honor can happen too long.
A poet of note had read,
Had read them his smiles
And spilled what was left
On the stage.
All of them nodded,
Tasting this fame
And forgot how the poems said nothing,
Remembering just —
We heard him,
That famous name.

During the next twelve months she submitted poems to a number of the more prestigious literary magazines and by the fall had received several more acceptances: *The Hudson Review* had agreed to publish "The Double Image" [TB], "Elizabeth Gone" [TB], and "You, Dr. Martin" [TB], and *The New Yorker* had taken "The Road Back" [TB]. By early 1959 not one finished poem remained unsold. That April, Houghton Mifflin signed the contract for her first book, *To Bedlam and Part Way Back.* And in 1960 Anne wrote "poet" under the occupation column on her part of the joint income tax statement. Even her children began reporting to teachers and friends that a mother was "someone who types all day."

But her success with her poetry could not block out personal crises. Anne tried to care adequately for Joy, who had just returned home after a three-year absence; she fought to balance her relationship with Kayo against her embryonic career. In February of 1957, Mary Gray Harvey had developed breast cancer, and several months later Ralph Harvey had suffered a stroke, from which he made a slow recovery. Anne's mother moved into the guest bedroom at 40 Clearwater Road. But in October of 1958, her cancer metastasized. For the next five months, Anne numbly monitored her mother's slow decline as she visited the hospital room daily. On March 10, 1959, Mary Gray Harvey died. Three days later she was buried in the Mount Auburn Cemetery, Cambridge.

In April, her father announced plans to marry again. Anne was appalled. She attempted to intervene, but he stood firm. Early in June, several hours after he had lain down for his customary Sunday nap, the maid found him dead of a cerebral hemorrhage.

Within four months, both Anne's parents had gone, leaving a small legacy for their third daughter: a mink coat, a diamond, a few rare books, a ruby, and some stocks and bonds. They could not know that the richest inheritance they had left was an abundance of unvoiced emotion which would fill Anne's poetry for years to come.

[*To Mary Gray Harvey*]

[*40 Clearwater Road*]
Christmas Day — 1957

Dear Mother,

Here are some forty-odd pages of the first year of Anne Sexton, Poet. You may remember my first sonnet written just after Christmas one year ago. I do not think all of these are good. However, I am not ashamed of them. They are not in chronological order, but I have arranged them in a sort of way, in a sort of a story. But not too much or too well. I have tried to give a breather between the more difficult ones that use a more modern idiom. A few are obscure. I do not apologize for them. I like them. Mood can be as important as sense. Music doesn't make sense and I am not so sure the words have to, always.

These are for you to do with as you wish. If you want to send them to that man in New York — do so. Simply put them in a manila envelope and address and fold (inside the other with the manuscript) another return envelope. (enclose some) Take these both to the post office and have them weighed and put postage on both. I feel that this is the only gracious way to ask anyone to read (and then return) poetry. And do the same with Merrill Moore. I sort of hope you won't separate and fold some for mailing in a regular envelope as then they will never get back together again. However, do as you wish, they are yours (short of telling someone to publish them).

I know that they are lousy with typographical errors but I did my best — am not a graduate of Katie Gibbs and have a peculiar lack of spelling know-how.

I think my favorite poem is the first in the book (this may be because it is fairly recent — poets always prefer their latest things I hear — and it seems so). As you can see I have developed no one style as yet. But at first it is better, and is sort of chain verse. Both of these were difficult but fun — rather like a crossword puzzle. There are no sonnets. I am not ready for sonnets yet, somehow.

I hope you can have some fun with them. Now if you meet some interested person you will have these to show. Although it is a rarity to find anyone even willing to read poems — or poetry of my voice. Although there is nothing new in the manner in which I have written these, it seems new to most poet tasters. I do not write for them. Nor for you. Not even for the editors. I want to find something and I think, at least "today" I think, I will. Reaching people is mighty important, I know, but reaching the best of me is most important right now.

I did not win the Ingram Merrill Foundation Contest. However, this is just a start for me ... I imagine I can always get printed from the psychiatric angle with preface by Dr. Martin — but he won't talk about it until therapy is over — and by then I may not want to do it anyhow ... There are lots of contests for first books of poetry that have real merit — most usually no money but a real start ... I hope I am going to continue to improve and if I do I'm going to aim high. And why not.

I love you. I don't write for you, but know that one of the reasons I do write is that you are my mother.

Love,
Anne

As the workshop with John Holmes drew to a close in the spring of 1958, she gained the confidence to send her poetry to well-known journals. "For Johnny Pole on the Forgotten Beach" [TB] was accepted by *The Antioch Review* in late May when she received a letter from one of their editors, Nolan Miller.

She liked to say that Miller and *The Antioch Review* discovered her, despite the fact that she had already published elsewhere. But it was true that after her *Antioch* appearance some of the better-known magazines in the country did begin to publish her work. Through Miller she applied for and received a scholarship for the Antioch Summer Writers' Conference in August, going expressly to study with W. D. Snodgrass, then her favorite poet.

[*To Nolan Miller*
THE ANTIOCH REVIEW]

40 Clearwater Rd.
June 1st, 1958

Dear Mr. Miller:

[...] I am twenty nine (am not sure if this qualifies me as a "young writer") and have been writing for about a year. I have been published in *The Fiddlehead*, *The Compass Review* (reprinted in *The New York Herald Tribune*), and have just received an acceptance from *The New Orleans Poetry Journal* (for a really long poem — which is pleasing). I have started to get quite a bit of encouragement from various editors; i.e., Ralph Freedman at *The Western Review*, Karl Shapiro at the *Schooner*, and *Accent* and the other morning received a phone call from one of the editors of *Audience* asking for more poems (ten, he said) as they liked one and wanted to print more than one. I have about twenty rejection slips from Howard Moss at *The New Yorker* saying "please send more" (am not sure what this means as they add up each week, after week — but it seems encouraging) also a couple of personal letters from Anne Freedgood at *Harper's* and also *The Atlantic* . . . I didn't mean to get going on what might happen but hasn't, however the list of published looked so small.

I had been thinking of applying for your scholarship before I received your letter because it looks like the best one. However, did not because of the long trip out there which is an expense. I had even asked John Holmes (we are in a workshop together) if he would write a letter for me and he had agreed to do this. However, I guess I don't need his letter now.

I would particularly like to meet W. D. Snodgrass because his poem "Heart's Needle" startled me so when I read it, that I just sat there saying "Why didn't I write this". I admire his style and know that I need to study with someone I feel this way about.

Am writing this in a rush so that I can mail the revision of "Johnny Pole" [TB] tonight. I excuse this hurried and rambling letter (to myself at 1:00 A.M.) by saying that poets just aren't expected to write sensible letters — just poems. Hope also you will forgive the fading type — am in need of a new ribbon.

Many thanks for giving me the chance to revise this poem as I knew it needed it — just needed someone to tell me.

Sincerely,
Anne Sexton

When Anne met W. D. Snodgrass at the Antioch Writers' Conference, she fulfilled one of her first ambitions: to establish personal contact with a worthy mentor. Immediately following her return to Newton, she began an intense passionate correspondence with Snodgrass which set the pattern for many later friendships-by-letter.

[*To W. D. Snodgrass*]

40 Clearwater Road
August 31st — [1958]

Dear Mr. Snodgrass honey —

I have three pictures of you (and others) on my desk — they are placed there for inspiration. They do not work. But they will. You look sleepy in this one and Jan [Snodgrass], beside you, looks earnest and sweet with that one curl promising something. In another you are busy telling a bunch of sitting ducks something from your desk. Here you are looking young and rather handsome by the mike and Jessy West. She must be telling you how [illegible] genius you are or something — else why do you look so humble and pretty? I like your pictures — otherwise I wouldn't believe it . . . some funny dream I walked through . . . I do believe it because you were real. I was afraid that the "HEART'S NEEDLE" man would not be real. Thank you for being — and Mrs. Snodsy and Buzzy too. [. . .]

Once I said to Dr. Martin that I didn't care if I were crazy forever if I could only write well.

Somewhere, sometime at Antioch this plan seemed to fall down. Everyone seemed to like my poetry and the doctor was right. It isn't enough . . . That was another thing about meeting you — I was afraid to find out what you were like. I loved your poetry — even this was dangerous — but unavoidable considering the unconscious area of my guilt. Then I met you and unavoidably you were special. So now I love you and your wife and your Buzzy and your Cynthia and — well, "it makes me nervous." (Jarrell? I think, you quoted this).

Are you going to answer this? If so I'll ask some questions — like where does Robert Lowell live — if I knew I'd write him and ask if he would like me as a student for his graduate course in poetry writing. It says in the catalogue that students may enter without degree with instructor's o.k. . . . There are six Robert Lowells in the book.

If you do come to Boston you had better come see us, or visit if you like. Would you have a place to stay — I could put you up — though we have no real room, could shift about — could the three of you manage in one room? Warning: my

husband is not bohemian (sp?) but is at one with the world
like the farmer — at one with a conventional world — but
good man. Have been thinking that he is just right for me.
He is solid; I am lonely. Why do I ask him to be lonely too?
He doesn't know what I'm talking about. I have stopped trying to change and started to appreciate . . . (all because of your
devious analysis of the "FARMER'S WIFE" [TB]). Come to visit
if you can.

I enclose yesterday's poem. I have so much I could write
about that I do understand — but could only write this rather
trivial thing because I didn't understand. I'm not sending it
because I think it's a good poem — but in case your analytic
bent has been frustrated lately and you'd like to figure this
out. The only thing I can guess is that "I'd like to be there,"
but can't because I'm dead and the poets know they are dead
— or maybe?????? I don't know — better get my analyst back
before I fail all understanding and go back to thinking portraits do talk.

Wasn't Ruth [Soter, another writer from the Antioch work-
shop] cute to call you? We had a mutual farewell analysis and
drinks on tuesday (she left Wed.) . . . George Starbuck (in our
Boston workshop) is also up for the Lamont Award from
Houghton Mifflin. John Holmes says it is a tight year (talked
with him and told him all about Antioch). He is on The National Book Award committee — or judge of whatever you call
it.

It is late at night — but no excuse because I always write
sloppy letters. I forgot to ask you — did you really live next
door to the jail — or what does it mean? Why do I associate
this to mental institution? (is it only MY association? or not?)
— it is followed with "when I grew back from helplessness
when I grew able." —

Hell, I'm never going to stop writing you tonight — there is
just more to say.

I have avoided mentioning some of the things you said
about "By Nameless Flesh" — first of all am still too confused
about its real meaning . . . I keep (even now forgetting to tell
you this one true part — so will do so quickly before I forget

it again). After *I* got out of my jail (institution) they said I wasn't well enough to have children . . . But got the oldest five months later (as I told you) . . . Some months later I thought my only chance for emotional survival was to leave my husband. He said that if I did he would take the children — that no court would give me (dangerous mad me) custody of the children . . . Everyone said I wasn't good for them (my mother-in-law mainly) — but the oldest proved very unhappy away from me (various symptoms) so could keep her. The youngest, Joy, was only eight months when she left. Did the poem mean, nameless — ie. you have no father — I am your only parent — ? Did the poem try to give her up? How many times I read your poem, crying, and not knowing what and why. "you visit me sometimes" — they would bring Joy down for the day — she would cry for her Nana . . . I don't care (I would pretend she wasn't mine) which worked until "and still you are my daughter" . . . also, "you wheezed for breath . . . drowning there." — Before I went inside the jail Joy had been very sick with a croup-like attack. My husband went on his first trip and one night I heard this funny sound like a dog choking — went into Joy's room and she was almost dead — no air. I didn't even know what croup was — had never heard of it. I took her into the bathroom and tried to breathe into her mouth — no time to call a doctor — then finally I turned on the hot water thinking steam would help (like a stuffy cold) — maybe I had read about it — sometime — All that night (it was — just realized it was Easter —) I held her in the bathroom — rocking her and thinking "she will die in my arms" — I didn't dare leave her because she would stop breathing I thought — I don't know why — but am just beginning to understand this! You said, "Easter has come around again" and when it did — three years later (from that Easter night when I watched the light come slowly up through the steamy bathroom window) I just went down and got her.

I do not dare write this true poem — it is too mixed up with the influence of your poem. My "Nameless Flesh" was my fictional way of feeling my way out of it. Maybe now that I've gone this far I will write it again — I will, if I have to . . .

If so I will have to be a "shore rocking" your lines off. I like
them too much.

Sorry to have gone on so long and easily—

Love to you and Mrs. Snodsy —
Anne

In September, Anne applied to Robert Lowell's graduate writing
seminar at Boston University. A week later, she received a letter from
Lowell, a leading American poet and author of *For the Union Dead*,
accepting her.

The class met on Tuesdays from two to four in a small room.
Although smoking was forbidden, Anne lit up furtively, defiant as in
her high school days, using her shoe as an ashtray. In the seminar she
worked again with the poet George Starbuck, then an editor at
Houghton Mifflin, and met Sylvia Plath, who had recently returned
from England with her husband, Ted Hughes. All of them were
struggling for recognition and publication.

After each class, accompanied by Sylvia and George, Anne drove to
the Ritz-Carlton Hotel in her old Ford. There they sat upstairs on the
mezzanine with snowy shoes, umbrellas, and manuscripts, ordering
martini after martini while they "workshopped" their poems. Then,
they moved from the muted elegance of the Ritz to the vinyl and
plastic of the nearby Waldorf Cafeteria, where they dined for seventy
cents each.

At this point in her career, Anne was making the friendships that
were to shape her life as a poet.

[*To Robert Lowell*]

[*40 Clearwater Road*]
September 15th, 1958

Dear Mr. Lowell:

What a fine letter you wrote me. I am considering framing
it to prove to all comers that poets are people. I am so pleased
that you think my work shows promise, that I shall need no
new proof for possibly a month.

Since receiving your letter I have been busy begging money
from old fat relatives. Today, with 90 dollars in my fist, I
called the registrar's office. However, it seems they are not
bouncing with joy at the thought of "special students" with
no particular degrees. A Mr. Wilder said I would have to wait

until after registration and see if there were too many students in the class. I forward this information to you because I gather he will present you with the problem. I hasten to add, since he may forget my name, that I am one of the vagrant applications that awaits your decision. He asked me if I were connected with any publication. I am not. In fact, I am totally disconnected from everything. I did not mention my slim list of credits, thinking he might wonder WHAT I was talking about. I am supposed to call him on Friday morning at eleven.

If this doesn't pan out I can always try for the second semester. I am even tempted to sit watching your lovely letter of praise and forget all about the work and criticism and growth that I would enjoy working with you.

I am more than a little shy of great factories of humanity, like B.U. and it will take considerable moral courage to get on with this complicated application, registration and these new hurdles. Somewhere, I hope I will get to a classroom where Robert Lowell is talking about poetry. I don't want the three credits, I am not sweetened with a background of knowledge, am even defensive saying ("I don't know anything.") — but if you can squeeze me in, I will be there.

You do not need to answer this letter. I just wanted to let you know the meanwhiles and if so's. If I do not make it I will surely meet you sometime.

> *Yours sincerely,*
> *Anne Sexton*

[*To W. D. Snodgrass*]

> [*40 Clearwater Road*]
> *Thursday now*
> [*circa October 6, 1958*]

Mr Dear Mr. Snodgrass,

How in heaven's name can I write anything when I seem to be constantly writing to you. Who says this is a waste of time — I have given up poetry in favor of letters anyhow.

Lowell just called and says the poets' theater wants you on November 9th. I imagine he will write you to this effect. I want to announce that I will be there clapping and also that on November Ninth I will be thirty years old. I am crossing the margin and may no longer plead youth as my excuse. I don't mind being skinny and wrinkled but I do mind, resent really, years wasted with my own neurotic living and my dull mind. I have really been alive for only a year . . . but my natal date is november 9, 1928.

I shall never write a really good poem. I overwrite. I am a reincarnation of Edna St. Vincent . . . I am learning more than you could imagine from Lowell. I am learning what I am not. He didn't say I was like Edna (I do — a secret fear) — also a fear of writing as a woman writes. I wish I were a man — I would rather write the way a man writes.

Don't mind me. I have been, in truth, very depressed lately — tho I am adroit at hiding behind the verbal and pretty mask — still, I am depressed. My mother is dying of cancer. My mother says I gave her cancer (as though death were catching — death being the birthday that I tried to kill myself, nov. 9th 1956). Then she got cancer . . . who do we kill, which image in the mirror, the mother, ourself, our daughter????? Am I my mother, or my daughter? Snodsy, I am afraid to love. How do you love? Teach me — you are a good man. I feel you loving your daughter . . . I felt it when I first read that poem . . . don't answer all this . . . I am not taxing you with my turmoils [. . .]

Ah Snodsy you are famous.

You don't SEEM famous. I looked at your wild handsome overgrown face and thought "of course, of course, this is Snodgrass!" AND SOMEONE WAS THERE.

ANNE (THE HUDSON REVIEW
MADE A MISTAKE) SEXTON

[She enclosed a critique of Snodgrass's poem "The Red Studio."]

[*To W. D. Snodgrass*]

[*40 Clearwater Road*]
Sat. 7:00 A.M.
[*circa November 15, 1958*]

Dear My Dear Mr. Snodgrass.

When I was a little girl I had a funny little club called "THE TENDER HEART CLUB" . . . I was president. My mother was treasurer and my Nana was Nice President (I meant Vice Pres. but 'nice' is better) . . . The point being, that I am a tender heart still, vulnerable, never wise, but tender hearted. And although the club disintegrates slowly, although time makes madmen and corpses of some, I am still the President of my own club in my own way. My Nana went crazy when I was thirteen. Then she was only a crazy tender heart. At the time I blamed myself for her going because she lived with our family and was my only friend. Then at thirteen I kissed a boy (not very well — but happily) and I was so pleased with my womanhood that I told Nana I was kissed and then she went mad . . . I tell you this not to confess, but to illuminate. At thirteen, I was blameful and struck — at thirty I am not blameful (because I am always saved by men who understand me better than I understand myself). I am not immoral. I am not wise. But still, I am not cruel. I have no place loving you and because I let you be my god for a while, I was in need of loving, of giving love, and not wise, nor cagey, nor — just walking around wearing my womanhood and trying to keep us all sane. Failing this entirely, I give you back to yourself, with all the tenderness I have ever known for you and yours (my good night clerk in your emotional hotel).

I wrote Will Stone [a coastguardsman she had met at Antioch] a reply that is so fine that I think I shall correspond with him forever. I think he loves me — tenderly and encouragingly. It has nothing to do with my life or living, and is just there, to taste when I need it. Today I need it, as I lean toward madness (such an escape, such a simple childlike full believing state) . . . But if I live long enough, if time keeps me whole enough and a living reading writer of my day, perhaps I will go to some conference . . . The future is a fog that is still hanging out over the sea, a boat that floats home or does not. The trade winds blow me, and I do not know where the land is; the waves fold over each other; they are in love with themselves; sleeping in their own skin; and I float over them and I do not know about tomorrow. I am a mixer of obscure metaphor by ill habit like many minor and unmentioned poets.

Kayo left for two weeks trip this morning. I need him —

"women marry what they need — I marry him" (beg pardon to Ciardi) . . .

I have been a tender heart with Will Stone and he does not feel guilty any longer (I mean, I tried and I think I helped) . . .

My two girls play with itinerant mices and their small furry fingers hop over my eyes in the morning when I am not admitting that I am awake. After you left I washed "snodgrass tattoos" off four arms. One a picture of you. You came off with soap! The house misses you — Snodgrass is part of our family, it seems.

If you misread this I will be very angry!! I am not saying anything!! Except that Will Stone wrote me a crazy nice letter and I am writing you the like because you are a night clerk, because you are home with Jan and Buzzy and because I hope you are recovering and *because I never meant to confuse you,* least of all!

Also when you read my poem I want a critical opinion *NOT a friendly one.* Poetry is special, is something else. As a poet I admire (not as my night clerk love), I want your real idea, unclothed from your feeling for the writer . . . Poetry has saved my life and I respect it beyond both or any of us. I love Maxine but when her poems stink I tell her so — because I love poetry and because I love her.

I am going to a mental institution today. I am hearing voices. I am never sane, you know — I pretended to be for your visit and THAT was kind. Although you didn't know it. I really do not want a "nice" letter from you — but a critical opinion of "The Double Image" [TB] (if I knew what was wrong with it I might be sane again and get back to writing it).

                  ⊘haste
     In chaos —— df453679¢;!.!'¢#!!!!
                  Anne

P.S. Please allow me the luxury of writing you this kind of confused letter without you misinterpreting it.

[*To W. D. Snodgrass*]
usual rush

[*40 Clearwater Road
circa November 26, 1958*]

Dear De,

Here is the poem, done for the moment ["The Double Image," TB]. Apparently my short trip to "the sealed hotel" helped unblock me on its writing. I only want to know if you think this works, if it has a reason for its violence, a reason for being written (or rather read) aside from my own need to make form from chaos.

I KNOW you are exhausted and have little extra energy for others' poems. A poet, in the long run, must be selfish; if he wants to be a best writer he can't spend time on friends' work. But I am not sending you all the stuff I've written since August (dozens) but just this — that you told me to write (tho maybe you didn't know what you were saying or what I would HAVE to write about)... You told me I hadn't found my voice. But this poem has a voice. A changing, lame, but real voice, I think... Whether it is my best voice, I am not sure. It is the voice I HAD to use and maybe your opinion won't change me — still, if you can find the time, I would enjoy your opinion, pro or con.

Snodsy, let's be friends! Let's be poets first — all else is unessential. Return this when you are done with it unless you want to keep it because it is a bother to type. Only some of the sections are syllabic count — the others being freer and looser, despite the looks of the thing.

We are enjoying your record. I am such a dullard I forgot to thank you. And the children love their mouses. Kayo keeps building them a "mouse house" out of cardboard and they spend considerable time on all this.

Went to Lowell's class yesterday. I guess I forgive him for not liking me (if he didn't like me as I thot) because he has such a soft dangerous voice. He seemed more friendly yesterday. He is a good man; I forgive him for his sicknesses whatever they are. I think I will have to god him again; gods are so necessary and splendid and distant.

Don't answer this. Just write: yes, no, possible, perhaps, sort of, ... or whatever ... about this poem. At least I am done with it. Thank god for that ... My father is now ill with a cerebral hemorrhage and so I have that to worry about, now. Though I shan't write a long poem about it. No guilt there — sorrow is easier than guilt.

I am sorry I keep writing crazy letters. You should not have crazy friends, my sweet night clerk, but sane and uplifting friends. Thank god you have Jan. Be good to yourself and think of me kindly enough.

And give me a one word statement about this "voice" I've got here for two-hundred odd lines of confession and art. (Art I hope?) The difference between confession and poetry? is after all, art. That poem of yours about "The Red Studio" — I can't forget the lines "but his own room drank him" and "there was no one there" ... If you get two lines so good they keep ringing in my head then the poem is, of course, a success. So you see what time does to my judgment!

Naturally, Anne

[*To Nolan Miller*]

40 Clearwater Rd.
[27] Nov. 1958
Thanksgiving

Dear Nolan,

I have looked everywhere for my large envelope containing "letters from famous people" and cannot find it. However, I am answering your fine letter, at long last, despite the missing envelope. As a matter of fact I have had copies of poems typed up to send to you for two months now.

Today, being thanksgiving, I give thanks that I have finished my "long" poem ["The Double Image," TB]. I have not written before because of that damn poem and because I do want your opinion and crit on it. I sent the others along (to show you I am still writing) and for any passing comments but I really care most about "The Double Image". It is a kind of a voice; but is it a good voice? You know, Nolan, people keep telling me that I haven't found my "voice" yet and I have spent considerable time fishing around in my desk drawers and under old ms. and have found no new notable sound. Therefore I wrote this long poem on my best bond paper as if it deserved it from the beginning. Etc. Etc. What I mean is something like, "what do you think?" etc. etc. [. . .]

I enjoyed Antioch so much. I am glad you discovered me and I hope you can wade through my long poem and give me your opinion.

> *with all best wishes,*
> *Anne*

please forgive this inahurrytogetinthemailbox letter

[*To W. D. Snodgrass*]

> [*40 Clearwater Road*]
> *day after thanks-giving*
> [*November 28, 1958*]

Dear passionflower tender,

I was just looking out the window at the truck that was delivering two bottles of whiskey and it was, yes it was, snowing. I am young. I am younger each year at the first snow. When I see it, suddenly, in the air, all little and white and moving; then I am in love again and very young and I believe everything. Christ is in his manger and Santa in heaven. I am a good girl and the man left two bottles of booze because my mother is rich and she ordered them. She is staying with us because my father is ill, in the hospital with a stroke. My mother keeps telling me that soon I will be rich because they will be dead (she is greedily wordy about this) and I listen to her and think about a poem by you about a mother . . . she is like a star . . . everything MUST center around her.

And I write in a hurry because it is snowing and because this morning I received a letter from you and because I would rather write to you this moment than sleep with Apollo or even go outside and measure the snow on the walk. I write to you because you understand my letters and do not take them TOO seriously or too casually. And because, after all, I love you and you are my best god anyhow.

Did I? Why do I forget everything! send you a complete

copy of my "Double Image" poem the other day? I sent it to someone that I cared about. But was it you? Who else could there be, that I care about — about reading it??? I think I did. If so — read it. If not — let me know.

I also received a nice letter from Jim McConk taking two poems for *Epoch* (it's about time) and saying such nice things about my work and when was my book coming out (I didn't believe that but it looked nice on the page) and all. That sweet ladypoet from Rochester took two poems for *Voices* (don't know why I sent there — but did — one of the ones was a new one, "Obsessional Combinations of Ontological Inscape, Trickery and Love" . . . why am I rambling on? Now I know why I am really writing you so promptly. I have a question —

How do I go about applying for Yaddo? Would John Holmes be enough of a recommendation? Who else could I find? Would Nolan Miller (he thinks he discovered me) help? Or Hollis Summers [a novelist from the Antioch summer session] (he writes me letters) — I might be able to go. I think the first thing to do is see if I could get in — do you think, perhaps, it would be better to wait a year (in view of that fact that I'm such a "new" writer) . . .

John Holmes is having a small party for John C. Ransom next Wed. night and has asked me so maybe I will meet someone who will decide to discover me. I will be on the lookout for a possible famous soul who can recommend me . . .

But how do you go about it, dear night clerk; the future is my own. I am trying to steer. I paddle my own craft with toothpick oars . . . thank you for quoting my letter . . . I will write you dozens more someday. I doubt if I can use it in a poem (but there is lots more where that came from). I am a romantic and am full of tiers of tries of all that.

let me know about Yaddo —
yours Anne

[*To Nolan Miller*]

[*40 Clearwater Road*]
Wednesday 11 Dec. 1958

Dear Nolan:

You are my favorite famous person! And what a nice letter and such splendid enthusiasm, after all . . . and thank you, as always, thank you.

I am set right up by your discussion of my voice, and which voice works etc. Because, I agree with you — and I feel more capable of steering the craft. You are my radar, my double check and now it's full wind ahead. [. . .]

I don't know who could beat Snodgrass as poet-teacher for next summer. His talk was amazingly fine I thought. His class was good too — tho I don't know yet, if he is the best "teacher". I got more actual crit. from my conferences with you and Hollis. Still I learned something about poetic sincerity from Dee that may be just as important. I like James Wright's poetry and have met him. Or maybe Donald Hall (I haven't met him tho) . . . Still, neither of them have the wild genius way that Dee seems to radiate. Eudora Welty sounds great. By then I may have some prose to submit. [. . .]

Per your advice: I am writing a new poem in my own symbolic world of the half-sane, knowledgeable insane . . . and I am really stimulated by your remarks.

Before you leave please drop a note and advise me where I ought to try "The D. Image" [TB] thing. Maybe I should try *Poetry* — tho Dee says it stinks . . . ? . . .

Thank you Nolan Miller, as always . . .

Better Best's . . .
Anne

Since the spring of 1958, Anne had submitted sixteen poems to Frederick Morgan, editor of *The Hudson Review*. All were rejected; then in October he accepted "You, Doctor Martin" [TB] and "Elizabeth Gone" [TB]. Anne was overjoyed. Having worked all fall on the intensely painful and personal poem "The Double Image," she submitted it to *The New Yorker* but it was returned. Finally she mailed it off to Morgan on December 11. His acceptance arrived on December 30 and in her next letter to him she called it her "best Christmas present."

She agreed to delete the subtitle, "A Confession," referring to it as "a hat on a naked lady."

Expansively, she soon made *The Hudson Review* her favorite magazine. With trepidation she went to New York City to meet Morgan and his wife Rose, and in August she and Kayo were their house guests in Maine.

[*To W. D. Snodgrass*]

[*40 Clearwater Road*]
Jan 11th 1959

Dear Mr. Dear W. D. . . .

I hope that all went well in New York. I have kind of been looking for a letter from you — but just now thot that since our letters crossed neither owes either. And of course I love you. And sometimes I worry about you. Mostly I just worry about myself. However, today I raised my head out of a long three weeks of damn depression and now realize that there really are other people. There is someone there. I had just forgotten. (Not really forgotten about YOU — that's impossible) . . .

I got a nice letter from *Poetry Northwest* and they are considering the stuff I sent. Thanks for writing them about me and so forth. I am beginning to run out of good material (not quite but almost all the best have been sold) . . . But am still writing new ones — or was before the depression gloomed in. Right now I ought to be writing as [I] have a couple buzzing my brain. But first had to send words to you (I'm the crazy one who thinks that words reach people). [. . .]

I have stuck my poems together as if they could be a book and Lowell is looking it over. Did I make a mistake? I don't know. Still, he seems receptive to the idea and said he would tell me frankly if there was enough good stuff for a book. (tho God knows how you get them published —) He seems impressed that *Hudson* took "The Double Image" [TB]. So long (240 lines) and all. And then in the next breath he said, "But I knew they would take it. It was just a question of where to send it." . . . ???? . . . He is difficult to figure. The class is good. I am learning leaps and boundaries. Tho I am very bitchy acting in class. I don't know why but I am very defensive around Lowell (I think I am afraid of him) . . . so I act like a bitch with these sarcastic remarks . . . The class just sits there like little doggies waggling their heads at his every statement. For instance, he will be dissecting some great poem and will say "Why is this line so good. What makes it good?" and there is total silence. Everyone afraid to speak. And finally, because I can stand it no longer, I speak up saying, "I don't think it's so good at all. You would never allow us sloppy language like that." . . . and so forth. But I don't do this for effect. But because the line *isn't* good. What do you do — sit there and agree and nod and say nothing . . . ? . . . As you say, I do act aggressive. I think the trouble is that my mind, my thinking mind, *is* aggressive. I am a machine of ideas. I adore (in a funny way) to think. I mean in a class like that I am very stimulated . . . but in fact, I do not mean to really be there after I have spoken . . . I often think of your analysis. I would like speaking, but not being there. It would be like your "Red Studio." And that turns us back to figuring YOU out. I like figuring you out. You are so human and puzzling and my splendid oaf.

What are you writing? If you send me a copy I promise to keep THE MACHINE silent. I will only love it and wonder it and be glad your words are barking along at the top of the sky.

I got a whole mess of books for Xmas, among them Philip Larkin's — which I enjoy and Randall Jarrell and Frost and others. Where is your book? I want to buy it!!! I want to buy it quickly so you will be rich and famous and lapping in luxuries and touring the world with Jan at your side. And also stopping at places to be the night clerk, as always.

Midst the rubble of this place my daughters still play with their mices (for which Kayo made a house) and the aura of you remains, remains, remains . . .

Ugh, I think I am missing you, & *right now!* I don't know why — you are such a contrary creature. But I do. We do. Should I invite you again? I mean, you do know that you are always welcome here. Don't you?

If I have a copy I will send it along — of a recent poem I

have & will enclose ["Some Foreign Letters," TB]). For your reading or not reading?? Just to let you know I'm still writing.

And Happy New Year, my darling, and all good things for you and yours,

fondly,
Anne

[. . .]

[*To W. D. Snodgrass*]

[*40 Clearwater Road*]
FEB THE FIRST [*1959*]

My dear night clerk

How was Yaddo? I hope it was good and that the writing goes well. I can't find your last letter to answer in kind so (I ought to know it by heart — I read it a zillion times) will do my best.

I can't tell you how your advice etc. helped when I went to New York. I mean, *I think* it helped. I am never sure. I might have axed myself — but I don't think I did. At any rate, it was very easy to be easy with Fred Morgan. He didn't SEEM shy or difficult but charming and very warm and friendly. I tried NOT to act suave (as you said) but this was difficult because part of my well-worn mask is being suave . . . I tried to tone down the mask and, as you said, "be myself." If there had been time I would have written you back, "which self????" . . . but there wasn't time . . . Still, I was pretty much my own self's self, booming with enthusiasm about this and that and (now that I look back on it) mostly enthusiasm for your work. One thing sure, I raved about your genius constantly. I hadn't planned to or anything — but it happened that way. And not, De, that you need it . . . For me, now, you are not a God (you are right Lowell is taking THAT spot over), but you are an honestly lame real genius (and there are few enough of them writing around). I noticed in the trend of conversation that you have been mentioning me to Fred and that it didn't hurt any. (unlike you — I do need it) . . . And many thanks . . . Why are you so nice to me, Snodsie . . . do I deserve it? as a writer? . . . I WANT to deserve it, but I wonder in passing at such miracles and devotions. And anyhow, forget the question — but take the thank you. [. . .]

Is this letter strange? or more sensible or extra flat? I am trying a flat mask to hold my sanity up . . . my life is falling through a sieve . . . With all these good fine things happening to my poetry (and I haven't told you half of it yet) I'm dropping out of myself. Partly because my mother is dying now and I . . . I know it's crazy, but, I feel like it is my fault . . . Now don't lecture to me, De, I'm just telling you how it feels. My father, since his shock, is not the same; he acts about ten years old, and keeps crying and begging my mother not to die. I don't know how long this will all last, maybe a week, maybe two months — they won't tell us for sure. She is in the hospital with cancer now in her liver, stomach, lungs and bones . . . (I feel guilty. Remember the letter I wrote you about hating her) . . . What do we do with our old hate? I feel as if, now, I were taking each one of her bones, separately, and carrying them to a soft basket. It is hard too, when people die slowly, slowly, slowly; bone by bone to the soft basket . . .

And analysis goes poorly. I think the guy thinks I'm psychotic. Or something . . . I have this crazy new symptom (he calls it a symptom) where I pass out, black out actually . . . and sometimes stay out for 24 hrs. Once crossing the street in Boston during a snow storm, they found me in the gutter (GUTTER) — out —— for 18 hours and so forth. No physical reason. A hysterical type of thing, I guess. Tho once, half-waking up in a strange hospital I heard the nurse say "looks catatonic to me" . . . all quite frightening. And by the way, don't mention this to anyone . . . with most people, I prefer that they think of me as normal or as normal as possible . . . and even you, my dear, I won't continue with all this as it's very discouraging. And I am very discouraged about it.

The thing that seems to be saving me is the poetry (I refuse to misspell that word, at least) . . . Lowell is really helping me, De, as kindly as possible and I can't figure it out. I am always so startled by goodness. He likes the looks of my "book," with some critical reservations, and has shown it to Stanley Kunitz and Bill Alfred) who both, he says, agree with his enthusiasm (and his reservations). He is going to show it to somebody Ford at Knopf this week to see if he would be interested. And Houghton Mifflin wants to see it. He thinks that I ought to make my final goal Sept. — at which time it should be ready to be printed. Tho, he says, I might not be lucky — but then I might. Still, in total he likes my work a lot and ... isn't that something, De ... I mean, I am — jeepers creepers about it. He means by Sept. that I might get it accepted now, but should still rewrite and work out the poorer stuff and write some new ones to fill their place.

I am confused and delighted with this — and time and the publishing market will tell the rest. But, I remind my self's self, I've got to stay sane to do it.

By the way (and by the way of asking your opinion), he (R.L.) thinks that "By Nameless Flesh" is one of the "poor" poems and should be omitted. I remember that you liked it and once said, "well, it doesn't matter about the magazine that took it — it will be in your book someday" ... Do you still think this? I am about to take it out of the "book" unless you still feel it is good ...? ... I have changed it a little since you saw it, flattened the over-statements, etc. But apparently that isn't enough. Have you an opinion?

With all of this I am ready not to get *too* hopeful and am willing to wait my 4 or 5 years. If my mind stays intact and the writing progresses as it has been, then I really don't care so terribly about "success." The "next" poem is always THE thing, the question, the fear. I really do feel that the only true thing about me is possibly a good poem or a good line — aside from that it is "mask" ... even for you, most always, mask ... (I don't mean YOU. I mean when I am *with* you, even you, it is a mask. Old rudderless mask. And still I love you. Love you for being your own self — not quite as marvellous as your own poems but so kin to them, as amazingly real as they are ...

And enough of you. It's just that I won't give up loving your work. Won't won't won't. So there ... Perhaps, after all, it is better to love someone who is very far away (like Scottsville is farther away than I can get to). It is as if I could say to my desk's soul that THERE IS SOMEONE THERE knowing this is safe because it is the *idea* of you that is there, here, every other elsewhere.

Whoops! I'm forgetting I was going to write a plain howdy-do flat letter.

And Joe Bennett said, "O, do you know Snodgrass" and I laughed and replied, "Know Snodgrass! I love Snodgrass!" and we all laughed. I told Fred about your genius talk at Antioch and how the audience fell down in praise, etc. I also mentioned it ought to be printed . . . and it should . . . tho I expect you want to talk it a few more times. I wish I had a copy of it. I NEED some poetic tact. Would you, my dear, send me 1/2 lb. of poetic tact, post-paid?

I AM being kind to Lowell. *I promise.* I take everything, anything back . . . all of it . . . etc . . . he is being kind to me also. I was never unkind to him anyhow. Don't you know, De, I am not an unkind folk. I am (despite cracking mask etc.) a gentle heart. I will nod from now on. No matter what he says I will just nod. I always knew he was teaching me a hell of a lot — it was just the nodding I minded. I wondered if it could be stimulating to teach a class where no one questioned or even answered YOUR questions . . . just a bunch of nodders. But if YOU just nodded then that is for me too.

Actually, Lowell can not have influenced my work with his work as I haven't been reading his stuff . . . just listening to his ideas about other people's work. I do not feel he is influencing me — but teaching me what NOT to write — or mainly. Christ. This IS getting to be a long letter. I liked your comments on "Some Foreign Letters" [TB] and have changed one line per your advice. Tho your advice wasn't too specific. I like crit., you know, or otherwise wouldn't ask for it. I've left the ending tho. I think I *do* want it to end, just the way it does. Kind of rough, but the way I intended, really . . .

Forget the bridal veil. As of now you owe me one bridal veil. And that takes care of THAT. To be returned only in kind — !

Got my stuff back from *Virginia Quarterly* yesterday (in

case you haven't — I was the last of ten known poets around here to get it back) . . . not that I care. They can take their crummy 500 bucks and . . .

Do you have the energy for two poems. In case you do. [. . . "A Story for Rose on the Midnight Flight to Boston," TB]

This is fairly new and I feel that I would like your general opinion on its success or failure. A yes or no.

And here is another ["Ringing the Bells," TB] that I, myself, like better. Or maybe only because I've had it to look at for a couple of weeks and it wears like an old hat. It isn't so old as all that seeing as I wrote it from a recent (the calendar says it was Jan 6th) trip to the "summer hotel" that is rapidly becoming a winter jail . . . one good thing is that they don't keep me in there too long anyhow. Tho if I don't watch out, my Dr. says, I'll be committed for 6 months . . . at any rate my book's title, so far, is *To Bedlam and Part Way Back* . . . and this is another "bedlam poem." [. . .]

And that's all. Let me know what you think of them if you can. As much or as little. They are not great. I know that. For the moment I have ceased trying to be "great." Lowell told me to write ten more really good poems and now he has said THAT I can not write, hardly. So I gave the idea up and am doing as always, just writing what I can, what I *have* to. My stuff is always just what is actually going on. I can't make it up any different. I fear I will have to write one about my mother dying. Tho, don't WANT to, it is such a common boring subject.

Have I told you I love you? No. I just rattle on and on. Consider your moustache twitched. I wink at you. You are magnificent. I will buy three dozen copies of your book in April. Give my best to your good wife, your dear children, all of you and yours. Kayo passes by the typewriter and sends his best. And Joy and Linda too. You have walked through my universe —

                                        let me know about Yaddo.
                                        love, Anne

[. . .]

Early in 1959 Anne submitted several poems to Carolyn Kizer, editor of *Poetry Northwest*, who rejected and returned them with a letter full of incisive commentary. Kizer dared to question Anne's work and thus earned her respect; in days when praise came easily, honest criticism was invaluable. Over the years she and Anne continued to write sporadic letters packed with poetic critique and warm-hearted gossip. When Kizer moved to Washington, D.C., in 1965, they preferred to communicate by phone. This early correspondence reveals one of Anne's greatest strengths — an ability to welcome constructive criticism.

[*To Carolyn Kizer*
POETRY NORTHWEST]

> *40 Clearwater Road*
> *5th of Feb.* [*1959*]

Dear Carolyn Kizer,
I want to thank you quickly for your fine letter and all the comments. I like what you have to say and in most cases I think I have profited from your crit. Everyone needs GOOD detailed criticism and I know I do. Although I have many "poet-friends", they are so used to my extra flamboyant stuff that they have missed reminding me (in some cases) to flatten it down. Which, in total, you did. And thank you. [. . .]
Within my small experience I have never gotten such a nice and worthwhile letter from an editor. Any editor . . . Furthermore, I am pleased that the poems interested you enough to bother. and etc. It might interest you to know that your level of criticism seems about like Robert Lowell's (and he is a good critic I think) . . . or, at least, what you said was about what he said about "The Death" one. (why the hell didn't I change it when he told me??? I don't know. I just don't know. Maybe it takes a woman to tell a woman for god's sake don't do THAT) . . .
I hope you will bear this messy letter. I never bother with "letters" (simply NO control in this dept.) . . . though I do try with the poetry.
I do not know your work and wish I could see some. We seem to be running in the same track. I have a long thing (240 lines) and two other shorter ones coming out in the

spring issue of *The Hudson Review*. I think the long one would interest you greatly as it is surely the most super charged thing I've done, and is entirely about the "mother child" relationship. A feminine and directly emotional piece that will make most readers flinch and probably the men! most of all. So perhaps it is a bad thing that it did get in there as I tend (now) to think I can get away with it . . . when, after all, I should remember to (as you say) turn down the volume knob. If you have a chance to see it, let me know what you think. I would be very interested. In fact, if you don't run into a copy and would like to read it let me know and I will send you one. [. . .]

The reason I was in a hurry is that Lowell is pushing me to send out fat groups to the big places. and I am getting short of what he thinks constitutes a "group" . . . Being a "poet" in Boston is not so difficult except that there are hoards of us living here. The place is jammed with good writers — it's very depressing.

As you may note I can't spell. And at this point my husband insists I put the children to bed . . . so it goes . . .

I look down at your letter and an underlined sentence jumps out at me "the phenomenon is the poem" . . . and I say to you, Carolyn Kizer, the phenomenon is NOT the poem at all, but an editor, like you.

> *a million thanks and best wishes,*
> *Anne Sexton*
> (no pen around here)

[*To W. D. Snodgrass*]

> [*40 Clearwater Road*]
> *Feb. mon something or other*
> [*circa 11, 1959*]

Dear Mr. Dear De,

Bride's veil received today. But no letter. Am I off the list? Am [I] a bad girl that didn't know she was being a bad girl? I don't care if you don't write, really, but can't bear to be a bad girl.

I NEED communication from you because only YOU know if I axed myself with Fred Morgan in N.Y. . . . now I think that

I must have and you don't know how to tell me. Please tell me, De. I must know if I'm axed or not. I trust you to give me the real scoop. Who else can I trust if not you, my good night clerk in your emotional hotel. Who else? The world is full of faces and dozens of liars. Zillions of men and all, but no one TELLS me. I have all sorts of would-be lovers but no one but Snodsy to trust. My dear trustable friend. Write me.

I don't give a shit if you don't read all the poetry I send you and ALL THAT STUFF. De for God's sake, don't stop writing because you can't find time to plow through my lengthy letter. Just write me, a post card and say "axed" or "not axed" . . .

Enough of that. Thank Jan for the bride's veil. Linda is now wearing it. They both have these bride costumes and parade back and forth beside the typewriter wearing them and singing as I tip tap type away . . . I have been working all afternoon on revising that "By Nameless Flesh" and grinding all the lyrical and overwritten stuff out. It is kind of like sandpapering a sunburn but I'm doing it. Lowell is very good for me; I mean his advice is good. A hard task master, but it is good for me. I THINK I am learning something. You know, De, I just adore learning things. I can feel my mind expanding like a pulled elastic band. I was always a dope in school (never paid the slightest bit of attention). I failed most things. (a real juvenile delink) . . . (or a real neurotic mess — depends on how you want to look at it) . . . I was afraid to succeed. Didn't even try . . . Jesus god thank you for psychiatry. Without a second chance (or last chance really) that it gave me I would be impossible-er . . . Of course I could always write somewhat — but it's this business of writing BETTER that continues to fascinate me. Today I feel encouraged (revision of poem has gone well) and I'm hoping inside my mind, thinking "I will get better! I will learn! I will write!" — you know the feeling, I am sure. Of course there is always the let-down when you guess it was all a fraud anyhow — but I won't worry myself with that, now.

I don't know why the hell I'm writing you. I must like to, or something. I think I pretend you are real.

Nothing else new. Lowell's class starts again tomorrow.

My mother is still dying. I go to see her every day (being a
good girl you see) ... Have been asked to read March 1st at
the poets' theater with two other poets. It doesn't mean anything actually but will be good experience.

Did I do something wrong? I am always doing SOME
DAMN THING WRONG. If so, let me know. Did I say
something wrong about you to Fred or, or or, anything? Is Jan
mad? Or Fred mad? Or Buzzy mad? Or Mary Emma mad?
Or Snodsy mad?

If so, I don't care, I love you anyhow. It is too late to turn
you out of my heart. Part of you lives here.

love, Anne

While studying with Lowell at Boston University, Anne also partici-
pated in an informal workshop with other Boston poets — Maxine
Kumin, George Starbuck, Sam Albert, and John Holmes. Drawing on
the criticism she received from her class and her workshop, Anne
gradually began to develop her own style and voice, and wrote many of
the poems which were to make up her first book, *To Bedlam and Part
Way Back.* Her poems were intensely personal, revealing much about
her family problems and her own mental illness. Holmes, who had
been her teacher a year earlier, did not approve of her candor. Early in
1959 he expressed doubts about such public confessions, warning her
against exposing both herself and her family. She replied with a letter
and the poem "For John, Who Begs Me Not to Enquire Further" [TB],
explaining that she could not help herself. Later, her choice of a
preface for *Bedlam* reflected this conflict with her earliest teacher:

It is the courage to make a clean breast of it in face of every
question that makes the philosopher. He must be like
Sophocles's Oedipus, who, seeking enlightenment concern-
ing his terrible fate, pursues his indefatigable enquiry, even
when he divines that appalling horror awaits him in the
answer. But most of us carry in our heart the Jocasta who
begs Oedipus for God's sake not to inquire further ...
            – from a letter to Goethe by Schopenhauer

[*To John Holmes,*
possibly draft]

[*40 Clearwater Road*]
LINCOLN'S BIRTHDAY
[*1959*]

Dear John,

I have spent the morning writing you a poem ["For John, Who Begs Me Not to Enquire Further," TB]. And now that's that. I could have written you the volumes that raced defensively through my mind, for two days now. Instead, a poem; the condensation of it all. I let one word speak for many.

Of course there are other poems that I did not write. I didn't say that, although we seem to be strangers, that I wave to you from my distant shore, that I send semaphore signals that you may find my signal no matter how foreign the language. I didn't say that you have taught me everything I do know about poetry, and taught me with firm patience and a kind smile. And I didn't say that poetry has saved my life; has given me a life and if I had not wandered in off the street and found you and your class, that I would indeed be lost. I didn't say that I *have spent two years wishing* that you would like me and feeling that instinctively you did not. I didn't say how I cried the day this summer after leaving your house, because you were such a good man and your home seemed to radiate. I didn't say that I am surely a fan of yours, a lesser but a firm fan. I didn't say how welcome you make me feel in your home when you think to include me to a party. Or that Doris is great — and Doris really is so great, so likable and fun.

And then I didn't say that your criticism of me as a person was difficult, was perceptive, but bitter, or that I would like to cry, "but I don't know how to be anyone but myself", and that I felt ashamed . . . and then I knew that I had forgotten the affection and the courage that wrote the letter. I do not know how to be what you would rather have me be. But I will try. Of course, I will shuck off this shell; of course I will change, will grow to look around instead of inside. But in case it takes a little while, I hope that you will wave back to me from your distant shore, and understand the signal — if not the words, will see the gesture and disregard the lack of sound.

And because you can see a young light within me, hidden but possible and I can see your special sensitive light, always constant . . . I will blink in your direction. And that is a bridge, from my window to your window (no door!) . . .

In the midwinter of 1959 she sent "Some Foreign Letters" [TB] to Philip Rahv at *The Partisan Review* and "The Road Back" [TB] to Howard Moss at *The New Yorker*. Both poems were accepted. She wrote to Moss: "Despite many successes nothing has been sweeter. (I mean yippee)."

As the friendship with Snodgrass developed and the tutelage under Lowell continued, Anne worked with more intensity on her book. She later remarked that Lowell didn't teach her what to put in a poem, but what to leave out: "What he taught me was taste. Perhaps that's the only thing a poet can be taught." Following his suggestions, she cut out fifteen poems and replaced them with new ones.

[*To Nolan Miller*]

40 Clearwater Rd.
sunday Feb. 15th, 1959

Dear Nolan,

I was so sorry to hear from Jud about your Mother's death. It was so sudden; that is always hard. Easier for her, of course, but so difficult for you. I meant to write you right off and tell you that I was thinking of you day by day and hoping for you. Now I hear that you are back. I am sure the trip helped a little, as time will, as all things of life do help a little. I know how close you and your mother were . . . and there is nothing that I can really say. I remember reading an essay by Theodor Reik in memory of Freud . . . and Freud said something to him that he remembered more especially after Freud had died. The last time he saw Freud, he knew that Freud was dying, and he felt unable to speak, Freud took his hand and said, "People that belong together, do not need to be glued together." . . . and I remember it too. I mean, I kind of like it and I kind of think I will not forget it either . . . I always have this desperate feeling about time, time passing by

and not being able to catch it. But, now that I consider it
again, I try to remember that people who belong together do
not need to be glued together.

Do I make ANY sense. I doubt it. But the gesture is sincere. [...]

Recently I gathered up my stuff and piled it into a book of
sorts and gave it to Robert Lowell for his opinion. Now he
tells me that he showed it to Stanley Kunitz and Bill Alfred
and they like it (with some critical reservations) and then he
left it with Harry Ford at Knopf ... So lots is going on. I
hadn't meant for him to do anything but read it and give me
an idea of what was wrong. And now I find it is resting in its
bastard form at a publisher's. I feel it will axe me. The book
is a mess, though since have dragged SOME of the lousy stuff
out and have written some new poems. Lowell is very enthusiastic about my work. (But I haven't forgotten WHO discovered me) ...

I am giving a reading at the Poets' Theater in Cambridge. It
will be my first real reading. George Starbuck and Maxine
Kumin are reading with me. Also Houghton Mifflin seem
anxious to see my book (though I doubt they would want it in
its present form) ... But I do seem to be getting help from all
sides. Writers and writers' folk are the best of all in this big
world.

I have tried to follow your advice and crit of my work and it
has helped me, has steered me quite a bit. I have been so busy
with the poetry that I have not given any time to prose. I will
because I will have to, sooner or later. I do have a feeling for
stories, for plot and maybe the dramatic situation. I really
prefer dramatic situations to anything else. Most poets have a
thought that they dress in imagry imagery (I just can't spell.
I'm in too much of a hurry.) But I prefer people in a situation,
in a doing, a scene, a losing or a gain, and then, in the end,
find the thought (the thought I didn't know I had until I wrote
the story) ... This is, in fact, a major criticism of my poetry.
But still, I think it makes stimulating poetry and poetry need
not be dull. And anyone can think of images, most anyone. I
like a good image; I use them often enough — but I want,
usually, more than that. I wonder, rocking on the tight rope

of my own proclamation, if I am right. I announce my belief
and then doubt my position in air. (Speaking of those anyone's images). [. . .]

And forgive this hasty letter. I save my grammar and spelling for the poetry and just don't have time to write a decent
letter.

with my best,
Anne

[. . .]

[*To W. D. Snodgrass*]

[*40 Clearwater Road*]
Feb the 24th the 59th year

Dearest Snodsy,

[. . .] Am writing like sixty, lately. Alternately depressed or
up. All my personal life stinks as you know. Mother still
dying away and Daddy acting nutty. Thank god for my good
sane husband. He holds me up. He is a wonderful good man.
I am lucky. He is the . . . god knows what I was going to say.
Have been interrupted . . . cup of coffee with Sandy and Les.
Now it is time to get lunch. And you know.

I hope you had good luck on the job interview. I wish you
would find one around here.

My book is taking shape. Though will probably reshape itself a dozen times before I get it accepted. Still, it doesn't
look bad. I am about to write an article in defense of sincere
poetry, saying more than you said. I guess because I am starting to get attacked on my kind of poetry. I guess this always
happens when you do something out of the norm. John
Holmes thinks my book is unseemly, too personal, tho
talented. So I have been firing the burners in defense of myself. I have one comment to make that might interest you.
One comment that is essentially a personal comment. And
that is . . . J. Holmes wasn't impressed with "Heart's Needle"
. . . and now I have figured out why. He is afraid of something
that real. People are afraid of people, especially poets. As I
said to Fred Morgan, in discussing how I came to know you
and how I first came to be influenced by you . . . I read
"Heart's Needle" and I changed. It made me see myself new.

In seeing you, in feeling your marvellous restrained sense of immediate loss, I saw my own loss in a new color. And I changed. I said to Fred, "A poem isn't supposed to do that! It isn't supposed to be that vital!" . . . meaning, of course, how unusual, how much genius and the fine grip of talent, is in such a poem that reaches down and touches the inmost part of the reader. A writer, showing himself, in his true light, and doing it so well, has indeed done something so great that one might be afraid. Afraid of the writer's truth and their own truth . . . That's what I think you did. That's the great thing you did. And who would expect it from a 'just a poem' . . . I don't mean to imply that I have written anything as good. I have not. But I would, if I could. I damn well wish I could . . . Tho Rose Morgan said to me, about "The Double Image" [TB] "Thank you, Anne, for writing that poem" . . . it meant something quite real to her tho I don't actually know what. Something about being a woman and a mother. and Fred said, in talking of it, in talking of the final insight of the poem, in the last lines, I quote "I, who was never quite sure/ about being a girl, needed another/life, another image to remind me./ And this was my worst guilt; you could not cure/ nor soothe it. I made you to find me." . . . he looked kind of funny and said, something about those lines really got him. And how he guessed he understood better why his first wife kept wanting and having more and more children . . . "She made them to find herself — but couldn't" . . . What I'm trying to say is that, I think a poem that can do that to people, make them see themselves through yourself, is valid . . . not unseemly, not too personal . . . but worth it!

Christ. I'm off again. Talking in circles. My darling, the peanut butter calls.

You will write, won't you . . . Nothing else is new. Got an acceptance from *Accent* . . . two old rather cruddy poems . . . though one you will recognize from Antioch and down at that tavern ["Portrait of an Old Woman on the College Tavern Wall," TB]. Maybe I sent it to you a long time ago, I forget. Will be out for the winter issue if you happen to run into it. But I forget you never read the mags around.

You really wouldn't like it around here. There are always

these parties after readings that The Poets, the good, the almost and the best all go to and muck around. It is politics
and as bad as the University itself. See Cal at them, but avoid
hanging onto his jacket... People like Phil Booth (who I
think very phony by the way) go... Last week for Dick Wilbur, John Holmes had a party. After most had left (Cal, Stanley Kunitz, John Brinnin, and Isabella Gardner) we sat around
and read our poems aloud (dozens of others must have been 50
people there!)... Wilbur, Holmes, Dave Ferry, Phil Booth,
Maxine, Me, George Starbuck and some others I forget. and
that was kind of fun. But still all very political and "who do
you know" and "do you have a new book in process" And...
Wilbur, by the way, is a doll. Very handsome and handsome
himself. His wife is a go-jus creature, curvy and all, expensily
dressed...

The kids are jumping on my feet. MOMIE we want some
lunch.

fondly,
Annie

Her mother died of cancer in early March. Each day Anne had sat by
the bedside of the woman for whom she felt such ambivalence, playing
cards and talking until time ran out. She poured out her grief in "The
Division of Parts" [TB], published by *The Hudson Review* in 1959.

This winter when
cancer began its ugliness
I grieved with you each day
for three months
and found you in your private nook
of the medicinal palace
for New England Women
and never once
forgot how long it took.

In June her father died. While in letters Anne could bear to mention
the loss of her parents only in passing, in "All My Pretty Ones" [PO]
she mourned within the strict walls of her art.

. . . My God, father, each Christmas Day
with your blood, will I drink down your glass
of wine? The diary of your hurly-burly years
goes to my shelf to wait for my age to pass.
Only in this hoarded span will love persevere.
Whether you are pretty or not, I outlive you,
bend down my strange face to yours and forgive you.

[*To W. D. Snodgrass*]

[*40 Clearwater Road*]
Marchsnowingout [*11, 1959*]

Dearest De,

How really splendid your letters are for me. I kept your last letter in my notebook to give me the strength to be myself and to hell with the rest of them. We read again at the Poets' Theater this Sunday night because it was a sell out the week before. And was again, this last time. In fact, tho most of the really important people came the first time — the second reading was a greater success. Maxine read much better and I had really organized my stuff into a coherent whole and said a few words about — well about "loving," which seems odd I suppose. I tied my reading up on the statement that someone had said the week before about there being no love poems read . . . So, after saying that I WISH I could read a love poem (as we know them) I went on to say that mine were, in fact, love poems — and/or poems about finding the way toward love . . . and etc. but it did work out into a whole and went well. Still read "The Double Image" [TB] which seems to read well and moved both sundays' audiences. There was a sweet gray woman in the front row crying when I read it (later find out she is Mrs. Marquand — wife of . . .)

Then last tuesday Lowell did the complete "Double Image" in class and what's more he made ME read it. I was quite unprepared but he was adamant — I *had* to read it out loud. (I *think* this means that he liked my reading and now likes the poem better. More better. As a whole it has a good dramatic structure — but many faults when picked apart — He didn't pick it apart tho . . .) . . . When you do read it, *and please wait until it comes out in Hudson . . .* it will remind you, in

its like ways, of "Heart's Needle" because there was some experience so alike; the letting go of the child; the visits of the
child . . . But in main, now that I can be objective about it —
I do not feel it is an imitation of your great poem . . . (I was
afraid it was, you know) . . . But it ain't really. It is much
more twisted, less objective, more caught up in its own sickness — and then, it resolves like a story. I can never add nor
subtract to it. — Does this seem odd to write you about
this???? Maybe I do because I think you don't want to read it
because you love me and don't want to find me copying you
with my own like sick inventions pasted over your true
poem . . . And if you feel that I have, when you do read it, I
can only say that when I read your poem, that first time, leaf-
ing through the anthology, and it walked out at me and grew
like a bone inside of my heart. So, if the bone shows, it will
only add to your fame and fortune. Now that it and even you
are a kind of terrible part of me — I do not know how to dis-
organize myself. I have grown into this. No way back. No
way at all.

This letter is disjointed. I am slugged with tranquilizers today. My mother died last night. I have just returned from the
undertaker's and viewing the body and picking out the
gaudiest baroque (but cheapest) casket. And will leave here, in
a minute, with my sister to go down to Gloucester and pick
up some pieces. De, I am going to lose myself — or else, the
chance is that poetry will save me. (That is even the reason
that I am writing you right this very minute in the middle of
ghoulish death — because you . . . no. I won't say. I am
over-effusive. You represent something to me. So rare. Is it
too dumb or trite or feminine to say I love your soul? . . . I am
just beginning to learn to love at all . . . you taught me with
"Heart's Needle" . . .)))

The mail just came. Fred Morgan has taken another new
poem with great enthusiasm. He is a doll. A real love. I forgot, somewhere in New York about what he was thinking of
me, and found I did like him. and whatismore he really does
like my poetry. He took "A Story for Rose On The Midnight
Flight To Boston" [TB] — did I ever send it to you??? I forget?
It doesn't matter.

Also got a swell letter from Nolan Miller who wishes I would come back to Antioch. He is most enthusiastic over my work (which I send him as I write along) and his comments are good ones too . . . I might . . . But it costs. And I can't take the time to go everywhere, lest I lose my husband.

I would like to go [to] Yaddo. What should I do? Can you find out for me (unofficially) if I could get in . . . and if so, when. After, or around the end of June is better because I could have Sandy [Robart, a next-door neighbor] take the kids. But if it must be in May, that luscious of all months, I could try to find someone else. Would it be possible to go for only ten days or even just a week . . . I would like to get some real work done . . . and Antioch just isn't the place for it. But I don't care to go to Yaddo if there isn't some dear to talk to in the evening. If I write all day, I prefer to get smooshed in the eve. a bit anyhow . . . I prefer Yaddo cuz it is all free. But could probably get into MacDowell easier. Russell Lynes (*Harper's*) made the offer . . . Write me your complete thots on this. You wouldn't like to try and write a verse play (maybe a small one-act thing) together would you??? I think I'd like to try it but think that two poets could do such an unusual job of it, if they were of such a mind to do so . . . Maxine and I have discussed it . . . But can't seem to get her away from her text books . . . The theory of the 2 voices working with and against each other amuses me. And I DO have a real feeling for drama and know I could do it if I set out to . . .

If nothing pans out I know I'm going SOMEWHERE ANY-WHERE AWAY FROM HERE. Quick.

Got a letter from Knopf. Harry Ford seemed luke-warmishly encouraging about the book. And asks me to submit it when I've done all I can. (I asked him to send it back as it wasn't THAT ready for submission) . . . A friend at Houghton Mifflin is dying to get his hands on it . . . Oh well — who cares. A book is a book is a book and if it isn't really good who wants it on the reviewer's desk. Not I. Not till I'm strong enough to take it. You are right. I run around begging everyone to approve and like me and then sneak back to my desk and write this stuff that people either adore or detest. It don't make

sense. Ford did say he would be interested. But, he didn't say
how much — I guess that's the trouble. I want everyone to
hold up large signs saying YOU'RE A GOOD GIRL . . .
  Have got my money out to buy your book.
  And my mother is dead. I'm in a state of shock. It will
wear off, in time. Don't worry about me. Be your own night
clerk . . . I don't want you to worry about me, just to be you.
just like you are — stubborn, oaf . . . I wish I could make your
reading. I will think of you. Fred wrote and asked if I could
come. What large friends I have.
  What think you of Yaddo?
                            I adore you (I door you, as Joy says)
                            Annie Pants

[*To Carolyn Kizer*]

                            [*40 Clearwater Road*]
                            APRIL FOOL [*1959*]
Dear Carolyn,
  May I write you a long diffuse, misspelled letter? Here I am
liking you so much and feel indeed as if we are kindred
spirits. I do not think you will really like and approve of my
poetry once you get a real gander . . . but I think You'd like
me. There is such a slight, small band of lady poets with guts
that it is impossible not to want to draw closer and form a
band of understanding although we all play different notes on
our own horns.
  What I mean by all this is that since last writing you I was
constantly tripping over your name in print, your poems in
print and find that I must have sounded like a goop to say I
didn't know your work. Now I do — a little anyhow. There
is no reason for you to know mine as most of it has been accepted within the last year and isn't out yet. I'm the most
about to be published poet around I think. Tho *Hudson* is due
soon, I hope. Then people (poets) will know my work and
now that I think on it, I am afraid. The stuff I write is so controversial. NO ONE WILL LIKE IT. Of course, you don't write
to have poets like it. I don't. But I wish they would anyway.
And they won't. The whole trouble being that my writing has
guts, but I do not.

I like your work. Your poems are well coordinated effects of texture and emotion. They do not *seem* like attempted rape. In fact, for me, they need more *goose* left in to take away my breath. DO NOT CHANGE THAT LINE. If you do, you have nothing left of Kizer, but a rather commonplace thought. You do not slug too hard for me. I rather like being slugged; to walk away from the poem with old wounds reopened and . . . let the poem bruise me. Without the damn *goose* I walk away unchanged and even bored.

To get to what will really interest you, Carolyn, I will forgo the rest on my bits and ends of by-the-way thoughts. I received your letter yesterday and as I was about to see Cal Lowell in the afternoon, took it with me. I gave him the copy of "A Muse of Water", saying, as I tucked it into his pocket, "Here is a poem written to you by a lady poet." There were several people standing around and he bent his head over, the way he does, (the crooked man by the crooked house) and fumbled awkwardly for it. I told him that you had written it after seeing him at a party a year ago. Still fumbling the pages he smiled and said, "Carolyn Kizer is a beautiful girl." — (How do you like that!) I told him that I did not know you but that we had a slight pen pal going. And amidst the people and all — we parted. And now there are several more people who know C.K. is a lovely creature.

But this morning he called to ask me what's the scoop. So I told him mildly how we had written a couple of letters and that you had written this for him after hearing his remarks on "lady poets". He likes the poem. I said that I couldn't imagine "A Muse" would come in for that kind of crit. I mean, it seems a careful poem to me, no rape or danger and still not the usual weakness displayed by the female poet. He agreed. I told him (I hope it was okay?) that at first there were more references to him, but that now all that was left was the "Charles River" . . . We laughed at this. It strikes me funny that all that is left of Lowell is a river, running through a water poem. Of course, there *is* more, only you've generalized him.

But the main things I caught from our phone conversation is that: he likes the poem better than others of yours; that when

you come into a room you change the entire atmosphere of
room (a real dynamic kid) . . . I am not sure if Cal is a good
judge of poetry. I wish I could make up my mind about it because he is influencing me to such an extent. I probably am
making a mistake to let him be my super ego (or critic) as my
stuff seems to unhinge him and then he ends up thinking it is
good tho violent. But I have talked quite a bit with him about
various poets [. . .] and he dismisses so many so lightly, with
some remark like "accomplished but slight" — or so forth. If
he BOTHERS to criticize someone it means MORE than if he
thinks they are mildly adroit. And he has bothered to be
bothered by you. If so it means something. [. . .]

I am just not sure about Lowell. He has been very kind to
me and gone to bat for my work at great lengths and showed
it to Jarrell and such, much to my surprise. But he is very
shy. We hardly speak when we meet publicly. Then he will
call me up and we will both enjoy a frightfully stilted conversation as he tells me he has shown some poem of mine to this
one or that one and they concur with his high opinion . . . It
is so strange that I can't explain it. I think he may like my
work because it is all a little crazy or about being crazy and it
may be that he relates to me and my "bedlam poetry".

However, when De Snodgrass was here in Boston he stayed
with Cal for half the time and with us the other half of the
time. And this was early fall and Cal acted as if he couldn't
stand me. (or was I being paranoid?) . . . But I think that the
woman is a direct threat to the man-man friendship. Maybe?
And at that time Cal expressed open hostility to my work . . .
and then, later, seemed to convert to it. This is just by-the-
by guessing and for your added information and insight . . .
Cal has been so kind to me that I cannot think of him un-
kindly. [. . .]

My two children keep interrupting my train of thought for a
cookie, girl scout variety. I have two girls, age 5 1/2 and 3 1/2,
and a good husband who is not the least a poet, and very
much a business man — but all in all a happy marriage in the
suburbs. I have only been writing for a little over a year. But
have really put great energy into it and would be no one at all
without my new tight little world of poet friends. I am kind

of a secret beatnik hiding in the suburbs in my square house on a dull street.

I read your letter to a good friend fellow poet who really related and is sending you some poems for *P.N.* I hope you don't mind. She has published almost everywhere and is pretty good. [...]

This is a jerky letter as I'm in a lousy mood but I did want to write and tell you Lowell's reaction. [...] I think I will apply for poet in residence at the local summer hotel (institution) as it is so fashionable and all. Cal and Snodsy both have books appearing this April. Tho I haven't seen Cal's, I hear it is full of personal poetry and think that he is either copying me or that I'm copying him (tho I haven't seen his new stuff) or that we are both copying Snodsy! and that is true enough . . .

If this letter is awful, please forgive. I have wrenched it out of a clearly depressed day. I am having the dry heaves over a poem I don't want to write, but must write. It is too personal and not good enough and still I keep trying. I will muster the strength to type out some copies of my stuff which requires no thought and will soothe me perhaps, tho I'm sick of all of them. It does get that way with long much worked poems. Please send me copies if you can bear it. I would enjoy seeing what you're doing.

All Best Regards,

[*To W. D. Snodgrass*]

[*40 Clearwater Road*]
April in Wednesday [*1959*]

Sweet De,

I am glad that you wrote me. I thought I had died or something.

I understand your letter in kind. In all kind. You are right, I think, I must shuck off my poetic parents. But I have. Didn't you know that? "The Double Image" [TB] was written this fall. Of course it shows your influence. And this IS difficult, but not unsurmountable (how do you spell that!) . . . It is funny — the line Lowell thought most like you is "watching the yellow leaves go queer" and you say it is most

Anne-like. I think the main trouble is the theme of the child
as a visitor. And a few other tricks of yours that I incorporated into my technique. But different, essentially, because
mine is a wrenched story ... I don't know. I really don't.
The trouble is that we (you and I) are alike in a funny way. I
feel we are simpatico. In many ways.

But that was the fall. Now it is spring and summer gains on
me and the ground changes itself like a perfect machine. And
I will continue to change myself like a wrenched machine.
"Some Foreign Letters" [TB] (soft white lady of my heart) was
a Christmastime poem. And I have written dozens since. Tho
one of late that is reminiscent of "Double Image" [TB] in its
personal quality. But a common theme (not special like the
visiting child) but the commonplace of the dead mother (mine,
not me) ... O Snodsy, I love you; what's the use. We are
trees glued to the same forest. I ask you Snodsy, what's the
use/to even think of other trees/when we can see lots more of
these/good spruce ... That's a poem too.

Yale Review took a poem of mine for the June issue. It is
getting so that I have almost no unsold poems. The mail gets
thin and dull and only your letters cheer. Still, I am writing
— but I don't think I like any poem of mine as well as "The
Double Image" [TB]. Maybe that is only because it was so
wretchedly hard to write. I am trying to gather up a group to
send to *Poetry* mag. since the publishers tell me the credit
looks good for a book. How silly! How silly it all is. I am
beginning to think poetry is some sort of racket. I would personally rather send everything to Fred Morgan (he is such a
fine soul . . . I really like him a whole lot . . . not in THAT
way, but in a real-kind-for-special-folk) (you too of course) but
I guess you are supposed to add credits like some sort of badge
to wear.

So I will take your advice. At least I think I will. I am so
changeable and all. Nolan (to my surprise) nominated me for
a fellowship to Bread Loaf. Maybe I'll go there. No one interests me to study with ... I mean so few poets really fire me
with enthusiasm. I suppose I will never recapture the terrific
thrill I had when I read "Heart's Needle" and became your fan
and went to Antioch just to meet and speak with that great

poet man, W. D. Snodgrass. There are no new Gods to find.
So I must convert to myself. Or Christ. Or whatever. And
now I meet young poets and they think I am someone to copy.
I find this is threatening. (a WHO ME!) Ouch! My head is in
the mixmaster just as you said. And I'm being sorry for myself because my poet parent is pushing me out of his warm
safe arms and into the cool street.

OUCH! But, okay, because you is you and I do understand.
Only one thing, De dear, let me return sometimes for a visit.
Good idea? . . . And I know we will be uncomfortable until
we are on a like level of growth. So I'll just get me up and
grow taller. I am a bean sprout stretching toward you. (You
see, you can't make me be angry. I do not know how.) Will
you send me one visitor's permit in the next mail. I hereby
apply for a permit to visit your soul, on and around the date of
need. I am a soft lady and will not bristle nor mar the atmosphere of said soul and will, in fact, honor its scars and shine
its perfections. If you will award this permit, I will accept it
without specific obligations on your part and hereby promise
not to be influenced, comprimised (can't spell it), or reminded
that this soul is the biggest rooming house, with the softest
feather beds. In fact, Kind Sir, if you can allow me the honor,
I will be a level lovely loving friend . . . so much for that. It is
a fine thought. The trouble is that I love you and I just
WON'T be thrown out. In the first place, I did kind of walk
out on my own and you didn't even know it. (I mean you
haven't been reading the other poetry of mine carefully enough
to see it has changed) . . .

Why don't you write the Yaddo people about me or something. John Holmes received an invitation to go there. And
he is going to go when he can get the time. It would be easier
if I thought I could get in. I mean, if suddenly, I found I did
have the time to get away sometime — then I wouldn't have
to go through the rigamarole of getting passed. (or is this
never done with unknowns such as I???) Whatever you think
best.

Ted Hughes and his wife (Sylvia Plath) are in Boston this
year (he is an english poet) and they are going to Yaddo for 2
months next fall. She wants to know what it's like if you can

drink and etc. She is going to Lowell's class along with George Starbuck (poet) (and publisher at Houghton Mifflin) and we three leave the class and go to the Ritz and drink martinis. Very fun. My book is at H.M. now. Tho only in a half way sort of way. I don't think it is ready to be a book quite yet. It is tempting to go to Antioch and then Nolan and others, you and people, could see the book and advise me. But, in the end, I think I will know when it is good enough. And Lowell is a great help and very kind to me. [. . .]

I forget what poems I've sent you but will send some along. I guess this is a lousy letter. I'm depressed. God knows why. I'm sick of figuring me out. My head is in the mixmaster.

HOORAY FOR YOUR BOOK. IT LOOKS GOOD. DAMN GOOD. I will write more about it when I've had a full chance to digest it. As a matter of fact you are the greatest.

love among the mixed metaphor and mixedmaster.
Annie

[*To W. D. Snodgrass*]

[*40 Clearwater Road*]
[*April 1959*]
the next day

Hello again,

I wonder if I wrote you a horrid letter? Gosh — I didn't mean to. I mean I mean I mean, I forget what I said or how it sounded. I just must begin to censor my letters — they are getting out of hand. No super ego in them . . . or something. And too, I write very fast.

In the first place I've got you all mixed up in my mind with father-psychiatrist and god like folk. You mustn't mind me, really De, I'm too mixed up. I mean to be straight and simple. But I'm not.

I think I am too mixed up to ever be a good writer.

What I want to say is that yesterday I did (you warned me but it did no good) feel kind of rejected. Fool! Fool that I am. Grrr, at myself . . . and whatismore, Snodsy dear, you don't owe me anything so don't let me make you ever feel guilty. I think, unconsciously, that I was trying to. So cancel it.

Youse is a good boy. Even with a great dane which doesn't prove much (I mean having such a BIG dog) but if it was free who could resist a free BIG DOG. Not I. Not even a free little one.

Do you know Carolyn Kizer? She has converted to my poetry I think. Lowell says she is beautiful. I have never met her.

The trouble is that I am crazy and the room, ah, my own room drinks me,

and youse is such a good boy that I don't know how to blame you . . .

O dear, this letter is getting THAT way again.

Maybe I'm just frustrated. There is a rather nice poet in Boston who is in love with me. I guess I'd better give up and sleep with him. Then I'll have something concrete to fret about. But then, lust is so inadequate. And loving exhausts me.

I guess that small success (i.e. acceptances from lots of mags) is like taking dope. At first it worked wonders. Now it is never enough. And have no mana with which to get more.

Frankly, De, I'm lost. And it's my own fault. It's about time I figured out that I can't ask people to keep me found.

Tear this letter up too. Even my letters are incoherent. I meant to write a sensible note. But can't. I'm not in love with you but I seem to keep acting that way. If I ever figure it out I'll let you know.

> *yours without comprehension,*
> *Anne*

[*To W. D. Snodgrass*]

> [*40 Clearwater Road*]
> *April 11th 1959*

Mr. Dear De Snodgrass,

Because such things only happen once and because it happens again, a twice of admiration, of a being struck down dumb with the poem . . . because I hadn't EXPECTED to be found out again . . . because your book [*Heart's Needle*] is the loveliest book in the whole world, because the words in your book are new, never discovered, never seen pieces of language and living . . . I am your ardent fan.

The god damn splendor, the just right simplicity — It is a needle in anyone's heart. You will be great and famous, but it doesn't matter. What does matter is the book. You have done a perfect thing. I hold the red cover in my hand and the pages are as full and sweet as a first child. If I ever have borrowed your voice, I have done nothing but improve my own. By god man, you have it!

You know I said that I would never recapture that first experience of reading your ten part poem. But I was wrong. Tho I know the poem well (at least the parts in the anthology) it comes new in the book. It is the finest printing job I've ever seen. Three cheers for Knopf, they did you justice.

Whatever I have written you, disregard. I have no right to offer you my mumblings. They mean nothing — just the miasma of madness. I'm just writing as a poet. And as a poet, and person I'm bonged on the head. And even this is unimportant. The thing that matters is that anyone wrote it ever.

As I linger over the poems, I think to myself, "I must not read this. I like it too well. I am being *influenced*." . . . But truly, De, I love this book more than I love myself. I don't care about my poetry. I just don't care. Zillions of us writing the damn poetry. It means little. But what you have done! I am richer because I read it and love it.

Is Jan proud? She must be. You know one poem that I didn't know and like so much — "A Cardinal" . . . that's a fine piece. And I don't dare read it all carefully. Your things say so much without excess words.

Oh De, you are the most. I'm glad you are what you are and that your book is so fine. Now I'll put it tenderly on the shelf and resist watching it live in me. But before I did this, I had to let you know.

So now I'll go back to my own dry page and poke at it like a rough goat. Fool! Fool! I fumble with words for a mother and lounge in sad stuff with this love to catch, or catch as catch can.

But I'm so pleased and moved by your book. Knopf has been good to it. Now you just continue to be good to yourself.

And I give you permission not to tear this up. I mean it now and tomorrow.

On May 19, 1959, Houghton Mifflin Company of Boston accepted *To Bedlam and Part Way Back*, offering an advance against royalties of $200. Her close friend George Starbuck was to be her first editor.

[*To Nolan Miller*]

[*40 Clearwater Road*]
May 19th, 1959

Dear Good Kind Sweet Nolan Miller:
What wonderful bouncy encouraging letters you write! Your assumption that I could just sit down and write a novel — it is things like that that endear. Something, even, to cherish. So I will; both cherish and sit down and write a novel. And furthermore, just because you think I can.
Yes. But aside from all that. You must give me more time. I haven't even READ any novels lately. Not, as you say, that I need to. But, because I want to know what I am doing, a little bit. I can still be a mushroom, but I've got to have texture, smell, taste, and a place to grow. Sure. I'll grow from the ground, my ground, untutored stuff, but there are still things to test and learn. You know my first poems, my very first poems, were undisciplined, lacking in substance and technique. I have LEARNED this technique and not only from writing; but by keeping my ears to the ground the page and the critic. Only after I had learned a few techniques could I (and did I) start writing a mushroom at all. Before that it was crab grass. I don't want to waste as much time with fiction. And I will, if I don't stop and watch what I am doing. But the point is . . . I've been putting this off. And I won't any longer. Now I'm starting . . . but give me a little time, time for less crab grass etc.
If not this year at Antioch, perhaps next — I can't tell. I have just started (you see). The book of poetry has been accepted by Houghton Mifflin (as of today — I was awaiting their final decision so I could write you an answer). It won't come out for a year or so — but it is taken. So much for that.

I wish I might come to Antioch so that you could look at the book and to get your suggestions. (You see, Nolan, I trust YOUR intuition plenty!) ... I am pleased about the book, really. Tho since the *Hudson* came out I have had letters from two other pub. houses asking if they could see my book.

It has taken me, from the first poem, 2 years and four months. (to today) ... It took me one year and four months to my first acceptance from *Antioch Review* (and that was my first *real* acceptance). Therefore I think it ought to take me at least a year before I can really write a decent piece of prose. I've got so many new horrid mistakes ahead. But then. It's worth it. I know I must sound strange making a kind of "program" out of it. But this is how I set myself goals etc. It pushes me to work harder if it isn't just an empty void of writing into nothing. When I started to send poems out to magazines I said to myself, "I'll get a poem accepted SOMEWHERE within two years" . . . and then set out to beat my goal. . . .

Of course, the goals have matured. Now and long since when the magazine acceptance ceased to work — now it's got to be a Good Poem (worst critic Anne Sexton) ... The reason I go into all of this junk is so you will understand what I mean when I say I've started. I have a new goal. I won't tell you what it is. No. I will too! I must; you gave it to me. I am promising myself that I will write some fiction (I think I will start with short stories tho) and sell it within a year from Christmas. And maybe I can beat the deadline. And maybe not. If I write anything I think is half way good I'll send it to you. Okay? [...]

In fact, I will write you a sensible letter soon. I wanted to hurry off a reply to your kind letter. You just went and cheered me up. Thanks. Thanks. Thanks.

Love,
Anne

[*attached to preceding letter*]

I've had this letter on my desk for two days, hesitating to mail it and planning to rewrite it. It sounds a little conceited or "I can do anything" ... and since this is only a now and then mood (soon lost), perhaps I am Manic or something, I didn't want it to go out ... But send it anyhow. The buoyancy was your doing and most of my letters are depressed and full of self doubt.

The words I write in letters are never real anyhow. I hook into my mood and drain it onto the paper. The doubter is back today — but sends this anyway with love — the fact is — I have [not?] written for a month —

[*To W. D. Snodgrass*]

[*40 Clearwater Road*]
June 9th, 1959

Dear Dear De,

2 nice letters to be answered. You cheer! I'm so glad you do like the final version of "Division of Parts" [TB] — god, how unsure I am always am; needing constant reassurance that new things are good (good enough). It is indeed, a marathon, a marathon with yourself to outrun your last distance or something. And too, the vision is always unreachable; not ever realized in the result. But, when YOU like it, I feel surer. (tho I WISH you wouldn't keep telling me it suffers from Lowell's voice or your voice when, of course, I'm so sure that I haven't borrowed anyone's voice. Or, at least, sure about the Lowell influence. I've been so careful not to read his work. If anything, [I] have been influenced by his critical sense, his teaching — you know, just sitting in class and keeping my big ears clean and open. And YOU told me to. And I did ... Jesus, I'm a defensive creature! and in manicy moments I say to myself, I'm better than Lowell! — How is *that* for poetic conceit. ! ! ! You know, De, I never WANTED to take a course from him because I always heard he had such mixed imagery [...] These were *my* faults and I didn't want to be influenced by my own weaknesses. But, when you told me you had studied with him ... Still, I'm damn glad I did. He taught me great. It was as easy as filling an empty vase. After all, I didn't know a damn thing about any poetry really. 2 years ago I had never heard of any poet but Edna St. Vincent ... and now do know how to walk through lots of people's

poetry and pick and pick over ... god, is this still an
aside.)))))) ... And now that little argument is over. You
are a good boy. You are good for me.

I'm glad you're glad the book is sold. I will not wait for the
Lamont. I want to get it out and out of the way. My first
book, all about my own madness, is an encumbrance. I wish
that you would look at it. Would you? Do you have the
emotional-intellectual-time for it??? If I paid you a pittance
would it help??? I would be glad to if you wish ... Lowell is
gone. I do not trust *all* the poems in the book nor the poems
that Lowell told me to take out. There are about ten poems
out of it that could go back in. I don't care especially about
line-by-line crit as much as a heavy hand (a trustable one)
marking "take out" "put in" on the pages. I have taken out
the seemingly lyrical, early, Lowell-won't-allow-such-things
out of the book. And what is worse. There isn't one (not
even a little one) love poem. Imagine! A woman, her first
book, and not a love lyric in the lot. Except in the way that
"D. of Parts" [TB] is a love poem to a dead mother etc. I
know that this kind of thing is more of a love work than the
stereotyped kind. But still. I enclose for your casual glance a
couple that I have taken out. Wondering, if they are too weak
to include????

And, directly, let me ask you, would you look at the book.
Would you have the time? I would pay you $20.00. I mean,
that's not really anything. But I would if it helped.

I drag on with poetry talk and you NEVER tell me what you
are doing and writing. Why don't you send me copies? You
OUGHT to care about my opinion. I am your first and a devout fan and your severest critic. (and I'm not a bad judge
either. You really weren't famous when I picked you out. I
had no one else's opinion when I read "Heart's Needle" —)

I have been having a terrible time lately. A week ago at this
time I was in "the summer hotel" (local institution for nervous breakdowns [...]). God knows what was wrong with me.
I just sat in there and cried. For 3 days. I didn't eat or sleep. I
just cried. Then I got hold of myself and got out. My Doctor
is against institutions and always persuades me to leave. For
3 days it cost me $92.00 ... ! ! ! Pretty expensive tears I

would say. I haven't cried since, at any rate. I got out on Tuesday. Got home and started putting my pieces back into place. Read your first letter, looked at my book again, at letter from Fred Morgan taking 2 new poems (one being the "Division of Parts" [TB]) . . . and was about to get the girls back on Wed. morning when my sister called and told me that my father had just died of a heart attack.

So now he is funeraled, cremated, and I have no parents left to run away to Calif. from. Some misty god has shoved me up the ladder and I am my own inheritor . . . I am going to try and NOT write a poem about it. God damn morbid life I've been leading, that's all I can say. How can I write anything positive? My old gods are tumbled over like bowling pins. All is an emotional chaos. Poetry and poetry alone has saved my life.

The trouble with everyone just up and dying like that is that there are no faces left to throw your emotions at: love or hate. What do you do with the emotion? It's still there, though *they* are gone?!!!! . . . (I'm not really asking you; just confiding my every puzzle) . . . But, this has been one hell of a year. I don't know how I ever managed to write as much as I have.

Maxine has sold a children's book to Putnam's. It was written in the form of a poem. 80 lines and a $500.00 advance! That's the way to make money, boy! . . . I will try it myself, perhaps. If I ever get my life in place.

I am glad that Phil Booth likes my stuff. He called, one day, to tell me. I told him (he hadn't seen it himself) that I was your great admirer and "Heart's Needle" reader. (I should have kept my yap shut. He had no idea I *knew* you . . . I guess I want to hide your influence on my poetry. But, I notice, I did not; in fact, I offered the information. Credit where credit is due. My love.)

I met Philip Rahv a month ago and he is very cordial and friendly and father-figurey, kind of. I complimented him on printing your GREAT article . . . I also like Diana Trilling's thing. Did you? You both looked like those real toads in the imagernary garden. (you don't mind if I don't bother to spell . . . I'm sure).

Stop sending me written "pinches." I need "pats" and am not the pinchy type. Last year, at Antioch, you told me (I bet *you* forget) that I was a "great lady" . . . You did! Well, just put me back there and stop pinching me via the stamped envelope. I have forgotten your bodily self. It is too long ago. Only the soul remains. And that is for the best. It's so safe and at the same time, so true. Oh well, enough said — my soul sends your soul a pinch . . .

luv
Annie

[*To Carolyn Kizer*]

[*40 Clearwater Road*]
July 24th,[1959]

Dear Carolyn,

[. . .] I am going to study with Roethke this summer as I have received The Robert Frost Fellowship at Bread Loaf. He probably won't like my work. And there we'll be (you and me) with our Cal and our Ted, not liking our work enough (sobbing in our own private caves of womanhood and kicking at the door of fame that men run and own and won't give us the password for) . . . Perhaps not. Perhaps we can exchange famous poets' admiration, back and forth as if it were coin or old or solid. Eh?

I am going to see Fred Morgan in August and will mention your poem to him and twit him for missing a masterpiece. Okay? I leave in a week and have no more time to write another page.

Yours,
Anne

After visiting the Morgans in August, Anne and Kayo went on a fishing trip to Maine. In her thank-you note to Frederick Morgan, Anne remarked:

I really didn't have too much fun in the woods this time. The trouble with the woods is that you take yourself . . . only more so. I don't know what Thoreau would say about it. Perhaps I'll write a poem about it sometime: living in the deep woods is no escape. The trees become mirrors and only

your voice answers back. The deer is not my brother, nor
the trout as I pull him in, slapping at death.

Anne went to the Bread Loaf Writers Conference in late August, and
discovered an old friend from the Antioch conference, Hollis Summers.

[*To Hollis Summers*]

> *40 Clearwater Rd.*
> *August 31st, 1959*

Dear Cousin Hollis,

My suds, I'm back in the suburbs, the children are having
an acorn fight on the front lawn, it is 95 in the shade of the
acorn tree, a ham is cooking itself and me in the oven (my
desk is situated in the dining room, but at the door leading
into the kitchen . . .)

All things being equal (and they surely are) I am beginning
to feel and speak like a human living woman that I am. My
voice, as it descended from Bread Loaf, had a terrifying whiskey tone (gin I guess — but the same bloodstream voice) . . .
My doctor said that I'd been on a binge. I mean, he knew I
hadn't — but I certainly attended one and did indeed partake
thereof. [. . .]

I don't think I had a chance to say farewell to you. But I
liked your speech. I mean, I heard it. It seems important for
you to know I listened. And besides, you know perfectly well
that your yankee cousin does not like saying goodbyes.

So I have been settling back since my return on Wednesday.
Music, music, music . . . my life and music music music . . .
and your book OF COURSE! . . . and have even written a poem
which I will enclose for your approval. It is only one hour old
so don't be too critical. Though I have been trying to write it,
bits and starts, for six days.

Answer me or I shall cry.

> *Best,*
> *Annya*

Chapter II

All Her Pretty Ones

October 1959–December 1962

A woman who writes feels too much,
those trances and portents!
As if cycles and children and islands
weren't enough; as if mourners and gossips
and vegetables were never enough.
She thinks she can warn the stars.
A writer is essentially a spy.
Dear love, I am that girl.

A man who writes knows too much,
such spells and fetiches!
As if erections and congresses and products
weren't enough; as if machines and galleons
and wars were never enough.
With used furniture he makes a tree.
A writer is essentially a crook.
Dear love, you are that man.

Never loving ourselves,
hating even our shoes and our hats,
we love each other, precious, precious.
Our hands are light blue and gentle.
Our eyes are full of terrible confessions.
But when we marry,
the children leave in disgust.
There is too much food and no one left over
to eat up all the weird abundance.

"The Black Art"
from ALL MY PRETTY ONES

The next four years were prolific and exciting for Anne. She began to refine her gift. Although her sporadic outbreaks of mental illness continued, as did her therapy, the family learned to ride out the episodes. Now Kayo wore the Santa Claus suit from Abercrombie and Fitch, and the children left water and carrots on the back stoop for the reindeer who couldn't land on a modern pitched roof. They even weathered the trials of housebreaking a Dalmatian puppy. Her daughters brought her happiness: each year they measured the width of the chimney to see if Santa could still fit down that narrow brick tube — after all, they reasoned, wasn't he growing too? Linda marched through the house reciting the multiplication tables. Joy tap-danced dents in the kitchen linoleum. When Linda won the lead in the children's musical, *Sarah Crewe*, Anne taught her nine-year-old to belt it out, despite her own inability to stay on key.

Kayo had advanced in business, and now, in the summer, the children went to day camp. In August, the Sextons rented a cottage in West Dennis on Cape Cod. But the greatest self-indulgence was free; Anne loved the sun. No matter when it shone — even in winter, stripped to her underwear, wrapped in her mother's mink coat, she would sunbathe atop the backyard snowbanks. Finally, as Anne earned more in royalties and from grants, they put in a small swimming pool.

To Bedlam and Part Way Back came out in March 1960, receiving many favorable reviews, and a few fan letters slid through the mail slot at 40 Clearwater Road. Anne answered every one. Meanwhile, *All My Pretty Ones* had begun to grow. She wrote steadily, aware that her poems now would find immediate acceptance. Her letters to the editors of various magazines reflect her maturation; her earlier tentative cordiality was replaced by an easy, familiar tone. But, though she enjoyed her new status, the more notice she received, the more exposed and vulnerable she felt. She wrote to Carolyn Kizer in September, "I think I am aging fast. By the time I get to New York in October to read at YMHA I will be an old, wrinkled, yellow woman leaning on a stick." Nevertheless she plunged on, determined to explore and experience and record.

[*To Frederick Morgan*
THE HUDSON REVIEW]

[*40 Clearwater Road*]
Friday Oct. 16th, 1959

Dear Fred,

Many thanks for your letter that relieved me of all neurotic worries about you being angry with me and that told me to go ahead and try for the Guggenheim. I did try for it. So time will tell.

I have had serious troubles since (why is it that writers can't have slight troubles. But never. Always some big damn thing) . . . So I just got out of the hospital having had an operation . . . not exactly a hysterictomy (can't spell that one, for sure) but half a one kind of. They also took out my appendix as long as they were in there and an ovary and a cyst the size of a grapefruit. Ugh, the medical is so explisit. (can't spell anything today. Too weak.)

I am typing here in bed. I have a nurse to take care of me and mind the children. Which helps and will, I hope, help put me back and into New York in two weeks. Somehow I will stagger down there — if I have to lie down on the floor and read prone! The Dr. isn't enthusiastic about the idea of N.Y. but I shall be there nevertheless.

The minute this happened I started a new poem. I had to go to bed for a week previous to the operation as I had pneumonia at the time. In fact I rushed the whole thing because I wanted to have the op. in time to recover and get to N.Y. So here I am. Better and worse for the whole thing and not knowing if I have cancer or not.

I have written a short story that I want to work on and I have this poem started that looks like it will be a long one. If only I felt well enough, my creative spirit is boiling to get going. I will enclose the start of the new poem for your interest, though it will see new changes in even the beginning I am sure. I always work and rework to get things just so . . . Oh, dear, here I am with a soul full of energy that raps against my skin, my old paper bag skin that holds me together — just barely.

George [Starbuck] and I have reservations to fly over on Thursday morning, the 29th. I am staying at the Gotham if you want to contact me ahead of reading time. I shall be very nervous. Oh suds, I would like to read well. I will try to. Lee Anderson (he records poets all over the place for Yale or something) recorded me and liked my reading so maybe it won't be too sad after all. George is really a professional reader and will go over well I know. Thank you for asking him to the party.

I don't think Kayo will come over to N.Y. as his business is so demanding at this time of year. But he might, if I were still quite sick.

Enclose the start of new poem. All best to Rose and You.

p.s. Have just read Louis Simpson's new book and think it has some of the best poems of our generation in it. He is great. How I envy his way with about ten of those poems which will live forever. Maxine says I am getting didactic (sp?*) but I can only reply that I just know when I know. And one thing I know is that he is good. Though, I admit sadly, I did not like "The Runner" — felt it a failure, but then it was nice he tried to do a long one. On the other hand I thought (and did before) that "The Bird" is one of the best pieces, in fact the best war poem ever written. (Didactic? I suppose. But you have got to have opinions, don't you? I do. At any rate I wrote him a fan letter in care of Hudson. Was that awfully gauche? I am not in practice on fan letters but thought it rather homely and straightforward to write one.) [. . .]

love and kisses,
Anne

p.p.s. Should I read "The Double Image" [TB] do you think?

Anne published her short story *"Dancing the Jig"* in the 1960 issue of *New World Writing.* Sterling Lord, a New York literary agent, read the story and wrote to her, conveying his interest in representing her. The idea of an agent was new; Anne was flattered. So began an association which would last throughout her life.

[*To Frederick Morgan*]

[*40 Clearwater Road*]
Sunday, November 15th, 1959

Dear Fred,

Here (enclosed) are my proofs. I so glad I didn't suggest what order I wanted them in — because I didn't the last time nor this and both times they look better than I thought they would. I'm glad though, that you did include "The Expatriates" [TB] because I like what it does for the group.

Now! Here I am weeks later, and I haven't thanked you for all your kindness, your introduction (that I didn't hear one word of — but I know it was good), your fine party, your always assuring presence etc. etc. But don't think I'm not appreciative, Fred, because I am, I did, I do. You are the most!

Not much news here, except that (as I think I mentioned to you) I wrote this short story in Sept. and the first place I sent it to, took it! *New World Writing*, that is. As I said, I didn't dare send it anywhere that I was known as I was afraid it was so amateur that I would axe myself there. But maybe not — maybe not? I can judge the poems pretty well, but I'm quite unsure with fiction.

Because of all this I have had a letter from an agent who would like to represent me. His name is Sterling Lord. Do you know of him and do you think I ought to have an agent??? Any advice you might have would be a real favor as I really walk through this literary world with innocence.

I am reading at Harvard, a Morris Gray Reading, on Dec. 10th. This time it will be by myself and I haven't thought how I will fill 50 minutes with my own stuff. I wish that I had some light verse to read in the middle; just to relieve the tension of my fisted poems. Have you any suggestions for improvement of my reading? I know you *said* I did a good job; but now that it's over I wish I knew what I did wrong. Was I too dramatic? I think I tend to project the poem too much.

I haven't finished that "operation" poem ["The Operation," PO] that I showed you. Maybe I never will; maybe I've said it all. Time will tell. I have been working on a new short story, but it lacks the force that the first one had.

The new *Hudson* looks good. I love the easy way that

George Elliot writes. And the ending of that thing — that egg part — was perfect! I was very interested in Joe Bennett's review, but I think this is more his problem than Lowell's. But it may be that I felt the thing fell down when he started liking Betjeman's book. I think that Tennyson would have cringed at his style. And furthermore, he is a snob (Betjeman) in his own way. Though I thought Lowell's book [*Life Studies*] was a kind of failure (and did not like the prose) . . . Oh well, how can I be impartial? Lowell gave me a very nice quote for my book which Houghton Mifflin is sticking right on the front flap (they don't ask *me* about these things — they just do them).

In the usual rush. All my best to you and Rose.

Yours,
Anne

[*To W. D. Snodgrass*]

[*40 Clearwater Road*]
Nov. 18th cold out [*1959*]

Dearest dear De,

I *think* I owe you a letter. But perhaps it is you owing me? Whoever — it is too long since I have poured out Some Anne and offered it up to you. It is too long since I've let myself love as you (as is my natural habit).

So here I am. Do you know that I've been very sick? I just can't remember when or what I've written. Well, I was — awful sick for about a month. I had pneumonia and a major operation (removal of one ovary, one tube, an appendix) — both of these at the same time which made my recovery from surgery more precarious (the pneumonia I mean) . . . But still, just three weeks after the op. I made it to New York to read at the YMHA (tho it nearly was too much for me) . . . I read pretty well, I think, despite my appearance which was pretty skinny (lost about 15 lbs. but they're padding back on now).

Kayo is on a hunting trip (bear and deer) this week. He loves to kill. Oh dear, I wish he didn't. I wish him more tender but then, people are always wishing other people things. Be different! Pause as I give thanks that he isn't destructive toward me, my female core, my important ego, etc. etc.

Linda is learning to read. I wish I were in the first grade again, resting my head on the desk while teacher reads the story and drinking milk out of straws, that funny middle morning milk taste. I have written one children's story which was rejected 2 places and has sat at Lippincott for 3 months so far. It isn't a good story anyhow — but I could use the money. The poetry comes much harder. I am working on a new thing that may not work (an operation, death, cancer, mother, me) thing. Damn thing. I could really write it if I could just die at the end. Full cycle. Mother dies her ugly death and now Anne follows, trailing her guilty gowns down the last aisle ... One good writing thing! I wrote a short story and I sold it to the first place I sent it to. Namely, *New World Writing*. It will be in their first issue (they stopped and are starting up again, brought out by Lippincott this time); it will be #16 actually. It is a rather rather sick story — but who am I to complain when it sold?? Perhaps I ought to have sent it to better places first, but I was afraid to show it where I was known (*Harper's, New Yorker, Hudson*) as I thought it might lower their high regard for me ... And still it might have.

You are applying for a Guggenheim and you ought to get it. I hope, tho, that you won't move to New York. I think the rat race will kill you. I think you are a special person and ought to live on an island and let the world visit you. Don't you go visiting the world (you can't have those lines. I just made them up and I like them. I will use them in my elegy for you if you move to New York and then commence to kill yourself.) Mary Emma [Elliot, managing editor of *The Hudson Review* at that time] and I had a long talk about you at Fred's party after the reading and we agreed (so that's how friends are — always telling you what's what and interfered their thoughts into yours) ... If I were you (that means take my advice) I'd write in some pretty place and spend any extra money on a slight bit of analysis somehow) ... But I could be wrong. That's visiting yourself and that is difficult (I know. I do it all the time), but poemwise it has been very productive. It might be for you. Maybe?

Poemwise I should be working and not writing you. But this is a missing you, where are you, hello and necessary for my soul. I also applied for a Guggy but won't get it. I just did it in case. I really do need time — there are too many people in my island. I need to have one or two days a week when I can hole up somewhere and work. Here the phone jangles, the kids exist from my plate, my husband pats my fanny, and poemwise I haven't enough left. A matter of energy. Dear Mr Guggy — I need money because I must pay someone to be a loving substitute while I write, an apron with arms would do. . . . I fear Guggy won't care. After you get yours I'll list you as a sponsor. If I live long enough, if you live long enough. [. . .]

On the back cover [of my book] they have a terrible soulful huge head picture of me, under which they have in big fat black letters: ANNE SEXTON. I gave them a choice of pictures (fool fool!) and the cover, besides having that long title, & Lowell's quote, has a drawing of a mother and child holding hands . . . And the inside print is too small. And . . . oh, I wish it were over with, done, done, and the terrible reviews out, out, out, so that I might carry them in my knapsack like heavy stones.

But you got only praise. But I know, praise can be heavy too. Yes. I understand.

A little while ago I read H. Gold's story "Love or Like" and thought it the best thing ever. I talked with him later at Fred's party and he mentioned that you had liked it so much. I can see why. Though why I should is not as plain. It's the destructive element between people that I recognize. Maybe it's my mother and me — some such I guess.

I am rambling, on and over and about. Must get back to something at this desk. My best to Jan and all of you and yours. Write me quickly and kiss me back. I miss you.

XO
Yours, Anne

[*To Frederick Morgan*]

[*40 Clearwater Road*]
Friday [*November 19, 1959*]

Dear Fred,

Was it only yesterday or maybe the day before that I wrote you to say I wouldn't send you anything more until I SURE.

Well whenever it was and time means nothing to me; I have
no idea when I write things (letter things anyhow). Sure! I
know all about time when I've sent you a poem that you've
got to like. And you are so gracious as to realize this and answer promptly. You're a good man. I send nothing to anyone
else, except a few little ones to *The New Yorker* or *Harper's.*

Well. I've been working this over for months since you saw
it and asked for it in August. But just this week I changed it
right. Right enough to send along. I hope you still like it.
I'm pretty sure it's a "pretty one" and I'm not in a terror of
fear as I was with the operation poem. So, herewith, I submit
"All My Pretty Ones" [PO] and hope you want it as much as
you did this summer.

Aside from that I've been trying a new tone (if you can call
it that) on some little poems. I don't want my next book to
be as boomy as the Bedlam one. A little more restraint and
never a false shriek. I wish my poems were gay sometimes. I
am tired of my gloom and death. I have been reading
Katherine Mansfield's letters this afternoon and wishing I
were Katherine Mansfield. And this morning I read all of
Elizabeth Bishop's poetry. Therefore I could reason to be discontent, as I am.

Here is the kind of thing I am playing around with. [She included a draft of "I Remember," PO.] You might give me your
opinion in an offhand way. I'm not submitting it. I haven't
written it, really. But it's on my desk and walking in and out
of my pencil box ... [...]

> forgive this messy wordy letter.
> *Yours,*
> *Anne*

[*To W. D. Snodgrass*]

[*40 Clearwater Road*]
Nov. 24th, 1959

Dearly De,   **IN HASTE!**

Your letter cheered me this morning and I am writing right
back. It is good to hear from you. In all this world, at this
moment, you seem nearest and rightest of anyone talking to

me. And also because I am so pleased that you are starting with an analyst. Good! I knew you ought to, but it is hard to tell someone else (aside from telling yourself) that's what they need. [. . .]

I wish I might try classical analysis as my psychiatrist is not doing me the good he ought to, or I ought to. I've wasted a complete year blocking out everything and trying not to talk about my parents being dead. Mostly I fight with him in an underhanded way. One day though I broke out and picked up all the things on his desk and threw them at him (including a lamp and an ink bottle). I'm better some, though. I don't go around trying to kill myself all the time as I once did. (Just him. Ha!)

But my writing is in its beginning of trouble because I just have the most difficult time forcing myself to write about what I won't work on in therapy. My psychiatrist wants me to write short stories as you have to use more ego in order to write them.

I don't think I'll get the Guggenheim but it would be good for me because I need the status in my family life. I need to hold up the money and say, "See. This has *got* to be for writing and I've *got* to have the time." Then I can call in a babysitter and pay her with Gugg dollars and turn in peace to my desk. It's that simple. Writing isn't that simple (we know), but I have other problems that hinder it in this way.

Louis Simpson's book *A Dream of Governors*, Wesleyan Press . . . Anne Sexton's (out March 1st, '60) *To Bedlam and Part Way Back*, Houghton Mifflin.

I will try to get better — I'm some better but depressed today. Thank God for your letter. It made me human again.

> *I adore you and snuggle the*
> *page I send obsessively . . .*
> *Anne*

p.s. Joe Bennett's review of Cal was very damning, called Lowell a snob and a sloppy writer. You ought to read it. I think Joe's poetry is terrible, the worst, the possible worst — a cultured "Howl" about the world ending. I like him tho — but it makes me wonder at Fred's judgment. I'm not so sure

Fred has so much judgment anyhow. Are you? Maybe I think that because he likes my work. ??? (It's a typical reason. Jesus, I hate myself) . . .

Not much of a postscript, that. But see, your letter asks about Joe [and] I couldn't resist airing my opinion (for you, no one else please).

dearly,
Anne

[*To W. D. Snodgrass*]

[*40 Clearwater Road*]
Feb the 1st [*1960*]

Forgive this jerky letter! Maybe I even wrote you a while ago — I have NO memory left. —

Dearest De,

I was just sitting here, trying to write a poem that I'm not in the mood to write and looked around my desk for something in god's name to think of or to pick or to love or to watch (at least I might watch if the brain would not obey the need to write) and I picked out, by chance, after glancing at magazines which had printed my first poems (Ha!) (and that didn't help) pictures of everyone at Antioch. I looked at Hollis, for a while, considered that, after all, it seemed he had buck teeth (which I do not recall from a couple of kissing him) and then I saw you (naturally I'd have *three* pictures of YOU) and I looked you over, remembering your vulnerable smile and your dear moustachio and I looked at Jan (also in my pictures) and at you and decided (how's that for spelling) that I MUST WRITE YOU DEAR SNODSY WHO I HAVE NOT WRITTEN FOR HOW LONG ANYHOW?

How are you, my dear, dear? Are you okay? How was N.Y.? Do I owe you a letter? Maybe I haven't written for months? I never remember who I write and when and if [I] owe or don't????? But all I know is that I've looked your picture over, read some of my old poems, sat here and as usual not been able to write, been lonely, been sadder than sad toads would be if they are as sad as their blinking eyes seem to be, and I thought direly of you and wished I had a letter here at my desk from you, my dear, to read and to console me. (I'm writing long sentences tonight and fast ones too. Hope you can keep up with me. I think I drink too much. Have had, as usual, 3 martinis tonite). And so it goes.

My (fucking) book comes out March 1st in case you've forgotten. I haven't seen a copy yet. But that won't help I know. Nothing seems to. I've written just a little since this fall. Some. But not much. (I won't send you what I've done as you've enough problems without mine.) But I have thought of you, De. In fact I wrote a not so good poem to you. It was two weeks ago that I wrote it and I have almost forgotten it was to YOU (of all people). I guess I was thinking about your problem (the one that has to do with being a success. Thinking that it was important to have touched the sun. That what you've done is all that matters, no matter what happens next.) But the poem doesn't sound just right, doesn't sound like much. This is it (even tho I just promised not to show you any. I won't mind, if you prefer to skip it. I'm typing so fast I won't know if you read it or not . . .)

(now if I can find it in this messy desk here . . .*) ["To a Friend Whose Work Has Come to Triumph," PO . . .]

Well. I know you haven't written me since N.Y. as you haven't told me how it was. In fact I don't recall anything about you since Cal told me you had taken back your Guggy application which you should have still applied for no matter where you want to live. Oh my dear neurotic friend. The things you do!

Not much new with me. Kayo is well; is away for a week at the moment. Mostly I look at the night movies on T.V. and cook and care for Linda and Joy who continue to delight and amaze. Why can't I write a poem about loving them? Or Kayo? I don't. I just write morbid (my Doctor says I write "grim" poems and stories, that I only write with one small segment of my unconscious). I told him to get the hell out of my writing life! I'm better tho. Haven't killed myself for a year or over. (except in socially acceptable ways like drinking myself to death or taking sleeping pills each night but those don't count) . . . (also not writing anything *real* lately) . . .

I guess I told you I've written a couple of stories and sold the first one to *New World Writing* (out this spring).

I'm depressed now. Maybe this is the last letter I'll ever write anyone ever. I have nothing to say, really. I'm at my desk and my desk has nothing to say. I'm lonely. I guess I need Kayo around to pull me upstairs to watch T.V. . . . lonely lately. I certainly don't believe in God either and that's rather sad of me. Ruth Soter has converted to Christianity and goes to church all the time, she writes. She will be back this July. She still loves her husband, she writes. When she writes.

Enough. Enough. I have nothing left to say in all this world. Write me though.

Here is another newish poem ["Young," PO] to fill out my unfinished page (I'm very compulsive and always fill out that page). [. . .]

Goodnight, Dear De, yours,
Anne

[*To Louis Simpson*]

40 Clearwater Rd.
March 7th, 1960

Dear Louis Simpson,

You are wonderful and I have treasured your letter. I wasn't going to answer as I thought it was presumptuous of me to start a "correspondence". You know? But I am a fool. I have been rereading your book for the 10th time and in it I have placed your letter and have again reread your letter. It is rather a mean timid soul who would not answer such a letter! I will not be that. I mean, I didn't intend to be that. I was too busy thinking of being self effacing to think I OUGHT to answer. Of course, I wanted to. But that's something else.

What I'm trying to say is thank you for your letter. Oh stupid stupid that I didn't answer in November. Yet maybe my instinct was right. I wrote you in the first place in a terrific burst of sincere admiration and thanks for your book. I didn't want to start an "admiration exchange", I didn't want to seem social or poetry ~~pliciteal~~ (this is a bad day, the typewriter won't spell) political. You know?

Now — the time has passed for a chance of all that. It's

time now to wave back to you and even throw you a kiss. And what words can I send along with the kiss? Perhaps there are none left. How special it has made me feel to think that you did know of my poetry and even liked it. Of course we all care. We want someone, most especially someone we admire, to like our work. Like you (when you got my letter) I said to my husband, "nothing matters now". And there we all were. I don't know how long it lasts, this "nothing else" — perhaps until you reach out from your desk again and wish "please, oh please, something else now"? Or perhaps forever. I hoard your letter against the day of reviews of my own book when I fear I will be ripped open and found unsightly. And then, if I should lose your letter which praises ME I will always have your poems. They can't die. They live in the mind, by themselves, hardly belonging to you any longer. When you love poetry (as I think we both do) you want no 1. for your own to be good and no 2. for anyone's poems to be perfect, alive, . . . We are all super critical and that's why it is so honest a delight to meet poems (a whole big book of them you dreaming Governor) that arouse all senses.

I have written a new longish poem called "The Operation" [PO] which is (damn it as I really don't *want* to write any more of them) a personal narration about my experiences this fall. I mention this as you are in it. Well. Your name isn't. But you are. Toward the end, where I decide I will live after all, I say "All's well, they say. They say I'm better./ I lounge in frills or, picturesque,/ I wear bunny pink slippers in the hall./ I read a new book and shuffle past the desk/ to mail the author my first fan letter" . . . and it goes on. I won't send the whole thing but you will perhaps read it sometime in *Hudson* as they've taken it and I'd rather not send out new poems to people when my book is about to appear. Still, I thought you might like to know that you are *there* in my mind and told me to get well, that there was life and great beauty left. Let me dare say what my "Operation" doesn't (it would sound phony) After nothing but pain and fear and the problems of guilt, your book burst over me and made me want to live . . . I know, how overly dramatic that sounds and so I wouldn't dare put it in a poem, but I do to dare to tell you.

So thanks and thanks. And, looking over your letters again, so shoot the guy who said that about my poems in the issue of *Hudson* where you had your long long effort that will be famous, for its very perfect historical poetical G.I. self. I will not let *them* put us in competition. We are not. We are different. I would write just like you if I could. As you know I don't at all. I do what I do because I don't know how to be someone else. Therefore I dedicate myself to write my best self, and in this minute to thank you for writing your best self so well and giving me a hand out of my foolish "death bed".

I'm sure we will meet sometime. I look forward to seeing more of your poems and to the day I may shake your hand. Until then, I wave a kiss.

Yours,
Anne Sexton

In March of 1960, Anne's father-in-law was killed in an auto accident in Florida. George Sexton had long since forgiven Anne for taking his son out of college and was very much a parent to her. His death, especially after the loss of both her parents the previous year, stunned her. As she wrote to W. D. Snodgrass on March 25:

> Kayo's father was more fatherly toward me than my own father ever was. He has, in fact, paid one half of all my psychiatric bills for these past 4 yrs and one time that I tried to kill myself he was the one who stayed at the hospital. They won't let you stay alone if you've tried to kill yourself and they refuse to let any nurse be responsible for you. It has to be a member of your family. Kayo was away and my mother and father said they wouldn't come ... Well, it doesn't matter now ... Just to explain why I mind so much about his being killed.

[*To Hollis Summers*]

[*40 Clearwater Road*]
March 16, 1960

Dear Love of a Hollis,

I do not think I have written you in too long a time now. But, I told George [Starbuck] on the phone yesterday that I didn't think I would write you again. (all I need is to make a

foolish statement like that to prove it almost at once a false bit of words . . . He said, "Have you been writing to Hollis?" and, "I just had this nice letter." And then he read it to me and it was as always a "hollis letter" and then we talked of you and your pleasant charm and your specialness and it was then I said I was done writing to you who I couldn't "communicate" with you ((((as you may have gathered, it DOES provoke me that I can't seem to reach you under your mask of charm)))))
[. . .]

All I'm trying to say is that I *am* writing. And for no clear reason that I can rationalize as you do seem to refuse to write me back. Why do I bother with you? Christ knows! You ARE a bother. I throw real misspelled and true words at you and with the exception of your always honest and appreciated comments on my stories and poems, you answer me with . . . I can't describe what it IS, only knowing what it isn't.

Would you like better if I did not? Why don't you answer questions like that, Hollis? Why? You must be afraid of me. I think you are. Am I so scary?

I, frankly, do not mind you not being in love with me. Really. No need to be in love with me. But must you be frightened of me? Or perhaps my soul (that word I can't learn to avoid) is not to your liking . . . ? If so, damn it, tell me. I wish you would be frank with me about the condition of my soul when I throw it at you helter skelter and you act as if this had not happened when it has. Is that supposed to mean "go away Anne soul. You are not pretty enough to linger aside of for a while" (and only on paper. My suds (((as I say to my Linda and Joyce)))) it is only on paper.) Maybe even on paper is not so pretty. Not so pretty enough for Hollis's soul. On paper. Hmmmm?

If you find it impossible to answer these questions I will understand that your silence leaves you your gentle mask and the answer is "not pretty enough" . . .

My book is delayed. It will not be out until April 22. "Dancing the Jig" comes out in *New World Writing* April 1st. Have you not heard from the Guggy yet. My father-in-law, who was my best friend and paid all my psychiatric bills was killed in an automobile accident last week. So many dead. I

am tired. But I continue. I am not well yet. But hope I'll
make it . . . Let's see? What else? Ruth Soter comes home in
July. She called me from Tokyo when I sent her that story
"Hair" [BF] which she liked . . . Four of my worst poems got
in an anthology by Conrad Aiken . . . I have a very real honest
type correspondence with James Wright (I recall that you and I
agreed on the excellence of his poems) . . . He is just as wonderful as his poems which is almost impossible. But true . . .
Do you like Saul Bellow's *Henderson the Rain King.* I am
reading it. Right now I would rather read it than breathe (of
course, I'm writing you right now. For some reason though I
said I wasn't [typing runs off the page]
Dear Hollis, another p.s. I don't mean, really I don't, to sound
not grateful for all your comments about my story and both
stories. I was. I am. You are the ONLY ONE who will give
me the straight talk to on them. I trust your judgment over
all people and I do appreciate your giving me your advice. I
do! This is about something else.

I guess I'm saying I want an honest letter from you and if I
can't have one I will cease to write except for news and, as
always, to trade our new poems and stories and such. I mean,
if you do not want Anne soul words I do not have to always
keep sending them. Already I am beginning to feel stupid and
lonely because your answers are so covered and well-dressed.

Is it necessary to wear a hat and gloves with you?

Well. Is it????

Anne

Tillie Olsen's classic short story, "Tell Me a Riddle," appeared in the
same volume of *New World Writing* as "Dancing the Jig." Anne
praised the other woman's gift in a letter which led to another important friendship.

[*To Tillie Olsen*]

40 Clearwater Rd.
April 5th, 1960

Dear Tillie Olsen:

I have just finished reading your story ["Tell Me a Riddle"]
in *New World Writing* and I must write to you. My eyes are

still crying and I cannot possibly tell you how much your story has moved me. I am also going to write the editors of N.W.W. to congratulate them on finding and printing the best short story of years and years. That story will never die. People will be reading it in anthologies for many years to come. I feel proud of you, although I do not know you. I have heard Nolan Miller speak of you with such pride. But mine is different. I want to sit down and say "thank God someone (anyone) wrote that story!" There is not one wrong word in it. It is all one key, a human key. How I envy you your talent and yet I am proud, more alive ... well, this must sound stupid. I don't mean to sound as foolish as I must.

I mean to send honest thanks for that somewhere and never very often found sense of having touched the middle of a heart on a printed page.

I am actually a writer of poetry and not short stories. I admit that I do have a story in N.W.W. ... But now that I have read yours, I wish mine could melt right out of the book. I have only written two short stories. I know nothing of the technique and my stories are really experiments. However, my poems are better. What I guess I am saying is that I am not as lousy a writer as it would look from that issue where your story shines out like a miracle. The reason I explain is so that you will realize that I can do something and that my opinion is worth a little more than it would seem. (Which is a stupid thing to try to explain, but I'm sure you will understand.)

Well, enough of that.

Please accept my thanks, my admiration, and my need to write you in a rush.

All best wishes,
Anne Sexton

[*To Frederick Morgan*]

[*40 Clearwater Road*]
May 6th, 1960

Dear Fred,

[...] The only thing I can really say quickly and honestly is that the worst thing about a mental breakdown is that someone changes. Or at least (I don't know *really* how Kayo felt but I know that this was my reaction when it happened to someone that I loved) . . . where was I? About the "changing" — It is somehow like a nightmare to see someone change in front of your eyes, to become a stranger and not to be able, with just your love, to make them that familiar person again. Maybe I'm wrong. [. . .] But I do remember Kayo visiting me (and I loved him before I got sick and I love him now, more if such is possible) and saying "Anne, I just want you back — the way you were" . . . And also, I remember not understanding this and not understanding him, nor anything for that matter. But, in time, he got me back (only I changed a little, not much, but a little. I am a poet now and wasn't before.) But I'm me (whoever in hell a ME really is) but still, to him I'm the Anne he wanted back. And the poetry, the writing are a gain, a something very good from a something very terrible [. . .]

The book is out. Lots of people like it, lots of people don't . . . Louis Untermeyer writes: "Anne Sexton's *To Bedlam and Part Way Back* is a book of which any publisher — and any poet — can be proud. It has a singular beauty, an unusual poignance of feeling as well as phrase, a fusion of pain, suspense, and exaltation. It is a book that is not only an excitement but a reward to read — and I hope that many people will read it."

Marianne Moore adds (this is from a H.M. Co. printed up thing to book sellers and I'm quoting it the way they put it) . . . "I am in sympathy with the spirit of the poems but not equally with the diction. The quoted headings reveal an attitude to prize. And nothing could surpass the presswork."

And Dudley Fitts comments: "I had seen & admired some of these poems in various reviews but I had not expected the extraordinary power that they take from one another when collected. This is a completely engrossing, completely moving book. Mr. Lowell is quite right. Her poems do stick in the mind. And they appall me, too; especially those in the second section; but it is right and salutary to be appalled in this fashion."

. . . .

And so it goes. I will be interested to see Louis Simpson's review. I admire his work, love his last book, but George Starbuck tells me that he (Louis Simpson that is) did not like at all my first group in *Hudson*. I didn't know that. Too bad. But then, they can't all like it, it IS appalling. I am always aware that my poems are appalling and wishing they weren't, wishing I could make them beautiful. But you can't force it. When I try to the result is stamped with the word PALE and other words like NO GOOD or HOW COULD YOU! or ADDRESS UNKNOWN. etc.

I am glad you like and are taking "The Truth the Dead Know". Good. This makes me happy.

One last thing from old Wisdom Sexton here [...] I think that writers [...] must try *not* to avoid knowing what is happening. Everyone has somewhere the ability to mask the events of pain and sorrow, call it shock ... when someone dies for instance you have this shock that carries you over it, makes it bearable. But the creative person must not use this mechanism anymore than they have to in order to keep breathing. Other people may. But not you, not us. Writing is "life" in capsule and the writer must feel every bump edge scratch ouch in order to know the real furniture of his capsule. (Am I making sense? I am trying, but I have never expressed this before). I, myself, alternate between hiding behind my own hands, protecting myself anyway possible, and this other, this seeing ouching other. I guess I mean that creative people must not avoid the pain that they get dealt. I say to myself, sometimes repeatedly "I've got to get the hell out of this hurt" ... But no. Hurt must be examined like a plague. The others can run, take bottles of Miltown etc. But I think we (let's say we have no name, this literary bunch) have got to hang around and know just what's going on. [...]

As ever,
Anne

When W. D. Snodgrass received the Pulitzer Prize in May 1960 for *Heart's Needle*, Anne wrote him two letters: one of appreciation and one of stern caution.

[To W. D. Snodgrass]

> *[40 Clearwater Road]*
> *May 10th or 11th not sure*
> *[1960]*

Dearest De,

I am happy for you. I am proud of the world of poets. I knew. Of course, I knew. In fact I knew three years ago when I read "Heart's Needle" for the first time. Today I will not praise you and make you nervous (does it, by the way, make you nervous now?) . . . instead I will praise your book which I praised one year ago anyhow. It is no better now than when you wrote it. It was magnificent when you did it. The only brilliance that has been added is to the prize. You glorify the prize; make it young again and alive. Every young one who writes is proud of you.

I am too. Was proud that anyone could write it. Proud perhaps to know you (but then I've been that ever since I saw your bushy mustache and your oafish face) . . .

One thing I hope is so. I hope your parents are sitting up and taking notice. I would wish that for you. For them to know. Even if you hate them; still, you would care. Awful, but I know you care. Well they damn well better notice. I always think prizes are for parents so they'll know. Only a prize will convince them sometimes. And if not. Well damn them to hell.

Things will be easier for you and harder for you. I hope just easier. When you get what you want, what is left? Such a responsibility to get what you want.

I like very much your new poems in *Hudson*. Good. Glad to see you are still working. You write rather as if you'd written nothing and then spring forth in print with your usual strength and as always, your original voice.

If I had to say one thing I'd say that your poems have an integrity. Also they are so there. So impossible to forget once you've read them once.

When did I last write? I didn't wire you (I was going to) that Cal was fine now. I'm sure he was. He was wasn't he? He is beautiful and wise.

My personal life has been hell lately. Nothing to do with the book which is out and is getting some good quotes and one good review that I've seen (saw it before its publication). God knows I'll see plenty of lousy ones in print before I'm done. But hell. It's out. A few people have bought it. Some like it. What more can I ask. The life of poetry is saving me (I hope) as some things are as bad as I've ever known. I am sometimes totally lost from the world. Maybe I am crazy and will never get really well. God knows I've been working at it long enough.

If you find the time to read my book and *if* you can think of anything good to say about it (without forcing the issue) you could send it to H.M. Co, 2 Park St. Boston — they are trying to collect some quotes for an ad. I would rather you just wrote *me* the TRUTH.

Or both.

Or, if none, it is okay. I understand you better than you guess and do not expect you to be able (particularly right now) to be capable of this task. I don't De, suggest it as a task. But, if you should happen to read it out of queriosity — you know? And then, if you feel like one thing or the other . . .

It would be okay. But also okay if you don't.

I am sorry to miss you this trip. I wonder if I'll ever hug your big fat self again. I am very fond of you. I am your bean sprout, you know. Though how the hell I can be I don't know. But still I am. I am stubborn. I AM!

My family is well. It's me that stinks. Jesus. But I won't trouble you with me troubles today. What are you doing/ going to this summer? Have you found an Island to go to? Or will you stick by your analyst? Mine leaves for Australia for three entire months on June 1st and for one summer I have no conferences to go to and no escape from being left. But then — it would be relatively simple if *that* were my only problem.

Oh suds. Enough of my hurts. My book is out. How can I complain? De, dearly De. I am so damn glad you got The Pulitzer. Since I have seen you I have met lots of poets — but none like you. And read much poetry — but none like yours. Whether or not the world acclaimed you, I would have con-

tinued to do so. Still, good for the world. For a change, good
for it. It did a good job.

in haste
Your Annie
XO for winning

P.S. Write me — even a note — I need a letter!
PLEASE!   X OXOXOXOXO for existing

[*To Carolyn Kizer*]

[*40 Clearwater Road*]
May 23rd, 1960

Dear Carolyn,

Your letter cheers! God damn it! How pleased I am that
you like the book as a whole. And how extra nice that David
Wagoner likes it too. I think his poetry is great, as I am sure I
have told you. [. . .]

I didn't see the Kunitz-Roethke blast at Wesleyan, though I
did see Roethke at a party at Lowell's house. The party
wasn't too wild and I did have a small chance to talk to
Roethke (mostly about you . . . I mean, I felt *you* were the
thing we had in common) . . . He thinks your *Poetry Northwest* a very good magazine and I spoke mostly in praise of
your (you yourself, not your magazine) poems.

About De Snodgrass getting the Pulitzer. Of course, he IS
my good friend so I couldn't help but be pleased. But I have
never told anyone what you just said and I DO think you are
right — he has *not* cracked the shell of his own ego. Not yet.
I think he will, though. I really do. But not yet, not yet. I
know, because I know him. His poems are all truth (so to
speak) but not the real truth yet. (that is if you think the
greatness of a poem depends on its intrinsic truth to the action). [. . .] As you say, you've been there yourself, God
knows . . . But Carolyn, I rather like poems or stories about a
"contemporary dilemma". Why not? What other dilemma
would you suggest? . . . I (actually, personally etc) think he
could have presented the SAME dilemma a little better . . .
But then, I love him, in my way, and when I first read his
"Heart's Needle" (the poem) was terribly touched. — In a big

rush, but with love, — good luck on your book. I promise to read, buy and promote it all the way in and around Boston. Hope they do a good job with it (as you say, H.M. Co. did do a swish job with mine and I'm quite happy with THAT)

Write me news when you can.

If you get out around Boston let me know in advance so that [we] can meet.

I'll write a better longer more knowledgeable letter some time, if I can.

With best love,
. . . .
Anne

[To W. D. Snodgrass]

[40 Clearwater Road]
June 27th, 1960

Dearly De,

Hi Snodsy! I have just ten minutes in which to write you a quick note. I thought of you, suddenly, I had words that I wished to speak to you across the void.

I say them with love, as if I turned to you from reading a book and you looked up from yours and listened and understood that I meant them with love, with known fondness . . . as if we had been together for years and I just suddenly said them because I just suddenly thought them.

As I will show you thoughtwise it went. De. Yes De. He has written a great book and got the prize he wanted. But how is he now. With his prize and all. I hope he is good. But I don't know. Maybe he is unhappy or sick a little or just confused. I don't know. But, if it would mean anything to him, I'd say.

So okay. "Heart's Needle" is a great poem. But you have better than that inside you. To hell with their prize and their fame. You've got to sit down now and write some more "real" . . . write me some blood. That is why you were great in the first place. Don't let prizes stop you from your original courage, the courage of an alien. Be still, that alien, who wrote "real" when no one really wanted it. Because, that is the one thing that will save (and I do mean save) other people. Prizes won't. Only you will.

So okay.

Lovingly, dearly, with all beliefs in you, Snodsy who first saved me and gave me back my daughter — because his poem held me and hurt me and made me cry. And I hadn't cried and I needed to.

If this doesn't suit your present needs, ignore it as you should. I only mean it as a sudden sincere and tender thought to you.

Did I tell you that the new poems in *Hudson* were great? They are!

All my best, dear to you and Jan and

all of yours
Anne

[*To W. D. Snodgrass*]

[*40 Clearwater Road*]
August 6th 7th 8th or some-
thing like that [*1960*]

Sweet Snodsy,

Yes I forgive you always for not writing. So don't worry. I accept you the way you are. You are special enough to take the way you are (silent or noisy)... my good dear Snodsy. I *knew* of course that things would be bad so I wrote as a note of simple love. No more, no less. [...]

You said "forgive me for griping in this letter" ... Jesus! What have we got each other for if not to gripe. I have nothing but gripes. I seem to be much sicker lately and it is really throwing me. I wish I had the money for a real analysis. I have been going on this three times a week basis for over 4 years. Shit! That's all I can say. Just shit. I don't know what the hell I'm doing with my life anymore. What a mess.

Don't worry about reading my book. You'll get around to it sometime. I hope you'll like it when you do. I live in horrors of doubt about it... waiting for the lousy reviews. None lousy yet — so far anyhow. In your same issue of *Hudson* (crime and punish) Louis Simpson did a review of my book (the last book reviewed) and he liked it quite a lot. And I had a good one in *The New York Times* ... a long one there. But then ... more will come ... time will tell. And there is no guarantee that the reviews mean anything anyhow. But you know yourself that you can't stop *caring*.

Maxine's book comes out next year ('61) and she is up for the Lamont. I tell her it won't matter, but she is like you were — she wants it. At least I didn't go through that ... I didn't try for it ... my publisher's decission. Note that I can't spell anything today as I am feeling rather crazy. Only poetry saves me (and by poetry I don't mean getting famous but the writing of it) ... I am in the middle of work or attempted work and interrupt it to write you a note, to your unknown address, to a known human, Snodsy whom I love.

We bought Linda a 2 wheeler bike for her 7th birthday. She is thriving and can swim and dive and all that. She is not as shy as she was ... Joy is the same, a little buzz of life and love. Linda can read. I wrote her a children's story which she loves but that won't sell. I haven't made any money in ages! Are you going to try for a Guggy this year? If you don't I'd like to use you to recommend me. Is that possible? If not don't worry ... there are all sorts of people who like the book now ... Don't worry about not writing me or reading the book. I'd rather have you write me than read the book if you're ever faced with the choice.

> *All best love to you and Jan*
> *and all of your emotional hotel,*
> *Dear de,*
> *love from Anne*

That summer Anne took two seminars in English literature at Brandeis University, one with Philip Rahv, editor of *The Partisan Review*, and one with the critic Irving Howe. At this time she also met the poet Stephen Spender, editor of *Encounter*. With the encouragement of these men, she was finally able to do much of the reading she had missed earlier in her life.

[*To Philip Rahv*]

40 *Clearwater Road*
[*October 8th, 1960*]

Dear Mr. Rahv,

Here is a group of poems. I am totally unsure of them and wouldn't send them now except that: one, I am listing you as a sponsor on a Guggenheim application (assuming that this will be okay with you from our talks this summer); and two, that my psychiatrist says that I worry obsessively about failing. So I should fail!

Well, I told you I'd send you a group by Sept. 1st and yet I keep looking at this group and feeling that it is not good enough. I am not worrying about your returning it, but about your printing it. If you return it, I will be relieved, I think. The reason I go into all this is that ordinarily I would not send you a large group if I were not perfectly satisfied myself. However, I know it's not lousy — my trouble is that I want everything to be great. I think the last poem, "In the Deep Museum" [PO], of the group is the best (that means "great", I suppose).

About the quote ... do you think it works? I like it and would like to keep it ... but need your opinion. I am willing to take "A Curse Against Elegies" [PO] out of the group. I am least sure of its tone. However, please don't just take one of these and send back the rest as I would like them to be printed as a group. I would, however, be willing to shuffle, rearrange or discuss this group and any changes you can think up. (You see, I'm making you work as an editor.)

If you feel that this group is not quite good enough please return them as I would rather wait and print only a very good group in *Partisan*. Although you mentioned that it would help me get a fellowship to have a group "featured" in *Partisan*, I now realize that the poems themselves mean more to me. That is, I want a fellowship because I am a poet — not that I am a poet because I want a fellowship. There *is* a difference.

I hope you don't mind that I listed you as a sponsor without asking you formally first. I started to send these to you in

September along with a letter . . . but, as I said, I became worried about being "great". And so it goes.

I hope it won't take you terribly long with this group . . . certainly not as long as it took me to send them in!

I enjoyed the course this summer. I am still reading . . . Mann's essays at this point.

All best,
Anne Sexton

[*To W. D. Snodgrass*]

[*40 Clearwater Road*]
October 11th, 1960

De Darling,

What awful news! God! Can I help! I could lend you $500.00 if it would help? Would it? I have enough right now that is sitting untouched but will eventually go to my psychiatrist. But won't need it until after March 1st. Would it help . . . ? For time being? You must continue your therapy! Of course! And someone, some grant or foundation or something will come to your aid. But, if in the meantime you can't get the cash to pay the Dr.'s (for both of you) and could use a loan. Then the next mail will bring my check. Really. I don't mean it lightly, but truly. !!!

Oh, dear dear De . . . you come to my help so readily when I send you an "I need you letter" . . . is there anything I can do for you? If there ever is and I ever can, please send me an "I need you" . . . okay?

What's wrong with me? you ask. Jesus, it has been too long since we have talked, too long and too complicated. To put it simply I have had the Flu since Sept. 1st and want a Guggy but was getting exhausted trying to write to sponsors and explaining the whole thing. I felt that you were the one person I need not explain to. Okay?

Aside from the Flu which is just now getting better (damn sick with it for four weeks) . . . life is complicated. My Dr. went to Australia for four months this summer and this almost undid me . . . you know, in those awful emotional ways . . . But, I am still trying. Am going to him again now

and slowly getting back to work (on that Cross) . . . This
summer I took two courses at Brandeis . . . one with Irving
Howe and one with Philip Rahv. Howe had written me a "fan
letter" about my book . . . so I got a fellowship for the two
courses. Rahv is a very exciting teacher. Howe says he may
do an article about you and me (!!!!) for some mag. I forget
which. Stephen Spender also gave a course there this summer.
He is very nice. I didn't take his course but he asked me
(when I met him) to please send him some poems for *Encounter* which I haven't yet. Rahv asked me how I liked being
a success . . . and I started to shake all over and couldn't even
light a cig. All very neurotic. My Dr. says I am obsessed with
the fear of failure and so don't dare send out my poems now
as they may not be any good. And so it goes. So-called success frightens me as . . . oh, you know. I think you do, anyhow.

At any rate, if I could get a Guggy it would help on the
home front among other things. Kayo (who we all agree is
better than I deserve and all) does resent the poetry and sometimes I feel chained to this place . . . not to him . . . but to this
suburban place. If I could go to Europe for three months with
Joy and Linda it would help me become unchained, grow up,
look around, become a me without him (not leave him . . . at
all . . . I don't mean that. I mean becoming me without always leaning on him and his mother who lives, almost, at our
house) . . . all very complicated. It has something to do with
identity. I am getting to be a better mother though . . . much
more sure of myself than when you were here.

God! I hate Wayne Un. for you! The Prix de Rome, a Ford,
a Guggy and all. You are famous! But then, I knew all that
when I first read "Heart's Needle"! I'm glad though, that
everyone can recognize real genius when they see it. I think
(privately) that it is unfortunate that they ever compare your
book with Lowell's. (Yours is so much better — !) I don't find
them the least alike. Do you? (truthfully, I mean).

I know this letter is all mistyped but I'm writing in 15 min.
and must go fast. Hurry, hurry, hurry . . . hear me! Dear dear
De, thank you for your good letter. It restores my faith in all
of humanity!

"Anne as a baby – Sister (Blanche), hand (mother's!)," c. 1929

Grandfather Dingley's "Aerie," at Squirrel Island

"Anne – on left as child in summer at Squirrel Island," Maine

Anne (left) with Jane, Arthur Gray Staples, and Blanche, at Squirrel Island cottage

c. 1946-1948

With friends at Rogers Hall,
c. 1945-1947

"Anne in Chicago nightclub at 17
– with boy from Princeton –"

"Anne at 17 at ranch in Montana –"
1945

Posing à la Jane Russell in The Outlaw

"Kayo (20) and Anne (19) — outside church — just before our wedding — (forgot to pack white shoes) — Kayo forgot to pack his belt — see pants — August, 1948"

Anne and Kayo at Virginia Beach on their honeymoon

On a fishing trip, c. 1951-1952

Anne's mother, Mary Gray Harvey

Anne with her father, Ralph Churchill Harvey

Christmas 1952, with Joan, Kayo, Wilhelmine, and George Sexton. "Sexton Family at Xmass 1953 (Am pregnant – a little – with Linda)"

From Anne's modeling portfolio, c. 1949–1951

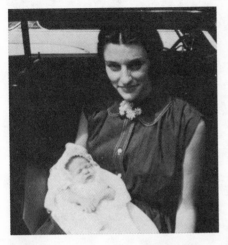

Anne returning home from hospital with her firstborn, Linda Gray, July 1953

Pregnant with Joyce Ladd, 1955

Holding Linda and Joy, 1955

Anne, Kayo, and Linda, in backyard at Newton, 1955

The Sexton family, c. summer 1957

Self-portrait, oil on board, c. 1950s

Anne at Antioch workshop, with Hollis Summers and Ruth Soter, August 1958

Breadloaf Writers' Conference, Vermont. Anne and George Starbuck (on her left) listening to Robert Frost. August 1959.

W. D. Snodgrass, 1961

Sylvia Plath, 1959

Robert Lowell

"posing — 1961 or 1962"

With James Wright, Long Island,
August 1960

The Sextons, June 1961

I liked your article on Dosty [Dostoyevsky] — most especially because I had just finished reading *Crime and Punish-
ment.* I had never read any Russian stuff and just love it. It is
right down my alley!

Since last June I have written 7 bad poems. I *know* they are
bad. I have reworked them until I loathe them. Finally, in
disgust, I sent them all out. I am tired of trying to be great.
My Dr. says I will have to learn how to fail. So out they go.
Let the bastards print them and then everyone will know I
stink! (how's that for being a mess?) . . . But what else can I
do? I keep thinking I have lost it. But what is it? I didn't
used to be afraid. Now I am. When you get to a certain point
editors just take your stuff, no matter if it is good or bad and
then you have to be your own super ego. I am scared of being
my own super ego. But then . . . *The New Yorker* took one of
them for $250.00!!! Of course, *The New Yorker* isn't anything
really. But that is one reason I could lend you that $500.00 if
you wish. Still, I don't feel as if *The New Yorker* were an effective "super ego" . . .

But these are just minor worries. All so trivial. There is no
one new who is dead, at any rate. And that is something for
me as I seem to specialize in dead people. Guilt. Guilt. etc.
I guess I told you that Kayo's father was killed this March.
The girl across the street died of cancer this August ([. . .] *I*
said that she ought to die) . . . why don't I keep my big mouth
shut!

Dear De, dear dear De. I love your letter. Of course you
will swing lots of weight with the Guggy! I have 11 other
people but I like your weight the most! So there. I don't really expect to get it . . . but it can't hurt to try.

I'm glad to have your address and phone number . . . If you
ever are around our phone has changed and is not in the book.
It is De 2-0101.

Lovingly,
Anne

in haste — hope things are better by now — write when you
can — my love to Jan & all your kids —

[*To Nolan Miller*]

40 Clearwater Road
November 14, 1960

Dear Nolan:

[. . .] Hello. Are you okay? I'm still here, not doing much
— not writing enough, not writing good strong stuff — just
coasting along with all my needles threaded, too busy worrying to sew. Worrying? Well, it is a difficult period . . . one
book out, most reviews in, and the feeling that I'm a fraud,
that I didn't write the thing but that I stole it somewhere.
New poems come slow . . . the fun's gone. Or maybe it's just
now, maybe soon, maybe sooner I'll get it back. I have about
25 pages toward a second book but some of it isn't too
good . . . I am allowing myself weaknesses that I wouldn't
have permitted a while ago. Or maybe I'm wrong . . . maybe
not weak. Hell-bell! I worry obsessivly (can't spell that one)
and can't seem to feel that I'm lousy or great . . . but both.
Have a feeling that they (magazine editors) take my poems
without reading or judging them . . . they *were* my super ego.
I have a large group coming out in the Spring (I think) *Hudson*
(some that you have seen) and they are okay I guess . . . also
have a group of 6 coming out sometime soon in *Partisan* and
they are the ones that worry me. Well, just today I made up
my mind that to-hell-with-it, and that I'm not going to worry
if they stink. They are a bad dream that I'll put away. Do
you think that is okay? Okay, I mean, to put away bad poems
like bad dreams even when you have allowed them to be
printed, revealed etc. It is all I can do.

Enough! Winter comes. No Guggy . . . no nothing . . . no
stories. The thing about stories, Nolan, is that they are so
damn big and my time is damn little. Another thing about
stories is that when my first one appeared in *New World* I
was ashamed. I mean, I read Tillie Olsen's story and I cried
and I was ashamed to have my story appear . . . She is a
genius. Her story will live. My story *is* nervous and only an
experiment . . . it's died right on the page.

What I have been doing is reading. And that is good. I've
been forming . . . Kafka, Mann, Dostoyevsky, Rilke, Faulkner,
Gide — etc. A mixed bunch, picking and delighting. I wasn't

kidding when I told you once that I had never read anything.
I hadn't. So I'm forming, eating books, words, thinking and
now and then worrying about all this intake and no output.
[. . .]
Write me some of your inner and outer . . .

Best love,
Anne

p.s. Tillie Olsen has written me a sweet note, that great
writer, that good woman. You pick the right friends . . . and
now your friends become mine. This is worth keeping.

Anne continued in the workshop with John Holmes, Maxine Kumin,
George Starbuck, Sam Albert, and others. She wished to maintain her
relationship with her first teacher, but this did not prevent her from
asserting herself when he challenged her.

[*To John Holmes*]

[40 Clearwater Road]
Monday, Jan. 30th, 1961
Dear John,
    It has taken me this many days to get over your letter —
that is, this many days to love you again and this many days
to love me again. For once, I'm not going to beat around the
bush. Your letter hurt me. More than you can imagine.
    What makes you believe that I am insensitive and that Sam
[Albert] is, indeed, sensitive? I hear that you also wrote to
Sam and I cannot know what he will reply but I can know the
truth. He was not hurt by my comments nor would I ever
hurt him in this manner. I have talked with Sam many times
about his work and I am rather sure of what his ego and his
deep heart can take in the way of crit. He, in fact, returned to
my house after everyone had left. Returned, not to make a
pass (wonders!) but to hand me a sheaf of forty poems to look
over and comment upon and to talk, standing at the door, for
one hour until I pushed him out. He was so enthusiastic over
the workshop etc. Is that a hurt ego? or a stimulated one?
You seem to think that my comments were thoughtless and
went on and on. I believe that Sam NEEDS to hear them over

and over. Sam is, in this way, much as I am. I have a hard
time getting it once . . . I need the same comments over and
over. This, of course, takes more time. I am willing to give
Sam the time . . . with constantly renewed hopes that he will
be able to HEAR. It is hard for Sam to hear. It was a compliment to his actual ability to go "on and on" over this point.

What kind of workshop is this? Are we mere craftsmen or
are we artists! I have felt that we have become increasingly
close, increasingly attuned to each other's needs — so individual — each needing something different, specifically different each time. I think this is a great strength and a great, but
mutual intuitive creative act each time it happens. It is hard
enough to be an artist (so called) without trying to be five artists at once. Yet, in our fashion, we do it . . . with each poem
and at each workshop.

I have talked about this with George and Maxine . . . I
haven't talked to Sam but I will shortly. After our last workshop both George and Maxine felt we had done an extraordinary job. Then your letter . . . you knew, of course, that I
would read it to Maxine . . . and by that time I felt I ought to
mention it to George (if only to find out if I had been as terrible as you suggested). Maxine has written to you so you know
how she feels. George felt that he got a "very good" workshop. George doesn't need a great deal of comment — his
poems come so finished — the personal reaction that Maxine
felt to one of his poems (a rant, if you wish) was enough proof
to him that the poem was doing SOMETHING. And the other
comments helped with details.

Neither Maxine nor I had had as much to drink as we ordinarily do. But we were more relaxed. I *know* that I was
rather manic . . . this can happen without drinking . . . I won't
say "I can't help it" because I try to help it — sometimes it
doesn't work.

Please, John, stop making me feel like a toad.

Damn it all, life is complicated enough with "the poets"
wrangling. This seemed like "one safe place" . . . where you
could let go. Now I feel as if I were holding on . . . if there's a
rail.

George says my trouble is that "I don't listen" and I try to

tell him that I try to listen, for God's sake! (like that)...
Well, holding onto that invisible rail, I'll try harder to listen
and not take up so much time. But I resent it. I resent the
idea that an almost good poem isn't worth any amount of
time if we can make it better and first the actual writer has
got to be able to HEAR. As with Sam. It takes me longer to
hear.

At the same time, I don't want nor mean to take anyone
else's time. I never have. Can't you perhaps help me with the
real problem instead of just telling me that I am rather selfish
and then in turn, thoughtless and then, what's worse, very
cruel. I may be noisy — but I'm not cruel and I never have
been.

In the long pull, John, where you might be proud of me, you
are ashamed of me. I keep pretending not to notice... But
then, you remind me of my father (and I KNOW that's not
your fault). But there is something else here ... who do I remind you of? Whoever he or she was or is ... it isn't my
fault. I am not them! (Perhaps I am all wrong, but I wish that
you would consider this for a minute and remind yourself.)

Now ... that is all hysterical raving. I thought, as you did,
that I had better express it than brood over it. And "brood" is
a mild word in this case. Well...

As for the drinking. You were wrong. We *were* that way,
but it wasn't from drinking ... just from personality quirks.
Workshop is so tense, so concentrated ... I doubt if I could
bear it without drinking. I know that YOU do and God bless
you... I know that it must be hard to put up with us but I
think we will have to continue it. (Perhaps I could try to
drink more and SAY less... that can happen if you drink
enough ... and it would have the same effect). I do not
WANT to be a toad, you know.

...I am, after all this, glad you like the revised poem.
Now, to yours... I think you have taken it into *your* hands
and made it *your* poem. It is not what I would have done ...
it gets kind of loose... It doesn't have the impact that it
might have had if you could have followed our ideas. But, so
what? Impact is not all. (I, myself, tend to forget this). Our
comments seemed to make you redefine it ... and in your

own words. You hide your impact inside it ... it drifts off, like a faint (but unheeded) call to children ... It is, perhaps, the right tone. I don't honestly think you improved it ... but I do think that you now OWN it. Does that make sense? It is a really good poem and worth the effort you have spent. I liked it in the first place ... very original ... I think it is right.

... I talk too much, even in a letter. Oh my, this toad suit is very uncomfortable.

[*To W. D. Snodgrass*]

[*40 Clearwater Road*]
Feb. 17th, 1961

Dear Snodsy,

I know I don't owe you a letter ... but I just typed up a couple of copies of the group of poems that will appear in the spring *PR* (march-april) and thought you might like to see what I've been doing. It is an awfully bitter group, I fear ... stark, in places ... But, it *is* like me, bony and stark in places ...

Untermeyer is taking five of my poems (one of them in this group, "In The Deep Museum" [PO]) and one other new one from the forthcoming group in *Hudson* and three from the book ... for a revision of *Modern American Poetry*. This, of course, pleases and surprises me ... In fact, it scares me. It will be like opening the bible and finding my name in it ... I suppose you are used to this sort of thing ...

I'm reading at Amherst next Friday (in a week) and it scares me because I shake ... but the money is great. This reading is a real racket ... a fine one! Hope you can make the B.C. thing ... so you can hold my hand if I shake. God knows who'll hold it at Amherst.

I've been reading the last 2 copies of *The Fifties* and *The Sixties* ... do you read it? I think [Robert] Bly is the only critic with energy and a goal ... very exciting, even when he's wrong.

I do expect to see you sometime this spring. Wait till you see the kids ... they have grown so. You were right ... Linda is like me ... you are awfully sensitive to people ... what makes you that way?

Despite all my seemingly good news and all ... I seem to be full of despair this winter ... each grim and bleak day follows another ... I wish someone were in love with me or that I was having a wild affair or something! But I'm not. (guilt-wise this is fine ... my Doctor says I am a moralist and although this amazes me perhaps he is right ... guilt-wise) ... Still, I wish there were some nonguilty escape from the self ... psychiatry is a dirty mirror ... How do you tolerate it? How do I?

... Well, here are some new poems, if you can bear to read em ...

Lovingly,
Annie

In 1961, Anne met the poet Anthony Hecht in New York City, over dinner with Frederick Morgan. Her first letters to Hecht date from April 1961, and he soon came to stay with the Sextons in Newton Lower Falls. Hecht became the family's favorite guest of the year; even the children fell in love with him after they spent a frosty winter's evening zooming down a toboggan slide behind him.

[*To Anthony Hecht*]

[*40 Clearwater Road*]
MAY DAY [*1961*]

Hello Tony! I have a sore (cut) thumb and it hurts to write ... type I mean ... but I really feel that I must write you on May Day ... not because I am any kind of a revolutionist ... but because it is, for me, the festival of little children running from house to house and leaving baskets of flowers and candy on their friends doorsteps ... this is my basket of flowers and candy ... and I leave them secretly on your doorstep ... (the way it's done here is to place it on the doorstep ... ring the bell and run and hide) ...

Hello Tony's doorstep ... OUT OF THE WAY CALL GIRLS THIS IS A FLOWER GIRL ...

Please don't say that I write with eloquence ... because it

shouldn't make you feel YOU need to. I am (I fear) eloquent by nature ... Most people I just won't bother to write letters to ... so when I do, when I must and like to, then I'm just naturally happy ...

I feel very special about you. I suspect it's your face ... but then, it's your manner ... your voice, your intuitive kindness and sensitiveness etc. ... Ah, that isn't it quite ... this is more what it is ... you know that poem of mine "Old Dwarf Heart" [PO] that I wrote to Bellow's lines ... well, just before the lines I quote it says ... rather the woman of Bittahness says to Henderson ... "World is strange to a child. You not a child, sir?" ... and then his reply ... "True, all too true. I have never been at home in life ..."

You make me feel at home. You make me feel that the world is not strange ...

What kinder gift can someone give another one? Is all this mere eloqeunce ... (sp wrong) or simple humanity ... simple love. Love, perhaps, should always be this simple ...

I really don't want our letters to become famous ... I want to keep them simple and true. Famous letters are ~~enither~~ (my damn thumb) neither ... or else they are only (simple and true) ... Letters are false really — they are expressions of the way you wish you were instead of the way you are ... (poems might come under this same catagory sp wrong) [...]

Dear, dear dear tony, happy spring, happy may day, happy doorstep,

Anne

[*To Anthony Hecht*]

[*40 Clearwater Road*]
May 24th, Wed 1961
5:15 P.M.

Oh Tony,
            oh.
What a lovely, full, rushing right day we had (see I like adjectives too). I have thought about it all day long. Every time I turned around I was thinking about it or, at least, I knew it every minute. How one day can seem like one hour ... it's so strange. Being with you is just like your face said it would be.

I feel today at home at home. You remember I said I didn't feel at home in life, well that was almost always any life — not just the outside world — more the outside than my house here. But sometimes, all my life really, I've stayed home hiding from the world. Hiding is different from being "at home". Today, just now, I was working around the kitchen singing at the top of my lungs . . . and I was just kissing Linda who came in for a drink of water and as I kissed her I thought again of you. They match really, for kissing my girls makes me feel pretty "at home" too.

And as I have spent this day rather busily with daily things, not at my desk except for one letter I had to answer, I have thought and rethought our "our day". Of course, I haven't thought it out with YOU DR. MARTIN'S help . . . but I don't need him for everything. I'm getting so I can do it myself . . . a regular do it yourself psychiatrist . . . And these are some of my thoughts (only some because there are so *many*). You said that I'd told you more about me than you had about yourself . . . Maybe. And yet, there are many ways of telling things. And, anyhow, my feeling for you outshone the few big sins I could throw out at you . . . by sins I mean those things you ought to hate me for and that if I don't tell him then I'll be lying by not telling him and he'll think I'm something I'm not. All that. And after all I exaggerated my sins. They aren't that bad. I'm not that bad. And in a way I was rather mysterious about them . . . telling the facts and not the reasons and the emotions [. . .]

Well, what I mean is . . . if it was going to matter to you I had to tell you quickly . . . Now, about you. The thing is, it doesn't really matter to me what you've ever done so you didn't *have* to tell me. The way you are is what you are. It's true even for both of us. I was afraid that the way I was wouldn't be true. But it was. I know it today.

God damn it, I have so much to say that I need to come right back to New York and have another day with you.

Tony, I want to be your friend forever and I'm glad that I didn't sleep with you. I mean, I'm glad in a total sense. I hope you are.

Later Thursday 10:00 A.M. Dr. Martin says that I am a

moralist — & maybe I am in a way. I do know this — I'm beginning to learn how to love without feeling it necessary to be
all things to the person I love. In other words — how to love
you without having to prove it by sleeping with you.

Does that make sense? I feel very happy — I should have
ordered snails for lunch — I keep tasting that garlic butter &
have developed a CRAVING for snails.

What does your Dr. say about me — ? Tell her I'm not
crazy when I'm with you. Tell her I'm your friend who loves
your face. That's what I am — There isn't anything sick
about us — I think we are healthy together — We don't have
to be healthy for each other — we just are. — also kind to
each other.

Anne

That spring, the Radcliffe Institute for Independent Study appointed
Anne Sexton and Maxine Kumin its first Scholars in Poetry. As usual,
Anne used the money for baby sitters and a housekeeper. The grant
also provided her with office space in Cambridge — a long-awaited
haven away from the children, which, once gained, she seldom used.

Another fan wrote Anne that summer — a monk from California,
Brother Dennis Farrell. She responded quickly. Religion fascinated
her, and she wrestled incessantly with her own need to believe. Her
long intense correspondence with Brother Dennis became at least as
confessional as her poetry.

The myth, the belief, and the mystery of Christianity intrigued her,
and she always talked eagerly with any acquaintance of the church. In
these years she called herself an atheist, and the Sextons joked that on
Sundays they went to St. Mattress.

[*To Brother Dennis Farrell*]

[*40 Clearwater Road*]
July 11th, 1961

Dear Brother Dennis:

Your letter reached me through various routes last Saturday
and I hasten to answer. It means a great deal to me. I am
pleased that my "four dark girls" ("Letter Written on a Ferry
Crossing Long Island Sound" [PO]) meant enough to you to
lead you into my book. In my book, I fear, there are no good

nuns drinking the sky ... and thus, I value your letter even more.

I am, at this point, working slowly away toward a second book — very slowly. I am afraid you will not like all of it ... but I do not know, I really don't. I want *someone* to like and understand ... and yet I wobble on a drunken sea, crawling between pebbles and slow fish, never knowing if anyone will like any poem. The poems that worry me most will appear shortly in the *Partisan Review* ... a group of six. I have no copies or I would send them to you right now. Perhaps you will see them someday and give me your reaction. I hope so.

I am pleased with your choices of favorites ... they are mine. I have hope that we can continue in accord, more or less. I don't know much about the life of a Monk (do you capitalize *monk?*) but I would like to. I asked a Catholic friend about monks and she told me ... but still, I don't really know. Believe me, I treasure the thought of your prayers and Mass intentions (in case it's true, I tell my Catholic friend ... in case it's true, I tell myself, and plead with it to be true, after all. No matter what I write, I plead with it to be true! Even if I can't believe it — nevertheless I want it to be true. That is true ... no matter how it sounds.) Well ... no matter ... you know, what a question. As long as there is someone like me, I am thankful that there is someone like you. There is a phrase that Guardini said, that sticks in my mind and that I might even use somewhere in my next book ... it goes ... "I want no pallid humanitarism — If Christ be not God, I want none of him; I will hack my way through existence alone ... "

And I am. I will enclose some new poems from *The Hudson Review*, printed this spring ... but they are not the ones that might interest you most. Still, by way of a gift, I enclose them ... for what it's worth ... and wish all my best wishes. I would very much enjoy hearing from you in the future if you feel like it. Your letter gives me great pleasure and great fear. I will now enjoy both of them; they are both important!

[letter runs off edge of page]

[To Anthony Hecht]

> *[40 Clearwater Road]*
> *Friday, Sept 15th, 1961*
> *noon time*

Dear Tony,

I think that I'm cross with you. I have just finished reading your letter, just now — and I have things to say back. I'd do it better in person, but this will have to do ... when you say that I am giving vent to a wild, romantic fantasy of a rather suspect kind ... etc. and that I tell you (too often) that "Tony, I feel so comfortable with you" ... Well, damn it, I'm going to defend myself because there really isn't anything *wrong* with a wild romantic fantasy and it is the warmest blurting forth to tell you that I am comfortable AND that you attract me (all at once). What I meant very simply is that I love you ... but that I'm not *in love* with you ... that it isn't necessary to be IN love with you. To be your friend, a good close friend, is not complicated by neurotic demands. This is unusual. Maybe you don't know it, damn it ... but there aren't many around like you (not any). For one thing you are kind, rather unusually so ... not kind like people are kind to Oscar [Williams] because he is pitiful (that's easy) but kind to a Joe Bennett when he hires a queer car and hopes we will laugh.

Besides it's all just a fact, what I said and I'm not sure what it meant except that it isn't as bad as you make out and, Tony, it may have been silly and childish to say ... perhaps it was and I don't dislike you for coming back with your feelings on the subject but I am very cross with you for not allowing me some room for a very female emotion that wasn't meant to bother you or tempt you or do anything but make you smile your nice smile. I wasn't talking about "fucking" (I'm really too New England to use the word with ease) and I don't suppose I was talking about who you really love. In fact, I wasn't trying to intrude. You make me feel as if I had intruded. You make me feel sad, I guess. Is everything a question of the one love or on the other hand "fucking"? Or being "pals"?

Jesus, what is anything? What I meant, if I meant anything real at all ... I meant that I have loved, really loved a few

people and with the exception I guess of Kayo (he is too complicated to go into) it always seemed to be tragic or something
equally neurotic. When I am with you I feel happy. I guess
that sentence says the whole thing and says what I meant in
the first place. It isn't only that you make no demands on me
as a woman but that you don't feel you have to and yet I still
feel like a woman. This in itself is a compliment to your
musculinity, I would think. [. . .]

It is late and I'm drinking my pills in a glass of milk. John
Malcolm Brinnin Inc, are putting 2 of my poems in that book.
You were right . . . "Her Kind" [PO] and "Letter on Long Island Ferry" [PO]. I don't think L.I. Ferry really a good poem of
mine . . . too sentimental. But perhaps I'm wrong. Perhaps I
ought to allow my female heart more room . . . it seems to be
the way I'm writing lately . . . my new poem too . . . but I'm
going to harden up soon I promise myself . . . stop all the
emoting around and get down to facts and objects. Can I send
you my new poem. You OWE me some good crit . . . though
this poem may not inspire it.

I'll type out the poem for you before I fall asleep here in my
brown study. You know, Tony, even if I'm cross that I love
you and bless you and wish you well. You make me happy
but that doesn't mean I own any of you. None of that is fantasy.

love
Anne

[*To Tillie Olsen*]

40 Clearwater Road
November noon [*1961*]

Dear Tillie Olsen,

Your letters look like poems and here I am typing on this
paper that looks like I run a business or that, at least, I knew
who I was. I wish my letters could look like a poem . . . your
writing is so tiny and perfect that it looks as if a fairy with a
pink pen and rubies in her hair had sat down to write to me.
And I . . . I must look like a rather stout man who sits by a
very respectable black typewriter.

Dear dear Tillie Olsen, you are a genius and a good woman.

I am thankful that you like my book. I think often of you too and hope we will meet sometime for talking. How kind to think of my face on your wall.

Do you ever get East? I wish you would.

My writing? Bah, it is terrible now. I dare not venture into any stories ... they are all experiments and I must not again feel ashamed as I did of my story in *New World*. Bah, I am a commonplace, or if not then why are the objects of my life not worth noting. And then, everyone is dead lately ... I shall type out a poem ["The Truth the Dead Know," PO] for you (so that my letter can look like a poem too). [...]

There are more poems, about 20 pages toward another book and all sold to someplace or other in the meantime ... but now, this now, this November now, there seems to be nothing to say. Two years ago at this time I was struggling with the poem, "The Double Image" [TB] and now ... Bah! Perhaps it is reading the reviews ... though most are good enough ... still it makes me feel that I am evesdropping (sp?).

I lived in San Francisco once, for three months ... I forget where exactly. My husband was in the Navy and it was federal housing. Out of our window we could see a little bit of ocean and a dump. At night the dump glowed on the water, burning its little fires. We had no furniture, but a bed and a table and I was pregnant with my first child and rather sick. All I could eat were radishes and carrots and with too much vertigo to read and too shy to make friends. Most of the time I watched the gulls. Once in a while I dressed up and we went into the city. I love your city.

Now I live in the suburbs. New England is a delight, its seasons are my seasons. I would send you a scarlet leaf but they are gone. Outside my window only the Oak holds on, dry leaves, the color of tobacco that only the ice will yank down in a couple of months.

Tell me your life, if you will ... and your work or any. We might talk by letter ... and perhaps get more said ... I feel suddenly much to say and you know that I will hold your words gently and honor them.

Yours,
Anne Sexton

[*To Brother Dennis Farrell*]

[*40 Clearwater Road*]
Dec. 22, 1961

Dear Brother Dennis:

Your Christmas letter, written on Gaudete Sunday, is beside me on my desk. I am deeply touched. I have on the crucifix, with a piece of package string as usual. I don't have a collection which you inferred with your happy sense of humor . . . I don't have a crucifix at all because I sent the other back to Ruth [Soter]. It made me feel too guilty to keep it; it was hers, she had worn it for years and I didn't feel I ought to keep it somehow. I think I was in danger of loving it too much. I will keep the one you have sent me . . . I don't know if I will wear it, or rather, continue to wear it . . . but please know that I will never wear it without a feeling of humility and awareness. Which is a round about way of saying, thank you deeply. And thank you too for the Thirty Masses and thank you too for liking some of the new poems in *Partisan*. I was afraid you wouldn't. I just sat here rereading them (over with you so to speak), listening to them with your ears.

I feel like sitting here and writing YOU a ten page letter. I promise to, if you'll send the one you didn't send. (Would you send it anyhow?)

Brother Dennis . . . it is dark in my room now and I can't see to type. It is now after 12 midnight . . . but I can see out of my window where tonight the landscape is fired by moonlight . . . it is covered by patches of snow and the frozen whistle of the air . . . and I am thinking of you somehow . . . because I'm wearing your crucifix, I guess . . . the sky is quite blue . . . the moon is on the other side of the house but before I came into my room I looked at it for a long time and thought a long time. Somehow, I can't spoil my thought by turning on the lights which would enable me to type this better . . . It is almost Christmas. I wish that I knew you better. I wish that I knew God better. I guess that your letter and all that goes with it, has made me want to write a poem . . . or to pray . . . I am still, in the dark, thinking more than I can type . . . all I can say is that I have been wearing that crucifix and I wish it would talk to me. I guess I'll go up to bed now

... and write more tomorrow ... or soon when I can ... tonight I feel your prayer. Tonight I will try one of my own. Bless you, dear Brother Dennis ... Bless you ...

...Dec. 29th ...

Time goes by ... my desk is heavy with work and letters and much too much. Write me when and if you can find the time. I have on The Crucifix ... I haven't taken it off since Dec. 22 ...

Always my best,

[*To W. D. Snodgrass*]

40 Clearwater Road
Dec. 27th, 1961

Dearly De,

I think maybe I *am* a bitch ... but I *do* think of you and I don't seem to have written. Have you missed me? Hope so! To tell the truth I've been so "fucking" busy that I don't know what the hell is going on. Also I keep losing your address every time I'm in the mood to type you a letter ... be sure to always put your address on your letters.

I got a grant from Radcliffe, I forgot if I told you that or if I'd gotten it ... no, I went for my interview the same day that we spoke at B.U. Well, I did get it ... so did Maxine. Weren't we lucky, both of us yet! Anyhow this is the first year they have given these grants (it's for mothers ... I mean, the grant is for *talented* mothers with a Ph.D. (or equivalent!)) ... well there has been so much publicity that I've spent most of this fall talking to newspapers and magazines. By now I could write an interview with myself better than they. Also I got tied up with a lecture bureau (Redpath Agency) and have been giving readings around hell and gone. It takes a terrible toll on me as I still feel required to get plastered before each reading. I would like your advice on the lecture bureau, if you've heard of them and if you think they are any good. One place I read they asked me why my fee was so cheap ... so I promptly gave Redpath hell and raised it to $250.00 plus expenses ... previously it was $150.00 plus expenses. I know that you have had a lot of experience with this and wonder how you handle it . . . ? Please advise. Of course I'm not a prize winner like you and it wouldn't seem to me that I should be able to get a fee such as you can . . . but I have no one to ask as no one that I know (know well) is in this racket except a couple of "old timers" like Untermeyer or people like that. What you advise, uh?

Jim Wright wrote that he saw you and that you spoke so well of me (you damn better speak well!! I'm your bean sprout) and that you went to see some belly dancers (so I gather you are still the same).

I wrote a stupid thing about Cal for *The* [*Harvard*] *Advocate*, quoting (I'm sure they wrote you) you very nicely. It makes you sound better than me, but you are anyhow. I have a new room to write in (thanks to Radcliffe) and am right now looking out on the blazing blue lights of the snow field . . . I'm still going to my Dr. and will be going for life I guess . . . I have enuf guilt to last for 2 lifetimes. How are you doing? And Jan?

George [Starbuck] is in Rome. June [Hill] is still here. He ought to marry her, she is a doll. I see her sometimes. Tony Hecht is coming here for New Year's. Do you know him? He is very nice.

I have written a few new poems. I tried a story but I can't seem to handle prose. Kayo is fine, also going to a psychiatrist twice a week (I'm three times a week). You can IMAGINE what that is costing us! But I think it will be worth it. He had to start . . . or else we couldn't have stayed together. It was getting terrible for various complicated reasons. Maxine is also in treatment. Jesus, where is someone sane?

Now here comes someone to visit me. I wish to hell I'd get a little time to myself. Now that I have this grant the whole god damn world keeps interrupting me . . .

Where was I . . . telling you everything all at once.

I signed a first reading contract with the *New Yorker*. You get $100.00 just for signing . . . but it hasn't changed my poetry at all. I'm not really their type, as you know. I did sell them one thing though . . .

Linda is learning to play the violin. She is so grown up. Joy is learning to read, but still a minx with fat cheeks and happy naughty ways. Linda is, I guess, just like me, which makes me alternately adore and loathe her, depending on which me she seems like (good Anne or bad Anne).

Write me if you can. Christmas, though nice in its way, always sends a great and almost irreparable wound to my writing self . . . I am left without a word to say and all the poems in the world seem to have drifted out into the Atlantic without once looking back at me. I hardly feel like a "poet" if I am one anyhow.

The kids are giving a puppet show in the next room . . . the unconscious is showing. I'm the witch who won't let them stay up all night (or so it seems) . . .

> *Love to you & yours,*
> *Annie*

[*To Paul Brooks*
Houghton Mifflin Company]

> [*40 Clearwater Road*]
> *Jan 9th, 1962*

Dear Paul,

I am delighted with your enthusiastic reception of *All My Pretty Ones*. I am mad for the fall publication date too! I think I have settled all my problems about that (those I mentioned in our pre-Christmas talk) . . . as *The New Yorker* has promised me to print "The Fortress" [PO] on Sept. 15th. So we will all be in safe for an October printing on the book. Hooray!

I have sent the contracts on to my agent, Sterling Lord, to deal with a little more officially, because the very sight of a contract confuses my poetic mind (as you might have guessed). I have been writing a little prose and Sterling Lord has been handling it for me. So, when he offered to handle this too I thought it would save me a little time and energy. I hope you will hear from him shortly as I am most anxious to get the book really underway. There are a few things (not your nice advance) that I would like to change and add, but they can talk to you about it.

I have written two more poems that I'd like to add to it and

I want to check your copy for typos that I have since come across in my carbon copy. Perhaps after we settle the contract we could meet for lunch and do all these things at once?

I am feeling very cheered up about the book . . . as I sent most of it to Robert Lowell for his critical evaluation and he likes it and because you (my friends at Park St.) like it too. I will quote you a few sections from Lowell's letter to me, although it couldn't be used for publicity . . . it might interest you to know what he said . . .

"The best thing about your book is its unstoppered fullness. I get an impression of increasing supply and weight; indeed your first book, especially the best poems, spills into the second and somehow adds to it. Perhaps, you shouldn't be too critical, and should have no fear, except the fear of losing your material and screaming off into vagueness. This you haven't done. My favorite still is the *Hudson* one on your father ("All My Pretty Ones"). I feel a passion and concentration here. I'm glad you've tried new things, the religious poems and character sketches. They are variously successful, I guess, but give the book a professional air of not just confessing, but of liking to write poems. Your final "Letter" (last in book) is a good idea and reads like one of your own letters. Maybe I'll find myself imitating it too. (Others have).

"Faults? I don't think they matter. Or perhaps they are unavoidable human limitations — yours! There are loose edges, a certain monotony of tone, a way of writing that sometimes seems to let everything in too easily, uninspired voice, poems that all one can say about them is they are Sexton and therefore precious. I sometimes feel that you are one of the few people who could write a whole book, like the *Spoon River Anthology*, where the little moments would prop the big moments and there's little waste. To an extent, you have done this, and have made your life your treasury."

There is some more but that is the general idea and awfully nice, I think. I don't know him very well at all but I respect his judgement of my work more than anyone else's. He is not easily given to praise (when sane) and so it means more than with most people.

Again, my thanks . . . I'm really counting on being on the
fall list.

Best wishes,

[To Robert Lowell]

[40 Clearwater Road]
Jan. 25th, 1962

Dear Cal,

You'd never know how much your letter meant to me because I didn't answer it. For one thing I was too busy reading
it over and over. You gave me the confidence I needed and as
always your thinking was clear and definitive. I have added a
few new poems to it — none that are important in themselves
— but give it a little additional weight. The book has been
accepted by Houghton Mifflin for publication next fall. I
haven't signed the contract yet as there are a few "extras" (not
money but hopefully an assurance of both of them coming out
in two years in a paperback edition) that I am trying to get.

I haven't written any poems toward a third book but will
soon, I hope. I worked over Christmas on a little prose piece
about Santa Claus ["The Last Believer"] (of all things!) and the
few new poems for the book. During the past few weeks I
seem to have gotten way off the road trying to write a one act
play. It is almost done — a bit too melodramatic I fear — but
I was seized with it completely. It isn't about me, but I used
some material that I knew something about and which moved
me greatly. It's called "The Cure" . . . four scenes, three
characters: an hysterical girl, a psychiatrist and a priest. (Now
don't smile!) It has *some* good lines. At the end, the last lines
of the play, I am using one of my own poems . . . I wonder if
that's kosher? — otherwise the play is not a verse play, except
for that one poem.

As you can see this Radcliffe Grant has fired me up a bit —
actually given me more time, which is what I needed in the
first place — I was fired up in the first place. I am teaching,
one day a week, a group of Harvard-Radcliffe students. They
are, for me at least, rather uninspired. I have one who has the

energy and latent talent to be a poet. But she is a senior and also a dancer. Anyway, I understand you will be teaching at Harvard next year so you will probably inherit some of my students and you will find, I fear, that I have taught them nothing. That under pressure I got soft with them and that their work is limp. I always wanted to teach, but it is more demanding than I had thought. Did you see my sentimental article about you in *The Advocate*? I wrote it the only way I knew how ... no masterpiece but sincere. De should have written it anyhow ... he was your student long before I ever wrote a poem.

The title of my book is worrying me ... someone has told me that the working title *All My Pretty Ones* was used in a book about models and call girls and maybe is going to be made into a musical on Broadway next year. I don't think *that* would help my book. I could call it *The Survivor* or *The Truth the Dead Know*. Got any ideas?

Tony tells me that your play is being produced and that you and Elizabeth [Hardwick] are fine and entertained him so graciously. I guess he has filled you in on his troubles. I pointed out to Tony that he and I are at opposite poles — he has troubles with his life and is in a way "the victim" while I have absolutely nothing wrong with my life and if anything am the victimizer (if there is such a word).

I will be in New York around March 30th and perhaps could see you then. I might be down for a reading before then ... I'm not sure.

Thank you, Cal, for that letter. I am still rereading it.

Anne

[*To Brother Dennis Farrell*]

40 Clearwater Rd.
Feb. 12, 1962

Dear Brother Dennis ...

You are awfully handsome to be a monk ... but then ... I'm glad you sent your picture because it is a distinct pleasure to behold. You have amazing eyes. Your letter is warm and funny and human. I am still laughing at your description of the wizened, bearded monk shuffling through drafty cloisters!

What had I pictured? I'm not sure ... a soul in space ... with no age, no beard, certainly no eyes like that!

How do you picture me? You who have had the advantage of reading my poems plus seeing a picture of me on the back of my book ... and in *Newsweek* too! Well, I guess you pictured me about the way I am. Though I may have a few secrets up my sleeve (I'll think them up some other time).

Dear, dear Brother Dennis I forgive you for not sleeping in a coffin, wearing canvas underwear (I love that!) or scourging yourself nightly with a discipline. I forgive you on one condition that is ... namely, that you'll forgive me when I steal all your lavish description and put it in a poem about "us" ... "the monk and the lady poet" or something like that. You write so well that I feel strongly inclined to steal your adjectives and your delightful humor. You'd better let me know fast if you, perhaps, stole it from someone else in the first place. So there! Having lost my lovely medieval romantic image of you I give you fair warning that I still find you to be a "soul in space" ... and your picture ... now that I have seen you with your face undressed before me, tells me that you are not a monk at all but a matador. Your face gives the whole thing away.

Your poems are very good. They are original and moving. You are awfully young to write so well. Perhaps it is due to all those hours of contemplation ... your poems have a certain maturity and a sense of style. "Existential" scared me. But that's because I don't like throwing up from too much cheap wine ... Have you written any longer poems. You must watch out for a tendency to let each poem be a "fragment" ... if you know what I mean by that.

I have been busy this last month trying to write a one act play. It is not good, but I might be able to make it good in time. There are three characters in it ... A 30 year old woman, a psychiatrist and a priest. The girl sees visions of Christ ... but is cured of them in the end. The title is "The Cure". The priest, you'll be glad to hear, is a crusty old individual who sips brandy most of the day and is rather bored with this girl's visions as he is pretty busy with the business

of his parish, altar boys with measles etc. He doesn't sleep in
a coffin either! In this case, it would be better if he did.

My second book of poems will come out next October ...
Houghton Mifflin ... title *All My Pretty Ones*. It is mostly
about the dead ... and love ... and sin ... but mostly the
dead. I hope you will like it. You have seen most of the
poems anyhow. I'll save my poem about you for the next
book ... I need something to write about, I think. Haven't
written a poem in the last month. I feel empty. And sad.

I'm awfully glad that you have found some "truth" in my
letters ... and that, somehow or other, managed to reveal that
I am I ... that I of the poems. It's not quite true that I, you
know. Though I've never lied to you; I often lie to myself.
It's the same thing, really.

Yes. You are right. You can't proselytize me ... even
though I wish you could. Still if you are praying for me and
you are, then you must know that you are probably the only
one who is praying for me ... since I can't ... so, therefore, I
offer you a sense of trust and a kind of devotion that you can't
turn down. I give you no choice ... you must accept my faith
in your faith. Probably I am a fool ... most poets are fools ...
but for some reason I love faith, but have none. The girl in
my play (who is after all, me) says, after she has been cured of
her visions "belief like that is like reaching up into the sky
and touching a live wire".

And it is.

... and one time the priest says to her "and would you
mock God?" and she says "God is only mocked by believ-
ers!" ...

I wonder if any of it makes any sense? Anyway ... if *you*
say that *you* "believe grace is working in" me ... well, maybe
it is and I just don't recognize it ... the same way I recognized
you but wouldn't have been able to describe your face.

I am awfully glad that I somehow saved you from the total
horrors of six units of lit. crit. It would be enough to finish
me, I promise you. I think that you can usually believe poets
... or, at least, believe their poems. Or at least, I find myself
believing the poet's poems that I love. Do you ever read Rilke

... I don't need a letter from him to love him and to know him. Did you ever read his book *Letters to a Young Poet* (Norton publishes it). I am very fond of that book and read it often, going to it when I am thirsty or lonely. Rilke himself was probably a bastard and a bum. Look at Dylan Thomas, an obscene despairing man ... but his poems are all grace, sparkling with his words and his love. What I mean is this — believe in what you love. You already know how to do that better than I ... you with that matador's face and that monk's heart!

Listen to this ... it's a poem by Rilke ["Lament"], translated by Randall Jarrell. [...]

Oh, how I wish I'd written that poem. It is so simple, so direct, so just right. Do you like it? I do.

Write me again. As you may have noticed I can't spell or type very well. As for you being "still in college" ... although Radcliffe gave me a grant and I seem to be trying to teach creative writing to Harvard-Radcliffe students once a week ... I never went to college at all! (see, I have some surprises ... minor, but still, some ...) ... keep working and get that BA. You are just as lovely and medieval and romantic to me as you were in the first place (only handsomer) ...

You know, in a way, you are more "in" the world than I am. Almost every day my desk is my world.

This is a much longer letter than I meant to write ... yet the words keep falling all over each other to get out on the page and off to you.

> with love,
> Anne

[*To Tillie Olsen*]

> 40 Clearwater Rd.
> [*spring 1962*]

Dear wonderful lovely Tillie Olsen,

Your letter that babbled was/is dear to me. I put it away thinking, I will write her when the first flower blooms and I can send her a petal or a something ... I will cherish writing her and not overdo every relationship. So please, please never worry about babbling ... you are very contained ... do not worry when you overflow. I am very uncontained and so try, sometimes, to put up measures, walls, rules, margins ... That's why I can't write prose, I guess ... it won't contain me as a poem will (sometimes, when I can write them).

I can't wait for your "stories" and I feel humble to think that you would want and did send me a copy. I will treasure it.

Well, I didn't write you when the first flowers came ... though they are hardly here, a late and sulky spring. But I many times think of you, have thought, do think. You are like a secret that I don't dare think about too often for fear it will go away. As a writer, I am jealous of your talent ... but then, as a writer-human-woman I am so glad of it and for it. And then, reasoning right now with myself, I know I have put it falsely. What you do with a "story" is the high point, the impact, the pitch ... it measures just what I want to do with a "poem". I want to be that good, that true. I want my poem to do what your story did to me. Having touched, sensed, the great talent, I know my own goals better. Deeper too.

Sick? Be well, please be. It is dreadful to be sick. The body is precious ... it is a luxury to be able to forget it ... a precious house ... And now you must work for money. Oh dear, there ought to be a grant or something for you ... have hope ... there will be soon. Perhaps under the hardness of having to leave your writing and work for dollars you will find new objects, words, new stuff for new writing? Or am I being faint ... It takes such time to build your stories and without the time ... how can you write? I have time right now, you see, but no new or old objects, words or stuff. My desk is empty, I stumble over it, paper by paper, not knowing my way nor finding comfort in old paths. Nothing speaks ... vague mutterings of ghosts ... they mutter like Macbeth's witches ... otherwise the radio honks in the background and children pound over the steps. I waste hours keeping my soul out of the cauldron (sp?) but near enough the edge to hear any important messages.

I have some new poems in *Hudson* that I send on with af-

fection. You have seen some. I think. I do not write stories.
If I could study with you I would. But I don't need to write
stories really — I will leave it to you.

Write me contained or overflowing . . . either way you are
lovely.

proud to be your friend — Anne

[*To Brother Dennis Farrell*]

[*40 Clearwater Road*]
May 17th, 1962

Dear dear Brother Dennis,

For just a quick minute — this note. This note that says I
love you, you of your feelings, you of your belief. Your letters
have a profound effect upon me! You can't imagine!

You are the reason I wrote the poems. I didn't even know
you were there — but you were. "There ought to be something for someone in this kind of hope" I wrote . . . but I
wasn't sure.

Now I am sure.

I will write a long letter soon and I will send the book and
let us never stop being friends. Please!

with great affection,
Anne

[*To Brother Dennis Farrell*]

[*40 Clearwater Road*]
June 21st, 1962

Dearest friend,

I haven't answered your last letter — not really. Somehow I
can't get it all in my head at once . . . I savor it. I think of it,
but I cannot answer it . . . yet.

I write now because I need you in some way that I can't explain . . . that, in truth, I do not know . . . in what way (I
mean) . . . Only that I reach out to you. I do not know why or
how, but I need your love, in the truth of it, the gentleness of
it, the Godliness of it. Knowing you, at times better than myself, I ask for it without fear.

Here I am with your truly fine letter and I ask for more.
Does that seem strange? Not really "more" . . . for there isn't

any more after such sincerity and impact ... but there is a now ... I'm in trouble NOW. Write me anything ... just words ... I need a friend. You are that friend.

Did you get *BEDLAM* ... can you keep it? I hope so. I would like it very much if you can keep it. I will, if I may, send you the second book this October. If you cannot keep it let me know.

Here, also, are two poems ... dated and recent. In the last poem I don't mean the "real" God. I don't think I do.

I shouldn't even be writing to you. I don't make any sense.

Forgive me for writing when I'm in such a dark room.

> *with love,*
> *Anne*

[*To Brother Dennis Farrell*]

> [*40 Clearwater Road*]
> *july 16th, 1962*

Dear ever present friend,

Please don't let any letter I write disturb or worry you about me too much ... or make you question our relationship or my response to you. If I sometimes sound vague about what my "problem" is ... then you can be sure it isn't you. Dear friend, I am a very direct person. If there were one thing, one small thing wrong between us, I would speak up. If I am sometimes reticent it is because it is too complicated to go into or too obscure ... if I am reticent it is because I must tell you I'm in pain or whatever ... but do not feel compelled to burden you with the specifics. Does that make sense? I will tell you this, my letters to you and my poems enclosed are real! ... and they all mean I trust you. Now let me say in A LOUD VOICE you have never presumed too much on our friendship. You could not do so. I trust you and I believe in you. Your letter telling me all — all you went through and your very personal response to my poems and letters — has let me know you ... has given your own secret self to me ... and you are valued and dear to me. Your letter strengthened the bond and your words put their arms around me and I felt like a child who feels safe.

Lots of words ... am I getting through?

Here's naked truth.

Your letters give me many things ... an aura of yourself, of God, of a different life, of a constant friend. I love you. I know you love me. I am, to be sure, afraid if you knew me that you wouldn't love me. But this must be faced ... I fear it in any relationship. Thus I am perhaps afraid to reveal facts about things ... or to say too much for fear if I make too much noise you'll drift away, pull down the shade of your ivory tower ... and all that. Afraid, I guess, that I'll lose you ... I keep losing people.

No. I don't have you on such an awfully high pedestal. I am deeply touched by your miraculous presence in my life ... that's the pedestal. That fact that you are a monk endears you to me ... it can't be helped. But the fact that you are a monk and are YOU ... that's the core of it all, all this reaching and gathering in. You see, I dare write to you quickly, pouring forth, badly written, all misspelled, any old way the words come. Only in a poem is the emotion intensified, sharpened, made acute and sometimes more than I knew I knew. Too much verbiage in a letter by Anne Sexton ... too many words, words all over the field like obstacles. Not meaning to, I get mixed up in them ... and nothing remains defined except the gesture, the pouring forth, the friendship and the aknowl-edgement of love. (how in the world do you spell aknowl-egdement fgfydusoepgmbnebs???)

I keep hearing the beautiful sound ... "I am black but beautiful ..." That is a true gift to me ... for perhaps it will become a poem for me ... it touches a chord ... I will wait for it.

Do you know about my room? It is quite lovely ... a wooden tower (ground level). We built it last summer when I got the Radcliffe grant. I used to write in the dining room, books, papers etc etc all over the place. My husband (Kayo) loathes poetry and does not care too much (at all) about his wife being this poet-person. So with the grant money we built me a wooden tower ... this room used to be the porch ... now a little larger (how large) maybe 10 by 6 feet ... I'm not too good at figuring those things out. It is made of plywood mostly ... the long window all one wall, looking out over a small back yard, that looks out over a golf course which really resembles a field, with very old (200 years maybe?) pine trees on it, and beyond that blue hills. The rest of my room is book shelves. I hoard books. They are people who do not leave. I think it is too bad that monks are not allowed to keep books ... I mean lots of them ... I have a filing cabinet ... a tape recorder (I will explain in a minute its function) a red chair, a straight chair for the desk when I'm writing and a softer chair for when I'm sitting at the desk, with my feet on a book shelf and I'm reading or thinking. I often sit as you saw me in that picture in *Newsweek*, feet up ... etc. I do not often face the view for I am busy with words and nature (out the window) becomes my enemy.

You want more of that?!?!? If you want I will go on and on ... and yet it hardly makes all that difference ... You know, Brother Dennis, I am actually a "suburban housewife" only I write poems and sometimes I am a little crazy (withdrawn for a time and then flashing into a manic excitement, wild words, wild talking) ... yet not quite as crazy as all that. I mean, if you wrote me I would promptly be myself. That is because I am myself when with you. Whereas I fear I am not myself here in my suburban housewife role.

I drink quite a bit. I'm not an alcoholic but I seem to rely on drinking too much (my Dr. says). I drink three martinis before dinner. That's really all. I might have a beer with lunch when I remember to eat lunch. The time I actually drink too much is when I go away as to give a reading at a college. Then I drink secretly in my hotel room for I am afraid to meet people, afraid of the audience, afraid of the deans and instructors etc and determined to impress them ... Which all makes me sound dreadfully shy and if you should meet me I would seem like an extrovert (but I would be so afraid to meet you that I would have 4 martinis first and that's where the extrovert comes from). At Cornell, I was there five days during a great conference, poetry festival etc.... they still tell stories (so people have told me) of Anne Sexton who was the last to leave any party, who after her reading took off her shoes and stood around talking to students with her shoes in her hand while the faculty drank coffee (and the students snuck in a beer for Anne Sexton)... In five days I could hardly sleep and my engine went only on booze. When I got home I slept for 52 hours straight. I must learn moderation in all things, my Dr. tells me.

You see, I am given to excess. That's all there is to it. I have found that I can control it best in a poem ... if the poem is good then it will have the excess under control ... it is the core of the poem ... there like stunted fruit, unseen but actual.

There now! You said "I only want to know you as you are — no pretenses/defenses". Do you still want it all ... I don't mind except I'm afraid myself you know. Don't YOU put me on some honesty-pedestal. I will only tell you this much for sure. It never occurred to me to lie to you or to deceive you in any way. My moods shift so ... In June I got quite upset... I had a rather violent fight with my Dr. (psychiatrist, "You, Dr. Martin" [TB]) and went into the mental institution for a while. Got better, a bit, and came out. I wrote "Flee on Your Donkey" [LD] in there. It needs work ... it needs the stunted fruit ...

We have a swimming pool in our back yard. We put it in this April. It is small but cool. Sometimes I go in without my suit which is like being reborn ... and my girls, Linda age 8 and Joy age 6 adore the pool. They think Momie is very naughty to go in without a suit. They stand at the bedroom window and watch me and they giggle and worry about it. We are all puritans in Boston ... me too, that's the trouble. To be a moralist without God is a lonely maze (and with no way out really).

Have I said "more" ... Have I been more me, more Anne? This is the effort for today for you ...

It's all so jumbled. I am not calm today. I need order. I am supposed to be listening to my tape recorder ... I tape (or rather he tapes) my appointments with the psychiatrist (I go to him twice a week, for six years now) and then I bring home the tape and am supposed to listen to it again (to put it all into order). Sometimes I have used it to record myself. Once, this fall, I recorded a radio program I was on ... it was taped at the station and on the air two days later so I thought I'd record it. All quite funny because, of course, I had three martinis with another poet at the Howard Johnson's next to the station before we did the tape. We were four, who were supposed to discuss something (they never defined it) about poetry. The moderator started with a long question (five minutes worth) and then said "And, Miss Sexton, what do YOU think about the state of modern poetry" ... which caught me unawares as I didn't know he was even asking a question and in fact I hadn't been listening too accurately to him ... so I said (it's on the tape) "Well, Mr. Morgan (or whatever his name was) the state of modern FOETRY ... I mean poetry ... " now, around Boston, poets greet me with a question about the state of modern foetry!!

Brother Dennis, I love you. All the time I've been typing here it has been thundering. Now the sun has come out. Such bright greenery! Such lush and extra leaves on all sides. I feel unexpectedly happy and clean. I am wide-eyed and rich!

This is a lot of pages and yet I wonder if I've said anything at all

   page FOUR!!!!!!!

... I lived in San Francisco once. At Hunter's Point. Kayo was in the navy (Korean conflict) and we had run out of money (he was a sailor) so we lived in the federal housing which was full of quite a few cockroaches ... but our window overlooked a small bay and a dump. At night the dump was lovely, burning in gray and scarlet fires out over the water. I remember most the rain, the rain, the rain. It was sept, october, november and december and it rained. I had never seen Christmas lights up over the streets in the rain ... I drove out to the coast in five days ... stopping seldom except once at Reno where I won about 50 bucks ... it was a wild ride. I love the mountains and those huge trees, the redwoods [...]

In view of the total disorder of this letter I'd like to close with a poem ["For Eleanor Boylan Talking with God" PO]. I've just been looking over the new book and chose one that I wrote to a very devout friend. She is the one I asked about "monks" when I got your first letter. She is a lovable and dear and humorous and talkative person. She is older than I am. We talk often about God and belief etc. She has no con-

cept or understanding of "sin" except as the church teaches
and knows it. Or perhaps that's wrong... I mean, rather,
that she is imbedded in a conventional viewpoint... I don't
really know. I love her, but I do not feel as close to her as I do
to you. [... she closed letter with a poem]

[*To May Swenson*]

> 40 Clearwater Rd.
> August 8th, 1962

Dear May Swenson,
   I was so pleased today to receive a copy of your letter to
Houghton Mifflin about my forthcoming book. I feel (as
readers sometimes do) as if I knew you... for I have long admired your work ... looking up to it and being, somehow,
proud of it ... for it *is* the work of a woman *and* the work of
a fine poet. I have counted you at the top of the list ... beside
Elizabeth Bishop...
   If I were to make up an anthology (and I don't plan to but if
I did) I would not be able to represent modern poetry without
many of your poems...
   So I am, of course, extraordinarily (sp?) pleased that *you* like
my second book...

> *With all best wishes,*

   Anne first appeared on television in the fall of 1962, with Peter
Davison. The two poets were interviewed by P. Albert Duhamel, a
Boston Herald literary critic. The occasion was noted in a letter from a
former colleague of Anne's at the Hathaway House Bookshop.

[*To Mrs. Willard Fuller*]

> 40 Clearwater Rd.
> Oct. 9th, 1962

Dear Mrs. Fuller,
   How wonderful to hear from you! I'm glad you saw me on
T.V. and thought I was pretty good at it ... mature and all
that! I'm really the same girl who liked the lending library
desk and who you taught many things ... about books and
who writes them and why etc. Also I remember you started

to teach me French . . . but then I had to leave for California.

I think often of Hathaway (of course I go there still . . . but I mean the old Hathaway with you at your desk and Mrs. Benner in the children's room). The other day I was thinking of it . . . thinking that I wish I was still working up there in the old aura (for me) of calm and order, the friendly people all pleading for a new mystery, the tea we would cook and all those books to read in between. Now my life is much more confusing than that. The two girls, Linda and Joy are 9 and 7 . . . and very busy and happy. I sit here at my desk and *try* to write some sort of "honest" poetry or else I dash over to Radcliffe where I am a scholar at their Institute for Independent Study. This is my second year at The Institute . . . I wish my mother were alive to see that . . . it would have impressed her greatly. I never went to college you know . . . the others at the institute have a "doctrate or eqivellent" (as you can see I still can't spell) . . . I taught last year, creative writing, and found it difficult but interesting. (hoping my students wouldn't find out that I can't speak french or even spell english) . . .

I have written a little children's book in collaboration with Maxine Kumin. It comes out this spring . . . called *Eggs of Things* [published by Putnam's, 1963] . . . also I have a small piece (a reminiscence of Santa Claus in our family) titled "The Last Believer" which is coming out in the Nov. or Dec. *Vogue.* It is nothing like my poetry. Kayo (my husband) said that it was "too healthy" . . . which, as you may have noticed, my poetry is not (or, not often) . . . I feel, sometimes, sorry about my poetry . . . not as far as "the literary world" is concerned . . . but as far as the people in Wellesley and surrounding towns are concerned. It shocks them and I can understand why . . . they say it isn't anything "like me" . . . "it is so depressing" or "cruel" . . . and I know that it is, in truth, like me inside. And, you see, "inside" is the place where poems come from. I don't know why I explain this to you at such length except that I always did love you and admire you and would (indeed) like your approval despite the difficult subject matter of many of my poems.

I'm pleased that you remember my mother and my nana

(Miss Dingley) so fondly. They are really "all my pretty ones" ... for I loved them the very most and miss them terribly.

No, I didn't know that Peter Davison sold you books. He never mentioned it ... though I guess I knew dimly that he began as a salesman ... (and me at the lending library) ... now we are *supposed* to represent a poet and a critic. Strange, isn't it!? ... At any rate I don't recall seeing him. After all, you always shut the door when you saw salesmen!

Your letter makes me very happy.

> *with love,*
> *Anne (& no pen at this desk)*

[*To Brother Dennis Farrell*]

> [*40 Clearwater Road*]
> *Nov. 19th, 1962*

Your last letter said waiting and always praying ... in deep ugly need a few weeks ago I tried to pray without knowing the rt words. I hope you aren't angry over my last letter. I don't honestly feel you are but that you are busy ... it is import to rem that we won't get angry with each other, there is too much trust between us, too much honesty and love ... still I don't know how to pray. I'm waiting and always without praying ... tho you say that writing a poem was a kind of prayer (as by mistake) and your letters are certainly an answer (by no sort of mistake) proof of something ... goodness, I think.

You are my friend of friends (and if it doesn't frighten you then by God I won't let it frighten me) really how strange it all is, your life is made up of belief and mine of doubt. How strange we should meet. It is a gift for me, a prayer in sickness that was answered ... me who opposes all authority, who struggles against misery and belief alike and even as I think of myself as an unbeliever ... then why do I love God? ... and the "love" such as it is (it being I suppose too sentimental) is not a feeling of surrender but a feeling of longing. It must be a diff. world ... to believe instead of longing to ... I am so rather hysterical that I have a feeling that if I did believe I'd lose all grip on reality . . . but then, it wouldn't be the same reality.

Do I make any sense? Talk to me!

yrs with affection

[*To George Starbuck*]

[*40 Clearwater Road*]
dec 18th, 1962, sat night

Dear George!

My God! What a wonderful Christmas present. A letter from you — so full and so dear, so George, who I've missed for so long . . . I have read it six times. I don't think I have let myself realize how missed you were . . . how everything was without word and words of yours. My good friend! My needed friend. In simple words . . . I have missed you badly . . . I just kept drinking up your letter like mother's milk . . . and there is so much to answer, to call back across the void [. . .]

God! I missed you. In fact, I have needed you for one whole year. You are the only critic (for one thing) that I respect and the few things I write lie untouched and not sent out . . . sad little poems of guilt and loss — with no passion or conviction left to them.

You've GOT to tell me just what you thought of *Pretty Ones* . . . because I need your thoughts (you discovered me, you know, and you have got to keep up my morale in that department . . . I don't trust the rest of them) . . . Please like *Pretty Ones* . . . it is all I really have. It won't cop prizes (I'm sick of wanting them anyhow . . . this year I didn't bother trying for a Guggy . . . shit on Guggys . . . their applications just aren't worth it . . . you have to crawl through a field of white worms to begin with . . . having done so 3 times I resign . . .) . . . No prizes. No awards . . . I want George's opinions . . . that's all. You count. For me, you just count. (s.o.s. newer poems no good . . . where do I go from here? Nothing any good anymore. Plays stinck . . . (sp?) poems now bad . . . . prose in wastebasket. Genius flew the coop. Alone with only book with black cover to go my bond) . . .

Pool covered with snow. No help. Linda plays the violin
. . . pretty good but rather sloppy. Joy tried to learn to read
but too busy day dreaming to bother. Kayo fine . . . happier
now he has been in therapy for 2 years (him almost done) . . .
Me still going to Dr. Martin . . . He is married (or did I say)
. . . it mellows him but I'm still in hock to him. Crazy. Crazy
as usual. (pills as usual and martinis at 5 . . . the f ococlack
(god look at that!) Martinis! . . . I write you this letter as fast
as I could talk (pretty fast) . . . with a rush of love and HELLO
THERE!

Paul Brooks (formal shy and awkward) has taken me to
lunch at Locks [the Locke-Ober Café, a renowned Boston res-
taurant] a few times. I puzzle him (and why not?) . . . read a
manuscript for them a few weeks ago (msc. by bad poet. told
them so and got 25 bucks reading fee. Hard way to make
dough . . . reading bad poems . . . sent my opinion all misspelled too. He thinks I'm a cookie (kooky?) genius who can't
spell . . .) . . . Read my poems at Cambridge Center last week
to overflow audience (me drunk as usual) . . . readings are a
show. Read all around now . . . big show . . . rather depressing
(miss you on show with me . . . us happy and drunk and not
caring) [. . .]

I want to send you new (bad) poems for help. If I call a
REAL help will you answer? (now Anne! just after you promised "no questions") . . . When you come back to U.S. I can
afford to call you and ask. Rome too much money and all
that ocean would get in the way I think.

The play I wrote is bad. If you read it you'd make a sad
face. I'm still Sappho's never-read understudy. [. . .]

At a reading in Cambridge last week three people (more but
these three stand out as rather typical for an after-Sexton tri-
angle) came up to me . . . a girl who was crying cuz she's been
in a nut house too . . . a girl who was proclaiming Jesus and
was trying to tell me "need IS belief" and an analyst who said
"if you ever get tired of your analyst I'd be very interested in
treating you"! (funny?) . . . I now make (if you can stand *this*)
250 bucks a reading plus expenses. Keee rist!!! So come home
and you can make your living reading (I think to *myself*) dead
and old poetry. (course it's not dead but it's not really RE-

CENT ... newborn as it ought to be ... or we all wish it were) ...

Maxine's father died early this fall. It was expected but is hard just the same. Me. I'm tired of all these dead. There are getting to be too many of them. Maxine and I wrote a silly children's book [*Eggs of Things*] and is coming out this spring. It is a limited vocab. We are going to do a sequel (sp?) this winter when she gets back from Puetro Rico (sp?) where the whole family went for 2 weeks. She has brought out a book of children's poems. They are cute and good and it is selling well.

I see June [Hill] now and then. She is just the same. She held my hand and boozed me up and took me over to the T.V. station this fall when I had to be on Duhamel's show. I had Peter Davison on with me ... it was awfully phony I thought ... but saw it later (being on tape) and it turned out fine. A few times June and I have gone over to Arthur [Freeman]'s and drank martinis ... I also saw Galway Kinnell last time he was in town. He is very strange, George, and I'm not sure I like him too well. He is too silent on purpose with hair in eyes on purpose. Also he is a big gossip type. He asked me if I had ever been in love with you! I said "no" but that I loved you. Found out later from June he'd asked her the same damn thing the day before. (maybe at heart he is an old maid gossip) ... Watch out for him I sez.

Enough gossip. I miss you. I love you (just like I said) and hope you'll write me that "other" page about all my pretty ones.

[*To Brother Dennis Farrell*]

[40 Clearwater Road]
Dec. 26th, 1962

My good friend, my dear Brother Dennis ...

Your letter, as usual, one worth eating up and I did. And your card, reminding me that I hadn't answered though I'd read seven times. I am your friend, that poet girl who still

    a. loves you
    b. reads your letters

c. saves your letters

d. thinks up so many answers that she can't contain them in any envelope

e. wishes you'd convert my doubt to belief

f. knows you won't cuz it ain't that easy

g. thinks, well, anyhow, he *is* praying for me!

h. knows that's a lazy way out

i. needs your friendship and love

j. yours, not just any monk

k. hadn't thought you (what you TOO) were in a nut house making those moccasins and weaving those useless mats . . . but now I know it makes no difference one way or the other except why didn't you tell me sooner.

l. (at least I think that is the alphabet . . . I can't spell and can't add or subtract . . . oh well.

m.

mnopqrstuvwxyz. . . !

I love you. E. E. Cummings is dead, bless him . . .

I'm writing but I can't really answer your letter. No. I'm not withdrawing from me! I couldn't. I'm just sitting beside you being quiet as a child might. A small child (mine are not always so quiet).

Job-like, your job, your ambition and all the clutter and waste of it all . . . Please do blow off steam to me. I would think it hard to be a teacher-monk . . . like trying to walk a picket fence all the way home. In a way more like a picket fence than a Cross . . . imagine carrying a picket fence! Despite the ambition that you feel you shouldn't have . . . and isn't that ambition for them as well as you? I mean, if you want your classes to be best so much . . . won't that (just that quality of ambition) make them better and if so won't your students receive more because of it? . . . You know, I confess to an extraordinary ambition myself . . . I want my poems to be better than anyone else's. I do. Because (one reason anyhow) I wrote and rewrote them . . . and now the reader (even such as you were a reader and found you "received" from my poems) finds the poems a "gift" . . . So perhaps this ambition to be "the best" and "to give the most" though it starts inward goes out and from you and from me and spreads out its

roots in other people. So, after all, forget the original mo-
tive . . . And please note how much easier it is for the poet for
people think poets are in touch with some mystical power and
they endow us with qualities we do not possess and love us
for words that we only wrote for ambition and not for love.
At least a poet is ignored, hated, or adored and strangely respected. Where as the teacher just goes around being taken for
granted and used . . . literally used like a highway. . . . If I'm
not being saccharine I'd say (or rather, perhaps being saccharine, I'd say) that I think the poet tries to be God while the
teacher somehow serves God . . . and ambition be damned.
The Pope was ambitious too . . . and it's a hell of a lot more
difficult to be ambitious when you know you are going to
carry a picket fence all your life.

Well, I'm quite ignorant about monks and teachers . . . but
that's the way I see it and maybe it will mean something to
you. I sit here at my desk which is covered with unanswered
letters, requests for poems I haven't written, haven't dared to
write . . . knowing that the vein I'm still tapping is so inward
that I dare not bring forth poems . . . that my ambition to
write good poems is going to stop me from daring to write bad
ones. But I feel a new confidence somewhere, a new daring
. . . to write for its own sake and give up the goal. I am going
(I hope) to love my poems again and bring them forth like
children . . . even if they are ugly . . .

I have been reading *The Way of the Cross*. I like it. I see it
twice, through my eyes and through yours. A double vision
. . . far richer! I think of Mary . . . I wonder what she felt.
How could I find out more about her? . . . I'm silly. I wish
Mary had kept a diary . . . and put down her thoughts. The
birth seems to be told too often in the same words and the
early life of Jesus . . . all like a fable that no one quite believes
or is sure of. Where can [one] read about Mary . . . ? What
was the weather and temp. in Bethlehem that night? What
was she wearing? How long was her labor? Things like that
. . . it is the poet in me that wants to know. The book is giving me a new insight and love and understanding of Jesus and
of his humanity. Thank you, dear Brother Dennis . . .

I'm glad you are not stable and I don't even want or need

you to be. My husband is so stable that he fulfills that need. He is so stable that he is a complete conformist, a middleclass lawn grower, good father, good golfer, nice all around guy (in other words also stable, just part of him to be stable). He doesn't ask questions ... even of me ...

I am so glad that you love my black book ... and if you think of me as the lovely lady on the back cover ... please remember that your devotion makes it so. There are a few great souls in my life. They are not many. They are few. You are one.

Now you can do me a favor. I will enclose a poem and I want your opinion on it. I don't think I sent it to you before. I wrote it last winter ... but dared not publish. I want to know if it insults Christ? I want your reaction to it ... your most honest thoughts. For I will change the last two lines if they do not work.

with love, as always,
Anne

[...]

Chapter III

Some Foreign Letters

January–October 1963

I have read each page of my mother's voyage.
I have read each page of her mother's voyage.
I have learned their words as they learned Dickens'.
I have swallowed these words like bullets.
But I have forgotten the last guest — terror.
Unlike them, I cannot toss in the cabin
as in childbirth.
Now always leaving me in the West
is the wake,
a ragged bridal veil, unexplained,
seductive, always rushing down the stairs,
never detained, never enough.

"Crossing the Atlantic"
September 1963
from Live or Die

Touring the college circuit all winter long, Anne gave reading after reading in dreary towns. Although *All My Pretty Ones* had been nominated for the National Book Award, William Stafford's *Traveling Through the Dark* won. In another attempt to make money, she began work with Maxine on a second children's book, *More Eggs of Things*, which Putnam's published in 1964. New poems came slowly during these cold months: "To Lose the Earth" [LD] in January, "Sylvia's Death" [LD] in February, and "The Legend of the One-eyed Man" [LD] in March. Spring brought "Man and Wife" [LD], "Love Song" [LD], "Protestant Easter" [LD], "Those Times . . ." [LD], "Two Sons" [LD], and "For the Year of the Insane" [LD].

Anne's winter doldrums broke with the arrival of good news: the American Academy of Arts and Letters had awarded her their first traveling fellowship. It came as a surprise — she had not even applied for the grant. The Academy offered Anne two generous options: travel abroad for three months or, with a larger stipend, travel for an entire year. A full twelve months abroad attracted Anne, but she also knew her own limitations; she depended too heavily on her family and friends to spend that amount of time alone in Europe. Kayo's job prevented him from going with her and he had asked her not to take the children. She decided to accept the shorter grant and take their next-door neighbor, Sandy Robart, as a companion. But Kayo, never content with second best, talked privately with Anne over a traditional Saturday night dinner of steak and Boston baked beans, and convinced her to accept the larger grant. He and his mother would care for Linda and Joy, now aged nine and seven. Soon Anne notified the Academy that she and a friend would travel for a year on the $6,500 grant. In late spring, she and Sandy bought a copy of *Europe on Five Dollars a Day* and planned their tramp through the cities and small villages of France, Belgium, Italy, Greece, Spain, and perhaps even Egypt.

[To Brother Dennis Farrell]

[40 Clearwater Road]
March 28, 1963

Dear good friend, Brother Dennis,

I was so relieved to get your letter today for I confess I was beginning to worry ... not worry about you not loving me anymore but worry that something might be wrong. I thought for a while that my last letter was just too "strong" (for your superiors if not for you) or that maybe you were sick (either mentally or at least on the verge of death!) ... such dramas of worry that I worried about ... and in a way, when I'd forget to worry I'd try being cross and wouldn't (as I do sometimes) listen to the evening rosary as I drove into Boston. Funny little girl that I am ...

My dear lovely friend ... I wish that your Dr. were around for you to talk this over with ... But I suppose that is impossible. What I mean is so complicated that I'm not sure I can say it right ... I hadn't thought about this, you see ... just hadn't ever occurred to me that you might be thinking of "leaping over the wall" ... for, of course, with the attraction of opposites I thought the wall wonderful and to be out of the everyday world, wonderful. I don't mean wonderful ... I mean escape ... but more than that ... it has something (in my mind) to do with a relationship to Christ that it wouldn't seem anyone could get out HERE. But I know so little ...

And since I know so little of monastic life and perhaps a little more about being a school teacher I guess I can only hold out my hand to you and say that I am your friend and do trust you will find happiness no matter where you go or stay.

Perhaps I know more about life "out here" (God! This is beginning to sound like prison terminology) ... I do understand, pretty accurately what you mean when you describe your old attitude toward yourself as an isolated-spiritual-eunuch ... I think I can understand it because it has qualities that would attract me.

But let me explain something ... rather complicated something too ... Our letters ... no matter how direct and human they may seem to you are not to be compared to a direct relationship. In a letter (no matter how quickly it is written or honestly or freely or lovingly) it is more possible to be loving and lovable, more possible to reach out and to take in ... there are no walls in a letter, no objects — the words can fly out of your heart (via the fingers) and no one really need live up to them. I mean this seriously and coldly and (as always) lovingly. You tell me "suddenly I found myself within a human relationship that I had often dreamed of, but never realized existed" ... Oh dear God. You must listen to me, for I feel I have somehow deceived you into thinking this is really a human relationship. It is a letter relationship between humans ...

You have got to believe me for I feel a strange guilt. You see, I'm pretty sure that no relationship like this, with the love we can have for each other, does exist in daily living. I'm afraid you'll take "us" as a kind of standard and go out looking for it. There aren't many of us! And even "us" wouldn't exist if it weren't for paper and stamps and the U.S. mail.

I knew an "us" once and after many more letters and even quite a few phone calls the "us" met and it crumbled apart like a rotten cookie. It was built on air and ghosts ... it was truly beautiful but it died ... because it tried to get real and it was never real.

I love you, but this is so.

Yet you should not deny your honest and good emotions! If you had been denying them you would never have written me the first letter ... nor would you have liked my first book much less read it. Because my poems are all emotion, goofed up, but still emotion!

You know, it seems like I've been out in "the world" so long ... for so many years and, of course, you haven't ... you've grown so much in between. If your ideals hadn't changed it would have been a terrible thing! But ... well ... I know you say that you have no romantic illusions about life on the "outside" ... probably far less than I have about life on the "inside" I am sure. But just the same, I worry that you are being romantic just for the reason that my letters seem to have made so much difference.

Only because I worry.

Well, of course, Anne ... (I talk to myself when I write to you)

... if I *had to* be completely truthful I would have to admit ...
that I like you being a Monk ... let's face it! Not for romantic
reasons but for safety ...

....

What have I said ... three hours went by; dinner, cocktails,
dishes, children, etc. and back here. Kayo (my husband) just
came in and took 5 silly polaroid pictures of me. I will send
them ... a matter of reality and how I happen to look right now
as I write. They are pretty bad but might amuse you for a moment. I meant to send you some others ... but I never did. So
here I am, for the moment ... just a person ... who is it that said
"It is by loving men that one learns how to love God"?
. . . .

And so I will not tell you any longer how our humanity (you
and me) is not real ... because it isn't exactly so ... for the love
is real, I think ... it is just that I worry, dear Brother Dennis, that
it won't be like this for you out in "the world" ...

And another thing ... I will lose you. Sooner or later you'll
find a wife and she won't let you write letters like this (unless
you are a poet or a crazy writer ... It isn't a very conventional
thing to do ... and it is amazing that the church can allow it ...
all I can say is that wives are a hell of a lot more conventional
than the Church!) ... so I will lose you ... But I think I can tolerate that (having thought heavily of it since reading your letter)
... In truth, I do want your happiness ... And this will take me
time to readjust ... to think, to relearn.

I'm not saying anything right but you do understand, don't
you, that I am trying, harder than ever, to be honest and direct?

Your picture is over my desk. You look very nice. Better than
I do at my desk. I have your picture over my desk as I write.

The reason I am replying so quickly (aside from the fact that I
feel moved to do so) is your Freudian slip "write now" instead of
"right now" that said something to me about ... well, it said,
either "I'm writing now" or "please write to me" and it seemed
like a hidden message inside your beautifully written lines ... a
hidden plea that I am moved by (but perhaps I am projecting) ...

... I love you. I wish we were real. We aren't, but we are just
as real as is humanly possible. If we met we would be awkward
and you'd feel awfully let down and you'd think "why, she's just

an ordinary woman . . . much like the mothers of those kids I teach" . . . that's what you'd think . . . I wouldn't be . . . but that's how we'd be. But there will be other people who won't be like that. It is just hard to get to know someone when you already know them so well. [. . .]

An hour later . . . Will this letter ever end!!!!???? I can't send it because I'm not sure of what I've said . . . I just sat here this last hour rereading all our letters . . . watching them become so full of understanding and of love; noting that they began that way right off; remembering how far we have come and how much, in our way, we have shared . . . No. I was wrong what I said at the first of this letter and because of that I have to keep trying to say it right. I just try! I notice, through all the letters, that we both keep asking the other not to think so much of "me" (the one who writes) as if we were afraid to be thought as good and true . . . afraid of the pedestal the other kept putting us on. Afraid to be loved when inside we both knew we couldn't possibly be lovable!!! That's what we keep doing. We are *both* afraid! And now I am . . . even more . . . because I am afraid I influenced you to think of a sort of a world that exists in our letters . . . But, in truth, for me, in my world, our letters *have* existed! Have indeed! And meant a great deal to me and have become an important part of my life. And all through the letters I kept putting you on some sort of a pedestal *because* you were a Monk . . . and you put me on a pedestal *because* I was a poet (or that poet). . . . In a way we were both snobs . . . *were*, not are. Something happened in between and it is real . . . Perhaps I'm saying that our relationship just isn't part of *the* world, but is part of mine. (make sense?)

. . . The next morning . . . I'd like, for some reason, to quote you from a preface of "Letters to Milena" by Franz Kafka . . . seeing as the subject of "letters" seems to have enveloped this whole LETTER . . . just fragmentary quotes . . . "writing letters . . . means to denude oneself before ghosts, something for which they greedily wait. Written kisses don't reach their destination, rather they are drunk on the way by ghosts."

And here is something else that G. B. Shaw wrote on his letters to Ellen Terry [:]

. . . "Let those who may complain that it was only upon paper remember that only upon paper have humanity yet achieved glory, beauty, truth, knowledge, virtue and abiding love."

. . . . .

And you know about Rilke's letters. But someone told me an amusing and telling incident about him the other day. He was so close and wise and giving in his letters . . . yet as an artist he was such a selfish and self-protecting human being. When his son got married he did not "have the time to waste" to go to the ceremony but asked if his son would drop by with the girl afterwards . . . some humanity!

. . . .

What will you do when you are "out" . . . will you live in Chicago . . . get a Master's? Have you any thoughts or plans?

. . . Well, even if this letter isn't very coherent I'll just have to let it stand and do its best for me. When I woke up this morning I thought of tearing it up and starting over but then decided that isn't the real point . . . and even if it is disorganized it is, at least, as much of me as is possible.

Lovingly,
Anne

W. D. Snodgrass had begun resisting the demands of Anne's long, involved letters in early 1962. Tired by the constant requests for critiques and reassurance, he had stopped writing her so frequently. The diminution of her correspondence with Snodgrass was paralleled by the development of other letter-writing relationships filled with the same exuberance and intensity. However, in time, each correspondence finally reached the same impasse; the writer could not reply as often, as promptly, and as thoroughly as Anne asked.

[*To W. D. Snodgrass*]

40 Clearwater Road
May something, 1963

De! Darling De!

It has been just so long since I wrote you, owing you a letter for *over* a year. Christ! And just now I was cleaning (trying) out a desk drawer and ran across your last letter . . . so here I am again, that "bean sprout" (remember that?) as always, etc.

The year a book comes out is always hell and has been again for me. If you don't have a copy of my book tell me and I'll send for though I asked my publishers to send you one they are not entirely dependable and I do want you to have one. It is called *All My Pretty Ones* and it *is* a good book even if it didn't win any prizes (I mean, I believe in the book ... even now ... it's better than the first, way better. Oh hell. *I* think it's a "great" book in its way. But then, I *would* ...)

Lots of readings and for the old (money disturbs me!) $250.00 with the agency taking a big bite, one third. But their main function is to turn down offers for 25 or 50 bucks. Readings really unnerve me ... they actually scare the shit out of me! But it *is* money and I have to have it. Actually I read pretty well tho I'm a little bit of a ham and I can't seem to cut that out and give them a "straight" reading. But of course if I'd try reading sober it might make a difference. But if sober I shake ... so what the hell. Fear, always fear.

Haven't been writing hardly anything this year tho ... a few that aren't good and that's it just about ... now I know what you were talking about. Jesus. If I'd get well or something, but I don't seem to ... tho a little better. Kayo is now out of therapy. His doctor says he is done and he thinks so too. And so I guess he is although I had hoped it might have tapped some of *his* unrealized potential. Still, our marriage is happier than it has ever been and that is what really matters.

Everywhere I read they talk of your reading. In fact everywhere I go they talk of you and it makes me feel close and happy. That is fine but I suppose it is irritating to all of [us] to have reviewers call Lowell, Snodgrass and Sexton (and now [Frederick] Seidel) a new school of conformity. I got a really terrible review from James Dickey in the New York *Times* blasting my work and saying this of us. The strange thing, for me, is that many reviews of *All My Pretty Ones* sound as if they were reviewing *Bedlam*. I mean, *Pretty Ones* is quite different and has a far larger dimension ... but then, they probably don't read it anyway!

Kayo and I did the craziest thing last spring. We put a

swimming pool in our back yard. It is canvas but it is *in* the ground and you can dive into it from one end. Great fun, for us and for the girls. Joy swims mostly and for three minutes at a time *under* water, more like a porpoise than a child. Linda can swim 100 laps (on top) and it's great fun.

Have you enjoyed your Renault? I have a Volkswagen. Never tried making love in it, either. Maybe tho you could standing up as it has a sun roof! . . .

Another crazy thing (and even my doctor frowns at this) is that I am going to spend next year abroad . . . the Am. Academy offered me the dough and I just couldn't turn it down (and strangely Kayo is the one who insisted I take it, saying "it is your chance of a life — Take it!") . . . so now, suddenly I'm going. Tho Kayo can't go or he'll lose his job and he asked me please not to take the kids . . . So off I go in August. I'm taking Sandy Robart (a next door neighbor, I forget if you met her) as a "keeper" or "chaperone" or simply as a friend. We sail (Christ! it scares me to talk about it!) August 22 on the S.S. France to Paris and pick up a VW and from there, God knows! France, Italy, Switzerland, Greece, Egypt, Spain, Portugal, England and last week I decided as long as we were over there (and as long as I'm scared anyhow) to go to Russia too, Moscow and Leningrad. In June Kayo will come over for a month and we'll drive around France, drinking wine.

My doctor says I'm running from therapy. He's right. I didn't know it when I accepted but I guess he is right. All I can think is that I've got to make it, stay well enough and all . . . it would be awful to accept and then not make it. In some funny way, De, I wish I were back to the old days when I sat hunched over the typewriter, doing the desperate and lonely and even heart breaking work of trying to write, and rewrite and rewrite "The Double Image". I was "true" then. Now I keep thinking I'm losing myself in some mad welter of publicity . . . Poems, maybe, should be published anonymously. You wouldn't get any readings but you wouldn't have to get so nervous. It is only a fantasy but it sounds so calm. [. . .]

Write when you can. Try and write before I go, (August) . . .

wish you'd come to visit! Kayo sends his best and adds you MUST come to visit and to have a swim. And please forgive the silence for you know, of course, the love is there.

> *still,*
>
> *still,*
>
> *still,*
>
> *Anniepance*

In the midst of Anne's preparations for Europe came a letter from the Oxford University Press in London, asking if Anne would consider bringing out a volume of selected poetry from *All My Pretty Ones* and *To Bedlam and Part Way Back.* Ecstatic about her first opportunity to be published abroad, she wrote back immediately. The poet and critic Jon Stallworthy eventually became the editor there to work with Anne and they developed a sizable correspondence. When later travels led her to London in 1966, they finally met. The extension of her readership to a foreign audience symbolized the accelerating popularity of her poetry; eventually her work was to be translated into French, Italian, Chinese, Japanese, and Swedish.

Selected Poems, published in London in 1964, was a Poetry Book Society choice, and as a result of its publication, she was elected a fellow of the Royal Society of Literature in 1965.

[*To Paul Brooks*]

> [*40 Clearwater Road*]
> *May 15, 1963*

Dear Paul,

I'm sorry that I had to be short on the phone the other day but when you called I was just about to leave for my daughter's violin lesson and it was impossible to explain to her that you are on my list as a very important person. I'm glad you like the review in *The New Yorker* (me, too!). Did you see the *terrible* one in the New York *Times?* Ann Ford hadn't and I called it to her attention. She certainly is on the ball. And newsmen are shuttling in and out of here daily. I wish the publicity would sell books but it seems that few bookstores stock my books (I bet you've heard that complaint too many times to find it interesting).

Paul, the reason I write is more specific. Oxford University

Press is going to bring out selected poems from *To Bedlam and Part Way Back* and *All My Pretty Ones*. They want to include new poems; I have about ten new ones but frankly I would prefer not to include them because they are part of a book in process (Slow process) and I hate to commit them into book form elsewhere. I feel that both my books of poetry have a certain wholeness and continuity and I have told them this and they say "it would be sad to miss the chance of putting in something new if we could persuade you to allow us to." If they do persuade me and I then later have a new book that I hope you will publish how will you feel about the ten poems that were included in the Oxford University Press publication? I'm sure there is a precedent for this or some type of copyright hitch or if there isn't, I would think you have some *feeling* about it one way or the other. I am very pleased about Oxford University Press bringing out my work but Houghton Mifflin is my first love and I assure you I will respect your feelings about this.

With all best wishes,

All My Pretty Ones had been much praised when it was published in 1962. However, the review by James Dickey in the *New York Times Book Review* on April 28, 1963, roundly damned Anne's poetic approach with the most cutting insults she had yet received:

> It would be hard to find a writer who dwells more insistently on the pathetic and disgusting aspects of bodily experience, as though this made the writing more real, and it would also be difficult to find a more hopelessly mechanical approach to reporting these matters than the one she employs . . . Her recourse to the studiedly off-hand diction favored by Randall Jarrell and Elizabeth Bishop and her habitual gravitation to the domestic and the "anti-poetic" seem to me as contrived and mannered as any poet's harking after galleons and sunsets and forbidden pleasures.

Characteristically, she paid more heed to this negative criticism than to the many positive comments; Anne was particularly perturbed because Dickey was a writer whose talent she respected. When the poet Gene Baro encouraged her to ignore Dickey's review, she failed to take his advice to heart, and carried the clipping in her wallet instead.

[*To Gene Baro*]

[*40 Clearwater Road*]
May 8, 1963

Dear Gene Baro,
   Your letter is hard to answer because I don't exactly know how to thank you for it or to tell you what it means to me. It came before I had read James Dickey's review but I have been told about it from more than ten sources. So I was prepared in a kind of hopeless way. However, your letter gave me strength and maybe courage (if that word is not too old-fashioned).
   What do you do with a review like this? It certainly was not written for me to read ... it was written for the readers of poetry (mostly poets themselves). If I were to listen to James Dickey I *would* stop writing. God, I don't know. Funny thing is, I think he's a pretty good poet and I suppose if I had written and told him so, the review would be tempered a bit ... that's the whole trouble with reviewing and so far I have not succumbed to writing reviews. Though God knows *someone* has got to do it and it can be a lonely road if you're honest. I must say I am tired of being grouped with Robert Lowell and Snodgrass ... I admire them separately but I really feel we're all quite different. There are lots of other poets you could lump together with us. But all these idle thoughts are beside the point. All this is wrong; writing a poem is a lonely thing, each word ripped out of us ... and you know ... and then later on the wrong things start to happen; you get to be fashionable or "a new kind of orthodoxy" and the only way to prevent yourself from going sour or becoming an art climber is to go back to your desk.
   You know all this anyway. I know you know it because of your poems and your letter. Thank you so much.
                                        With my best wishes,

[To Frederick Morgan]

40 Clearwater Road
May 17, 1963

Dear Fred,

If you are in New York and if (as I hope) I will have time to call you, you may see me before you read this letter. What all that means is, I'm in New York this coming week and have hopes.

Meanwhile, or afterwards, here are five new poems. They are a mixed bunch but I have the feeling you will like some of them. For one thing, this is to let you know that I have not stopped writing and that *The Hudson Review* is and will always be *my* magazine. This has been a year of gathering together of feeling frighteningly beyond myself and of retreat. I have been working for sometime on a long poem that so far stinks. But that is the kind of frustration I experienced with "The Double Image" [TB] and although I do not think I can reach *that* level of passion, I am trying to work out the unsayable say on madness. But that is another poem. I sure as hell hope I will send it to you someday. Meanwhile, here are these. The first one really hits me. And I, as always, await your critical evaluation.

In case we don't meet, my news is news you've probably heard but that I'd like to share. Anne is off for Europe and God knows where for a year and all this with Kayo's blessing. How in God's name did I ever get such a wonderful husband? Our marriage (it seems so strange and almost trite to say) blossoms. Fifteen years and more in love. Oh well, you'd never know it from my poems . . . But perhaps in Europe I will write long and lost poems to him.

Love to Rose and to you. And my best regards to Joe.

Affectionately,
Anne

[*To Jon Stallworthy*
Oxford University Press]

40 Clearwater Road
May 27, 1963

Dear Jon Stallworthy,

How nice to hear from you! I look forward to our work to-gether on the volume of my poems. And before I go any further, please let me say quickly how happy I am that you like my poems.

The problem of asking Robert Lowell for a foreword seems almost insurmountable; to begin with, I dislike asking him for another "favor". Therefore, when you write him please try to make it clear in some sort of gracious manner that *you* are asking and not I (this might make it easier for him to refuse and I want to give him every chance to do so). Now, sec-ondly, I have some advisors (those poets who write as I write . . . you know, those sometime and then now and rather good poet-friends) tell me, advise me strongly, that it would do me great harm to have Lowell introduce me to the reading public of England — for then the critics would come forward with axes that were meant to chop Lowell's head and not mine . . . thus, I would become more Lowell than Sexton . . . I would not be judged for the poems alone but for Lowell's reputation as well as mine own (feeble though it be).

However, you may ask him, using your own judgement for I am indeed grateful and happy that Oxford University Press wishes to bring out a volume of my poems. If *you* really think that a foreword by Robert Lowell would help (in the long run) instead of hinder, then, I suppose, you must write to him. [. . .]

Well, there it is and I don't mean to put [you] in a difficult position about Lowell except to say that I do not wish to coerce him in any fashion (nor have I ever asked him in per-son for an opinion or a blurb or a say-so but let Houghton Mifflin do the rather ugly job for me). Would it be possible to just use what he had said about both my books without ask-ing him to go to further trouble . . . or perhaps only asking him to go to not much more trouble . . . or perhaps only ask

him to connect both of the statements he made for the two
books. Oh well, maybe he won't mind. I loathe things like
this and, therefore, my natural reticence becomes obvious and
even troublesome. [. . .]

Yours in haste, but happily,

[*To Robert Lowell*]

40 Clearwater Road
June 6, 1963

Dear Cal,

My thanks to you and Elizabeth for all you did to make my
New York trip not only easy but a pleasure. The dinner party
was such fun and I will never forget the dinner table breaking!
I hope that it was fixable and that you are back in one piece
but I shall never forget the table in the midst of its earthquake
with Kayo trying to hold it up and undoubtedly making things
worse. It was a delight to get to know Stanley Kunitz and his
wife and the Sweeneys were delightful and there was Kayo sitting next to Lillian Hellman (and not, I think, knowing who
she really is, although of course, he knew who Marianne
Moore was). No matter, everyone was charming and your
apartment with that great window and those ladders up to
books is intriguing.

Cal, I do hope you will come out here and bring your
bathing suit. The temperature in the pool is 84 and although it
looks like the most extravagant toy we ever fell for, I have a
feeling it is better therapy than going to the doctor's (talking
about extravagance and being in hock). If you would like to
stay with us, we have a small room with a bed in it where we
would be very happy to put you up. All you need do is let me
know.

I think I have finished the poem for Sylvia Plath and I think
it is pretty good. I tried to make it sound like her but, as
usual, this attempt was not fruitful; the spirit of imitation did
not last and now it sounds, as usual, like Sexton. One of
these days, I will learn to bear to be myself and to be as
lifelike as a snapshot. I hope you will like the poem. And

Kayo joins me in the hope of seeing you sometime this month.

Love and thanks to Elizabeth,

[*To Brother Dennis Farrell*]

[*40 Clearwater Road*]
August 2nd, 1963

Dear Brother Dennis,

I do not know where you are? Are you there? Or are you somewhere else? Well, I imagine this will find you somewhere ... Your silence has been with me and I have let it have its say. I feel, as always, the same closeness to you which your silence makes into a kind of speech of its own.

Words bother me. I think it is why I am a poet. I keep trying to force myself to speak of the things that remain mute inside. My poems only come when I have almost lost the ability to utter a word. To speak, in a way, of the unspeakable. To make an object out of the chaos ... To say what ? a final cry into the void.

So much for that. The reason I mention it is that it has been on my mind what it is that writes a poem and what it is (so different) that writes a letter. Today I do both. One reason I am breaking the silence is that I have a poem to share. Maybe it will mean something to you, knowing me as YOU do.

And also to say farewell as I leave on August 22nd, aboard the S.S. France for Paris, Belgium, Germany, Switzerland, Italy, Greece, Egypt, London, Spain, Portugal. I will be home for a month at Christmas. I am terribly afraid to go. Aug. 22 is like an execution date. But that will pass I guess.

I think of you often and my love is with you wherever you are.

Anne

[To Nolan Miller]

                                              [40 Clearwater Road]
                                              Aug 5th, 1963
Dear Wonderful Nolan!

Your letter! And such a letter! I have been carrying it around with me but somehow not getting to answer. But now.

So reassuring, places, friends, hotels! I have a small notebook which is holding all precious information and your letter goes into it. After reading it I thought perhaps we might indeed to go Vienna and to Holland and not miss Bruges and many things you mention.

I like all the concrete details. And for being so "directive." I need you to be directive (now at least).

I forget if I told you. I am traveling with a next door neighbor, a friend, woman about 45 who is most sensible and ready to go along. Thus I will not be alone. Which is a good thing because I can barely cross a street in Boston alone ... much less an Alp! We have both read and reread your letter which Sandy says is, indeed, better than a travel book. [...]

Everything seems wild, hallucinary! I can't believe *I* am going, scared, the child says "stay" and the other says "go now". And I listen mostly to the latter for she should have her say now and then. Long enough in this one town with fear keeping me at its gates ... long enough the child in the woman's body. Each day one day closer. Each day I drag a new root out of the ground. So this letter is all confusion but to say thanks for yours.

If you think of anything after I have left my husband will forward mail.

                                                        Love,
                                                        Anne

On August 22 Anne said goodbye to her friends and secretly put small letters under the children's pillows. The family packed itself into the Thunderbird and began the drive to New York City, where the S.S. *France* was docked.

Arriving at the harbor they boarded and rushed to find the tiny cabin below the water-line. Two narrow bunkbeds crowded the stateroom

and there was an infinitesimal lavatory. Immediately Anne comman-
deered the lower bunk.

When the "visitors ashore" gong sounded, the Sextons and Robarts
filed down the gangplank onto the pier. As everyone cried, Anne and
Sandy raced to the ship's uppermost bridge and blew soap bubbles
across the widening stretch of water.

[*To Linda Gray Sexton*]

[*40 Clearwater Road*
August 21, 1963]

Dearest Linda,

I am writing to you tonight, the night before I leave. I have
just been up to your bed talking to you for so long and about
such important things. I was also talking to KITTY and telling her. And she knew! She knows and YOU know too, that
I love you.

All during the fall I love you. When the leaves change, when
the frost comes, when the cover goes on the pool, when the
Thanksgiving turkey is ready, when the stores put up their
Christmas lights . . . I love you.

I hope that you will enjoy your work at school, your violin,
your friends . . . I hope too, that you will be grateful to
everyone who helps take my place for this little while, to
Nana, to Daddy (who will need you) to Meme, to Mrs. Boylan,
to Rita . . . even to Kitty.

Don't forget it, Linda, your Mother, me, loves you very
much. And I won't stop loving you *ever.*

Mom
XOXO

[*To the Sexton Family*]

[*The S. S.* France]
Sunday, Aug 25, [*1963*]

Dearest Family (my Kayo, my Linda, my Joy),

Just a note, for the ship is ROLLING too much to do very
well. For 24 hours I have been strangely accompanied by Mal
de Mere [*sic*]. I make (just) the dining room and sit in a trance
of despair and eat rolls and drink wine and PRETEND that

things do not keep moving. Sandy is fine. We sit on deck chairs, altho cloudy, oyster gray ocean. Please call Maxine and read this to her as I have not the energy, but lots of love, to write to her on board. Martinis are 45¢ a drink (as I have said). I swallow them but listlessly. Please tell Max, tell the world that I have written a poem ["Crossing the Atlantic," LD] the first day out (when it was smooth). Poem talks about a calm sailing, over a flat sea. The poem is, I think, pretty good ... maybe for New Yorker even ... but sea no longer calm so can't work on it or even type it out. When you've got hold of a poem and can't type it out, well, then it must be rocky ... We sleep in darkness and daylight does not exist in here, wake at noon and have missed breakfast and today lunch. Strange! The ship, on stern, at night is glorious tho very windy and cold. Last night stood and watched the wake, booming barrels of foam, trailing out ... ever, ever. And moon went in and out [of] black clouds and out it shone darkly, dangerously and the wide waters. I love the ship, really ... but, well, you know. We can't seem to make definite plans about itinerary until Paris. We will be there five days, prob Lux 2 and 3 of Sept and Brussels (how long Brussels ... don't know?) could, for fun of it peek into Am Ex office there to see if mail by chance.

We think some of sending some clothes home ... so if packages arrive don't get excited ... only our old clothes (or books). Have thought of throwing books into the wake, I am still lame from carrying them half the way on board! I assume you will share letters with the Robarts too. Tell Rita I use her lighter and think of her with each drag (even if she has given up smoking). It is coldish in Europe (here too) 65 in Paris (Anne, what you so stupid for with white, two, dress!?).

I have shown your pictures to fifteen people so I guess I haven't forgotten you at all. Our table for six is nice, interesting lot of people. Our stewardess, arrives with smiles in morning (noon really) with lots of french and cute and brings us croissants and coffee and juice and a huge bowl of fruit. She said, today, good day to sleep all morning for it is dark and she is rolling (she's telling me!) She is a doll. However, I think this will be my last ocean voyage, but I am glad to have had one . . . or else how would I know! Sandy, right now is washing our undergarments and sends her love and says we are going through a period of adjustment and don't quite know where we are. We are, maybe, unwinding, she says (I say ship IS winding)

. . . .

I still love deck chair, Kayo, as in Canada and look much same with blowing hair (straight) peeking over kerchief, all wrapped in two big wool rugs. Saw a movie 1st night, Sophia Loren, good movie. Helped me get my mind off my stomache [*sic*].

I miss you all . . . must go for Sandy is now all dressed for deck and I'm in pajamas and it is two thirty in afternoon and have yet to see daylight (even if gray and cold) . . .

My love, my love
Anne – Mom

[*To the Sexton Family*]

Paris
Friday August 30th. [1963]

Dearest Kayo (and Linda and Joy) . . .

We are so busy here that there is literally not time to write letters home. I still don't really KNOW I have left or that I'm really in Paris. We still sleep so late that we waste half a day right there and each day vow to get to sleep early . . . or earlier but don't[.] We talk, walk to a cheap cafe for a glass of wine, lean out window, wash clothes or talk. I feel guilty that I am not writing better or more letters. Paris is just too much. I would have to be here for five months to explain its beauty and write of it or even make notes . . . it is overwhelming . . . and the thing I just didn't expect was the sudden sense of history . . . ! Oh, if I only knew more! Napoleon! And the buildings, the windows, the colors, the cobblestone streets, the, the . . .

Yesterday, with really sore feet, we set out to look up a writer friend of Nolan Miller. Just for the fun of it, didn't expect to find him, he had no phone, and it turned out to be only a block away . . . and the craziest top of a building with a French landlady who took us up six stories in an all open elevator to a thin dark corridor and down it, dark, to bang on his door, and call to him (just like a movie, her gestures etc) and Peter (his name) opens door to us (to strangers from U.S.) and he was most charming, an American writer who has lived here for 15 [years] and is married to a French girl (she works all day at Pan Am while he writes and does dishes)... We stayed all day talking and drank wine all day (but with never the effect of the predinner martini ... which I don't miss, haven't found time to miss) [...] — his wife charmingly cooked while we (another writer came too, a beatnik type) sat and shouted about writers and who was good. For years James Baldwin came to Peter's twice a week for dinner in Paris because Baldwin was starving ... now he makes about one million a year (and is not really a very good writer tho he is indeed in the headlines, even here, daily)... Poor Jimmy (they call him)... and yet, such luck, to be negro at that right time. We stayed late, drinking bottles of IMPORTED (15 cents a bottle) french wine.

Today we are going on a bus tour of historical Paris (save the feet it is called) ... we go without lunch to afford bus trip ... Your letters sound so sad ... so nostalgic ... ah, I feel guilty, but I do, very, want to be missed. I dream of you at night. Last night I dreamt you got a raise (what does that mean?) and we celebrated together. I think I am too busy to be myself except in dreams. Certainly no time to get depressed, but I already wish we had a house or apt. to settle into. Maybe we will in Italy or somewhere. I think that it is harder to be left than to leave, home without the other gets so alone, and here I have Sandy (who is swell) but more important a thousand things to see... I wish I were a movie camera, I can't hold it in and I can't even write it out. Also we are rather busy trying to save money as we pay about 14 bucks for this room with breakfast, but lovely with bath. Have cashed travelers checks DA31-348-790,791,793. Will write license of car when get, haven't even gone there yet, figure it is free parking until we up and leave. To drive in this city would be madness, and no place to park either. To walk is the charm, shanks mare (is this Anne?) miles and miles, as bad as walking yourself into Boston, I think. Nana used to walk twenty miles a day in Paris with my grandmother. If they can, we can. They could not afford a carriage, but perhaps tonight we try subway ... I am your Button, your Anne, your Mom

[*To the Sexton Family*]

Brussels, Belgium
Wed. Sept 4th, 1963
10:30 A.M.

Dear Family,
    (In her letters from Europe my Nana always wrote "dear home folks". So, I feel the same way. It means, dear "all", "All my loved ones" "all my home" ... I don't have time to write separate letters because my news is the same and the love, though differing in meaning is just as big for each of you ... However, your news is different sometimes and I'd love a letter from each if you have time and feel like it.
    ... Enclosed is our first traffic ticket gotten in Paris, not traffic but for parking in front of France & Choiseul. We are ignoring it (which is the custom for TT plates) and have skipped the country!! *I* drove us out of Paris and onto the ROAD. I drove for 2 and one-half hours and Sandy the rest. Drove from noon until seven so Sandy did the most and the worst. The drive thru France was delightful! All farm lands, a miniature Grant Wood all the way, with tall tall trees planted along the road (like in a french movie) and the land mostly flat ... [...]the roads not crowded, two lane or sometimes three lane with the old bother of when to pass. There were trucks, but not the largest variety that we have at home. Many of the streets were made of cobblestones, stretching for miles, all laid in by hand. Cobblestones do not make the easiest driving. We ate lunch at a small cafe which was fairly okay, beef, smoked ham sandwich. The toilet there was my first one with the footprint and not real toilet. It is like going outdoors because you just squat over it and hope you are aiming correctly. It flushes tho. But you must get all the way off as it flushes like mad all over the footprints. (Kayo I hope you have a good time explaining these footprints to the girls!)

When we crossed the border (with an extra six packs of
Salems, bought on boat for 20 cents a pack) more than we are
allowed per custom regulation we were slightly nervous) they
just asked for passport, driving paper that shows we are insured and asked if we were carrying "spirits" and we said yes
an open bottle (Billie's [Anne's mother-in-law] martinis) and
he waved us through. If only we had known we would have
brought all the cigs allowed into France (5 cartons each and
we only bought 7 in all having looked up regulation in Belgium) . . . Into Belgium we drove thru miles of bicyclists coming home from work. The Factory had just let out and there
were everywhere, Berets and lunch boxes. They dominated
the street. Belgium became one long city into Brussels and
almost all of it cobblestones. We were certainly in the "in-
dustrial" (as John [Woulbroun, a family friend] said) part of the
country. At times it looked like home, a worst of Waltham,
with on many corners a plate glass store, or anyhow much
more commercial than the part of France we had left and not
many painted shutters, in some parts miles of T.V. antennas
stretched for miles and then in one section that strange black
mountains that rise in their ugly fashion out of the flat land.
These are the unusable parts of the coal that has been heaved
out of the ground by men for years . . . a coal mountain . . .
very ugly for it makes you think of the sweat that brought it
up . . . and of the deep caves it left underground. I tried to
take a picture but got mostly Sandy's face for we were driving
along at the time . . . Now that we are in Brussels I would say
we got here by way of Dorchester. The city itself has long
miles of this . . . although we are in the heart, near The Grand
Place (one of the most famous squares in Europe). The Place
is a square of buildings that date back to the 15th century,
they were the guild buildings. The outside of them is painted
in gold and beautifully lit up at night. Our hotel (found in
Europe on 5 Dollars a Day) is on a tiny winding street, the
street is about as big as a sidewalk, we were afraid to drive
into it until we spied another car (all cars being foreign and
tiny. Your car, Kayo, would scratch its fenders on both sides!
In we walked NO Sandy walked. I stayed guarding the car

which looks like the Grapes of Wrath with all our stuff in it, but which is fondly called "the blue jewel" (pronounced the bloo jool)... Entrance to hotel is a very quiet and plain bar with food. Rooms (two adjoining) are 6 dollars a day. The John is down two flights (we are up three). I haven't seen a bath but there may be one, washbowl in room, but I note no hot water coming out of hot water faucet. We will heat our own with Eleanor's thing. And to get warm I plugged in last night, with extension cord (Billie, please note) but am not sure what voltage I should be on. The pad has two volt types you can turn to, I turn from one to other waiting to be blown up. Can't ask as they are very saving of electricity here (everywhere) and would frown or kick us out at mention of this expensive heating pad. Lights in hall turn off automatically in 6 minutes. So you push the button, run down stairs, go to John and get back up in 6 minutes or the light is out and you are thrust into total darkness (at night) to feel your way back. The toilet paper is like a Scott towel we use in kitchen, only rougher, maybe like crepe paper. Our rooms are delightful, clean, colorful, in a very old building with some history I suspect. Only about ten rooms here in all, everyone breakfasting in bar. As we sat last night in bar, empty but for an old cat licking her paws, filling out our passport things (in great detail in every city one must do this, date of birth, etc.) in the background madame was watching the Flintstones in French! Then we parked our car (for ten francs for overnight which is 20 cents) we came back to this street (Rue du Boucher) where our hotel is and the place where we ate (following *Europe on 5 dollars* ... it cost 6 dollars to eat because we had a fancy bottle of rosé from Luxembourg; Belgium doesn't make their own wine, only beer). We had a wonderful meal and were very tired and glad of it. We had Tomato Crevettes (tomatoes with tiny shrimp, never so so small, they come Ostend) and were very sweet. Then we had MOULES (marvelous). Moules are mussels. They were steamed in a vegetable broth, onion and celery and eaten out of the shell. Très bien! And then we staggered down to the Place for a look at it all lit up. It is lovely but we did not sit at a cafe and drink coffee and look at it as we were too tired. And so back to bed in a deep spongy bed where I slept well. Sandy had a double bed, her room a step down from mine. I am typing in her room which looks out over roof tops . . .

The coffee this morning (you have to get out of bed because you have to go to the bathroom and so we do get up and breakfast — has a ten o'clock deadline too) was the first drinkable since leaving Newton Lower Falls. We have tried hard to be good frenchmen and drink the coffee without complaint but I turned to tea the last few days in France. The french coffee is bitter bitter mud. Ugh. Even where you drink it half and half with hot milk (café au lait) it is ghastly. But today, still au lait, was far better.

My mouth continually is dry and almost dusty, perhaps from wine. In France I drank gallons of water with a great unquenchable thirst. Next door to our hotel there is a small market where we bought two oranges last night. We eat an orange a day to keep up on the vitamin C. This morning we haven't eaten it yet as we had to rush to breakfast.

The money *is* going fast although we are trying to hold back. Last night we switched to Belgian francs as I cashed a travelers check no. da3i-348-795. I think that 20 dollars a day is a *very conservative* estimate . . . but we will see. One thing for sure, it is certainly NOT necessary to pay 50 per day per Fran and A [family friends]. We can do this for about 25 a day I would think, going over only on special occasions or trips and extra gas. Or when we die for a Salem cig and run out of these, they cost one dollar or over a pack. But we are trying to keep it down and yet enjoy ourselves and we have been able to. The France and Choiseul was 13.40 a day (with bath you see, 8 without bath) . . . We enjoyed the bath, tho . . . and needed it as we will other times. I washed and set my own hair last Friday night and it looks pretty good, a little curly in wrong direction but passable) . . . I can't wait for Amsterdam and letters again. I have made Sept 12th the deadline for letters there and Sept 16th deadline in Zurich. Course those dates are just made up, but they sound good.

I love you and miss you terribly.
Anne–Mom

[*To Alfred Sexton,*
telegram]

September 5, 1963
OUR LUGGAGE STOLEN LETTER FOLLOWS-

ANNE

[*To the Sexton Family*]

[*Belgium*]
Sept. 4, 1963

BLACK WEDNESDAY

Dear Home Folks,

Oh, this is our day of great sadness. We are très sad, with tears flowing on all dies (interesting slip) sides. Just this morning we wrote a happy letter from Brussels and here we are, tonight, in abject sadness. I have cried into my squashy bed and we have moaned over another meal of Moules, but to no use. We have NOT been sightseeing in Brussels all day! We have not been the light-hearted Americans skipping about. No. We are the tragic pair. We have been robbed.

However, we are not starving. Sandy just found a piece of bread (with butter) that we stole from our breakfast — in *France* yet. We have ... well, right now we feel we have nothing. But we do have some. We, in truth, have retained (with our terrible luck) the worst of the luggage. We still have the car (I mean, I haven't looked but last time I looked we had it). It is still called the Bloo Jool. We have some toothpicks we stole. We also have the contents of Sandy's smallest bag (plastic hair curlers, two kotex, a box of kleenex, one heating pad, two pajamas, two bathrobes, my navy coat, her black and her white coats, toilet paper — two rolls, two pairs of pants, two bottles of my sleeping pills, two books of matches, my red suit is on me, my red print nylon dress, my Navy blue sweater bought in Canada, my list of addresses and of travelers check numbers, one coat hanger, my shower cap, package of lifesavers, one lace hat for a church, sanitary belt, bottle of foot cream, clothes line with nothing to hang on it, Sandy's sunglasses, vitamin C, News clipping about Luxembourg where we never went, two things of jewelry but one of Sandy's missing, two toothbrushes, cleansing cream and two comb and brush and two lipstick, deodorant, nail polish and clippers. Also polish and brush for Navy shoes.)

We was robbed! We had had lunch and were on our way to Claudine and Jacque's (John's friends who had *not* heard from him . . . John the bum) and we went to car that had been in perfectly respectable parking lot, called Esso . . . where, we read today on small print ticket, they are not responsible for articles in car, and mind you the car was locked tight as a drum, windows doors etc . . . we found the bloo Jool in its proper spot *without* the two medium bags of Sandy's in the back seat, without my books, the bag full of books all gone! Just without . . . not to mention the UMBRELLA . . . oh me. Most of our good clothes, carefully put in those two bags to wear in Knokke . . . are gone forever . . . In the front of the VW was my LARGE bag (repacked for both this time) with winter or heavy or useless clothes. It had not been stolen. But the rest was gone. They didn't take my Harvard bag full of what we laughingly called "the kitchen" (made up by Eleanor Boylan) but the rest was gone. We are trying to make a list (but can't remember) of what is lost. We wish to call you but feel too poor and anyhow what good would it do. Kazan told us that if we lost luggage (referring to insurance) we wouldn't get money for months if it were stolen so don't bother cabling him. Of course, we want you to start HAUNT-ING him from now on. Because lost it is . . . and it is up to him to take us from here. Naturally our record of slip of the bag insurance was in 2 stolen bags but he must have made a carbon. Oh Me. (Promising I'd never swear, I'll say, Oh Suds . . . oh damn Suds!) . . .

The parking people showed us how, on last night's stub, they weren't responsible. So on to police . . . worse than T.V. in time taken up and merely official as we made a statement in french of what had been stolen (and understated in amount of $ lost as we were in shock and couldn't remember all that must be gone) and after we signed it he, though most pleasant, told us we'd never get it back as thief is type who steals to make a living, slowly selling things . . . and thus we learn . . . about Europe or thiefs, and thiefs we have at home, we know, but we aren't so stupid as to leave two bags on seat at home. We cry, for home is where we live, where we can trust and believe and not lose. But. Didn't I ask for this in Paris? Oh me, and yet they took wrong bag, for large bag in trunk was full of things, almost, we figured we didn't need much and so wouldn't need to carry it. Why the thief didn't take it is, of course, clear to all. It was just too heavy to steal! (Moral — pack for an elephant to carry, elephants have trunks of their own) ... Oh, at last, I made up a joke, tho not too good, still a joke, to make us laugh midst this real unhappiness and longing for safety. I cannot bear to list what is lost ... it still hurts too much. [...]

Are we eligible for a CARE package? All my books are gone, even the rhyming dictionary, and all books I had to have in order to write. In fact nothing left to read except *Europe on $5 a Day.* We have the alarm clock. I have Joan's present (unopened). Gone the umbrellas. Still have our raincoats (liked umbrellas better with that history and so practical too) ... We have the hideous clods, the two pairs of comfortable shoes from the Barn which we both wear everywhere. Slippers gone.

In the large bag, in front of VW we found. Some things.:::::: my navy blue knit, my bright blue knit, my wool jumper, a blue matching blouse, my white sweater which is dirty and I hate it, my black lining for my navy coat, two pairs of wool socks, my white arnel dress with navy trim (that wore on *France*) minus its belt. All belts lost, in bag for Knokke for both of us which makes almost everything unwearable, my blue and white stripe, sleeveless dress that I wore in Canada so much, a navy jersey of Joan's, — sweater type, my navy heels both size, brown and tan shoes of mine, both our overshoes, my navy clutch, two pairs of stockings, shorts, shoe polish, orange jersey blouse ... of Sandy's we found, a navy knit dress, one chileco, one pair of stockings, two handbags, a pair of shorts, four blouses, two pairs of black heels, four pairs of *gloves* ... (she says she is really ready to go with her hands) ... Sandy has lost almost everything and I, too, almost everything ... all my best dresses, the navy low cut, the aqua two piece, the silk aqua print, the white arnel, the nylon aqua print sleeveless, the navy knit with white and kelly green top, slippers, all underwear except for extra pants, all hankys, two bathing suits ... one aqua print Moo-moo, receipts for baggage insurance we guess cuz can't find (for God's sake call Kazan and make big noise! We need some American noise right now! Can't remember what else gone. Sandy lost two wool suits, also a black knit given her with Les, plus skirts, sweaters, blouses, my harlequin sleeveless print). Well, we think and hope to make a complete list of what is lost for Kazan to start working on it. We don't know how to do it. Sandy insured to 500 bucks, me for 1000. But we didn't lose everything, but almost everything. The little bag was full of useless things (if I can call my heating pad useless ... never! but curlers, hell, they have curlers ...). We are awfully brave not to call you for advice but you wouldn't know. Tomorrow we go back to police station and probably waste all day trying to get a copy of his report and to add my bag of books to it. At first I didn't notice bag of books was missing ... too shock[ed] over empty back seat to fully assess the loss. Books themselves must be worth 75 to 100 dollars. But money not all of it ... so much a part of home is lost. Of course, we *did* have too much stuff but OH HOW WE WISH we could have selected what to be stolen, or even better, followed our plan to send home the big bag. We will buy a few things here to get along on knowing insurance & will come sooner or later ... but things we can stuff into tiny bag and huge bag (though we are really Goldilocks who likes the middle bed) ... for, in turn, what new we buy would, after all, have to be reinsured I guess. Ask Kazan. We talked to his fellow travel agent in Brussels and they were very nice and said to write Kazan a detailed report. (detailed? who remembers it all?). Whatever you do, call Kazan and keep after it. We need help! Oh, Sandy lost the lovely grecian white bathing suit. Oh well, all suits are gone and it's cold enough around here not to ask how will thief even sell bathing suits, much less ten copies of each of my books. Oh woe. This is, indeed, part of our Experience but how sad. Très sad. We are sliced clean, undone, half ourselves ... WE NEED OUR HUSBANDS! We need the faces of our offspring to answer back to our sadness. I need Billie to tell me what I've forgotten that I lost. (Can't bear to think of more) . . . (just remembered lost one garter belt. Mine. Sandy lost her girdle.) Now don't lecture us. It looked safe, brightly lit in a good place near Place. We didn't know. We do now. Nowhere without HUGE bag and TINY bag. We have our cameras, this typewriter, some film (as of now) film and kitchen still in locked car, give thief a haul for second night? . . . Claudine came right over to hotel when we called her after police. Brought her two peppy sons and then drove us to shops where they have clothes and to her house for a scotch, and then Jacques drove us back here. Very nice, most attractive couple. Listened sadly to our woes and saw us without letter from John and was most charming.

Oh KIDS, oh *woe*. I didn't lose new poems in manuscript for they in briefcase I brought to room, which is some good. We are some homesick . . . we are little lost babes . . . the "adventure" turned sour.

And even the umbrella. Where will I find one so good here. Bought hankys today for xmas presents, but need them to cry into. Oh, how is our home, it is so cold and rainy here. It never suns or gets warm. We are lonely. We write, tonight, out of desperation and fear and loneliness . . . We miss Clover and Deery [family dogs] for their sweet consoling eyes . . . we missed being kissed and hearing "it's all right now" . . . and at least we have this typewriter to send our love which is our total belonging. Your almost naked but loving girls.

[. . .] We say to each other — all good experiences — umbrella in Paris was comic opera. Luggage in Belgium tragedy like Shakespeare. Our recovery of spirits in a true Freudian light — not bowed.

[*To the Sexton Family*]

[*Belgium*]
BLACK AND WHITE THURSDAY
Sept. 5th, 1963

Dearest Home Folks,

Well today, with such rushings, went by without mailing yesterday's letter. So this will have to be part of it and too all.

But, by now or almost now you have gotten our cable, of course when you read this, but as we write we think of you knowing NOW of our tragedy. We sent out word over the waves. Our luggage stolen, letter follows. Hope it did not throw you ... but we needed to share so you wouldn't continue to picture us in some sort of European idle.

... This morning, with not enough sleep, we groped out of bed and ate breakfast ... called the Embassy to say we'd not be at le Zoutte for a few days, told Madame (so kind, speaks English, so très nice and fat and funny and likes the "americans" and more of her later. She told us, at length, just where our clothes would be for sale. In the Flea market and she told us where. We wrote down directions for flea market for later). First things first, we returned to police station to tell them we needed a copy of our complaint for insurance and to tell them we had forgotten to report a third bag stolen (all my books) worth $150.00. This complete and with no hope, they said, of ever getting thief we got back to Bloo Jool with still our kitchen in it and drove to flea market. We had forgotten our cameras which is a pity as flea market something. A Place de Flea! (place as in glass not as in face). There in an empty square everyone sets up shop, bringing their goods in old wagons. Things, clothes, shoes, spoons, tires, mattresses, umbrellas and old real flea sweaters, racks with fine looking coats, racks with odd dresses, and mostly on old bedspreads are spread out the articles for sale. So went we, like two rather old and wrinkled female Perry Masons, to spy for our lost clothes. To put the suspense down, they were not there! They are certainly *lost*. We are not good detectives and have lost the scent. We, true women, found something else. By that I mean, that laid out on top of a pile of old and really dirty clothes was a fine looking houndstooth suit that fits Sandy. It is true chic and looks very Peck and Peck only perhaps with more style. Of course it is stolen goods, being used and obviously wearable ... but most things are "rags" or stolen, so we prefer the stolen. Perhaps tonight in some other hotel room in Brussels someone is putting on my navy blue low cut dress that they bought at the flea market. If so we could not find. It occurs to us a good idea to buy our own things back after claiming insurance. The reason this would work is that one gets very little money for stolen (hot) merchandise and so it is also sold cheap to public. Sandy's suit (it's true) cost 2 bucks. I priced a very pretty red dress but only got them down from 7 to 5 and that was too much for that place. Don't mistake the prices in Brussels, they are for normal goods, high and ordinarily higher than in the U.S. Belgium is booming and prices are up and up. I can tell you this like a comparison shopper for the rest of the day spent in the Bon Marché (a cross between Filene's and Peck and Peck and Jordan's) and the 5 and 10 buying things not available at Flea Market (before we left it Sandy bought me Sherwood Anderson's *Winesburg, Ohio* in paperback for 16 cents to start a book collection over again) . . . such as . . . one girdle (Sandy) one bra (Anne) one garter belt (Anne) one black jersey top to go with suit (Sandy) one pair falsies (Anne) (foam yet) then to Haute Courteir (sp wrong) to buy me one dressy dress for Knokke which is having a "ball" on Sat. evening. I have no dresses left, Sandy has a white with thin straps left for it. My dress is blue, I think silk, print, too dressy, but very lovely. [. . .] Oh me — even in bedraggled condition after police dept. and flea market. I hate to say but it cost 60 dollars but can't be helped. It is being fitted and ready tomorrow.

So you see we have taken the reins into our hands, though it hasn't been the least easy I promise you, and are trying to muddle through this mess alone. We sent you the telegram after the Bon Marché, where we also bought a navy blue umbrella (oh Billie, (sorry Robarts, this old ragged carbon borrowed from Madame, Bon Marché doesn't have carbons) . . . and we had walked wrong way to Bon Marché and it was about ten miles both ways and we had been all over the damn store cashing checks, looking, asking, Sandy forgetting all her French . . . to think we had come to Europe to end up in a huge dept. store, hot sweat in store, full of counters and escalators that went up and up into the air, as up a mountain. We walked home in rain, going twice the wrong way, and then couldn't stand you, at home, not knowing what had happened [. . .]

Well, in we came, up comes our friend, Madame, who is so

distressed that we didn't find our clothes. We sit in bar (lobby is bar where Madame holds forth, fixes t.v. for customers, serves wine ... bar not a regular bar, bar is where only beer and wine is served ... cooks meals, gives change, rents rooms, advises guests, etc). We sit down and order glass of wine and tell her our tales of woe and of "finding" in flea market, finding SOMEONE'S suit anyhow. By then it is pelting rain and we too tired to go out to eat ... Could have used a triple hooker of whiskey but no real bars (that serve real liquor) in this neighborhood. So Madame says she serves small dinner and (of course for money but not much we don't think, we hope not) and what would we like. She has cooking, she tells us, some pork, some beef, some cauliflower with cheese, some boiled potatoes, some asparagus soup. HOORAY, we say! (in French) and all grubby and too tired to walk upstairs and even wash, much less go to bathroom, we sit and wait and Madame fixes us supper. We walk back and forth to kitchen, on left of bar, talking to Madame, showing her Sandy's suit and etc. while she cooks away. It seemed homey. Only one other couple in bar (speaking French.) Like a little family. Madame says it is too bad we are leaving tomorrow for tomorrow is her birthday and she would like to ask us to supper. Sandy and I think that over (by now almost in tears for someone is being kind to us). We then declare her "our mother" and decide to stay an extra day ... This is fine, not only for Madame's birthday dinner but because it will allow us more time to screw our heads on right and we think, to splurge and get our hair done and also we will buy Madame flowers. By this time Madame is getting nicer and nicer, bringing us each delicious course and telling us to eat and forget our troubles and that she personally knows the Chef of police and she will call him and tell him to watch for our stolen goods and she will slap him on bottom if he doesn't. Then we ask if we could have bath (Madame must light water heater beside tub for this) and she says we may have bath with no charge to make up for losing everything. And thus we come upstairs and wash and wash clothes (no hot water in room but we have sink and we have plug and we use El. Boylan's little heater, glass by glass to make hot water). Right now room looks like a laundry full

of drip drys. Sandy is sewing. We are très domestique! The
rain is pattering on the roof and Madame turned the heat on
for an hour to "take off the chill" . . . quite cosy. Madame put
blue scent bubbles in our baths to cheer us up. We are both
clean and warm . . . I looked hard and long at the pictures of
you, Kayo, Linda and Joy, today, tears welling up, missing you
. . . not just the clothes or books, but you. Sandy has only pics
of Andy and Sis and wish she did of others. Kayo, could you
take a polaroid pic of Robart family and send? Sandy would
most appreciate it. She longs.

Kayo, I worry terribly that I don't have time to write to
Maxine. She will be feeling rejected . . . and yet no other carbon and this is the whole story and THE whole strength. Tell
her I think of her as I write and it seems, almost, as though
she were dictating this to me and we were writing another
children's book. She is part of my fingers and they feel
strange not writing with her (or very guilty not writing *to*
her) . . . (Please call her, just for me!!)

We both miss our cats and our two dogs. But out of the
whole trip I think we are gaining great experiences . . . even
the true loss of luggage has its happier aspects (staying over
for Madame birthday or even the mundane time spent shopping which shows up Europe is more like America than we
dreamed.) I know that out of the worst, the unexpected, we
gain. Life is indeed, happening to us, over here, we are not
just "visiting it" or seeing it through the large-money-tour-
type eyes of most Americans abroad. The people are all kind
and so willing to help . . . You should have seen two police-
men try to help us open collapsible umbrella that wouldn't
open and would only collapse! Everyone seems to have more
time for the personal touch, even in the big stores . . . more
helpful, more interested . . . Knokke on Sat. morning and
there until Mon. or Tues. and then to Amsterdam and God
knows what. Right now the bidet is catching water from our
dripping clothes . . . we are making a home, of sorts and
Madame calls us . . . "how are my babies doing?" We took a
picture of Madame behind the bar. Tomorrow we buy her
violets and some other flowers sold in great bunches under
gay umbrellas in middle of The Grand Place. Buildings are

fine but the people are the grandest (don't count thief ...
there are thieves everywhere, must ask Joy! And we all learn.
I need lessons from Joy!) ... Sandy sends love to all and
misses greatly too. She wishes when you have finished their
copy, that Robarts wld forward it to Andy (telling him to keep
and return as we have no real journals, only our letters to
you)... I can find my way pretty well, now, in Paris and in
Brussels, car good for that. Soon I will know many more
cities this intimately (better than I know Boston). And more
about people. We have weathered a bad storm, we think, and
tonight after bath and a wonderful home-cooked meal, things
look better ... we feel in control. We love! We miss ... there
is true *pain* in not sharing with you (thus cable) all good and
all bad. (bloody but unbowed)

yrs
girls.

XO Mom — Your faces look so dear to me. Please write just
everything (good or bad) I want to know — (share letters
[with] anyone who cares. Tell John Brussels very lovely & fun
— His friends charming — MADAME TAKES THE CAKE. I
miss my home — (ie you)

[*To Alfred Sexton*]

Saturday night,
Sept 7th. 1963,
Knokke le Zoutte

Dearest Kayo,

I want, though not often, to write you a letter of your own
... ie. a love letter. It can be a drag to have to speak publicly
(to all, the girls and whoever, sometimes I feel to the whole
neighborhood) ... when, I often long for you and wish to
speak only to you. Naturally the news goes on, the road
moves, the travelerama continues ... and with it, with each
time I type are these almost unspoken words of love for you.
Kayo, my darling, I miss you terribly ... each food I taste that
I think worthy of your taste I miss you more. And more! Oh
Boots, there are times, despite the excitement of the buildings,
of the food, of the people, when longing for you wells up in
me ... and I want to be home beside you in the bed looking at

t.v. or at the kitchen table drinking a martini . . . (for God's sake now Sandy is talking and talking and all day she has been silent but when I start to write, well *then* she talks . . .) enough complaints. Actually we get along pretty well, except for a fight last night that didn't last long. I was typing out the list for Kazan and asking her how to spell and she sounded irritated and I barked back and told her to go to hell etc. She went out of the room in a huff and went to the john and smoked a cig. Good for me I sez . . . might as well speak up and clean the slate off once in a while. [. . .]

Kayo, the night before last I dreamt that you were having an affair with someone and I woke up crying. Awful! Please keep loving me! I love you so much and feel you are here with me all of the time . . . miss you more than I had thought possible. True, I am terribly busy, what with losing everything! And all. The shock of losing it all just doesn't sink in. I lost all the books! Even nana's letters from Europe and grandfather's too. I did value and love those two books . . . but they are in the thief's wastebasket I guess . . . and life must go on not backward (just this fact makes me feel better, the trouble with therapy is that it makes life go backwards . . . and I am so tired of that old suffering. I want life to go forward even if I have to lose all my books and clothes to keep it going in that direction. And in a way, life *is* flowing toward us . . . you and me . . . and the life we have, for each day that goes by brings us nearer and each mile does it too. I feel, sometimes, as if I were actually driving upon the map in our kitchen! I know I am here and you are there and yet, and yet, not quite. The sound of the ocean reminds me of the night in front of the house we rented on the Cape. Do you remember that night on the beach?) . . . I keep missing baked beans. Do you think you might send me a care package of baked beans? It is the first meal I think of and long for. Tonight in Knokke at our hotel (meals with room . . . a nice summer out of season hotel . . . typical dutch bourgeois hotel resort, very nice) we had tiny, two or three inch, lobster as a start and then steak and marvelous sauce and french fries. The french fries all over Europe are wonderful. I have become a lover of french fries (not frozen, not HoJo) . . . The poetry festival is a farce, à

la New Eng Poetry Club only from every country ... perhaps
better but not much, arrived today and have taken no part really, sat in café outdoors by beach and drank an apertif, sea
too lovely to bother with a building full of poets. And, I must
admit, that it is perfectly awful not speaking French. I mean
it is useless ... French is THE language! If *you* really want to
tour France — you must start now taking French lessons ... I
am serious, Berlitz on Sat. or something. You can't do it
without it. It is like a car without gas. Sandy speaks. Thanks
God for we get in the right direction (though I have a better
sense of direction and usually find out way home or "back")
but when she has a discussion it is in French and I stare at
floor and wonder what the weather will be tomorrow. Otherwise (if you don't have time or won't) we had better stick to
Spanish speaking countries ... for I am serious, no speak no
live (except a la Fran and A and who wants that) Sandy says to
tell you that he [you] would be proud and overjoyed the way I
am bouncing around from place to place and taking it in my
stride. But you know, Kayo, I always did have a "wanderlust"
and it wasn't JUST A NEUROTIC wish to flee responsibility ...
but to see new things. And I do love that. I don't have the
time or energy to get depressed or anxious ... if anxious I
seem to have four miles of walking in front of me and that
takes care of THAT. Tonight we are suppposed to be at the
Poetry Festival Ball (for which I bought that damn expensive
new dress in Brussels) but which I don't feel like going to.
The sea has undone me. To hell with the ball. The dress I
will wear on New Year's eve and you will fall in love with
me. That's what I want the dress for. Meanwhile I'll wear the
few rags I have left. We have a copy of what we sent to Kazan
as a list and will send it later, perhaps from Amsterdam (right
now using mailers) for you to check. I wrote it out quite correctly, be sure to check with him and see what's up and tell
him clothes all new for trip and not to devalue them as
"used" ... some never worn. Kayo, my boots, please keep
loving me. It is hard to go so long without letters from you.
Every night before sleep I read the ones I got in Paris but then
you had never heard from me ... the time lapse is painful

(that's why the cable) . . . You hear from us more regularly, but it is hard for me to wait this long, I become fearful and afraid, afraid I'll lose you. I know that IS silly, but there it is, in all its little ugly unsureness and with its open love. Europe is fascinating. I am truly interested and excited but I miss you very much and love you with all my heart. Usually I must write the large common letter. But tonight I must say my special say which goes for always but must be said once more. I love you. [. . .]
love you. love you. love you. love you!

[To Alfred Sexton]

> *Amsterdam*
> *Sept. 19th,*
> *(wishful thinking? Sept. 10, 1963*

Dearest Kayo,

At last! Mail! [. . .] I WANT MAIL. I AM HOMESICK. I WISH I WERE HOME. It isn't that Europe isn't just wonderful . . . It's just that actually Dr. Martin was right . . . I belong with you and away from you isn't quite right. In fact I'm crying . . . I'm sitting at a table in our bedroom that overlooks a canal in Amsterdam. Sandy is sitting across from me, writing by hand, (I'M the selfish one, using a typewriter . . . I'm used to the machine now and like it) I am even drinking a martini (from the bottle your mother gave Sandy). It is warm, of course and I hold my nose to drink it. We had a drink out of it in France one night (with ice then) and never thought of it since. Nothing but wine or beer since so I guess I'm not an alcoholic! . . . I guess I'm sad because I was hoping for letters from you and there they are sitting in Brussels! Gosh oh gosh. Me button. Me sad. And maybe even the letters I got made me even more homesick. Your voice is so clear in my head [. . .] and then I think of the rooms in the house and oh. It is worse (and in a way better) than when you were in the service. Worse because I know just what it is I miss and belong to . . . better because we have made a home, an "our place" and there is no question of its stability. But oh, I miss it. Oh! It is just now sinking in. Maybe Martin was right . . . much bet-

ter for a month with Sandy and a month with you. Oh! Oh!
If I acted on impulse I'd leave tomorrow! For HOME! YOU!
YOU! [. . .]

I worry that you are going to take Maxine out to dinner and
that you will kiss her. Please don't kiss her, just as a special
favor to me. I know a kiss doesn't mean anything . . . but if
you do kiss anyone it should be strangers, not my best friend.
See . . . I'm jealous (but that's no news) . . . I'm glad if you go
out with her . . . but please, Kayo . . . (it is silly for me to beg.
It is just my mood and it isn't the martini . . . perhaps might
be time of month. I forget. Nothing has happened anyway.
Am I overdue? I guess not. I wish I were pregnant and then I
could come home.) Enough! I just miss you terribly and I feel
lonely for my home and my husband and my children. It reminds me of camp . . . There was lots to do at camp but I
wanted to be home. Well I've been in Europe for 2 weeks and
have loved it, now I want to go home . . . though there's lots
to do . . . I'm homesick. [. . .]

While I have written it has gotten dark out. Soon we will
go out into the city that Anne Frank could never go out into
where she stayed for four years in her one room listening for
the tread of the Nazis. And they came. She is for me the Joan
De Arc of Amsterdam. [. . .]

So this is Amsterdam . . . a lovely city . . . and I feel like
Anne Frank not Anne Sexton . . . I want to be home. And so
did she. Tell El I haven't written a poem about lost luggage
yet . . . but will I hope. [. . .] Well, honey, we sure do worry
about each other. I guess we need to be together and next
time an "opportunity" happens I'm going to say to hell with it
and take the opportunity of staying with the man I love. But,
I'll stay on with this. I'm stubborn and stay I will. If I started
I'd better finish. And I don't feel sick, just awfully homesick
. . . it really just caught up with me today . . . in the worst
way. I think I kept looking forward to Amsterdam (where the
mail was) as if it were actually going to be you. I was driving
toward you and now you're not here, but thousands of miles
away . . . Please tell your mother to keep writing as I loved
her letters and all news of kids needed and wanted. Don't

have time to write her a separate letter. Please read appropriate parts of this to whoever you wish or whoever would be interested. Kayo, I even miss Clover! Please give Clover a kiss for me and tell her I'm proud that she is growing up to be a good dog (even if she did dig thro to Grants') . . . Hope her tail still wags the same way in the kitchen at night when you walk through. Can't imagine her being big enough to bark to be let out at 11:00 P.M. Love to think of it. And really can't get over the story of Linda's cooking! Good for her. Tell Billie not to forget Joy in all this . . . (Remember that. Joy could cook too and needs to have something just as much as Linda) . . . Also glad Meme [family housekeeper] is happy . . . but what will girls do in winter without friends in to play . . . ???? Just in the cellar or something. If Meme can't stand some times to have friends in then I *had* better come home . . . the girls won't like that for long . . . or it will put them too much with your mother which I would rather not, rather they lead almost normal lives. Are they? Aside from being "good" are they playing with friends and doing normal things. To hell with if they are neat. Are they happy? I mean in the old way? I want them to be neat but I want them to grow the way they have been . . . Oh hell. I worry. I'm the mother and I should be home, not in Amsterdam, not away. This is all wrong . . . [. . .] This isn't normal . . . no wonder I'm unhappy. Oh boots. Write often as you can. Tell El Boylan to write too as her letters make me laugh.

Kayo, I love you. Please stay. Please be okay. Please pat my place on the bed next to yours. I'll be home soon, if not sooner. Why did I let you talk me into this???!!!

Your traveling Button who will now walk somehow down the stair and out of her tears.

Anne

In Newton Lower Falls word had arrived that Anne had received a Ford Foundation grant to continue work on her new play, *Tell Me Your Answer True.* When Anne and Sandy picked up the mail at American Express in Amsterdam, they were jubilant; Kayo had sent the news.

[To Alfred Sexton]

> *[Amsterdam]*
> *Sept. 11, Wed. night*
> *[1963]*
> *8:00 P.M.*

Darling Boots,

I'm writing this on a cocktail table in dim light — We are at the Bali — an Indonesian restaurant to celebrate the Ford Foundation grant — and the day, time of the month (all's well) & — and, cheer our spirits. I have a martini and I feel, once more, real — you know! — Yes? — I won't finish this here — too noisy — only love to you at this moment — oh! How I miss and love you! —

Just a note again before I go to sleep. I am typing on the bed, the double bed where we are going to sleep tonight. We moved today to this new place and are now in new place . . . very tiny room with double bed, me with heating pad going . . . small room with no table or space but the bed. It is hard to type. I have cramps and a sore throat . . . but my spirits are up nevertheless. It helped to find I could get the letters you sent to Brussels. You can't know how much mail means . . . perhaps more than it means to you for you are at home . . . I'm not sure what that means except I'm more insecure than you . . . and mail only comes in certain places and I seem to live for them. At first this was not so. I think the anesthesia wore off this weekend . . . and only now am I realizing that I have really gone and how much I long for you . . . at first shock, and now truth. Even the lost luggage didn't sink in. Nothing was as real as this . . . this need of you and of word of you. Lovely here and actually warmer today than any other . . . Goodnight, my darling, I love you . . . Button . . .

> *Sept. 12, Thursday night*
> *11:00 P.M.*

Darling! It is unbelievable. I am typing with this thing on my legs, sitting on edge of our bed. Very difficult, I assure you. And I have so much to say to you . . . I got all your letters today, forwarded special from Brussels and also two more that just arrived from U.S. from you. God! Letters are food! I have lots to say but will save most for tomorrow A.M. when I plan to be alone and have all the bed to write upon. Our room is as small as a minute and no room, even on floor to type. No table either. Today was spent in looking up pep [people] for Sandy in connecting with retarded child. Lots of rides on the "trams" where Sandy's wallet was LIFTED. Another sad story for us. Gone her 35 dollars, gone her Traveller's Checks (which *she* did not have listed elsewhere) and gone about 30 bucks of my money in guilders. Gone! But I can hardly care about money because today I had such mail, such warmth, such love! To hell with money ... hooray for love. I bought Sandy five scotch and water to cheer her up ... and also for my cold, bad throat etc. All your letters make me want terribly to call you and cry out my love. And the few words that the kids dictated too ... Oh. oh. oh. I flirt with the idea of coming home a little early ... but don't know ... the Alps are next and I must concentrate on that. God knows our real route ... Zurich next mail stop anyhow. I've told pep [people] the 16 of Sept. will be last date in Zurich ... but we seem slow on our schedule, not leaving here until Sat. the 14th ... and I'd think it might take two days, at least, to Zurich and be there for perhaps three at least. Next mail to Venice (in case we think to skip Austria and just make for Italy) ... does this help. I wish I could think more clearly because you can't know what mail means to me. It is food! The thrawl (sp.?) of new places is passing ... only the new and terrible longing for you takes its place. I keep trying to remember this is my chance in a lifetime. But it doesn't work. Perhaps I am only just now realizing how much I love you ... it isn't need ... for after all I have Sandy (even if she can't read road maps and loses everything all the time) ... still, she is nice and is *there* and I don't simply need you ... it is not sick, this longing ... it is just one thing and the name of it is love. I love you, Kayo, and know it is an entirely different way than ever before. ... Is that why I came? To find out ... perhaps ... if so I'd like to bounce home into your arms ... I don't feel as if I'm in a different or exciting country ... no, I feel that I'm

only a little away and only a wall separates us and my need is
to open the door and walk through. Perhaps for the first time
in my life . . . *I know it.* I want to open the door and rush
toward you for I love you and I love our life. If I needed
foreign cities to tell me this, then I'm glad I came. Now I
know. This time I know — the love isn't sick . . . no, indeed,
it is health, the giving force, the outward reach instead of the
inward grab. I see much in perspective that I couldn't before.
Do you know I don't miss Martin at all. Nope. Just you and
Linda and Joy. YOU are my life (he is only my past). YOU
YOU YOU. Here I am with a cold and cramps in a strange
city, losing $ etc and all I can think of is your letters.

xo Button

[. . .]

[*To the Sexton Family*]

Zurich
Sept. 19th, 1963 Thursday

Dearest Homefolks,

[. . .] Oh! sob sob. Gee whiz (!) I'm sad. There is no one
lonelier than a girl with dark hair and clod shoes on, standing
in front of an Am Ex clerk as she shuffled through the "S"
pile of mail and then says "none for you" . . . Oh what words
of sadness! Oh dejected! As I walk out and sit in café next
door while Sandy reads HERS. Oh. It's not your fault, but just
so you'll know.

To tell you the truth I'm getting more homesick instead of
less. Now I really *shouldn't* be . . . but there it is, the bald
and naked fact: I wish I were home. I'm sorry I keep writing
such sad letters but there is no controlling or hiding it when it
is there, and no amount of travelogue will hide it in the end.
Perhaps I am growing over here but I can't feel it. I hurt too
much! [. . .]

Sandy is being very funny to cheer me up, suggesting we go
down town again to see the new Richard Burton Elizabeth
Taylor classic. When we left Boston it was the aura of their
romance that cast our parting Cleo-mood and now to Zurich
there they are again. So I say yes. But am holding things up
to write you . . . for if I don't write I'll cry and this is better

choice for time being. Sandy says she refuses to be sympathetic to my sadness or then she'd just join in. But she says she was prepared for it (to be sad herself) and so she continues *to be so positive*, almost *nauseatingly* so ... but then, she puts up with *me* and (as she calls them) my mungy kleenex. That's a good name for all the kleenex ... I use up. Sandy today has a cold which she protests is not mine, but her own.

I wish I could get more letters ... (I know it is my own fault — some gypsy! All I do is cry!) To hell with the view! I take your pictures out and study them and study them ... I reread your letters, Kayo, until they are in tatters ... and then I come back and type my heart out to you. I think perhaps I need to be on the road where I get so tired I can't feel sad. I don't know. Last night at 2 A.M. I staggered downstairs in this ark of a place, dragging Sandy after me, to the phone booth in the main hall to call you. *I was determined!* No one was up. But no matter how I tried I couldn't get anyone on the phone. Switzerland is the only country where you don't put your finger in the Operator's hole and get an operator (I know that is funny ... it is my only humor of the day, as shady as it is ...?) ... But even with the aid of telephone book, all in German, couldn't figure out how to get anyone on the phone. Today I don't dare ask as I'm afraid I'll call and you know how much that will cost and what good will it do really ... only make us all sadder I guess ...

Well, just so you'll know where my late at night inspiration goes. Now listen, everyone, *if I don't get a letter from two people named Linda and Joy by the time I get to Venice I am going to be a very sad mother.* I need letters from you girls and in your words. If you want to dictate it to daddy, okay, but whatever you do, you must write to your mother. If you don't well then I'm not going to send another family letter at ALL ... the rest will be just to daddy. I want you to be busy and to be having fun, but I want you also to remember me and more than that to write to me. For every letter you read you ought to be writing one! This is something you ought to learn and if you haven't ... I am the loser ... and you two are the losers ... for how else can you learn about love ... it is giving *and* receiving, but it works like a swing, it must be pushed both ways. You are old enough to give the swing a little push. I sound cross because I love you so much and long for your words. You would feel the same way if I didn't write to you. Just think how you'd feel! I know you wrote a little bit once on Daddy's letter ... but only once ... a letter a week from both of you would be *little to ask* ... if you go away some-time you will know how I feel and you will expect letters from both Daddy and me ... and you will get them. But I am not getting them! ... Okay! Get the idea! It is all love but I want a little push on the swing from both of you, SOON! ... Today I bought Joy a Christmas present! It is very pretty and I have looked at it 16 times since returning from town. It makes me happy. Perhaps in some other country I will find something just right for Linda. I'm sure I will! Nothing yet for Daddy ... Except the news, quite real I hope, of a week's earlier return home. Today I wrote Martin I'd be home Dec. 11th. Of course it will depend on schedules and airplanes and all that — but we can head for it can't we ... ? *And without* failing! Forgive the sadness ... this is Anne, Button, Mommie, who is in Zurich on some crazy endurance test. Be-lieve me, it would be far easier to get sick and come home. I am trying mightily not to take the easy way out ... Please someone quick write me some encouragement! SOS ... send encouragement to some address ... My cold is better, weather mild though cloudy ... can't write poems, only letters ... too sad to make a poem out of all of you ... you are too real for such as poetry ... too close and, dear God, too far, too far. Need I say I love you and am proud of you? Need I say any-thing more than this desperate sad letter that has no new scenery in it and no new sounds and nothing nothing but the plaintive cry of a homesick wife and mother?????

                              love,   *Anne Mom xo*
                                                          xo
                              Anne   *xo*

[...]

[To the Sexton Family]

7:00 P.M.
Sept. 20th Friday, 1963
Zurich, Switzerland

Dear Homefolks,

[...] How can you be so far away? Tonight I have been with a family again. How can you know what it means to be with a family! Four weeks of rooms and of paid meals ... and then into a home! To, for so long, be a sightseerer (I think I am starting to talk like, Otto ... what you think Kayo!?), only a sightseer ... is lonely, is to be an observer of life and not a participant. A strange alienated thing ... watching but never being. At home, without new sights and of course missing me, at least you do take part, live in and belong in the home. Here, there is never a home, only a temporary dwelling place, a borrowed bed, a paid for meal ..., no matter what the sights, they pall ... so tonight to be with a home, a family, a table, the warmth and of friends ... is good, was good.

Yes, Otto and Trudel are very fine. She is really very pretty, a hearty glow and with much more warmth then I expected ... for he is so extravagant that I thought she'd be shy. But she did not seem so. We talked and talked. Otto had gone out and bought gin and vermouth and had me mix a real martini for me and Sandy. Then we ate, a marvelous (the best I ever tasted) omelette and then Italian (home-made) pizza. [...] When we sat down for dinner Sybil said grace and then the whole family held hands ... just the way we do with "hands around the table" ... it isn't a German custom anymore than ours is an American custom ... a family custom. Isn't life strange and wonderful ... to think that countries that tried to kill each other were sitting at separate parts of the world, praying to win and trying to love with the same hands around ... makes you realize the war is made up by someone else ... not by these people ... you realize that America is your home, but so, again and most now, is the world. And if not then there will be no people holding hands and perhaps they are all that matters, no test ban agreements, or trade barriers, but the families ... I see this, in the home of a "Nazi" ... and I wonder ... and I know.

Enough for tonight, the ribbon is too weak to type on the reverse side of this aerogram. Last night late when I stuck letters in mailbox home I leaned against it and sobbed ... I wanted to crawl into box and be sent home airmail. This means I love you very much, all of you and with all my heart.

xo xo xo
Anne Mom

[*To the Sexton Family*]

ITALY!
So now it's Lake Como and it's
also Sept. 25, Wed. 1963

Dear Homefolks,
Over the Alps! Yes, it is really over the Alps, the St. Gotthard pass and what seemed to be many mts. thereof. [...] It was pouring, pouring rain out and we drove out of Zurich with our radar going as one could not see far ahead. It was awful! But who were we to be daunted by rain after all, it was only the Alps ahead! [...] The blue jool went like a snail, up and up! But this I must say has its advantages for if we had known where we were going we might not have gone. Who knows when they drive into a cloud how far away the ground might be? Who? Not us, the two ladies from Boston ... no, never us. So climbing and winding roads, (to call it a street is a private joke) like a snake, over and over a complete turn, hairpin it's called, but it is worse ... almost have to back and fill even with a VW. And American cars *really* have to back and forth it around a "curve"... So up and up. Finally we see through the driving rain signs that say "St. Gotthard" ... and "Andermat" and we are nearing the pass (already so high but not to IT yet) ... and so we stop for lunch and a "watering spot" at about 2 P.M. We run in from car into small alpine hotel full of Swiss soldiers and we find table and eat, all cosy with German-Swiss music playing away and it seems like a movie, all tucked away so high up — We ask (as Otto told us to) the conditions of the pass ... "Is it safe? Is it snow UP there (very cold even where we are. It feels like sleet!)... We ask, but no answer. No one understands us. All they can say (even at Esso station) is "okay". But "okay"

what? We don't know? ... "Okay" you buy gas? ... Or "okay" you order meal? Or just "okay" that you are American and we like you and your bucks? Or merely "okay" you pretty good looking...? Well! We don't know and no one we speak to knows so we eat and decide "what the hell" we have come *this* far and we will go *farther* ... we will drive it *anyhow!*

WE DID! We drove right straight up into clouds and drove, in snake fashion, over nothing but *height* ... until one hour later we came into blue sky and sun. Slow but sure, the other side of the Mt. is sun ... coming down, half way, we could see. Wow! I was driving the pass and if I'd known where I was ... but coming down (in 1st and once in a while in 2nd gear) I SAW WHERE WE WERE AND WE WERE ON TOP OF THE HIGHEST BUILDING IN THE WORLD CALLED A MT ... it was great. We tried to take a few pictures, but they are not good I fear. Too quick as I scream at Sandy "take it! take it!" as I wind around a bend like the letter S ... At top we had all clothes on, coats, mittens etc. and slowly, hour by hour as we descended in small s's we peeled them off. Not hot here, but mildish ... but fineish ... Or anyhow better than the winter that was going on UP there. Believe me I have never seen such scenery in my life. It was JUMPING CATFISH AND JUMPING JAMPOTS (please read to Maxine that one) all over the place. Breathtaking view, one after the other! Down, through little villages, past huge waterfalls, past Heidi villages on each side, past the light brown Swiss cows with bells, as always, donging on their necks, down, s curve after s curve, through huge rock faces, and places where avalanches had taken place with miles of rocks instead of rivers, past red rocks or brown rocks, black green of pine, into valleys of green lakes, a green I've never seen before, as one born from a palette ... reflecting the green pine I think ... past 1000 copies of an M.I.T. A FRAME [family name for Woulbroun's country house in New Hampshire] ... past and past ... into country that got strange, with dark winking men, into streets that crumbled more and where the sound of the Opera sprang up out of Switzerland and indeed it was not Swiss but Italian (though still Swiss in name) ... where the motor bikes started

to breed and the women grew stocky and big breasted. Into
Italy before Italy. That is Switzerland . . . it is no country. It
is Germany with mountains and France with mountains and
Italy with mountains. Lovely but never belonging to herself
(except for her prosperity and that she does have) . . . Finally
into Italy Lardo (sp wrong) the lake country and then into
Lake Como. This is spectacular bar none! The mountains
rise out, straight out of the lake! Tonight all lights flicking up
and down mountains and on lake. We have okay room and its
window peeks out on lake . . . I love you! My radio at this
table plays American songs . . . Glad to know from Linda's
note on El Boylan's letter that you went to the A Frame. It
made me happy to know where you were and what you were
doing. All through the Alps, looking at "other" A frames I
thought of all of you up there and the fun you would be having. And, you know, it makes me happy to know just exactly
what you are doing all the time. This is "the happiness that
is a small note" [. . .]

All this from your girl who drove the Alps and wasn't afraid
even in the high thick muddy clouds of freezing rain.

    Oh! Love to you all,
      my Kayo,
        my Linda,
          my Joy,
            my cats (two)
              my dog (one, named Clover!)
                Anne
        much love and all kisses and hugs
      Anne   *Mom*

Love too to Billie and Joan who I
hope you share letters with as often
as news is fit to share. Of course!
They too are "The Sexton Family" . . .

[. . . illegible]

[*To Alfred Sexton,*
telegram]
                                    September 27, 1963
VENICE IMPOSSIBLY BEAUTIFUL YOUR LETTERS BETTER
THAN WINE STAYING 8 DAYS PLEASE WRITE HERE JUMPING
CATFISH LOVE

[*To Alfred Sexton*]
                                    Venice, Italy
                                    Sept. 27, Friday [*1963*]
Dearest Kayo, My Boots,
   Your letters! Dear God how I treasure them and eat them
and pat them to death. Can you know? ... Now out to dinner
in Venice after an orgy of mail reading in the piazza san marco
... back here to *go* and now having reread now Sandy has her
coat on and is ready to go ... More later.
   My dearest... can it be *you* who writes such eloquent letters! Can it be? And, after all those blameful from me in
Zurich ... oh Boots, you must remember that for one week no
letter came to me ... and I did not know. I wrote from faith
and my faith grew weak. Forgive me. That is why (one reason) I called today ... so you would know that all was well.
But after your letters, what can I say ... that love is "well"
and that it is YOU I LOVE! Kayo, before I forget please date
your letters as well as the day as reading I don't know what is
going on. I realize you don't know our exact dates places and
is why I wired it today ... (I am so full of ideas that they rush
out, please forgive the manner in which they do so) ... I
wasn't being too hard to ask that the kids write ... not under
your supervision but at least under Billie's or someone's. Not,
certainly, after you come home. But on their own. Once a
week I think it possible and necessary for my soul as a
mother. If you were away for this long you'd know how I felt
... not to put stress on you, but the responsibility of *love*
upon them! Nana could help them or preferably encourage
them in this! No reason why not ... I realize the homework
and the rest ... but too, I know, they could, though not in the
habit, form the habit (when their mother is away) ... and I

expect them to be responsible . . . not you. Linda is 10 — not a baby . . . She can and so can Joy (in a smaller way). I think THEY can . . . not you forcing them. Enough. Even a mother in Europe can make demands (Can be effective! Can cry out and be known. Even.) . . .

And you, my love, my husband . . . oh god! How can I say? Your letters, at least (after the terrible mistake and silence of Zurich) come over me and fill me. I should not doubt and worry, but I did. I am too afraid of life and of love to know how to trust. Forgive this and understand. I have been terribly lonely without you . . . more than you know. But I HAVE HAD TO KEEP FLAG FLYING if not for me then for "us" . . . and whatever we stand for . . . Some of the words in your letters, my darling, are unbelievable in their intuition and their beauty. Could that be Kayo? Can I really know him? Oh, dear love, I love what I know — but how much more of you is there really???? What you has spoken? And how well and fully may I speak back . . . love, love love. And even when I doubted (as in Zurich) it was the same, never changing, never stopping. But now . . . my darling, I (the poet) have no words . . . the bed you pat I cannot. The room you see, I cannot. The moon, I cannot. All mine are different . . . infinitely strange and perhaps wonderful . . . but not part of you . . . except that everything *I* see is part of you . . . all I taste and smell and watch is part Kayo . . . oh god! I miss you. Quick! Listen! I'm here in Venice and today I sent a wire and it meant that Venice is the most lovely thing I had ever dreamed of in my whole life . . . and I refuse to spend all our time in France. Whether you like it or not we will come here. It is magic! Never! Never! I mean, my God. Sick or not this would make me well . . . Kayo, please know, that it is your letters and the truth of them that keeps me going over here, nothing else. I can't live without you! I just can't. Venice, I say on arriving, deserves at least a week. And so we stay on. I don't want to leave it ever (except for you) . . . I have never seen anything like it! . . . (This letter is no good . . . but it says so much love for you that I can't say . . . I'm not really a poet, just a button, who loves you forever and wants to be

home . . . though finds Venice the place she will force you to
come to) . . . That's it, my darling. Please play records and Hi
Fi and think of me, please wait for I will hurry and will stay
in your arms as long as you ask . . . in fact, seriously consider
a double bed. I am getting to be calm sleeper and wish to
sleep only within your precious arms. No matter where.
With you!

Oh! Boots! — I'm your Princess Anne — (as you call me)
who wants only to be your button)

[. . .]   *love your princess Button in Venice*

[*To Alfred Sexton*]
                    Section 2 of other letter,
                    Sept. 27th, Friday, Venice and all that . . .
                    [*1963*]

Well, darling, I lay on the bed while Sandy was typing a letter to Scot (I have to take turns with precious typewriter) and
I reread *all* your letters and I just couldn't let my last letter go
alone . . . for there is so much more. [. . .] but more I must
say . . . Share what is worth sharing . . . nevermind, this is
just to you. I love you so. Your letters to me are for each
meal, each second of hidden time, each time when I can't
bear, each moment that I want to share . . . I carry them with
me always and pick them up constantly! I'm just *looking* at
Europe, the person I'm listening to is YOU. (Understand?)

Boots, I was sick in Zurich . . . terribly lonesome for you. I
stood, one night, and cried into a mailbox slot until Sandy got
out of car and pulled me away. That's the way it was. And
then finally I grew hard with sorrow, not knowing why you
didn't write, and wrote all friends asking why you didn't write
. . . thought you were sick or unfaithful (I'm a nut, but I *do*
have such an imagination, boots!) . . . My radio plays beside
me, home songs, songs of you. Oh! And Sandy gets me irritated . . . but of course . . . I won't go into it. But she does . . .
Not now, but often enough. Not too often, but often. [. . .]

. . . Boots! You know what I wish . . . I wish I didn't get
Ford [Foundation grant] so we could have a baby and I could

stay home next year having... I sit here with head in hands, outside boats paddle by my window and I'm speechless ... what kind of writer am I? With all this love and no words for it? And then too, the wonderful letters from Linda (dear traveling Mom) and from Joy (who won't walk ding toed anymore) ... oh, how I love! Want and miss! ... *Kayo, I'm in Venice!* I can't believe it! *I can't believe you aren't here too!* But I'll fix that next June. You *HAVE* to come here ...

Paris is nothing compared to Venice. We will fly here, forget the cost! I can't bear it if you won't! Nuts to every other place! Oh Kayo, you are my King — you are ... and I am only your princess ... do you know? Do you know that you are the father that never loved me, the lover who made me a woman, the friend who taught me how to enjoy life, the brother to share laughter with, the son I'd like to have. Do you know? My life is so much your life ... and so strange and sad to see things without your arm next to mine. To live and yet — not to live.???? Please, when I come home, don't forget the "soul" ... and I don't mean "sweet sayings" ... I mean the truth, the sharing of our inmost thoughts, good or bad ... lost or comforting. That *is* the soul. I think it. The soul, is I think, a human being who speaks with the pressure of death at his head. That's how I'd phrase it. The self in trouble ... not just the self without love (as us) but the self as it will always be (with gun at its head finally) ... To live and know it is only for a moment ... that is to know "the soul" ... and it increases closeness and despair and happiness ... My life with you increases all things because I value it so much. Oh sweet, my darling, my boots, my King, I'm your wife. I love ... always, each minute. Write me always and know I miss you so.

Anne

P.S. We have chamberpots in our room blue and white china — to empty in canal!!

Letter to Linda and Joy tomorrow and thanks for their letters. They made me so happy! A happy Mom!

Hope pics. from here come out — they ought to be great!
Such a city on water! — xo

           xo

              xo

                 xo

                    xo

I keep hanging out the window — can hardly sleep — too
lonely —

[*To Alfred Sexton*]

                              [*Venice*]
                              Oct. 2nd, Wed., 1963

Dearest Kayo, my Boots,
    Ever since your letter of yesterday I have been thinking and
worrying about you. Thinking what can I do to help my boots
who is hurt and alone and tired and cannot sleep? First thing
I thought of yesterday is how fine it would be if you could go
on a hunting trip. Is there any way (even if we had to use
money from my acct. for it I think it would really be worth it
. . . you could call it my little present) . . . Then last night I
kept thinking about it and dreaming crazy dreams of distress.
And then this morning talking with Sandy, not about you, but
about me and being very philosophical. This is what I am not
writing you, I fear. I fear you get the travelogues, the amazed
and wondrous cries of delight and then in the next letter the
lost and despairing little girl. So this morning I'm writing a
little to tell you how I am and where I am. For you say that
each night you climb the four walls alone worrying about me.
    Darling, why all this worry? Nothing bad can happen to
me. You realize that in this separation I have the easiest role
for if I can't stand it, very simple, I come home. As easy as
that. But if you can't stand it, you don't feel you can tell me
to come home. I see your point. But, may I add, that if you
really can't bear it, home I'll be. Just ask. It is both our trip,
my darling. I felt this from the beginning when you insisted I
go . . . that actually I was going for and with you . . . never
leaving *you* really. That you wanted so much for me to go (I'll

never really know why) . . . but want you did and so I'm here.
And my being here is partly for you in some strange way.

It has not been easy for me . . . and the hard times, the cold
I got, the cold (not heat) and the various thievers were all part
of it. But they are the very things my strength is and is being
built upon. Then too the sights have amazed me and then too
I took a strange perverse liking to the very real physical dis-
comforts. To prove to myself that I could withstand them,
rise about them and go on with it. It is the part of me that
you first fell in love with . . . the girl who kept swinging the
club even when she couldn't hit the ball. Stubborn, keeping
on with it. This is a good thing . . . I want to prove to me and
you that I'm not a quitter. But I feel I already have. I do! I
have missed you more than I ever thought possible and when
in Zurich and I didn't hear I got worried, thought you were
sick and didn't know . . . Why then, I asked Sandy, is he *worrying* about me. You mustn't worry, Bootsy, I am all right.
Nothing can happen to me over here, nothing bad. Each day I
stay on stubbornly I am gaining (perhaps not pounds but they
are easily put on with steak and beans at home) but strength,
an inner guts. And I'm doing it for you because you wanted
me to. I'm not being shot at (as I worried about you in Navy)
. . . I'm driving very carefully, I'm not even looking at attractive men. The luggage being stolen was sad, but we were insured, it's not the end. The worst was losing Nana's letters
but it is over now. What more can I say? I'm sitting here in a
brand new navy three piece knit bought just yesterday for only
30 bucks. Outside the sun shines and perhaps we'll go to
beach. I bought a darling bloo jool color bathing suit that looks
like a little girl's gym suit. I smile. I smoke. My face in the
mirror (write on dressing table) is not gaunt, but pretty. It is
your Anne who looks back at me. It is your Anne over here!
Always!

Do you think that always sitting in my room listening to Hi
Fi is maybe just depressing you and that the T.V. might be
more fun and more distracting? Don't you think if you
cooked two hot dogs you might sleep on full tummy better
than *two* bullets? (what we doing, getting two drug fiends in

one family) ... Who am I to talk ... but still Dr. L. said you
didn't have a good reaction to them and ought not to take
them. [...] But I'd rather have you take one than not sleep.
Oh darling, you are so tired and with big stinko, and all ...
Oh mr. Boots, cheer up. Don't worry about your Anne, and
she is *your* Anne ... I am doing quite well in the overall ...
and soon I'll be home. And we (you and me) will discuss at
length whether I'll go back at end of Feb. or March or whatever it is. So it's really only about two more months ... and
we can make that, bootsy, I know we can. And I do want to
know just how you are ... worry is my right and so it is
yours. I'll never lie or cover up anything ... You are here
with me. Put me there with you. Pat the bed and smile and
say that's a good girl, Anne, and I'm proud of you and I'm
with you and you're really here with me. Also pat your bed
where I put my head. For God's sake your hands are getting
out of practice with no head rubs to give! But not for long!

Darling, do you feel you never quite know where I am? Well
I'm in the old world, or at least I seem to be ... that's where.
Don't feel so much you've lost me. Each day you are gaining
me. This is the biggest joint project we ever undertook ... to
rip ourselves apart on purpose, maybe a mistake, but we must
look *together* at the gains! ... Oh I hope you are less
exhausted when you get this! You NEED a hunting trip (but I
know *I* can't convince you, you also are pretty stubborn.)
Also why not go to Hathaway and stock up on books ... I buy
paperbacks over here and they really save the day. T.V. is
maybe too lonely alone but as I tell Linda, a book is your best
friend. Honey! Bleat! Bleat! I love you with all my heart.
I'm glad you told me how you felt. Sweet dreams

Anne – Button

[*To Alfred Sexton*]

Florence, Italy
October 6th, Sunday [1963]

Darling,

I think, today, a lot about us, pondering our relationship,
wondering how WE are doing ... with all our love for each

other, all our longing to be together. I do love you . . . but why do I need to tell you? Don't you know already? Haven't you known for a long time?

I sometimes feel that you need reassurance about me, that you feel you do when you don't at all. I mean as though you worry unnecessarily about my love for you. So I want to tell you how it is with me and how it is with my love for you . . .

I'm not feeling poetic or soulful in partic . . . but that is good for I want to say a plain say of love, of my love . . . perhaps that will be even good, putting aside the clutter of "romance" to tell you who Anne is.

Anne is your wife. It once was a new word (15 years ago) but now it is an old word (but the age gives it not only color but a truth) . . . For now, my dearest, I know what being a wife *is*. I know what loving you *is*. It is not a dream of roses growing in the garden, of just a hi-fi playing low, of just a darling baby in the crib, or the rosy wonderful house with the darling kitchen. All those things are dreams. No. Love for you is no dream. You are not the man of my dreams. You are my life . . . And even this isn't an ideal. I have seriously, at times, thought of leaving you and have tested the thought of other men as my husband . . . and I made a choice, an adult choice. You are that choice. You are my mate for life. But not from romance . . . from truth. I am proud of you. I like to live with you. I feel love for you at the most ordinary times and the most special. I am aware that you are handsome, but it is not why I love you. The you that is really you is other than handsome. How can I explain what I mean. I mean, in a funny way, that being "your princess Anne" delights me . . . but worries me. For, Kayo, I am not a princess . . . and I'm often ugly . . . and I need very badly to be just me. I can't live up to your romantic ideal of me. I worry about this at times. I have struggled to be a mother . . . yes, I fought obstacles for it . . . but I wonder if I mustn't fight harder for you. No. Not for your constancy or adoration or faithfulness . . . but for the love we really share and perhaps you don't know it. Kayo, we are old, no longer a prince or a princess . . . We are really rich! We want so much for the other, we have grown up together . . . we (us fighting the world) are a unity. This is our

strength ... Long ago I realized that no other person would be
to me what you are.

You are my life and what I breathe you breathe and ever so.
But not for romantic songs. For reality and the common daily
life. All things of myself I want to share with you. I try to
do. Sometimes it is hard to get through, but I always want to.
Despite all my sickness, I have grown. In my growth I learned
some important things. One of them is that I pick you. Not
just that I need you (for I do) but that even without the need I
can make a choice and the choice is you. Only with you
could I share the days, the children, the evenings ... I think
perhaps you worry that I will change or "outgrow" you (over
here or in therapy) ... But that change has taken place (even
if I'm not all well) and I have made the pick. It would have
been a little redundant to tell you ... for after all we were
married. But there came a time when I picked you and knew
it to be my happiness. You say you'd love me even if I were
ugly. Kayo, sometimes I *am* ugly ... age can make ugly ... I
will grow ugly as the years go by ... And so will you. But
you are who I want to grow old with. Kayo, I'm trying to become a person over here ... and with your blessing ... I don't
think I'm doing too well with it, but I *am* trying. Trying for
you as well as me. (Just as you're trying to make do without
me, for me and you!) What I mean is hard to say ... a tes-
timony of love, man and wife ... a life to live together. What
I mean, as can't put properly is that you must get into bed, pat
my side and say "Yup. Anne. We are doing it together, getting strong together, making the trip, both for my travelogues
and your strength." My strength comes only from the knowledge of our deep love and so does yours. We never had this
before. We have come through the Navy, three major deaths,
growth and my sickness. We have made it, stronger than ever
in our love. Without this I would give up the trip. It actually
is not a happy trip, Kayo ... yes, full of new sights, but I am
at loose ends, Sandy is difficult, I can tell no one ... Still, I
have always your confidence in me. That is the thing that
drives me to stay. How can I say it and make sense? I will
never leave you, not from a lack of choice, but from a decision. I want to become MORE than Princess Anne (much as I

want to be her) ... I want to become a woman who lives side by side with Kayo. Not a princess, not a queen, but a friend who fell in love with you. For that is the way it happens. You can't know how strong my feelings are! Let us grow to meet this challenge! Let me not forsake it from weakness and longing. The trip itself is nothing — only your attitude toward it makes something. Together (tho apart) I want this for us ... I haven't made a word of sense, I'm afraid. I'm telling you what I tell myself, I must learn to be a woman, not a child. Yes, I'm your princess and want to have you say it ... also your dearest friend, your companion, your mistress, your mother. I'm me. Anne, alone and homesick but with a great ideal about us. forever.

Your Wife, Anne

[*To the Sexton Family*]

[*Rome*]
Monday October 14th [*1963*]
Dearest Homefolks,

We had a "mixed" day yesterday ... starting with the most marvelous, the pope at noon on sunday ... We stood with the crowds outside St. Peter's until "The Papa's" window shutter was opened and they put a red carpet on the window sill. Then he appears at the window, just a white spot but the crowd cheers "Papa!" ... (me too) and over a loudspeaker he speaks (or prays) in Latin and everyone responds, the crowd speaks as one ... then everyone kneels, right in a huge square. I was holding onto my rosary and thus it was blessed. Quite something and moving to me (tho perhaps not so much for Sandy) ... The size of the crowd and the total effect of love and awe and ... well, it was something! Everyone waves and cheers and then he blesses everyone again and spreads his arms wide. I was waving too! PAPA! PAPA!

Then we drove to beach ... water was warm and I did really swim. [...] Then back to desk to ask Guido [...] if we have time to get to sound and light thing going on at forum. We go, all in rush ... Forum all dark with strange lights and music. Creepy, mystical wondrous, transplanted back in time ... Never! Never thought it could be so good. Making you want to cry. We also walked into the Colluseum (sp?) at night with blue lights on it here and there. It was almost empty. I felt like a Christian martyr or something (mostly something) . . . I haven't space to describe . . . It was haunting . . . the forum too . . . I sat frozen to seat, clutching new gloves that are now lost, not even thinking to smoke or hardly breathe. I touched pebbles on the Col. and wanted to pick up and send home to you in a box. Imagine! I mean, really . . . ! During the sound and light they narrate history with sound effects and different lights going on and off. It sounds phony but isn't at all. First of all it can hardly be phony in that place, decaying around you, but so much preserved, so much kept, so many hundreds of years and of kingdoms and the fall of kingdoms, the beginning of the Church (as it's called) . . . the beginning of The Eternal City (as it's called) . . . and the death of Caesar and of so much . . . After Col where we wandering for about half hour we made our way home quite sedately, being filled with wonder etc. Now please, get ready . . . here comes the clincher (tho not the final) on our misadventures. And please, Kayo, don't go climbing the walls with worry. We are handling things well. Not that I don't need you. My darling, I need you in order to be happy, not just in order to "fix" everything . . . we are driving along and CRASH. Accident. Bloo Jool and Bus. Big bus. No one hurt (I scraped my knee as usual that's all that happens to me). Sandy was driving so I can't swear to the partics . . . was looking other way. But crash it is and suddenly there are 50 Italians around car, all talking at once, we are out talking at once. Bus Driver is shouting, no police (no, no, don't call the police, some people who can speak Eng tell us. No police and you're in trouble and cause big trouble for yourselves by holding up traffic. No police unless there is blood!) I still demand police but no action. Scraped knee does not oblige and give forth any blood even tho I pinch it a little and try it out . . . no blood so no police. Great arguments and etc. and everyone on our side. All the Italians hate the Busses anyhow cuz they take up so much room and are hogging the streets. Bus driver very noncommittal and says we will have to move. This goes on for one hour, meanwhile traffic backing up all through Rome and everyone getting out of cars to come and join in the big interesting discussion ... and try out their English. Several witnesses say not to worry, it is bus's fault. Bus coming from left on blinking yellow light, we on straight long busy street proceeding on it. Hit in middle. I don't know. I believe Sandy and like Italians now and HATE bus. But still no police (they hiding I think) ... god knows what. They don't come despite a terrific traffic snarl caused by the fact we refuse to back up from middle of bus and bus can't move or it will drag us with it! Jumping Catfish! All this and the Forum too! Finally we agree, in all sorts of languages to follow bus to its station so poor people on bus can get there (we have been told a terrible crime to hold up public transportation, etc.) After all, just a few days ago they had a communist riot a few streets down and we thought we had not better stay over [illegible]. So ten men pull out front left fender (squashed completely) so it won't rub tire. Another man (cute) gave us the bumper guard that was knocked off ... we kicked aside broken glass from (headlight gone) and followed bus. At stop, last stop, the same thing happened. Driver no help. No one help. No police anywhere and no interest in them. Get Bus no. Gather huge crowd, all people from bus came to join in by now, and anyone else walking around. Found quite a few half english speaking men who were only too glad and off we went for another hour of talk. It was funny, looking back on it. Anyhow ended up with nothing except finally info that a policeman was riding the Bus and he had told driver it was our fault ... (it wasn't) ... Finally home, sad and tired, to sleep after 2 P.M. Today told Guido our troubles and he suggested what we were going to do anyhow ... go to insurance rep here. So did. So we have 50 deductible and that's it. Doubt Bus will ever pay. Insurance man says it takes 5 years in court to prove Bus is wrong. He shrugs and says "there was no blood" ... (I love the blood talk, but pinching knee did not prove effective) ... Insurance man drives us to a garage that "says" in Italian they'll make it good as new by Sat. It will cost something like 160 bucks (insurance Co. we think pays all but 50 ... THEY BETTER OR ELSE I'LL GO TO THE

TOP TOP MAN) . . . The hood in kind of a mess . . . it never works too well in VW so hope they can fix. Horn is out too. Only thing mechanic understood was when I said "no Beep Beep". That he knew. In Italy there are lots of Beep Beeps.

End of Saga. Have a new cold. But letters letters letters came today right at Texas [their Pensione] as well as some at Am Ex where I have to stand one hour in line to get mail . . . Gosh, letters! Kayo, my husband, your answer to my princess versus wife was a true and wonderful thing for me. I am both. But most of all I'm YOURS. That's the truth and that you must remember. You must try to keep it in mind, always. Everywhere the house must echo this statement!

Joy Sexton! You went to the library yourself! Gee whiz, am I happy! Jumping jampots and all that! I can't tell you how happy this makes me. Now you will be free in a way you have never been free. I mean now you can go to the library and find a friend anytime. It is my happiest time almost, the time when I go to the library. Although the Newton Lower Falls branch doesn't have enough books that I am interested in, still, even there I usually end up taking out three or four books. Of course I might be a little bit silly about books, seeing as I try to write them myself. But long before I ever thought I would write one or even try to write one . . . long ago, when I was your age, I loved most to go to the library alone. To me it is one of the most important steps in growing up. JUST as special, I think, as getting breasts and all that kind of thing.

Linda, I mean to write you a letter of special encouragement about Sara Crewe. But I may never get the time. My darling, you do know how much I wish I could be there. When you sing "Emily You're Named For My Mother," just think a thought for me . . . although I'm surely not dead, just gone until Christmas time. But still, I love that song. Not only my love for you, my love for Mrs. Boylan but even my love for my mother (who is really dead) comes to me when I hear you sing. So, you see, it makes me cry even tho it is a happy proud kind of cry!

[. . .] I have often thought I'd never last over here this long so feel pretty proud of the date these days. The hardest date will be Nov 2 and 3. If I can last through that I've made it. [. . .]

My weekly letter to Martin is missing this week, so must get to it. I have written him once a week . . . and that goes well. Important to remember that coming over here is not end of therapy (were you thinking it would be Kayo? I will write you more about this when I have time, but meanwhile, think on that.

If so, I understand, better, your motivation for wanting me to come, but want to say that you will be awfully disappointed when it doesn't work out. I am in therapy as much for your (our) sake as you, were for mine (our))) . . . Please give my love to Peggy and John. No time to write them but assume you fill them in. Thanks for forwarding Annie's letter full of pictures. She is a dear. Maxine's letter today is happy happy. She is my most dear of friends. I could go on writing forever but must go down and take part in cocktail time and Sandy urges me to go to sleep early to take care of cold . . . Dearest Kayo, you're in my pocket like I used to put "Kitty" in your shirt pocket. I love you always and each minute . . . Oh Love to Linda. Oh love to Joy. Oh send a picture of Clover. Oh kiss for all

love, Mom – Anne – Button

[*To Alfred Sexton*]

[*Rome*]
Friday October 18th [*1963*]

Dearest Kayo,

This is a very serious and very short letter. I just don't think I can make it over here. God knows I've tried. Tomorrow we leave for Naples . . . by train (car not fixed yet but will be mon or tues) . . . We will leave most of our luggage here and then come back mon or tues (depends on the weather) . . . I don't know if it will make you happy or unhappy to tell you that I am considering driving from Rome to Paris and home. And I don't know for sure if I will. There will be no time for you to write me back in any event of any decision. So I'm on my own.

My darling, on my own it is not so good. I mean seriously that you are the one I miss. But it is not just for you that I would come home. It is for my sanity. I too had the thought that if I left Martin I'd get over the silly dependence upon him. And I have. Don't miss him a bit ... only miss you. However I am just not well. Let's face it. Help me face it! Will I never be well. I ask myself ... But, honey, I'm not yet. When I don't know. I promise to try awfully hard to get well. But wife, princess, button ... whoever she is ... hasn't made the grade yet. (Oh Kayo, I know, I know how you are feeling as you read this ... so unhappy ... But Martin said it wasn't even very well for me to leave you for this length of time ... and perhaps not. I think not. But more, I know that our marriage, our understanding and our love have profited. I know this.

Need I tell you that I am very depressed about my failure "to make it". Need I tell you that I feel I am coming home in defeat? Need I tell you all this? Do you know how I feel right now? Throwing it all up ... not on a whim, but because it is, has been, increases, gets worse. That if I don't come home I'll be done for. Can you understand me? Yes. Yes. I know you can. But I wanted to give you something precious ... and now I return, not in a state of glory but a state of despair.

Some princess! Some wife! Some button! Oh! Some silken gown! ... I have done a lot a thinking about myself and about us. I feel very good about us. Except that I try so desperately to live up to your idealistic view of me. I try, so often, to pretend I'm not sick or something ... Kayo, something has got to give. Your sense and need of perfection ... mine too ... they are getting in the way. Darling, I need therapy ... I don't care if it's Martin or who it is. I have got to start getting well. This wasn't and hasn't been the way.

If you want me to need you (and I always will for I very simply love you) then this time ... know my need is your understanding if I do come home. Right now I need quiet. I need even (god forbid) Westwood [Lodge]. I need to lie down and sleep and see none ... I need our house and our quiet ways. The beach is nice, the monuments are nice ... I have weathered every robbery and car smash ... But myself I cannot weather. She came along. She needs help . . . love, she already has. The arduous work of therapy god damn it (I wanted to stop myself . . . you know, it *is* why I came) . . . But without your total support I cannot do it . . . Oh the awfulness of it, to come home with no flags flying, flags dragging like a sick dog's tail. But there you have it.

Joan [Sexton] wrote me about a party on Nov 1st. I wonder if I'll be home by then and how (in this condition) I can get through a party . . . If I am going to do this (and I'll decide within one week) I would be home for SARA. That seems to be the day before the play. ?????????? A strange time for a party . . . Linda will need rest. But anyhow . . . this letter will really leave you in limbo for I'm just speaking out, for a change. The real truth (not what you want of me but what is there of me) . . . I decided today to come home but am taking a few days in Capri to see if I can't restore . . . and find a way . . . If not there will be lots of red tape with car (will store in Paris for time being) (thinking I may work something out in therapy and get back to Spain later.) . . . and the tickets and all that. Don't climb the walls, boots, they are so uncomfortable. I've been on them all along. Only now you know. Rome is so lovely. But inside is where one must find a real monument. I find that out . . . Who knows maybe I'll last it. But I think not. I think I've had it . . . can't eat, or sleep. Even the sun, the lovely sun does no good . . . To tell you I love you seems silly. The letter is all truth and all love, every word. Who you are is who I love. Who I am is something else. I had better go home and start working on it. Here I am . . . and just that licks me . . . Oh Boots, I am so imperfect, can you love me when really my soul is deformed? Will you love me anyhow? I have learned much about us over here . . . and something about myself . . . I need help. I wish it were different . . . don't worry if I don't write for a few days. I am thinking, thinking very hard.

love you, my dearest, my Kayo . . .

[*To Alfred Sexton,*
telegram]

October 22, 1963

ARRIVING BOSTON SUNDAY OCT 27 3:25 PM ALITALIA
FLIGHT 624   AM OK BUT CANCEL PARTY

Chapter IV

Flee on Your Donkey

November 1963–May 1967

I have come back
but disorder is not what it was.
I have lost the trick of it!
The innocence of it! . . .
Anne, Anne,
flee on your donkey,
flee this sad hotel,
ride out on some hairy beast,
gallop backward pressing
your buttocks to his withers,
sit to his clumsy gait somehow.
Ride out
any old way you please!
In this place everyone talks to his own mouth.
That's what it means to be crazy.
Those I loved best died of it —
the fool's disease.

"Flee On Your Donkey"
June 1962
from LIVE OR DIE

The months following Anne's return from Europe overflowed with recriminations; no one was spared. Anne struggled daily with the need to accept the defeat brought on by her own inadequacies, and to cope with the ensuing depression. Even the prospect of the Ford Foundation grant failed to cheer her.

Her work with Dr. Martin resumed. Still complaining of the "leaky ego" which had brought her home from Europe, she faithfully transcribed the tape recording of each therapy session into a green spiral notebook by hand. She made a valiant effort to delve into her past.

Anne was a demanding patient. Dr. Martin had used hypnosis with some success and had allowed Anne lengthy hours for consultation instead of the customary fifty minutes. Her case was complicated not only by repeated suicide attempts but by various forms of hysteria, including trances, as well. Moreover, Anne tended to focus subtly on fee reduction and to insist on additional sessions, while denying that she had the slightest interest in either, and Dr. Martin's marriage had added complexities to her fantasies and dreams. Yet a bond of trust had grown between the doctor and his patient, and their work had gone forward despite the threatening nature of their discoveries.

In the winter of 1964, Dr. Martin announced that he was considering moving his practice to Philadelphia. Panicked by the thought of his departure, Anne filled the next several months with hysteria and anger. She had relied on him for seven years, through many crises, including the death of her parents. Her dependence was deep. She found the idea of transferring to another therapist unthinkable, and repeatedly tried to dissuade Dr. Martin from leaving. When he told her that he would definitely move in August, she grew bitter, convinced that he was yet another in a long line of loved ones who had deserted her.

Finding a new psychiatrist was not easy. Many doctors were reluctant to cope with such a complicated patient. Finally, after months of interviews with prospective psychiatrists — which Anne referred to as a marriage brokerage — she decided she could work with Dr. Samuel Deitz. In July 1964, they began the long, slow period of adjustment.

The psychiatric ward of Massachusetts General Hospital and Westwood Lodge grew more and more familiar between 1964 and 1967. Anne's mental illness was no longer novel and she grew bored with her anguish. She had written enough about "sealed hotels" and wondered if she would ever get well.

As she poured her energy into staying alive, she found it harder and harder to write. As far back as October 1963 she had written to Dr. Martin: "I think I have been getting to be an almost cheap artist since the first Radcliffe grant. Perhaps success is not good for me. I am beginning to think so. I am losing the innocence with which I began . . . "

She began filling a new black folder with poems placed in the order in which they were written; she remarked that they read "like a fever chart for a bad case of melancholy." Even so, another book was not to be ready for publication until 1966. She called this third volume *Live or Die*, since it reflected her struggles with the daily process of living over the past five years. For several months after she had titled it, the book waited, unfinished. She needed a capstone, a positive statement with which to end it. Finally, in February of 1966 it came: the poem "Live."

[*To Felicia Geffen*
The American Academy of Arts and Letters]

40 Clearwater Road
Nov. 5th, 1963

Dear Miss Geffen and Dear American Academy,
This is a letter of failure. If you can bear with me I will try to explain why I am "home" and not in Europe. I could, I am aware, just tell you that I am home under doctor's care and that he forbids an[y] further extensive travel.

And yet I think there is a point to my failure. As the salmon fight upstream to spawn I fought to stay in Europe. Everywhere my eyes and sense were stimulated and excited. But I began to feel smaller and smaller, unreal. There is more to it than that. It is called in psychiatric terms "impoverishment of the ego" . . . for someone with my history staying was becoming an endurance test, and in the doctor's word a "luxury" a "skating on thin ice".

You, I know, did not intend the trip to be that way. Even when I said "yes" I knew I'd have trouble (but I have trouble at home) but I wanted, desperately wanted to see, to know, to find out with my own eyes.

Perhaps now I have learned only one thing, a very American thing — that to fail (the endurance shattered, broken into small unimportant pieces) is the ultimate humiliation. How does one muddy oneself with failure in this "literary marketplace" and survive? There is something about it that is not respectable . . . to crawl home, shrunken, hardly a wife, hardly a mother — and the "writer" has fled. I left suddenly, the thin ice was breaking under me . . . left clothes and books and my car in Rome.

I was most honored by your award to me — and have still no wish to dishonor it. That is why I write you now, although I am still incoherent — because I felt you deserved to know first — not via the grapevine "Sexton cracked up" and all that. I am sure you know what I mean. It has become quite popular in our time (perhaps even other times?) . . . for this news to create interest and even a technical excitement.

My doctor suggests that I would be able to return for two months with my husband next spring. However, I am quite aware that this does not fit the terms of the grant at all. Please know that I understand your position in this matter. The rest of the money must go to someone else; let it be combed out of my failure and let it become something of its own. At this point in my life I have no idea if my months in Europe drove toward a new recognition in my work. It is a matter of mending, waiting and persevering. Damn! It is hard to send you this. A bludgeon to my pride and even worse, to hope and to that bright place "a year abroad."

I know this letter isn't very official in tone. I could not. Drowning [is] not so pitiful as the attempt to rise.

With sincerity,

Felicia Geffen graciously replied that the Academy wished Anne to keep the remaining grant money. In June, Anne and Kayo were to go to Rome, Capri, and Venice on "an eating tour."

[To Felicia Geffen]

> *40 Clearwater Road*
> *December 12, 1963*

Dear Miss Geffen and American Academy,

There are no words — how can I express my gratefulness? Very simply, let me say that your response to my letter is helping me renew my faith, not only in myself as a person but as a writer.

When all the world seems dead, I do know this ... the Academy is alive.

> *Yours sincerely,*

One night at the Radcliffe Institute, Tillie Olsen introduced Anne to Anne Clarke, a psychiatrist from California. They immediately formed a strong friendship which survived over the years via the mails.

Their correspondence began during Anne's crisis over Dr. Martin's impending departure. Clarke insisted that she could not replace Anne's doctor; nevertheless, Anne's letters constantly elected Clarke to the role of consulting psychiatrist with verbatim transcripts of her therapy.

Clarke suffered from the incurable degenerative disease lupus, and Anne was drawn to her by her own empathetic fascination with death. Once reassured that the disease was not necessarily fatal, Anne knew she had found a friend who would not desert or limit her.

[To Anne Clarke]

> *[40 Clearwater Road]*
> *jan what the hell is the*
> *date ... I guess it's prob the 21st or*
> *something ... no 22nd ...*
> *1964*

Sweet Anne,

I love you. Do you know how I look for the mail and it is your letter that I hunt for, that I spring from the desk for when I hear the mailman slip his letters thru the lock. Yep! It's your envelope I hunt for. Yep! It's your voice. Your cadence!

Okay? [...]

Anne, the thing that really is bugging me, putting me,

mouth at the wall (I *mean* wall) is that Dr. Martin is leaving
... Christ. I can't. I *mean* I can't. That's all. I just can't.
Christ's sake! How can I explain ... it would take too many
pages ... hours ... get the picture, Anne ... eight years of
therapy ... At start me nothing ... *really* nothing ... for two
years me still nothing ... and then I start to be something and
then my mother dies, and then father ... a large storm ...
then recovery and that slow and trying to both Martin and me
... I mean "hell" not just "trying" (and, for him too) ... (I'm
a very difficult, acting out patient) ... and I'd come quite
far , , , , but now ... now ... if he goes next Sept. and he
thinks he will ... I have had it. I can't make it (the intense
trust, *the* transference all over AGAIN) ... Anne! Please!
Help me! Don't be my doctor ... but for God's sake be my
friend who is also a doctor. I could use that. I mean, I not
only could use it ... but it might be essential for me for a
time ... I HAVE GOT TO HAVE SOMEONE. (Am I too
dramatic ... after all, I know I'm not dying ... not really ...
but it [is] so close ... as you said, just as you said. When you
die you are really alone. I mean no one is going along with
you and you'd like to do it without losing control, to maintain
a little pride, a little respect ...) ... Anne, I feel so alone. I
think, between you and me, that I'm half so well and half so
sick ... and I don't want the sick to win ... to lose all control
... but ...

but ...

alone ...

I was thinking more about the facts of death (real death)
after I read your letter and I thought, after your words, that
this was, Indeed, the awfulness of dying ... that you must do
it alone. I remember well being right beside my mother as she
died, and trying to help her, to stay there, *right there* so she
wouldn't have to walk the barrier alone ... to go as far as I
could into that dumb country ... I wanted to hold her hand,
as one holds a child's hand, to take her across, to say "It's all
right. I'm here. Don't be afraid." ... And I did. And then she
was gone. She was in the nothingness ... Without me.
Without *herself!* ... Thus she made the transition from

something-ness to nothingness . . . but what good was I? With all that love (longing) I couldn't stop the hours or the pain . . . I couldn't matter. No. Pain mattered more and it was, dear God, pain that rocked her out. Not me. For all my longing and my wanting, not me. And now she is a nothing. Except for me . . . for me she is a big something . . . a something I love and hate and still react and talk to. That is what keeps us alive. That living thing we leave behind. That['s] the flame. But that the body should be gone, a piece of furniture only , , , that dear body . . .

Oh anne.

Oh hell.

I feel awful. I tempered my suffering about "them" because I had "him" — good and bad and as doctory as he is . . . he was the first to believe in me . . . the first to care . . . the only . . . (it seems) and for him to leave is . . . is to leave myself. Do you know?

If I could run. If I could only. If I could put it out of mind . . .

Oh nevermind, Anne, what good will it do to talk about.

. . . Blah. Blah . . .

By the way, when I said "what is death for you, something angry" I meant for *Me* (the you talk meant another voice asked it of me . . .) . . . but you and I are close enuf to mix up. Only in that little "drawing" it was a dialogue between me and me. Ya know?

For god's sake don't let Doc Martin mind his own store. He is about to leave it. I'll still be standing in it, looking around, wondering where in hell "this is" . . . Talk to me serious as much as you feel like it . . . it's half way like death . . . I need someone, aside from pain, to rock me out, away, alone. (Sorry this letter so sad. But it's real Sexton and thus, as always, real stuff . . . which means real LOVE

[*To Anne Clarke*]

[*40 Clearwater Road*]
SUNDAY feb 9 1964

Dearly Anne,

A few words on a Sunday. One I note that my anxiety about us is quieter. I think it was the aftermath of worrying about the letter from you ... I am much calmer today.

I'm writing to share a couple of ideas. Not to write about them but just to say them to you.

From Camus' notebooks ... "an intellectual is someone whose mind watches itself. I like this because I am happy to be both halves."

And from something I read a few months ago and the source is forgotten ... "the uncommitted life is not worth living."

... That's really all I have to say of any import.

My therapy is degenerating to SEX. Boy, there *are* some things that I do avoid, avoid, avoid! But we got to it by the back door, starting with the poem "Wanting to Die" [LD] ... and the discussion of the sex of death. When (to me) death takes you and puts you thru the wringer, it's a man. But when you kill yourself it's a woman. And it goes on from there to his discovery that 1. I don't really think the dead are dead 2. that I certainly don't think I'll die even tho I'm dead 3. that suicides go to a special place ... asleep for instance. 4. that suicide is a form of masturbation!!!

Well, my rationalization for today is that if "an intellectual is someone whose mind watches itself" the same could be said for masturbation or even better for suicide. Bow wow! How's that! I look at it this way (magically) that there are those that are killed and the few who kill and then the other kind, those that do both at once ... I do think that killing people for any reason is perfectly terrible. I don't care what they did, even Hitler for instance. And I think that being killed is perfectly terrible, even dying softly in your sleep. But (I rationalize) when you take both things at once, then you have a certain power ... power over what? Well, life for instance ... and death too. I guess I see it as a way of cheating death. Doc Martin says (Christ I forgot what I was going to say??? INSTANT REPRESSION. For god's sake! Damn me. I was interested in what I was about to say ... thinking ... trying to remember ... I KNOW. He sez it's a way of "staying alive" ... and also (now I really remember!) a way of cheating pain. Killing yourself is merely a way to avoid pain despite all my interesting ideas about it.

It is a blue sky! A white snow. A yellow sun. Pretty nice out my window, rolling off into the distant pine trees ... Sandy and Les are about to come over for a drink.

I shall now go out to new kitchen and prepare shrimp and cocktail sauce.

Anne Anne

[*To Anne Clarke*]

[*40 Clearwater Road*]
Feb 12th, 1964

Dearly Anne,

[...] I'm working like mad on this (now appearing) section of poems on death. Maxine says I'm going to exorcise all my death wishes and get rid of them. I think so. I don't mind either! Pretty damn good idea. And nice also to do something with it. I see already what a strange poem I wrote last year is all about (death) and am rewriting it enough to make it a little clearer. I think I'll make a section of them ... I like making sections of poems that interrelate. Maybe I'll call it (the section) "The Wood of the Suicides" (from Dante's *Inferno*) ... I am fascinated with the whole thing and as I work on it I create it (instead of doing it) ... a fine substitute!

Doc Martin also thought it was interesting that I sent you tapes that showed me being angry ... anger is a rarity ... I'm really not (he agrees) an angry patient. I would say I was a little bit too much of a loving patient (Clover type) ... but really, he Martin *is* great ... I dig him ... He is my good parent. He cares. I keep thinking no one else would.

Enough of that. This just note to say I'm sorry for the hysteria of yesterday's letter. Yesterday afternoon I broke the spell (sadness) and the security rules and went with a friend to the bookshop. God! Do I love bookshops. I went on a buying binge. I now own: *The Exploration of the Inner World,* a study of mental disorder and religious experience; *The Second Sex* by Simone de Beauvoir; *Mere Christianity* by C. S. Lewis; *Paul and Mary*, two case histories by Bruno Bettelheim; *Spoon River Anthology* by Edgar Lee Masters; *Notebooks 1935–1942* by Albert Camus; *Young Man Luther* by Erik Erikson; *Death of a Salesman* by Arthur Miller; Stanislavsky on the Art of the Stage; *Who's Afraid of Virginia Woolf* by Edward Albee; *The Member of the Wedding* by Carson McCullers; *The Inferno* by Dante; *A Season in Hell* by Arthur Rimbaud; *The Three Christs of Ypsilanti* by Milton Rokeach; and *The Crackup* by F. S. Fitzgerald . . . How's that. (In case you wonder what I'm reading) . . .

love you
Anne

[*To Galway Kinnell*]

[*40 Clearwater Road*]
Feb 20th, 1964

Dear Galway,

Thanks for your letter about my poem on Sylvia Plath. I'm pleased that you liked it . . . I agree that perhaps I could have cut the last, if not the last two, sections with "our boy." I thought of it . . . and then couldn't. A poor excuse! But sometimes a poem says "stop fooling around with me. I'm okay the way I am." That's what this one did. So I listened and let it go its own way, a little flawed, perhaps a little overwritten, but belonging more to itself than to me.

I notice that you have a book coming out this spring. I also noticed your very fine poem in *The New Yorker*. The ending of that poem is superb! Power and grace! Starting with section 5, I quite fell in love with it — true insight.

Do you recall the lunch we had in Harvard Square after my book came out? I remember that you said that publishing was almost next to dirty . . . that to, for instance, have a poem in *The New Yorker* was next door to prostitution and a few things like that. I had the feeling, almost, that my book (the one you were holding) was also dirtied by publication.

Well . . . ? What happened? Your poem, in *The New Yorker* does not seem to me less a poem, less a true thing because it was printed there. I do not think so. I think it doesn't matter where it is printed or if it is . . . the poem is the only thing that counts. It can be little affected by publication or criticism.

I'm not arguing the point now . . . but just wonder if you remember what you said that day? Perhaps it was only the hangover you were suffering and I took it too seriously. I do have that bad habit, so female, of taking people at their word.

. . . All this pretty trivial now . . .

Do let me see a copy of your book. If that poem is any sample it ought to be powerful.

Best wishes,
Anne

[*To Anne Clarke*]

[*40 Clearwater Road*]
thursday feb 27th, 1964

Anne!

[. . .] So, you're obsessional about stamps and stuff like that. I'm just a slob, myself . . . obsessional only when confronted with terror and then I make up little magical acts to save me . . . as how does one get on a J-bar lift when sking (that word!) (how spell it?) without being smashed on the rear, tumbledover, cracked on head, and left unconscious. How does one keep a plane in the air when everyone knows the engines could fail? How does a plane take off when everyone knows it is too heavy to be dragging up like a bird? how does one walk down the street and not look conspicuous and strange? how does one function at a party when you forget everyone's name and want to hide in a corner? how does one ask directions in a strange city and then remember them if one has dared ask? how does one keep a car in control when this one has known a steering wheel to break off in your hand, or the brakes to fail? how does one prevent shaking while speaking in public? how does one walk over a high bridge when it might break in two? how does one swim in rough surf without being pulled under and drowned by panic? how does one go to sleep without pills? how does one live with the knowledge that death, their special death, is waiting silently in their body to overtake them at some undetermined time? how can this be done if there is no God? how does one not get struck by lightning when everyone knows it could and just might strike YOU? or tornados that suck you right up into a cloud?

And of course I could go on. That's about all that I can think of that really terrify me and thus I try useless little obsessional ways of handling terror. I.e., on J-bar lifts I had about five things: let one go by empty, get skis in line, look a J-bar straight ON, have Kayo follow directly behind to pick me up or push me out of the way if I fall; hang on tight, etc. in airplane pray when it takes off; drink while in flight, in fact drink before taking off, hang on hard to person beside me as if their arm were trunk, good solid trunk, of grounded tree. . . . On street, go fast, look like you knew what you were doing, count the steps, watch your feet . . . at party, don't go or drink before going or look very pretty or only talk with your husband or drink more. With asking directions there is only one answer, take someone intelligent along with you. With car, forget it or drive faster or stop the car and talk to yourself . . . when not driving but riding, count the telephone poles . . . speaking in public, have a lectern, be quite drunk, be manic, be very well prepared. High bridge? run across it. Rough surf? almost drowned the last time I tried that. now stick to calm water . . . Sleep without pills? impossible. take pills! death? have fantasies of killing myself and thus being the powerful one not the powerless one. God? spend half time wooing R. Catholics who will pray *for* you in case it's true. Spend other half knowing there is certainly no God. Spend fantasy time thinking that there is a life after death, because surely my parents, for instance, are not dead, they are, good god!, just buried. Lightning? wear sneakers, stay off phone. Tornado? retire to cellar to look at washing machine and interesting junk in cellar.

How's that? Neurotic? You bet. I don't even know if it is obsessional, really. All, I know, very common fears anyhow. [. . .]

Love from me on this kind of sad sky-blue sun-struck snow day . . .

The Boston Groundhog
Anne

[*To Tillie Olsen*]

[*40 Clearwater Road*]
March 1st, 1964

Tillie dear,

I thought I'd write you a note . . . because it is easier to type than to speak . . .

I know that I've told you before . . . but I have just been sitting wound up in my red chair reading, first, "I Stand Here Ironing" and then "Tell Me a Riddle" . . . I know them so well . . . Strange, but I don't think I have ever read anything over and over as often as "Tell Me a Riddle." I keep looking for its secret. Not as a writer, looking for your artistic approach, but as a human who becomes increasingly aware . . . I mean, but how can I say . . . ? I mean "Tell Me a Riddle" no matter on which page I might start (I don't always read it in sequence) hurts my throat. I start to cry. Work not to cry. I read and then I talk back to it and I say "But you are not my life. I don't understand you. I haven't really lived you! Why do you hurt; why fill me with terror and beauty?" . . . It is so alive that now I have lived it. A very strange, wonderful quality. I really mean, Tillie, that nothing (poem, novel, story) I have read before or since has done this.

Well, it still isn't said. But the effort and the continuing need to say it to you IS. I think (though I have no idea by actual count) that this is the THIRD fan letter I have written you about the same piece of work. I'm not in the practice of "fan letters" . . . but I have this conviction that you, Tillie, must say it. No one else has. If you didn't who would? You write beyond speech.

Lovingly,
Anne

I enclose a copy of poem

Although Anne had received word while in Europe that the Ford Foundation had awarded her a grant, unexpected problems cropped up. The grant was for a year's residence work with a theater; she planned to revise and refine *Tell Me Your Answer True* with the $9,000 windfall. Anne wrote Anne Clarke on March 15:

> I have a huge research thing going about my Ford grant for next year. It seems that they don't think our theater in Boston is good enough for me to take residence in. Must answer their letter very well, with a lot of ammunition, or I'll end up either not getting grant or committing myself to commuting to New York next year. Big problem.

But by springtime the Ford Foundation had notified Anne that the fellowship was indeed hers, and on her own terms. Working with the Charles Playhouse in Boston, under the direction of Ben Shaktman, she spent many long hours rewriting *Tell Me Your Answer True*.

[*To Anne Clarke*]

> [*40 Clearwater Road*]
> *Monday March 23rd, 1964*

Anne my dearly,

What's up with me? I hardly know myself. Your letter, received this Saturday, seemed to take so long in coming. (Not a reproach — just a longing) . . . I would have called, or would now in fact if it were not for the sum of my last phone bill which readily tells me that I am obsessed with SOMEONE who lives in San Francisco. Thusly I learn restraint.

About the Ford Foundation — all I can say is "FUCK" . . . I have spent the last two weeks dwelling on the damn thing and last night, after an entire week of false starts, I delivered (and I mean delivered) the letter to them. Research? Only research for my letter. The letter to convince them that, having received a grant from them this August (to start this fall of 1964 for a year — for a year's residence with a professional resident company theater) and was about to be assigned to one —

I can't type. Under my present circumstances I am becoming a drunk. Not an alcoholic but a drunk.

Listen. I got the grant. When I accepted it last summer I
kind of told them I would if I could stay in Boston. Their letter of two weeks ago kind of said there is no good enough theater in Boston. Thus research. Why? To con them. To sell
them me and to sell them Boston. In other words to lie. I am
tired of lying. But lie I will. But it took such vast energy that
I am now drinking away and away... I wrote it anyhow.
And it does me in. Why not tell them to go to hell? Well, because I REALLY WANT TO WRITE A PLAY   I COULD
WRITE   A   PLAY   AND   IF   I   HANG   AROUND   A
THEATER   ANY   THEATER   I   THINK   I   COULD
LEARN ENOUGH TO WRITE ONE. In hope. The grant is
for a YEAR'S RESIDENCE. A year? I hardly made two
months in Europe. I am a burden to my left hand. That's
what. And further, but not only, the grant awards me the
mighty sum of $9,000.00 for that year.

So be it. I feel like hell.

About Doc Martin leaving, about Doc Stein (Morton
Stein... very well known Doc in his field of community
mental health) I saw him twice and he said NO.

He was really quite nice, but he said NO. I mean No to me.
And if you don't think I am tired of spilling my life guts out
to these psychiatrists... oh annne! Jesus! Well, the NO was
because he is always away for 3 months each summer and he
doesn't think I would last. He right. But I am so tired of
hearing doctors say "really, Mrs. Sexton, I don't know you at
all" (this is after asking me some of the most personal questions i.e. "and what do you mean by ready for sex" and I blush
and stammer "well, I guess I mean wet" ... and then two sentences later they remind me they don't know me.)... Anne!
I don't care about the questions about sex or childhood or the
strange one that always asks "what is really *wrong* with you?"
... no, I try sincerely to answer... But it really unhinges me
to hear that they don't know me at all.

God, it seems to me that I know that too. And I feel so
lonely and so vulnerable and strange in their little straight-
backed chair. I feel so lonely. I feel worse — strange. And
when I leave on my thin and bony legs, with my big feet and

my awkward pocketbook I cry in the car. And I say to myself
that the trouble with life is that people are strangers.

Anne . . . people are strangers.

I don't know if I can go on spilling myself out to people —
those strange strangers.

As I may have said, I am not at home in myself. I am my
own stranger. But to be reminded that the Doc doesn't know
me at all, finds me a stranger, is enough to dissolve all my
feeling of personal identity.

Maybe you know what I am talking about? Hope so. For
God's sake don't listen with your right hand! I mean, be Anne
— not Doc Clarke. I love both. But Anne-Anne is never my
stranger. Not from the first glance.

So there. I poured some of it out. Jesus, I want to call you.
I feel lonely for the sound of your voice. [. . .]

I seem to be a ship that is sailing out of my own life.

Sad today. Please forgive.

> *I love you as always*   Anne

In next letter write your private phone out again. I keep losing it. Letters from you I never lost. Notes for myself always
lose

[*To Anne Clarke*]

> [*40 Clearwater Road*]
> *Wed April 8th in crying alley* [*1964*]

Oh Anne-Annie my dear, oh annnie my dear, I luv ya, I luv
ya!

Your letter came today. I feel guilty that I haven't written
lately. (Now don't lecture me about that guilt. I've got a right
to it. I feel guilty because I know full well that I have been
running like little black sambo into smaller and smaller circles around my ego . . . and not writing you. I mean, I know
how much your letters mean to me, I know how the heart
leaps with joy when your envelope slips thru the letter slot.
And you too. And I know it. So how come I can be so busy
on my own ego that I don't have time to write a letter for
yours. ? Thus, guilt. Not a big G but a tiny but annoying
one) . . .

Oh Dad, poor Dad, Ma's sent you away and I'm feeling so sad ... etc. Martin goes. Sooner than I thought! Oh too soon! My love goes too soon. My life is leaving me. I love him God damn it ... he is my friend at court ... July he goes. He told me last night tho I blocked my ears and sobbed, still he took my hands away and told me (though he held one hand because he is gentle and he loves me too in his way, his very real way). I went through one half a box of his kleenex and then thru another full one. By the time I left the office his waste basket was full of my tears, and also the tears that flow choked and ugly through the nose.

At home I cried up one of our boxes. Today, so far, I have kept tears locked in, with the help of the 25 milligram Librium I am taking.

He said, "Annie is in San Francisco and yet you don't feel she has left you." I said, "yes" but Anne writes, she is so alive that she vibrates from anywhere. (Doc Martin is not given to letter writing. But he said "you can call me just as you call Annie." He even thinks I ought to come to Philadelphia to see him "see my office" as he puts it. I said "no." I said I didn't need to visit you to know you were alive in my life. He said that he too would be alive in my life. I said (with a great renewed sob) "but Annie's dying TOO" (no I'm not romanticizing your illness. You may outlast us all. But you're not exactly the healthiest dear-good-one-of-special-loves that I have.) ... He said "What do you mean, TOO." he said loudly "I am not dying" and I said "for me you are."

Well, no matter. It's the feeling that counts. He is my mother-dad-Nana and when he goes part of my life goes. It's the essence of mourning, I guess. Lord love a duck! (as one of my "dearest" says) what self-pity and what true sorrows. [...]

However, thanks to you, thanks to Martin, thanks to Deitz, thanks to me and thanks to a lot of work on everyone's part, I did not ax the appointment with him [Deitz]. He *is* more flexible. Not much about fees but somewhat. It will be 25 bucks for the two hours a week. If I need a third it will be less (how much less I blocked the minute I walked out of his office. Was it 20 or was it 10?) Also he will see me in any dire need anytime. Also phone calls are IN. Also "acting out" (in his opinion) can be a sign of growth, as against the little girl (me) who sat in the closet and stifled her feelings and didn't dare have a tantrum but went underground. "Acting out" is just a temper and as such is a sign of greater freedom and growth that will lead finally to verbalizing (thus trusting enough) the feeling of "I don't want to play that game. I won't play that game." So, you can see, he is pretty relaxed. He is a pretty relaxed guy and actually a message from my unconscious that he makes me feel at ease is that I don't shake in his office. I don't feel transferred much . . . but that may be good. I would just as soon not be. (you might say how could you be transferred with one 3 appts. But you know me. I transfer fast, if at all.) [. . .]

About the little little whiz-bang piece (book, whatever) on psychiatrists. Don't worry that one. Strictly a way of mastering the powerless patient syndrome. Also, and more importantly, a desperate attempt on my part to write something that will make me some money. You see, Annie, I can't really afford Deitz's fees. Unless I get Ford Grant (haven't heard yet) or unless I cut out my cleaning woman (who is only 10 bucks a day 2 times a week), getting my hair done, give up drinking or eating out or baby sitters. In other words, drastically cut down on all luxuries . . . get it . . . needful luxuries like calling you and buying books. This book, if I write it (not with Max, she is ducking out. It *is* my theme, my idea etc. and she is busy writing a real novel . . . one she can put her name to[]). Mine is no such thing. It is supposed to be funny and awful and a little nutty, i.e. . . . not literature but rather a cheap but possibly commercial thing, supplemented with cartoons and all. I don't *want* my name on it. Not that my name isn't good enough but the book isn't good enough for my name (tentative titles: CRY NOW — PAY LATER OR A VOICE FROM UNDER THE CHURCH) . . .

Want to collaborate? It is okay with me! You have a whiz-bang sense of humor and lots of "in" information. I suspect you'd have Plenty to say too! But let me remind you that it won't be "great writing" for, frankly, I don't know how to write prose and my humor is about on the teen-age level. Or, if you don't wish to lend your art to this commercial and spiteful venture, then any hints, comments or stories you wish to contribute would be gratefully accepted.

As soon as I can gather myself together, juggling two SHRINKS, Linda's play that is put on this Fri, Sat, Sun ... a telephone lecture I give Monday A.M. and probably 19 more boxes of kleenex ... and get back to this wayward project I will write to you what I have written of it. As yet it is only notes, chapter headings, etc. (some of the best are (1) Comparison Shopping, (2) Casing the Joint, (3) What, no Garters? — or How the Hero is Dressed, (4) Getting to Know You, (5) Exits and Entrances, (6) Adventures in Acting Out, (7) The Big Cheat (positive transference), (7) The Fifty-Minute Hour and the One-Hundred-and-Eighty-Five-Minute Hour, (8) THE FEE, or Don't Let Your Swimming Pool Show, (9) Etiquette for the Couch, (10) Low Overhead Operation (small kleenex boxes on the Shrink's desk), (11) The Little King and Other Stories, (12) The Masturbating Secretary, (13) Prison Etiquette of Life Behind the Wall, (14) Legal Aspects of How to Outwit the Head Shrink (i.e., how to check out against their wishes and still be legal), (15) Taking a Dive, (16) The Rat-Fink vs. The Buddy, (17) Good night Sweet King, or Potions, Barbiturates and Tranquilizers, (18) The Mystery of the Missing Miltown, etc.

Dearly Anne, my dear. Take care of yourself and stop riding around in that truck with no brakes.

> *love you*
>> *from*
>>> *your cry baby babby*
>>> *nope it's baby*
>>> CRY BABY

[*To Anne Clarke*]

> [*40 Clearwater Road*]
> *july 3rd, 1964*

Anne Luv!

Happy happy to get your two (or one and a half) letters today. Actually, and as usual I surely don't have time to reply.

But as I was sitting here (all crampy) and in a judge of self
thoughts I thought . . . well, I said to myself, if you can afford
to sit here thinking (and rereading Annie's letter 3 times) and
then just thinking again, well you've got time to think
ALOUD to Anne.

Now what I mean when I say the word "thinking" is more
complex than it first appears. There are some things I am not
doing . . . not worrying about "through dooms of love"
(Maxine's novel) because it is all wrapped up until we get the
proofs back and have to go over it word for word. Not for
some time I hope. Also I am not thinking about Kayo and
myself because we are fighting all the time and we do not
communicate (but not hitting) and I am not thinking about
that. What I am thinking about is the kind of thing Linda
seems to be thinking about. Linda, that dearest garden, is
slowly withdrawing in order to wondrously observe her body.
I say to her with obvious delight "Linda, you're like a garden!
Something new every day!" (Linda smiles softly at this remark, a hidden flash of pride in her blue eyes, a tiny flicker of
the dimple and a shy shrug.) The remark was upon discovery
by me that Linda had three hairs under her arm. I didn't
count them OUT LOUD. But I mentioned them and she said,
sure, she knew about it. Well, you know what I mean . . . it's
so lovely and it breaks me up. (Kayo, naturally, is more reticent on the subject . . . but happy too.) Well, that kind of
thinking . . . Linda's getting born. And me too, getting kicked
out the womb you might say. It's enough to make anyone
thoughtful and terribly vulnerable. So. Thinking . . . thinking
. . . can I bear? Will I make it? Who will I be when I'm only
me and not his? Get it? Sure you do. And meanwhile back
at the ranch, I have had another huge fight with him and that
took time and (this was last thursday) I passed out for six
hours (don't analyze, but just for your direct info) and that
took time (but it counts up as thinking time because it ain't
sleep — more like a nightmare or more like anesthesia . . .
when I said this, this morning to Deitz he wrote it
down . . .) . . . and Martin and I have made it up and it was all
part of the game . . . false labor you could call it . . . and on his

part too. Not too easy for him to leave me. Anyhow, to indi-
cate the exact heat of my emotions I called Marianna [Pineda,
a sculptor friend of Anne's] today and asked her if she could
make me a little piece, maybe a relief called LEAVETAKING
(she had made, built, sculpted you call it, for someone else
who was going through the same birth-death trauma and I
loved it) . . . So I guess I can give him a little goodbye present
. . . and I know it will be lovely because her work has the
right feeling, my kind anyhow. I hope he will like it. I love
him. Plain as that. So I'm thinking about that and about the
tape I have to listen to and Deitz today and Martin yesterday,
Martin tomorrow, Deitz the day before, Martin the day before
that . . . and etc. Every day SOMEONE and then a tape and
these tapes can't be glossed over, too important content, etc.
And also, two or three days ago I started a poem to Linda and
I haven't had time to work on it. And today I thought of how
to begin a play about Nana and about me and about Venice.
And also I am trying to integrate what Deitz says before I
forget it, having no tape. And I do like Deitz. And he doesn't
scare me. And he knows what I mean when I tell him he has
got to learn to talk "language" which is a new term for what I
think I talk. (By the way, you talk language, but that's beside
the point. Or rather, you understand it, you don't always talk
it) . . . It is hard to define. When I was first sick I was thrilled
(a language word translate, relieved) to get into the Nut
House. At first, of course, I was just scared and crying and
very quiet (who me!) but then I found this girl (very crazy of
course) (like me I guess) who talked language. What a relief! I
mean, well . . . someone! And then later, a while later, and
quite a while I found out that Martin talked language (tho I
didn't name it until this week). And that's the story.

By the way, Kayo has never once understood one word of
language.

Linda does a little.

Maxine does. (Much more now than she used to. She used
to only understand it in a poem. But now she digs it in other
areas.)

I don't know who else does. I don't use it with everyone.

No one of my whole street, suburb neighbors . . .

Clover['s] eyes are full of language.

Doc Deitz doesn't speak it. But he is interested. Maybe that's a good sign.

Language has nothing to do with rational thought. I think that's why I get so horribly furious and disturbed with rational thought.

Language is the opposite of the way a machine works.

Language is poetry, maybe? But not all language is poetry. Nor is all poetry language.

That's the trouble with me.

Language is (i.e.) when I said "I have room." [. . .]

Who me? Sailing around like crazy in LANGUAGE whatever it is and then brought up short by reality (what is it, really?) . . .

If this is a crazy-sounding letter, dear one, please consider the turmoil I'm going through and the pressure of this constant one day one Doc, the other day the next, and etc. And the pressure of the end of July. (Goodbye Doc Martin and Doc Deitz will return from Brazil (he leaves the 11th) on August 6th or something.

And meanwhile the poem for Linda ["Little Girl, My Stringbean, My Lovely Woman," LD], the play for Nana, go unwritten, unborn, and I mumble language to the trees by the pool as if they knew and am fiercely resenting anyone who doesn't talk language (and now it's an obsession).

Well, nevermind. I think language is beautiful. I even think insanity is beautiful (surely the root of language), except that it is painful.

Language is verbalizing the non-verbal. (That's what makes it so complicated.) Holding hands is better than saying "I love you."

When Kayo shoots squirrels it is better than saying "I hate you."

When Sarah plays she is saying "I love myself again."

. . . that's part of language. Language in action is symbolic. Language in words is, too, but it is more difficult to follow.

To eat raspberries (I just ate a cupful) is to live. To take sleeping pills (four a night every night as I do) is to die.

To write you, even about this silly LANGUAGE is also to live.

you might say!!!

[...]

... thinking ...

UNDER A BLUEBERRY MOON
[Later retitled "Little Girl, My Stringbean,
My Lovely Woman"]

My daughter at eleven
(almost twelve) is like a garden.
Oh darling! born in that sweet birthday suit
and having owned it and known it for so long
now you must watch high noon enter
as last month in Amalfi I saw lemons
as large as your desk-side globe,
that miniature map of the world,
and I could mention too
the market stalls of mushrooms and garlic buds
all engorged. Or even the orchard next door
where apples are beginning to swell.
And once, in our first back yard, I planted
an acre of yellow beans we couldn't eat.
But what I wanted to say, darling,
is that women are born twice.

That's the poem for Linda, unfinished. And this letter too is unfinished but as I said a while ago in my language way, all my letters to you are unfinished, otherwise I'd have to wait up for the ash-can man.

Me

In August, another breakdown sent Anne to the psychiatric ward at Massachusetts General Hospital. This visit was to change her life substantially — for during her hospitalization Dr. Deitz prescribed Thorazine, a new antidepressant. Although initially Anne complained that the drug stopped the flow of her creativity, soon her life became more stable, and she was once again able to work. For the next few years the fugue states were eliminated and there were fewer suicide attempts. But photosensitivity, one side effect of Thorazine, was difficult for Anne to accept because she so loved the sun.

[*To Alfred Sexton*]

[*40 Clearwater Road*]
august 17 [*1964*]

Dearest Boots,

It is now after 2 A.M. I can't even type, the pills and all I took at 10. But I had to say . . . one, 16 years ago we were at the Hotel Cavalier and I love you. I love our marriage. It's sixteen times better than the childish dreams we had then. And more — we never lost the dreams, they just grew bigger.

But what I wanted to say is that I've been sitting here re-reading part of play Lucy [Foster, her secretary] typed and making changes again and of course, I thought I might tell you that I feel guilty about the play. Talk about rivals, talk about jealousy. This is a rival you can't call a Nazi, can't blame me for, can't throw up in my face to make me feel guilty. So you have to sit on sidelines, chewing your jealousy over and over. Alone with it. Who would sympathize? I'm supposed to be a genius or something. But I know, who wants to be married to that — you wanted *me*, not the sound, the frenzied sound of this machine . . . Whatever takes me from me, absorbs me, that will make you feel left out. I know. Jealousy is the same, corrosive thing!

What I want to say is that I'm sorry; that I know it's very self-absorbed, a shutting-Kayo-out. The play is simply using me up. But, Boots, if I knew I'd always be turned on this way I would force myself to control it — as it is I haven't been turned on for this length of time (and a large work requires a length of time) since I spent months, long evenings and into mornings, trying to write "The Double Image" [TB]. I didn't think it would ever come back — and I feel it's my rare chance to catch something good and get it down. It's leaving you out and I know it and I am sad for this but since there is only one me, since I must choose (that's a laf. some choice. The play chooses me and demands to be written. I didn't choose. I couldn't.) If it weren't for the pills I'd stay up all night and all tomorrow and forever, playing my violin while I've got one (you might say) . . . But it won't always be this way — someday I'll be back looking at T.V. with you, loving you, being silken gown with safe or no safe. I promise. Please wait for me. Meanwhile maybe the play will turn out good (even if Sandy and Les fell asleep . . . I'm working on it so they can't next time) and we can have yachts and whatever we want, summer camps, summer sailing camps, private school, or something silly-wonderful-extra. Forgive me, meanwhile for this trip I've made into a play that has, in reality, so little chance of success (any kind, either financial or literary-avant-garde)///// But I got to stay with it — it's the "Double Image" [TB] magic and that turned out good, after 6 months of work, turned out to be my best poem, a real poem at that. I've been hanging on its coat tails ever since, never really writing a poem like that . . . and it was written in 1959 or was it 58 . . . anyhow long time ago . . . 5 or 6 years. If the magic only comes around every 5 or 6 years I got to use it, just got to.

But I am sorry, sorry for us, sorry because it does leave you alone. No wonder other girls seem attractive, you don't even have one, all you have is a crazy acting typist.

But she loves you for real and Button will be back. I promise.

> *from Ike – Mike – Button & all the rest –*
> *Anne*

[*To Anne Clarke*]

> [*40 Clearwater Road*]
> *tuesday august 25*
> *6:00 A.M.* [*1964*]

Annie love,

Just a note . . . sitting out here in my room watching dawn come, seeing the mist rise off the golf course and the yard. Listening to early morning radio. They just played "I left my

heart in S.F." and I thought how I had left some of it there
and it was a long time since S.F. had heard a beep-blip from
me. Annie, dear-one — last week went to New York City
with Sandy and saw 7 plays in four days. Exhausted and poor
but it was worth it. Got my first check from Ford and spent
same. I am not seeing anyone or writing anyone — I'm on my
8th draft of this play and how many more — God knows. Boy
are the old fingers tired of typing! Plays, I think, are harder to
write than poems, stories or novels. I advise you not to try.
Do you realize how many unpublished unplayed plays are
written every year. About 15 new ones are produced per year
as against 5000 novels! This *is* madness!

Speaking of madness . . . manic me is under control thanks
to Thorazine . . . except for one day in New York when I forgot to take it and went out and bought a four feet high stuffed
DOG (for myself). He is very funny — looks great in bar at
the Waldorf and the Sheraton in New York. In a bar he is a
ball! Coming home he had his own seat on plane, strapped in
just like the rest of us. Dog enjoyed his first flight, via East-
ern Shuttle to Boston. Right now he is sitting in corner of
room with his red tongue sticking out at me.

. . . I think Doc Deitz is very smart, very intuitive. He
looks like a bookie but he thinks like a whiz. *And* he takes
my work seriously. Me too. All I do is work . . . not out in
sun much — can't anyhow cuz of Thorazine, Deitz very embarrassed he didn't warn me about that. He said "I thought
you said you were going home to work — I didn't think you'd
go outdoors"!!! . . . I told him I've been known to write-work
out of doors too . . . and especially after two weeks of being
sealed up in a locked ward with no air, no sky. So now he
knows . . . Wish I cld send you the play but it's too fluid . . . it
keeps changing, not the plot but the words. You can take one
page of a play, I find — *any* play and rewrite the dialogue fifteen times and learn from doing it. Try this — I recommend
it. This is Sexton's self-taught idea sent on to you in this
sometime correspondence school.

The foliage this year will be nothing but wrinkled brown
leaves . . . they are not turning, but just drying up. The
drought. No color without *some* water . . . . . I will give you a

few lines (favorites of course) from play. Daisy, our heroine, is
angry with Doc.

DAISY: Guilty! Guilty! That's what I am. Why don't you
           admit it! Admit it, Doc! (standing and pacing up
           and down). What makes you think you know eve-
           rything, Doc? You're a dog-god, a no good God
           damn dog or a Doc. All you do is sit here watching
           your precious little clock. Ha! (snatches up his
           clock) Hello little clock, Tickety-tockety-clockety.
           Who invented you anyhow? Freud, that fraud. Lit-
           tle clock, little clock what makes you stop? What
           you need is a sock, little clock (smashes Clock on
           his desk front) How do you like that, you — you
           little Doc Clock!

DOCTOR: Stop this right now, Daisy. I won't stand for it!

DAISY: Poor little Doc Clock, did someone hurt your face,
           bang it out of place? And your little hands, oh
           poor little Doc clock is hurt.

DOCTOR: Daisy, stop it! I'm not that clock. I'm the one
           you're angry with, not the Doc Clock. You act like
           a child, kicking her dolls.

DAISY: Dolls I kicked and walls I kicked but no one real
           did I ever do in.

DOCTOR: It was the real people that you wanted to hurt.

DAISY: Real people like you, Clock-Doc? Doctor Alex's
           clock with a face like a clown, brown clock, brown
           clown! Oh! you're a naughty clock of a Doc.
           What you need very much more than a sock is a
           KNOCK! (throws clock on floor and stamps on it)
           A knock and a knock and a knock.

DOCTOR: (takes her by arms and throws her on couch) Stop

it. Daisy. Stop this minute. There! ... There!
Stay there, for God's sake.

DAISY: Oh!

DOCTOR: Satisfied?

DAISY: You have no understanding. You're a locked up
            Doc!
. . . .

How's that, Annie — pretty active, pretty manic talking Daisy
... can't write you on onionskin paper — all gone. All paper
gone but this yellow. Figure you don't care if it's yellow long
as it's me.
                            with love as always . . . Anne XO

[*To Anne Clarke*]
                                    [*40 Clearwater Road*]
                                    tuesday . . . oct 13. [*1964*]
Anne dear,
    I just sealed the letter of friday for you. It stinks. Now I
write, marking time ... waiting for Dr. Deitz to call back.
(Having already typed out yr envelope. Not knowing. He sd.
he'd call back at 8:20 ... it is now 8:10.)
    Anne, I don't want to live. I'm only writing to tell you
about it, not to warn you. Him I'll warn. You I'll tell. Him
I'm NOT THREATENING. Who's to threaten anyhow, no
one. Only me do I threaten. Only me do I kill. No one else.
Now listen, life is lovely, but I CAN'T LIVE IT. I can't even
explain. I know how silly it sounds ... but if you knew how
it FELT. To be alive, yes, alive, but not be able to live it. AY
that's the rub. I am like a stone that lives ... locked outside
of all that's real. AY! That's the rub, locked out. Anne, do
you know of such things, can you hear???? I wish, or think I
wish, that *I* were dying of something for then I could be brave,
but to be not dying, and yet ... and yet to [be] behind a wall,
watching everyone fit in where I can't, to talk behind a gray
foggy wall, to live but to not reach or to reach wrong ... to do
it all wrong ... believe me, (can you?) ... what's wrong. I

want to belong. I'm like a jew who ends up in the wrong country. I'm not a part. I'm not a member. I'm frozen. And because I'm just so frozen I drink to simulate [stimulate?] it; a drug up too; I want to sleep all day and night (i.e., not live but not quite die) . . .

Oh hell. Not even the writer enough to fix up the unfinished. Oh hell. I wish, stupidly that someone but me would kill me and take the responsibility away . . . Oh hell . . . I wonder if I'll send this or even the last one. And if I send them what right have I to do it. Is it mean? Selfish? True? Or however this, is it kind?

No!

Well, Anne

is it fair to tell you this when what in hell can you do about it . . .

Maybe I can go back to the thorazine. Or something . . . Maybe, god please, it's all curable. If not . . . what can I do?

 Me needing permanent —
& pills of some sort —

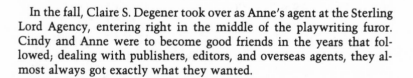 a stone

In the fall, Claire S. Degener took over as Anne's agent at the Sterling Lord Agency, entering right in the middle of the playwriting furor. Cindy and Anne were to become good friends in the years that followed; dealing with publishers, editors, and overseas agents, they almost always got exactly what they wanted.

[*To Claire S. Degener
Sterling Lord Agency*]

[*40 Clearwater Road*]
Nov. 16th 1964

Dear Cindy:

[. . .] I am personally quite depressed about the play. It is beginning to go stale in my hands. Since you and I talked I made the cuts you recommended plus some you didn't. Then The Charles Playhouse worked on the first scene and the very beginning which is a kind of prologue. Then I rewrote both. This worked very well and I would keep the play and continue this method except that they don't really have the time. It would take me a year or over. I find that I love working with actors and a director. Ideas bounce all over the place. Probably I could do a hell [of] a lot to the play if I were willing to wait. The director told me I could really rewrite two assignments (he gave me one) and I think I can. However, that was only once and meanwhile the play hot in my hand, waiting and then, over the weeks, slowly getting cool.

Believe me, Cindy, I've got a hell of a lot of discipline that I haven't used up for this play . . . but I need a sounding board, a real director who wants this cut and the other added. I've even got patience, but my instinct tells me not to let it (the play) get stale with revision after revision (this being the ninth or the tenth). Perhaps I need a major revision. But I need someone to tell me. Right now I'm beginning to doubt the whole basis of the play (One, that the inaccuracy of memory fools us all forever; two, that the idea of Christ fools us all, twisting life into little jigsaw patterns, leaving us all at the ever-resurrection terror of "The Place.") I *think* that's what I mean, and then some.

I think that's so but God Damn it I meant to be (not disciplined or patient) but just more stubborn about getting a good play out of Daisy. I think she has a story to tell. I still think I could tell it. But right now I need someone to tell me how to make it better. So let's take a chance that someone will. Who knows! Maybe magic hopes will work as well as discipline. ?????

I send a copy soon. What do you think???????

Yrs,

The Sextons' first Dalmatian puppy, Clover, was hit by a car in November and died. The entire family mourned and immediately sought a new puppy to make up the loss. Within a matter of weeks Angel arrived.

In December, the house in Newton Lower Falls ran out of closet space — or so Anne and Kayo told the girls. Actually they wanted to move to a better neighborhood and a better school system. They also hoped that a new house would be large enough to accommodate a live-in housekeeper. Even so, for Anne, the prospect of moving was traumatic. She had made a life for herself in Newton, having come to love her neighbors and her trees. But she forced herself to house-hunt.

At first she liked nothing: no matter what qualities a prospective house offered, she rejected it summarily. Then, driving through Weston, Anne noticed a house of an odd olive color. Kayo stopped the car. They got out to look and fell in love with it.

The day the moving men came, Anne lay on a sofa at the Robarts' and sobbed for hours. But by the time spring came around and the swimming pool was installed, she had adjusted to the move. Nestled between tall swamp maples and a huge rock in the front yard, the modern colonial at 14 Black Oak Road became a symbol of safety and security.

[*To Anne Clarke*]

                                        [*40 Clearwater Road*]
                                        Dec 10th, 1964

Dear One,

BEEP BEEP BEEP. I have tried to call you at least three times after nine at night (money!) and you are not there. Are you okay? I hope it means you are busy running around town. A class? Soon? Already? Work — any?

Personally I'd give ten thousand bucks to be a psychiatrist and not a writer. I hate being a writer (when I'm not writing). It's too fucking hard to write. I am very sterile now and don't think I'm a writer at all. I'd rather be writing something bad than nothing at all!!

So what [am] I doing? Well, I'm moving and you can just imagine what that entails emotionally as well as the whole damn house. Emotionally I've been very blue, dry, sterile. I go into the Charles Playhouse a little. They worked on the 2nd and 3rd scene of my play and gave me instructions to completely rewrite them which I did and did badly. Next monday, I hope, they'll work on the rewrite. The play is a dead thing now and will not revive for rewrite of any kind. I

have sent it to my agent to market in New York. Maybe she
can do something. I give up on it. It actually bores me now
and that may be my best estimate of it altogether. [. . .]

I have picked out papers for the house. It turns out everything I've picked is very dressy. I didn't mean for that. I
meant to pick things that were dramatic but now it ends up
too formal. We have a nice front hall. Room for ten people to
stand there all at once. So who has 10 at once[?] Not I! We
have a wonderful front closet. Room for ten coats (all mine)
and two new pair of boots I bought yesterday. I have shoe
boots, high hell and flat (get that! for high-heel) I wore them
to Dr. Deitz's today and guess what today, for first time I lay
on the couch. I'm still bewildered by it (the couch I mean). I
had my boots on too . . . I've been complaining for months to
him that therapy was no good and that we weren't getting
anywhere. So HERE WE GO. I'm starting to get into things
— "where" ever that is. For years I heard I was too sick for
couch, but I feel okay right now. If you want to know what I
am (sick-wise) — as if you didn't know — I finally got a word
or two from him on it. I'm everything!!! Hysteric, manic, depressed, schitz (spellomg spelling) etc. It all boils down to
him saying if I really wanted to know and work . . . a bit of a
straddler I, on the fence, a fence sitter. A couch lier with
boots on, boots with fur. [. . .]

Don't ask me why I'm moving. I've forgotten. So I can get
a swedish maid or something equally silly. It's not really
silly, Anne, but I don't know where all this money is coming
from. We had advertised in the Stockholm newspaper for one
(a mature woman) . . . What I need is a mother! WANTED
. . . A RENTED MOTHER!! U.S.A. . . . That is how the ad
ought to read. No answers as yet. [. . .]

As you can see I can't think of what to say. I'm drinking a
beer to go with my cramps. I'm in a little flurry about having
been "on the couch" à la Maxine, à la analysis, à la what I
never did before. The minute I got there I started to cry. A
very watery couch. I'm there to figure out why I want to kill
myself. I think that's a goal. I think it will be a miracle if I
don't someday end up killing myself. I'm right now hunting

down miracles. It was pretty rocky last month but I didn't
want to depress you with my depressions. I lack contentment.
No. I lack a mother.

When are you going to send me some of that journal you
kept in hospital? When are you going to send me something?

Write anyhow.

I love you as usual and as always.

Anne

[*To Tillie Olsen*]

[*14 Black Oak Road*
circa February 14, 1965]

Dearly Tillie,   Why don't
Your valentines re-   typewriters make
ceived! Read! Loved.   little hearts?????

AND YOUR NEW YEAR'S CARD FOR MY NEW HOME, MY
NEW PLACE

They (both cards, notes, actual things) mean a great deal.
Something to treasure. Your note says you are not feeling
well!! (But your book is. Hooray for the book) (that *is* important too). How sorry I am to learn that you are not. Annie
mentioned it too. All my catholic friends offer up their sickness to God. I wish that I might. Or that I could suggest you
do so promptly. Maybe you could offer it up to the Muse. Or
to Rilke. R. has some good (fine) things to say on the subject.
(as for me, I've got nothing to say but LOVE) which is all right
but not practical. When I hear you feel not well I say (simply)
Oh shit!

But that's not very poetic.

I have signed a lease with god that says I'm never very well
spiritually or mentally or whatever they call it. This
lease (I call it sickness unto death) is not actually very
serious, but it leaves me crippled. The g.d. tranquilizers
I started to take at M.G.H. this summer have completely
stoppered any original idea. I haven't had one since

the first madness of the play took over (and that
was before M.G.H.). Oh Tillie, dear one, I go
on and on . . . We miss you, here in Boston
town. My new home does not suit. It is
grand, roomy (no pool) and all. *My*
room is quite "public" with too many
chairs for any real privacy!

The letter from "Hannah"
your New York friend
gave me great happiness.
Such as I — with
majesty? And
composure?
Who?
Me?

(page other side)
///////// (those are little HEARTS) ie.
[drawn by hand, some little hearts]

Tillie, I did not see enough of you when you were here. What
one denies oneself. [illegible] Heart grows stingy and will not
allow. I don't know why either. Oh well, I am awkward with
people. Annie doesn't know that. And to be sure, I am not
awkward with Maxine. But she is my only sister, and it took
years and years to have that happen. She is very solid in my
life. I read, promptly, the *Herzog* section to her. And will
show it to her too. I didn't like the letters myself, but I liked
the *idea* of the letters very much. As you know, both Maxine
and I like Saul Bellow. It is even hard to dislike parts of his
work that one might in some one else. I like *Henderson* the
most. As I told you, once. To say, more true, I LOVE *Henderson*. I can not quibble bout the rest.

I thought of sending you a valentine. I started and then I
never did. There are no valentines good enough, I said.

The winter has had little snow. Out here, where I live, there
are Black Oak trees but since so much new building has been
going on in this neighborhood there are no birds. When I
hear a bird at someone else's house I want to go out and
kiss its throat. There is a fireplace in my writing
room and lots of wood to burn. No view at all. No
water. The kitchen is very sunny and I sit at the
kitchen table often in the sun and muse. I haven't
written a poem since this summer, since M.G.H. . . .
(have I been, unwittingly, lobotomized?)
Please miss us. You are always here,
in everyone's heart.
I'll return Hannah's letter when
I can put down her compliments.

Your valentine

[*To Anne Clarke*]

[*14 Black Oak Road*]
day after valentines.
65

Anne dear, your Jet plane letter today, full of your exhaustions
of the literary life and your mentions of the yellow note I
wrote that you carried with you to class.
I'm glad you liked my little note. It meant I love you.
It still does.
The music (Scott! [the Sextons' new stereo]) is playing
strong. I was just lying on the ouch (couch) in my room looking out casually and I saw with shock the roof, snow lined,
shining in the moonlight. When I saw that it hurt. I felt this
awful pain. Does that make sense. A winter roof in the snow.
??? There it was, beautiful and terrible. I thought I'd tell you.
It made me cry.
I don't dare walk outside where the sky must hurt even
extra with its full load of stars. The sky outside must ring.

Do you remember how winter snow nights could ring? You'd think the trees would fall to their knees with it all night long. Yet, they do not. And still the stars sustain such interest.

Such thoughts!

Kayo is away but a woman is here, a mother-like woman. She makes it okay which just goes to show how much Kayo is a mother-like man for me. I won't hit myself with that. A simple fact. A baseball bat of a fact! (For hitting mostly).

Rita [Ernst, her next-door neighbor from Newton] told me today that I've changed on thorazine. (Since M.G.H. thorazine). She says I'm more childlike. She also says that she bets I haven't had one original idea since then. [. . .] Rita right. No ideas. None. Of my own. NOT ONE.

Dr. Deitz suggests today that I need brain wave test (what the name of that I forget momentarily). Eppileptic me? (sp. prob wrong). I had this thing happen again on Friday night. Out with Maxine to a play, intermission, great play, smoking and talking madly, happy, great etc. . . . and suddenly, as has happened before, a sudden blackness, things going around, the floor moving, things double, black, black, Maxine pushes me to ladies' room . . . spirits of ammonia etc. and then heaving. All this within the space of three minutes. God, was I sick . . . Maybe the Flu. Feel less guilty if it the Flu. If it's just in my head I tell you I feel pretty guilty . . . to inflict this on friend. This used to happen all the time during stress appointments with Doc Martin . . . or once in a while outside of his office. But not lately. Now again. Like lightning! Martin always said "no brain wave test. It isn't THAT. It's *you!*" So allright already, I said . . . But Deitz asks, "why all these hospitalizations and never even a test?" So I sez, so I don't know? A terrible thing passing out stone cold or throwing up all over the place. I mean, it's really disgusting (messy) (inconvenient) . . . IT IS! For them as well as for me . . . Funny, I mean, strangely funny tonight as I look out at snow moon roof, to think it might be a brain wave not a "mee — wave" [. . .]

I am not going to take anymore thorazine. I want to write poems!

Listen, dear, lately I've been trying to tell Linda that she can hate me but she can't be fresh! (As I did this I thought of you and your admonition that I not be sarcastic) It applies! As a mother I say NO to her ... but as a child personally I don't know how to say NO to me. Linda hasn't figured out how to be angry and not fresh. She HAS got troubles. As I don't know how to tell her. I don't know either. Maybe two of us had better learn.

Oh dear one! Even if the room is small. Still, dear Anne-one, the room is full! (is that too cryptic?) Oh. Tell me it's plain!!! Tell me! It seems I'd rather die than think it wasn't plain and just the way it is, it is, it is ... IT IS. A small plain old fashioned room, rather small, not convenient or modern, pretty simple, pretty ordinary, old-used furniture ... with room to sit, to sprawl, to talk, to BE ... with a blast of love in it. A restatement. I HAVE ROOM. (restated now ... ie. This room: But full of love) ... Anne, the kind of a room I can make it. That only. But THAT with LOVE, with room ROOM ROOM for you

always — Yr [illegible] *friend Anne*

Dorianne Goetz wrote Anne from a mental hospital in June. She admired Anne's work and identified with it.

[*To Dorianne Goetz,*
postcard]

The June [1965]

Dear Doris ... Thank you so much for your note. I'm so pleased you like my work. I hope you can get a chance to see the new poem out in *Harper's* this month (June) called "For the Year of the Insane" [LD]. It is only for a few people.

I would like it if you could be one of them.

I wish I were nineteen. Not that it's better or worse to be me at 36 but it gives you so much more time to grow. Inside I'm only thirteen and outside I have wrinkles and a family and many who depend on me. How silly all this is when you are actually 13. That's what I mean "I wish." Time to grow — it's so needed.

Hope you still find Hillside "a wonderful place." I've been in so many that aren't. But that's another story ... Please send poems. I'd like to see them —

Best —
Anne Sexton

In 1965, Lois Ames wrote to Anne from Chicago; she complimented her on the poem "Sylvia's Death" and inquired if Anne could aid her in her search for biographical material on Sylvia Plath. Lois thought that perhaps she had known Anne earlier, but could not recall the place or circumstance. Although Anne did not remember her, she did reply with what she later called "that neurotic letter." They continued to correspond and met the following summer when Lois was in Boston.

[*To Lois Ames*]

[*14 Black Oak Road*]
June 4th, 1965

Dear Lois Ames:
Your letter isn't dated and the envelope is lost and ... God knows, that letter has been here long enough!

I meant to answer right off. But, somehow life/writing/my self got inbetween the answer.

Can you forgive? Please try.

Yes, Sylvia is dead. And already she has been dead too long. Many other friends seem to be becoming dead, too. I do not like this, parents, friends — God what next! One's own children, I suppose. Yes, that would be the hardest to face, yet many do. I, luckily have not had this happen.

About her death I know little — it is all gossip. It is certainly NOT gossip from her mother (who remains, hopefully, in the dark). The gossip-truth is that she killed herself, as she tried this once before one cannot be too surprised — by turning on the gas. And thus, she died. In England. [...] After all she had the suicide inside her. As I do. As many of us do. But, if we're lucky, we don't get away with it and something or someone forces us to live. Her last poems are amazing. True-blue things! I wish I might write her to tell her how [I] admire and love them. But one can't (altho I do in my poems) write to the dead.

Yes, I suppose you knew me once, or a carbon copy of me . . .
for indeed I grew up in Wellesley. As little said about the
child I was, the better. I was a fool who owned nothing but a
convertible and who never learned to spell or do anything. I
only started to grow at 28. So, if you do recall me, please
forget me. I started all over 8 years ago and would prefer that
no one knew about that other one — that terrible boy-crazy-
unhappy-foolish girl . . . I met Sylvia later . . . and if she had
known me in Wellesley I'm sure she would not have spoken
to me. My name was Anne Harvey.

I'm sorry I'm so late in answering. If there is anything more
I could tell you about Sylvia I'd be glad to do it. She wrote me
a few times from England — but always about her life. About
her death she was silent. Damn it. And then, maybe —
maybe not — it was her business. Everyone runs around con-
demning her for it and I say[:]

She had a right! . . . But it does leave friends lonely.

Best wishes, Anne Sexton

[To Dorianne Goetz]

[14 Black Oak Road]
JUNE!

Dear Dori Goetz,

I hate to let you down in any way but what you ask is impossible. Yes, I liked your poems but I feel you are just beginning . . . Once, I too, was just beginning and I am very aware
how much encouragement means at that time . . . But writing
is a lonely art and can be done, in truth, *only* by that one person and at their own rate. I cannot predict for you, your rate
of growth. But right now, for you, growth is much more important than publishing in a magazine. I have a feeling that if
you were somehow magically lucky enough to get some one
of your poems published that years from now you would regret it. It seems to me that T. S. Eliot and maybe Rimbaud
were around 19 or 20 when they wrote some great poems. But
that is the great exception. I started to write seriously (nine
hours a day) when I was 28. (Not counting my efforts at 16-
17-18) . . . I did not get anything published (although I wasted

some important "growth-time" trying to) for about three years. This was very quick as the "racket" goes. Usually it takes a poet five or six or even ten years.

Emily Dickinson never bothered with the whole thing. She was content to write them. I would not be only content to write and never to publish or share ... but some poems I do not send out (even when I could be almost sure they might get published) for I do not want to see *too many* mistakes in print.

It would or might be good for you to try to get in on some good course in Creative writing at some University. Even if the course stinks you will meet other poets and share the same interest, the same passion.

If you really want to send the poems out anyway try the magazine *The Writer* (in most libraries) and once a year they print all the poetry market ... it offers a wide variety and some of the places actually do READ the poems. That is how I started altho I collected about 18900 rejection slips first.

My life is so hectic that I could not possibly read your poems as they "roll along." I would not do justice to the poem or to you if I made such a promise. You see, Dori, I have so many demands upon my time — a family, two children, my work, my own therapy, the reading I never did, all the catching up to do — the growth-time still.

Your poems are sensitive. They show a great inner strength, a deep knowing of things. Keep it up — don't get discouraged and don't let my very realistic letter upset you. It also takes guts to be a writer. And discipline. And time. Give it all these. And do write again sometime to let me know how you are doing.

All best wishes, Anne Sexton

Anne's children were growing up. At twelve, Linda devoted herself to horses and spent her first summer at the overnight riding camp, Highlawn Farm. A few years later Joy joined her sister, and discovered that she, too, loved the camp. Anne's pain at the summer loss of her children often found its way into the letters bound for Warner, New Hampshire.

[*To Linda Gray Sexton*]

[*14 Black Oak Road*]
Thursday, July 8th, 1965

Linda dear,

How wonderful your letter is! Dishes, cups, silver and all! Also naps! (When in heck do you ever get to sleep at NIGHT?) . . . Nevermind, your letter, your Rachael [Linda's pony] are precious to us all.

Now, dear, I must tell you the hard thing. You must come home in August. We have thought it over thoroughly and at some length. Daddy and I have talked. Dr. Deitz and I have talked. Maxine and I have talked. Everyone is talking and talking. Now, that Daddy and I have made up our minds there is no questioning on your part. I know that you want to stay. At first, my reaction was "Linda must stay. She is happy!" and I ran around trying to fix things so that you could. Linda, darling, I would lie to you right now and tell you that you had to come home because Potama [a Massachusetts day camp] said they wouldn't give the money back. But that's not true. Also I could say that Liz [the director of High-lawn Farm] doesn't have room for you in August. But that's not true.

Since when have I lied to you? Since when haven't I given it to you straight?

Linda, there are many reasons you must come home for August. Yes, I was very enthusiastic about your reaction to freedom, your sudden response to the NEW LIFE and being all on YOUR OWN. Yes. And I do want you to continue on your own. However, there is a family back here in Weston — a family of four. None of us are ready to have you gone that long the first time. We can't get used to your absence.

And I know that in a way it stinks at home. There are jumping bugs in the pool. The lake at Potama is full of dead fish. However, many of your old friends from Potama ask for you, says Joy, and have been promised your return in August. Also, in a funny way, your mother was promised your return then too. And Joy. And Daddy. Your room is too empty to last all the way through August this first year. Part of growing up is going away and liking it. Also part of growing up is having to come home in August and putting up with a yelling but loving Mother, a lake with dead fish, a pool with jumping bugs.

Honey, at Highlawn Farm you are learning lots about freedom and lots about responsibility. Here, at home, you must learn these things too. I need you home. That is a responsibility but it is also a freedom. Freedom, because now you know that you're not just the baby needing the mother — but also the friend of mother, who needs you. There is freedom in this. There is growth in this. There is a song that is popular these days about "people who need people." I don't know if you know the song, but it says something about the way your family needs you in August.

We're all set for July. We love you to have your July at Highlawn this year. But we are not quite ready to put up with the empty room for August too.

This does not mean you can't go up sometime this fall with Maxine and ride. Maybe on Spring vacation you could even go up for a week. There are lots of times you can go up there and ride and do it all. But five weeks at once are all we can really (and in truth) bear.

I know this will make you sad. But I can only say that growing up does make people sad as well as happy and part of growing up is knowing that you are needed as well as the one who needs.

Make the most of your July. Have a ball! Try not to mind the dishes and concentrate on the riding and the fun and no one forcing you to go to bed at a certain time . . . and cokes when you wish. Try to be WITH it and do come home, my darling, with a good heart and a true wish to become one of us once more. I know I'll just be cross-Mom again. But even cross-Mom needs you around, your face, your eyes that are so unusually open to the world.

You must be very grown up to understand this complication. But I believe that you are that grown up. I believe in you. And remember that I could have lied about it. But how could I look into your wonderful eyes and repeat such a lie?

No! I don't think the truth makes us (me) look like such a great family to you right now. But I feel the truth will, in its own time, make us a really close one.

And I do love you
And what do you want for your birthday? We have shopping to do for your big year at Junior High. And we are all going camping on Cape Cod with Peggy and John. Wait until you see Provincetown this August. You'll Flip. It's such a funny place. You'll probably be the best at camping out down there . . . being so used to it now.

Linda, you are almost twelve. Please give me another year to grow up myself so that I can let you go longer. Meanwhile try to put up with me the way I am.

Tell me, when you have time, just what you are doing. The trotting and cantering and the walk-jog sound great.

I love you –
Mom –

Anne's fans never relaxed their demands on her time and energy. Envelopes arrived daily, full of poetry and prose, their unknown authors asking for critiques. They wanted her to tutor them, to know them, to promote their work with Houghton Mifflin, to support them through their nervous breakdowns. She tried to answer them all.

[*To Jonathan Korso*]

[*14 Black Oak Road*]
aug. 12, 1965

Dear Jonathan Korso,
Your letter was very interesting, hard to define, making it hard on me somehow to set limits for you, advise or help in any real way. First of all let me tell you that I find your poems fascinating, terribly uneven . . . precious perhaps, flashes of brilliance . . . but the terrible lack of control, a bad use of rhyme and faults that I feel sure you will learn not to make in time. I am not a prophet but I think you will make it if you learn to revise, if you take your time, if you work your guts out on one poem for four months instead of just letting the miracle (as you must feel it) flow from the pen and then just leave it with the excuse that you are undisciplined.

Hell! I'm undisciplined too, in everything but my work . . . and the discipline the reworking the forging into being is the stuff of poetry . . . the original impulse is only that . . . and perhaps often poets get that as a gift. But it is what you do with the gift that makes the difference. Everyone in the world seems to be writing poems . . . but only a few climb into the sky. What you sent shows you COULD climb there if you pounded it into your head that you must work and rework these uncut diamonds of yours.

If this is impossible for you my guess is that you will never really make it. And the route you take about publishing won't make any difference. In the end only the poem counts. I feel you should be concentrating on that and NOT on where you can get a book published. It would be good if you could study with someone persistently for three or four years, I would think.

As for madness . . . hell! Most poets are mad. It doesn't qualify us for anything. Madness is a waste of time. It creates nothing. Even though I'm often crazy, and I am and I know it, still I fight it because I know how sterile, how futile, how bleak . . . nothing grows from it and you, meanwhile, only grow into it like a snail. [. . .]

Advice . . .

Stop writing letters to the top poets in America. It is a terrible presumption on your part. I never in my life would have the gall (sp?) to write Randall Jarrell out of the blue that way and all my life I have wanted to do so. It's out of line . . . it isn't done. I mean they get dozens of fan letters a day that they have no time to respond to and I'm sure dozens of poems. Meanwhile, these poets (fans or whatever) should be contacting other young poets on their way — not those who have made it, who sit on a star and then have plenty of problems, usually no money, usually the fear their own writing is going down the sink hole. Read the magazines (you know them all) and write and make contact with others such as you. They are just as lonely, just as ready, and will help you far more than the distant Big Name Poet such as Lowell, Kunitz or Jarrell. The people you know at Amherst sound good and Honig too.

I'm not being rejecting, Jon, I'm being realistic.

Your drawings are marvelous, strange. Those perhaps you can let go on the rush of inspiration ... I think. But the poems and I take it you want to be a poet ... well then you must work. I talk as if I were sure of this. Well, it's my opinion that Honig is absolutely right. Rework or forget the whole thing. Spots of brilliance, associative imagry (sp?) is not enough.

I've been the whole trip myself. It wasn't until I learned to work my guts out that a true poem came into being.

If you come to Boston I might be able to arrange to see you if you have a car and can find your way out to Weston. And I'm not shutting you out with this letter but I sure am trying to tell you true.

I think privately publishing your book a waste of time. Get to work, man, and let the publishing come in its own time even if it's 15 years from now. No matter. Fight for the poem. Put your energy into it. Force discipline upon madness. You can do it. I did it. Why not you? Guard yourself from the easy thing. Push for the stars or, at least, go back and push one poem all the way up there. And then another.

Have you got Rilke's *Letters to a Young Poet!* You must. And read and reread. Read it like a Bible. I wish for myself that I could care [carve?] it into my eyes, word by word.

And good luck and write again.

During the summer of 1965 the Congress for Cultural Freedom awarded Anne a grant for travel in Africa or South America; Frederick Morgan of the *Hudson Review* had nominated her. She was delighted to be their first Literary Magazine Travel Grantee.

[*To Nolan Miller*]

[*14 Black Oak Road
Sept. 5, 1965*]

Dear Nolan how wonderful your good news!

                                        sept 30 . . .

well, you can see how far I got
with that letter . . . just now after

a rather protracted bout with the
flu, have I returned to my desk.

How strange to think you speak of my letter as "such a rich
letter" for I am getting sloppy and have no copies of letters
anymore and can't now imagine anything "rich." But if you
say so.

By necessity or needed I mean MORE that the poet needed
to write it. I mean . . . ie. The wife eyes her alcoholic husband and says "do you really need that drink" . . . so I (jaded)
look at many published poems and say do I (as reader) need
this poem. After all, we could all make a personal anthology
of our favorite poems (all an anthology should be in the first
place) and one begins to ask that question of much that is
published . . . I am saying it wrong on paper. It is something
for talk, not for typewriters to make clear.

I could give only my small instances . . . here and about my
desk are a couple of started poems . . . one "The Magic of
Things" another, "The Addict" [LD], another not titled possibly about a father and daughter walking in the evening . . .
. . . They will probably never be poems. They don't look
"needed." "The Magic of Things" looks already too cerebral.
"The Addict" (sp?) looks more promising, more interesting.
The father-daughter looks too watery, too easy . . . not
needed . . . But maybe I'm wrong. Maybe my need will make
them. Perhaps *I* must need them more. Maybe I have to be
ready to pay that cost of emotion . . . Oh, perhaps I know too
much in a way. Way back when I was at Antioch I didn't
know. I just wrote. The year preceding and the year after
Antioch were my most productive times. Or maybe the three
years after. It's hard to pin down. A third book is coming so
slow and I feel my best is behind me . . . and yet grants come
rolling in, never quite right but grateful to awarded. The first
Literary Magazine Travel Award (*Kenyon, Hudson, Partisan,
Sewanee,* and *Poetry*) sponsored by The Congress for Cultural
Freedom . . . to go to Africa or Latin America. I think I'll go
two months this year and two months the following. I'd really rather be teaching. Isn't that queer!?

This letter sounds so depressed — it's the silent for months typewriter that does it —

& again — how fine, how truly good your good news is. A miracle! Love, Anne

[*To Jon Stallworthy*]

[*14 Black Oak Road*]
sept 24, '65

Dear Jon Stallworthy,

No. I just can't face that woman, that Margaret Close (I think that's the name) with an accounting of my "life story." I did write that other rather sweet and old woman a letter ... but life story. DEAR GOD! It's nice to have fans ... but they seem a strange lot. One could read my poems and know a hell of a lot about me. Perhaps there ought to be a feature article done... The Life Story of a woman poet in America. ???

Well, I don't mind seeing the letters, rather enjoy them, but can't possibly answer them all. I usually try to answer (once) a fan letter here in America. But in cases such as this, and if you have such time in your busy editorial life for such as this ... I'd rather you gave out the life story.

I am 36, fairly attractive, a mother, two girls are 10 and 12, a husband in the wool business. I live nine miles outside of Boston. I do not live a poet's life. I look and act like a housewife. My daughter says to her friends "a mother is someone who types all day." But still I cook. But still my desk is a mess of letters to be answered and poems that want to tear their way out of my soul and onto the typewriter keys. At that point I am a lousy cook, a lousy wife, a lousy mother, because I am too busy wrestling with the poem to remember that I am a normal (?) American housewife.

I led an average childhood of rather well-to-do parents. I did very badly in school because I was (is this an American expression?) too boycrazy to bother. I attended public school (free) until the last two years when I was sent away to boarding school (where there were no boys). At boarding school I spent my time writing to boys ... (It's rather dull isn't it!) At any rate I eloped at nineteen and thought it a great idea. I am still married to the same man, by the way. Still . . . I wish I hadn't married until 30. I wrote poems, a little in high school, but stopped and didn't start again until I was 27. I knew nothing about poetry at the time. I had to start from the very beginning. My children were young at the time. I worked like hell, staying up until 3 or 4 in the morning to type out years of bad poems.

My family tree goes back to William Brewster who came over here on the Mayflower. It goes back further to William the Conqueror, to Peter The Cruel, King of Castile, to Sir Edward Neville who was beheaded in 1538, to Edward the Third who married Phillipa of Hainault, his mistress age 15.

I live the wrong life for the person I am. I'm tall and thin and that's all right with me, but my life is square and small and I wish I had a maid but that wouldn't help, and I wish I lived in Italy but that wouldn't help. But only important part of the story is that I started to write, and it was a solitary act . . . One might add that interviews and life stories give me the horrors. I'd throw it all out, like rotten apples, word by word, except for some of the [illegible] (love comes so easily) and old [illegible]

"her father was an alcoholic; her mother was chained to her diamonds?" Need it be said "She was locked in her room until the age of 5 when she started school." Or "She was unwanted, a third daughter used to cement a marriage that was unhinged" or "Her mother was a brilliant woman who excelled in all things and who shone brighter than the diamonds she wore" or "She was an awkward child, backward, breathing in Fairy tales and force fed on black market food" . . .

Isn't it all in the poems somewhere? Isn't too much of it in the poems, an almost shameful display and listing of one's LIFE STORY

I understand Kafka. I understand Rilke. Only through them can I understand myself. The life story or better named, the case history, is only the machine, a Kafka machine. It makes me want to hide, back in the room where I was locked. I spill it all out in this hopeless fashion because you are a poet and will know there is no "nut-shell bio" but I beg you, make one up out of all this. Hide me! Not necessarily from "fans" but from myself. Let me see the bio you make of it. After I was married I worked as a librarian and as a fashion model. Two facts. Only they are lies because I was locked in a cell. I mean, the poems hadn't come and the poems are my life. Please note I can't spell, but that is obvious. That you admire my work makes my life a better one. Please send me a copy of the bio if you [can].

In the autumn, Charles Newman, editor of the *Tri-Quarterly*, wrote asking Anne to do a small essay on Sylvia Plath. She accepted, and over the next few months worked on "The Bar Fly Ought to Sing," frequently calling Newman for advice.

[*To Mr. Charles Newman,*
Tri-Quarterly]

[*14 Black Oak Road
circa autumn 1965*]

Dear Mr. Newman:
    Please excuse the paper, but I have run out of my proper letterhead. And please know that I meant to answer your letter more promptly but that I was busy reading your issue of the *Tri-Quarterly* on Yeats and also, having just returned from a reading tour, busy on my own poems.
    I am very pleased to hear that you are going to put together a Spring issue with a feature section devoted to Sylvia Plath. I have already taken to chance that you wouldn't mind it and sent this information along to a girl from Chicago who I met this summer and who is hoping and working on a book about Sylvia's life and work. This girl, Lois Ames, might be able to add something — as she has started a bit of research. I did not know her before, but as she started her work she contacted me. I liked her and think she well may make it.
    As for me. Oh hell! I have no length or major emphasis to add. One might say quickly that I have no contribution to make ... However, I assume that you have seen the poem, the elegy, I wrote for Sylvia in *Poetry*. I sent it to an American magazine because I felt as you do — that not one had

noticed over here. I hope that you have read and perhaps
might reprint articles about her from Britain, by Alvarez, or
those in *The Critical Quarterly*. If you do not know these
please let me know. For they are important!!!!!!!!

I am writing late at night and my typing is more than poor.

I could add, for Sylvia, only a small sketch, such as my
poem. I knew her for a while in Boston. We did grow up in
the same small town, Wellesley, but she was about four years
behind me and we never met. We didn't meet until she was
married and living with Ted Hughes in Boston. Then she
heard, and George Starbuck heard, that I was going to a class
at B.U. run by Robert Lowell. Then they both joined me . . .
we orbited around the class silently and then, after each class,
we would pile into my old Ford and I would drive quickly thro
the traffic to, or near the Ritz. I would always park at a
LOADING ZONE sign and tell them "It's okay, because we are
going to get loaded" and off we'd pile into the Ritz to drink 3
or 4 or 2 martinis . . . often, very often, Sylvia and I would
talk at length about our first suicides, at length, in detail, in
depth — between the free potato chips. Suicide is, after all,
the opposite of the poem. Sylvia and I often talked opposites.
Ignoring Lowell and the poems left behind. After this we
would all three weave out of the Ritz to spend our last pen-
nies at the Waldorf Cafeteria — a dinner for 70 cents [. . .]
Sylvia's Ted was able to wait or did not care and I had to stay
in the city (I live outside of it) for a 7 P.M. appointment with
[Dr. Martin]. A funny three. I have heard since that Sylvia
was determined to make it — to be great. At the time I didn't
really notice. I was too determined myself. Lowell said, then
and later, "I like her work. She goes right to the point." I
didn't agree. I thought she dogged the point with her form
and with her difficult and far-flung images. I felt she was not
really making her own form or her own point. I knew she was
skilled. Intense, perceptive — strange, blonde, lovely Sylvia . . . From England to America we exchanged a few letters.
I have them now of course. She mentions my poems and
perhaps I sent her new ones as I wrote — I'm not sure. The
time of the loading-zone was gone and now we sent aerograms
back and forth now and then. George was in Rome. He never

wrote. He divorced and remarried over there. Sylvia wrote of one child, keeping bees, another child, my poems — and then in her own silence, died.

I could explain and better write such a small sketch if it will suit you. I can further say that I believe her later poems, her second book, is her really great stuff. I can add that I never guessed that she had it all in her. We were just two bar flies — talking of death — not of creation. What she did in her last poems, is I feel, worth a whole lifetime.

I know this is all mistyped and misspelled, but here you have it. Is this what you want?

I am greatly impressed by the *Tri-Quarterly* and thank you, more than you could know, for sending me that issue.

Please let me know if you want my Bar Fly sketch expanded ... and if you would or could use any advice. I want to help. I am ashamed of America — when I think of Sylvia's last poems. I read at many universities and yet no one mentions her work. Are they all fools? You are not, at any rate.

With best wishes,

[...]

Anne successfully avoided most literary controversies with adroitness and charm. But she had one bête noire: she never forgave James Dickey for being himself. The rivalry began with his brutal review of *All My Pretty Ones* in the *New York Times Book Review* in 1963. After a chance meeting in 1965, there followed a series of letters, midnight telephone calls, and encounters, all filled with anticipation and ending in resentment. Her acerbic references to Dickey over the years became so ritualized that they added a note of jocosity to otherwise mundane exchanges. Generous in her enmity, Anne never faulted the poet, only the man.

[*To James Dickey*]

[*14 Black Oak Road*]
Dec. 12th, 1965

Dear Jim,

How fine to receive your letter. It is strange — or perhaps it is not — that I wrote you one all by myself some weeks ago and then tore it up the next morning — a wastebasket corre-

Skinny-dipping in the backyard, Newton, summer 1962

"the Sun worshipper – 1962"

"day before I left for Europe – only Kayo smiling – only his face could lie –" August 21, 1963

"home from Europe, 1963 – Halloween –"

Capri, October 1963

Anne in her new study, Weston, spring 1966

With Tillie Olsen, in the study at 40 Clearwater Road, c. spring 1964

Anne with Linda on rock in front of Weston home, c. 1966.

On safari. Tanzania, East Africa, August 1966

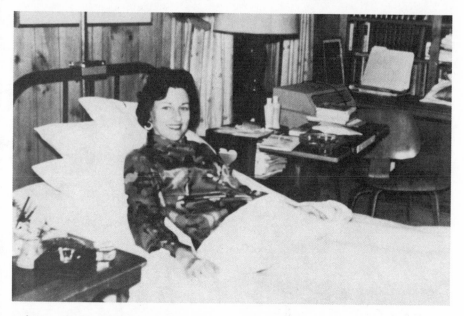

In her study, after breaking hip, Christmas 1966

By the pool, c. summer 1967

On Maxine Kumin's horse Xantippe, Highlawn Farm, Warner, New Hampshire, summer 1965

Anne and Kayo, spring 1968

Reading from "Eighteen Days Without You," Phi Beta Kappa ceremony, Sanders Theater, Harvard University, June 1968

Houghton Mifflin publication party for Love Poems: *Paul Brooks, Anne, and Howard Moss, February 13, 1969*

With Marian Seldes, at Sardi's, New York City, for opening night party of Mercy Street, *October 1969*

Honorary Doctor of Letters, Tufts University, June 1971

Anne Sexton and Her Kind in rehearsal, 1971. Left to right: Bill Davies, Theodore Casher, Anne, Steve Rizzo, "Hank" Hankinson, Doug Senibaldi

Maxine Kumin (far left) and Anne at party, Paperback Booksmith, Cambridge, August 1974

With Joy in backyard, summer 1974

1974

Anne, summer 1974

spondence? of some sort. Anyhow, I thought— "No Anne, perhaps he forgot that he met you or, forgot you, whoever you are." That's what I thought.

Wrong though. You wrote. And even after I had said that I had little time for letters . . . Yes, Jim, little time . . . my desk is piled high with letters to answer . . . but I wonder if I meant that. I'll tell you this, and in truth, I fear a letter relationship. [. . .] I once made the mistake of believing in a letter-relationship — I "wrote around" . . . letters, believing-God forgiven, water lost and sky found letters in which I believed. I sure as hell wrote around once. [. . .]

Well, now we can forget all that. I'm glad you wrote, *that* you being *you*. I would enjoy dinner with you this spring. I will be away a few times giving readings, myself. Let me know the date so we can be sure if we will both be here at the same time. I hope we will.

We can argue about your "ill-gotten gains" of Boston College at the time. Hardly, ill-gotten, I'd say. I would like to see you and have dinner with you — no matter who pays the bill.

I've been writing new poems — but none right-good enough to include. Here are some old ones from *The Hudson* (which you said you never read) . . . I check one that might (?) interest you. I know that it's all wrong, and yet it is all right.

Or toss it aside if you are busy. But not the letter.

"The Starfish" is fine (Joy) . . . so is The String Bean (Linda) . . .

[*To James Dickey*]

[*14 Black Oak Road*]
the end of December 1965
Dear Jim of San Fernando Valley,

I like your letter of today. I can't find your first letter — how silly, how very like me — the misplacer of the meaningful. Still, I recall well that it came and that I answered. And now, in hand, I have proof that you answered.

I like it.

I suppose we must go through the tangle of constant redefining of ourselves to each other — or "our relationship" in its own terms. To make sure the other understands. Also to just plain make sure.

To begin with — yes, I know well the letter that drains — the letter that begs "Please James Dickey, tell me I'm great. I wrote to Anne Sexton but she never answered and I know from your poems that you are more ..." Sure, I've got those, stacked up on the desk. Plus a horrible number from ex-mental patients who think they can write and even quite a few mental patients who are *in there* and think they can write. Fact is, some can write — just that I never advertised (though perhaps I did) that I'd be everyone's mother. Fact also, I can't take them all on, even the talented ones. There just isn't time or strength. An awful lot of completely sane people write me too. Categories are silly — too many people write that I don't feel I need to answer (need meaning the great impulse, the desire to respond, the want of it) ...

We (I) will forget them all in regards to you or to me. The desk of course gets cluttered — business too — but the human sympathy-tender-friend — doesn't really get in the way. Might say it adds to the trip — seeing as we are all on our way anyhow.

Now, to continue — I see for us — and if a miracle can happen once, then it can continue to happen if two people want it, really will it — a good friendship, a tender friendship, writing as we wish, back and forth, seeing each other when it happens that we can, as *decent, responsible literary folk and earthlings subject to social limitations!* I underline your words, so that I may reinforce my own. Tenderness does not require passion to make it real. Not for me. Tenderness is even unique and maybe it is far more valuable than passion. I would, in all frankness, hold it so. I do not want or look for a *mad passionate* affair. I would avoid one if it looked me in the face. I would run to the end of town to avoid it. Not because I am frightened, or because I feel it would be immoral ... but because I feel it might be wrong (self wrong — or him wrong — or life wrong) and because, please believe me, I do not want a lover. Sometimes, on readings for instance, I feel that everywhere I go I could find a lover — and I do not want a lover. I want a friend. One can look and look and still there is no friend. I would like, as a child might say it, to be your friend. After all, you say to me that "I don't know if this is what is going to happen" and I say to you, this is what I want to happen. Then, I add my miracle talk — if friends once, then why not forever. Why ask what will happen when we are the ones who can control what will happen. ?????

I cannot promise that I am geared to your kind of self. I think maybe I am. But I cannot promise. I do not know you well enough yet. I *can* promise that I will not hurt or presume upon the self you offer to me. I can tell you this as a friend who trusts — I trust that you do not lie to me. I trust what I met of you. I trust the (and now I must hesitate or will get into trouble) . . . but nevermind . . . say it, Anne, — the poet in you.

I am wondering if you got the job at Rochester . . . I knew, heard, you wanted one, but you do not say. I told what-his-name (Ford-frod-fraud) that you'd be good but I don't know how much my word stands for up there or across over there from my Boston-state. I have read there before and was the guest of (now I remember) george and pat frod? ford (keep making typo-s on his name whatever that means).

As a matter of fact, I am having a terrible time lately on typing (not to mention spelling which I could never do — from the third grade up) but now I can't type. My fingers won't obey. Maybe it's some disease. Maybe it's just foolishness . . . But even with poems typed out to *The New Yorker*, Howard Moss writes back two or 3 pages of mostly corrections of my typos. Perhaps my next book should be titled THE TYPO . . . Thus I must ask you to understand that the letters I do send to you may be almost unintelligible in some fashion. How will I ever get to the guitar at this rate????

Christmas has been very busy for my family — with the kids home and all of it. Still, very happy-time too. I wish I could have another child — and although I could medically my husband (who is as nice as you say he is) thinks not — in view of many things — me mainly. Still, I could!

I hope the holiday has been happy for you, your wife and your children. I know they are "good" as you put it, for they are yours.

Have I affirmed enough? Have I started what should be only affirmation — not a sermon on anyone's part — but clarity. Clarity is important, at the beginning — even always I guess. One must be sure . . .

although the affection came without anyone being sure . . . one must say hello to miracles — I think.

[*To Tillie Olsen*]

[*14 Black Oak Road*
circa January 1966]

THE YEAR OF ! (_____
OR THE YEAR OF !!??**
ACTUALLY THE TYPEWRITER DOESN'T
know everything

THE YEAR OF 1966
may it be happy and creative for you. I love your calendar and have it on my desk always and use it too. It smiles at me.

My work, at present, is [in] a dreadful slump. When one tries (what an understatement) to keep a marriage together that has been cracked and is as fragile as a cracked egg . . . when there are children who are growing and not growing on purpose . . . when you know that although you are *supposed* to be the sick one and are not and yet must play a constantly weak role to keep the egg from cracking open and out falls two chicks as well as 18 years of stubborness . . . when one's poems are damned for being tragic and confessional constantly from both sides of the ocean . . .

Thank God for Maxine. She is close by always and knows me. No one else who is within literal reach allows me to be real or to think.

Such complaints! Ugh. So mundane . . . I wrote a poem in October that I think is fair. I'd send it to you but I left my manuscript (all unprinted poems at Barbara's [Barbara Swan, an artist friend of Anne's] by mistake. How foolishly destructive one can be. I just called her and it's there, after frantically looking through this house. Anyhow it's not a book yet because I haven't written a book — just a bunch of ill-kempt poems that don't walk happily together. There are enough poems but not enough to say what I must say if I can ever say it. & even more confessional & tragic this time — reviews are bad for us — we should be blinded before we read such public praise or damnation. I meant only to write Happy New Year and look what happens — Oy! Joy is going to a psychiatrist now — too — that leaves only Linda, who, at 12-1/2, cries an hour a day — but I figure it's the age — the sensitivity — & also the world. Just a blue mood!

Sorry

Love

Anne

In January of the new year eight new members joined the Sexton household: Penny, the Dalmatian who had followed Angel, gave birth to a litter of puppies. A month later Anne had incorporated the joy of their arrival in her poem "Live," which completed *Live or Die:*

So I say Live
and turn my shadow three times round
to feed our puppies as they come,
the eight Dalmatians we didn't drown,
despite the warnings: The abort! The destroy!
Despite the pails of water that waited
to drown them, to pull them down like stones,
they came, each one headfirst,
blowing bubbles the color of cataract-blue
and fumbling for the tiny tits.
Just last week, eight Dalmatians,
3/4 of a lb., lined up like cord wood
each
like a
birch tree.
I promise to love more if they come,
because in spite of cruelty
and the stuffed railroad cars for the ovens,
I am not what I expected. Not an Eichmann.
The poison just didn't take.
So I won't hang around in my hospital shift,

repeating The Black Mass and all of it.
I say Live, Live because of the sun,
the dream, the excitable gift.

[*To Charles Newman*]

> [*14 Black Oak Road*]
> *Feb something or other,*
> *day after valentine day, at that.*
> *1966*

Dear Charles Newman,
Thanks so much for your call last night. It really helped.
And please don't get too depressed with Ted Hughes if he
never comes through. You can do it without him, after all.
Sylvia did! (I might add).

Yippie for all of us. I have just now finished my first draft
of my piece for you. I don't have the energy to retype it . . .
but think it won't be reworked or changed much. It's about
six or seven pages counting the poems. This is what I must
know — I suddenly had an inspiration and included another
poem of mine. It fits in perfectly and is right DIRECTLY to
the point of the whole thing. It has been printed before, but
only in England — printed in *The Observer*. May I include it
in my piece? Title is "Wanting to Die" [LD] and it has such
pertinent lines as "But suicides have a special language./ Like
carpenters they want to know *which tools*. They never ask
why build."

I feel the wanting to die poem is needed in order to further
show the desperately similar need that Sylvia and I share. I
could, I know, rework the wanting to die feelings into prose,
but the poem says it so much better.

What do you think?

I will sit on my first draft until I see Lois next week and get
her reaction . . . work, poems, prose, letters are piled high on
this damn desk of mine or else I'd take the time to type out
the whole thing right now. But I'm so damn tired and not
only that a daughter home for last two weeks with the flu and
eight dalmation puppies who are weaned and bark at ME for
food. How can I be a writer, or a poet as you call me. My
name is Miss Carnation Milk seven times a barking day.

Maybe I'll take Lois into the bar at The Ritz — if I can escape sick children and 8 puppies. I'll try. That Lois is smart and I'll place a bet on her. She's nice too. That always helps. I felt the same way about Sylvia, back then. Maybe my instincts are good. As you may have guessed, Ted Hughes doesn't turn me on one bit — but maybe my instincts are off?

How about that reading in May? Sounds like a good idea.

If Hughes writes about "the last year" I bet he makes it up anyway. Or maybe my hostility comes from Sylvia. I hardly ever met Ted ... maybe she turned me off. Her letters from England always sounded happy, tho.

O well, these are just musings. I'll tell the rest to Lois.

Good luck and stop hiding!

Anne Sexton

In March 1966, Houghton Mifflin accepted her third book, *Live or Die,* for an advance of $500.

[*To James Dickey*]

[*14 Black Oak Road*]
its march by god its march
[*1966*]

Dear Jim,

Just a note. Please don't be angry that I haven't written. I am out of this world busy and I've been sick and that just puts the botch on everything. Damn, anyway.

Your letter I received and liked — but was just going off for reading and then home soon as I got sick and I am getting to my work which pushes me hard, particularly after the sickness stuff.

Maybe we will meet in Baltimore. I know we won't sleep with each other. I know we *ought* to be friends ... and being friends isn't as intellectual as You think. It can't be for I have hardly a brain in me head and yet still I've got tenderness. I think tenderness can include touch — just shouldn't mix it up with sexuality. One need not. Really! [...]

Wouldn't it be nice to be friends, tho? I mean, I think it would. But it's easy enough to ruin, if that's what you really need to do. ... Write and I'll try to. [...] excuse the messy

typing — but no help for it — I'm on a ton of tranquilizers &
they make it all so impossible

Anne

[*To James Dickey*]

[*14 Black Oak Road*]
March 24, 1966
By God, it's still March
and it's still Weston

Dear Jim,

Well, maybe I'm all wrong and maybe I don't know what in
hell I'm doing, but my instincts keep going two ways about
you. One says it's O.K., the other says be careful. There are
long complicated reasons for this, for both of this, that have
nothing to do with what you have written about me, of
course. It's all very complicated. After I met you, in New
York state, I heard nothing but gossip about you. Things
rather nasty — not warm, not happy. As it went on, I thought
"Surely they are exaggerating, surely they are telling me this
to test me a bit.["] This so-called gossip made you sound like
Norman Mailer (and of course I heard all about you meeting
with him) in Batman's clothes and with a poison ring on two
of your toes, and problems I didn't need . . . Well, I decided to
forget all about that crappy talk and remember that I liked
you too — just as the person you were with me. When we
met, with the exception of one rather far-out statement you
made (statements something to the effect that you felt full of
violence that night and felt the need to kill someone or something) I, too, liked talking of children and family life and, do
you remember our talk of loss — about Randall Jarrell. We
were together. We were not opposed.

So, O.K., Jim, I won't bug you about the phone call any
more. I'll believe you. As far as I can tell I will be at Goucher
College April 19th speaking in the evening, Wednesday, April
20th speaking in the morning. I'm not sure what I will do
about the evening of the 20th. I may stay with some friends
in Baltimore, or I might stay at a hotel in Baltimore or in
Washington. However, I could meet you in the afternoon,
perhaps early, or for dinner, cocktails yum yum and dinner.

And then go on from there.

I put this down plainly so that you may look at your schedule and see in which way we might get together. It would be nice to meet for a drink at least. Will you be busy at dinnertime on Wednesday, the 20th? Seeing as we are both being paid, maybe we could go out dutch treat and talk with affection about our families and our worlds and things. I would like this, and I think it would be rather free and great — as you put it. I am not sure where I am staying in Goucher College on the 19th, but the name of the head of the English Department who has contacted me is Florence Howe, Towson, Baltimore, Maryland. You might let me know where to reach you in case we miss connections.

I am certain that if we discussed most things in person that we would learn to understand each other far better than by sentences on the typewriter or voices on the phone. I know, Jim, that my concern and anxiety are excessive. I'll give you one hint. I am more child than a woman. I am afraid of the dark. I am afraid of buildings. But not friendship, not my children, not my husband.

I have sold my book, *Live or Die*, to Houghton Mifflin. They are bringing it out in the fall. I finished the book because I wrote a poem called "Live." Good enough?

Yours,

Early spring found Anne trying prose again, for the first time delving into the mysteries of the novel. Although she never managed to complete the novel, a new onslaught of poems came in June: "The Touch," [LP] "The Kiss," [LP] and "The Breast." [LP] She had successfully bridged that difficult gap between the end of one book and the start of another.

[*To Lois Ames*]

   march 23 1966   14 black oak rd weston

Dear Lois of Chicago,

I luv yr letters. Even tho I did call so as not to break the record of constant calls. Right now I'm on the damn electric typewriter so excuse all mistakes.

I should be working on my prose (don't beshry and call a novel) I'll henceforth call itk my N, thus confusing it with my navel. This typewriter likes to write k and g every so often so don't mind them as they appear.

I should be writing, as I was saying, on my N. But sometimes I'll do anything but write . . . with prose that is. Not so with the poem. My tendency with the N is to keep retyping as it gets so messy all scotch-taped together and written over. Maybe I'm not a real N-ist anyhow! It feels so strange to have the book of poems gone and sold this suddenly. I feel kind of raped but don't imagine you could imagine the feeling. (Not the rape part, but the feeling of working for 4 years and thinking you'll never get it right and then within a month or is it two — anyhow, very quickly you write LIVE and type like mad and give it to editors and they take it. And it's all over but the clapping and not much of that . . . just reviews and a bunch of wasting-time crap.

So that's why the N seems important to be doing even tho I can't seem to pick it up again.

The "Black Art" [PO] poem could be a lie. After all, I never really tried it. Sylvia liked it but what the hell that means I don't know, . . . Maybe she just kind of liked it. Anyhow she lived it. I wonder if it's possible? The WURST would be marrying a critic. I'm sure of that. Two artists would compete unless they were in different fields. I think it would be quite nice (fantasy time) to be married to a painter only he'd always be around asking for lunch on a tray or something. I'm the one who wants that! I tell you! The best thing for a writer is to be married to someone awfully rich, who approves of their art, respects it and still thinks it's a bit silly, ole gal (so he doesn't take you too seriously . . . for writers DO tend to take themselves too seriously. I mean, of course, he ought to have a good sense of humor and also be a good father and also be nice in bed and also be cuddly when needed) . . . But very rich. With lots of telephones for long distance. The kind who calls up Switzerland to see what the snow conditions, ski conditions, are for the coming weekend and then sticks on the phone for half an hour while some infant says how school was today.

Silly, Anne. [. . .]

Mrs. Plath is now my friend and if I let it happen she might adopt me as a new but dangerous daughter . . .

Lois, lots to say, but never the time.

        now, you call me (and watch out for husband)

        anne

ps. have you seen the telephone bill???????

ain't it horrible.

one must learn.

my taxes this year were 1000 bucks $$$$ *I* have to pay in. price of fame! eh! and no joke. the dough not really here . . . Once was here but since then it vanished . . .

        love to Robert and the children and the Lois

        Anne

[To Claire S. Degener]

        14 Black Oak Road
        March 29, 1966

Dearest Cindy,

Subject: Your Trip

I hope that your anxiety about flying has not increased and let me reassure you again that there will come a day and it will shoot down like a bullet. I am a living example. And I'm here to tell it. Meanwhile, I give you my sympathy, my handholding, my heartknown knowledge that you will survive your terror, and come out grand, simply grand. Anything that I can do, in the way of reassurance or factually, from my own experience, for Chrissake let me know. You are not alone . . . but then remember, if I can survive it, and I'm well known to be the crazy one, then you can. Let's see, I should speak to you of God, seeing as you seem to have Him on your mind. Cindy, have you really read my books? There are all sorts of priests and nuns who think that I am religious. I have told no one of this fact in my town, including all ministers and priests, but I am pretty God Damn religious if you want to look at it. Once I thought God didn't want me up there in the sky. Now I am convinced he does. And you, too, and why not? There's lots of room up there.

Subject: My play. *Tell Me Your Answer True*

I had occasion to meet a Mr. Brice Howard of National Educational Television, 10 Columbus Circle, New York. Because he was doing a program for N.E.T. about me. Howard is the bossman, and came along with the producer, Richard Moore, to help him handle me because I made very difficult noises on the telephone. I told them they could never get the real Anne Sexton with their camera eye and their sound box, and that I was impossible and all that. So Moore brought his boss along, Brice Howard, to see if they could manage me. They did a fine job if it; and as we talked, I showed Brice Howard a copy of *Tell Me Your Answer True*. Moore and I were talking TV details. Next thing I knew this Brice Howard was talking to me of the possibilities of filming my play. [. . .] He had read the first act, and he talked real groovy about ways to film it. He kind of turned me on, but then maybe he was pushing the TV and didn't give a damn for the play. [. . .] I feel, although I might be wrong, that he was taken with me a bit — or rather, taken with the play. His ideas for filming were interesting and original, although he looks like a square.

Maybe nothing came of it. Once flying, I tend to fly too high.

The TV program they did was extensive. They will squash it down into a half hour or fifteen minutes, making me into an accordion. I almost fell in love with the producer, but that's par for the course. [. . .]

Subject: A Novel.

Cindy, I cannot possibly send you the first chapter of this damn thing because I am not sure if it is real. I have written three chapters, but they are not well-written. Still, if I have the time, and I am indeed dictating this to a Girl-Monday, I might send you a chapter or two just to let you know what I'm doing — but I don't want you to think of it as something set but as something that is started.

Subject: New Book of Poems. *Live or Die*
   Maybe I will be able to send you a copy. I'll try to. I see
that Houghton Mifflin has sent you the contract, and I assume
that I will get it in the mail before you get this letter. I think
I do know the poetry business, and as I swore on the typewriter and my Gideon bible and my Holy Bible Revised Standard
Version, you know about the other junk. Cindy, you have a
problem here. Poetry to me is prayer — the rest of it is left-
overs.

Love to you,

[*To Claire S. Degener*]

14 Black Oak Road
April 14, 1966

Dear Cindy:
   I am so glad that I talked with you before talking with Miss
Rhoades at *McCall's Magazine.* My Girl-Monday has just
completed retyping the unsold (first serial rights) poems from
Live Or Die. [. . .]
   Also, if you will stop being paranoid about it I am impressed
with your presence and your knowledge of the Big City. If
you can sell these poems, I will be even more impressed. [. . .]
I have a feeling the poems are splendid, but then, one has to
have some sort of feeling like that about their own work no
matter who prints it or likes it.
   I think you should be more impressed with my knowledge
of the poetry racket (although I have not got the NBA or the
Pulitzer, I am in almost every anthology with the exception of
one and have gotten a hell of a lot of money for writing the
truth.) I'd like those prizes of course — but it is mostly pull
or luck & certainly printing in *McCall's* won't bring them.)
The money I got was never, or hardly ever, for the printing of
the poems but in various grants, etc. Still, I am getting an-
thologied and if I can write good it will keep on going on, and
we'll all get little dribs and drabs of money for ourselves and
our children and their children. Do I sound like the Bible yet?
   I am in love with money, so don't be mistaken; but first I
want to write good poems. After that I am anxious as hell to

make money and fame and bring the stars all down. But if you respect me, you will understand that I know what I am saying when I tell you that *McCall's* does not bring the NBA or the Pulitzer. Maybe sales, maybe publicity. It's the only racket I know. Leave me some autonomy in it or in knowing my way around it. I learned the hard way, and I didn't crawl up anyone's back — much; or if I crawled, it took a hell of a lot of sweat and guts. As they say in the movies, I got here the hard way, with no education and no dough, and whatever I am I am because I wrote it.

So! Beautiful one, sell. Don't be put down by Palm Beach or even my synthetic words. I pray for the play. I don't worry about the poems — you'll do what you'll do. I have finished trying to sell them anywhere because they're mostly a secret. Time now to give up secrets and publish. If you can get *McCall's* to publish some of these poems I'll either eat this letter or my secretary. (Secretary says she's not worried.) However, I'll give you your positive thinking and let you get to work on it. After all, they're God damned important poems. Whether they like them or not, they ought to print them.

Luv,

P.S. You missed out on the novel again because it took my Girl-Thursday here three hours to type out these poems as per your request. I obey. I obey. I am a good girl.

In April, Anne gave a reading at Sweet Briar College in Virginia, with Linda accompanying her. There they met Philip Legler, a young professor and poet who immediately became infatuated with Anne's glamour. He wrote her an ardent love letter as soon as she returned home, beginning an intense correspondence which lasted for several years.

[*To Philip Legler*]

14 Black Oak Road
April 28, 1966

Dear Phil Baby —
   I am so glad you sent more poems. I want to tell you right off that "The Sweat Box" is a very good poem and you might

do well to send it to *The New Yorker.* I think the last two
lines could be stronger or, at least, they are obscure to me and
I also wish they were on rhymes — something I call slamming
the door shut at the end of a poem. Here, you have a cushion
with the off rhyme. At any rate, that's what I think, and I
think it about a damn good poem. Phil Baby, how come
you're still so smart and well to write poems in the nut-
house? And to go and rent a typewriter?? For Chrissakes,
don't be so terribly depressed. Tell that pregnant woman she
doesn't know anything about life yet. Tell your doctor he had
no right to be out of town when you were in trouble. Tell
your doctor that no wonder you're nuts when he goes out of
town and leaves you with a bunch of nuts. Tell him that it's
catching and that it's all his fault.

Phil, when I went in the nut house I was not "out of it" although I wrote that way. Sure. I was crazy as hell, but I
knew it. And knowing it is a kind of sanity that makes the
sickness worse. I would watch it happen and I heard the same
voice crying from the locked wing. I heard it too loud. It was
awful. They left me there and maybe I never recovered from
the sound of that loud voice and maybe that's a good thing . . .
Let it scream. Life screams in the head of every artist with
his typewriter or his pen, so let it. Check it all out. Write it
all down. When you get sane (if you can call what I am
sane??) you can fix what you write and prove what you write.
Anything you write now will be gold later so mine it and
don't make the God-damned baskets. And send me every
poem you write and every word you wish to write and I will
read it all and read it well and know that you send it to me
and forgive you and adore you and understand you. I know
you're depressed as hell and I don't blame you. About your
book and your second book and all of it. Of course your
poems care. You care and it's all over the place. Not every
poet gets instant fame and one can't expect it even though one
needs and desires it. God damn it, keep writing.

If I shook you up then know that you shook me up because
you are very intense and very beautiful and so are your words
and believe me I don't have the time any more to write letters
and if I don't write you every day it doesn't mean I'm not

thinking about you every day. I can cope with you. The problem is more how do I cope without you because such as you happens almost never. For Chrissakes keep writing to me even if I can't answer all the time. I need your letters like food. Don't show this letter to your wife. It's the kind of love letter I shouldn't write. But why not? We're both mad mad mad and I did see everything that went on and so do you. And it's awful but remember you're smarter and in a way that makes [sentence left unfinished]

Keep that typewriter going.   *Love from Annie Baby*

[*To Philip Legler*]

> [*14 Black Oak Road*]
> *MONDAY MAY 2, 1966*

Phil dear of the unnamed wonderful flower otherwise known as THE PHILIP LEGLER FLOWER

a rather nice name too. [. . .]

Let's see what my news of the moment is. Tonight I take part in a vast Anti-Vietnam read-in. I expect they will throw eggs, or my husband (the republican who hates my pink — he calls it — politics) says they may throw hand-grenades. Now, if I don't die tonight there is always tomorrow when I have an apt. with my O.B. because Linda took the pamphlet from the cancer collecting lady this Sunday and immediately read my symptom at William and Mary and the month before, namely I almost bled to death. Not usual for me so in I go to be checked over like a piece of meat. I would have forgotten it but Linda reminds me that I don't want to die. She also underlined HOARSENESS, as I almost lost my voice completely on this last trip. Well, my throat's drying up and elsewhere I'm hemorrhaging and so forth. As for the rest of the list I have all of them, as a matter of fact. Cancer at every hole! Eyes going bad also. Stomach, Kayo calls it my beer-belly, will, I fear, [end in] my throwing out of four very cute bikinis that I have lounged around in each summer. I'm the shock of the proper Bostonian neighborhood in my bikini suits. I think I'm going to Chicago next week if I don't die first. I love you, also and in amongst all this here things. Tomorrow morning

(P.M. for the O.B.) go to Joy's psychiatrist to see how she is. Meanwhile waiting for my husband's doc to call back and give me an appointment so I can see what's up with Kayo. His shrink has never seen me and finally I made a fuss so that even Kayo got mad and now he says he'll call today but I haven't heard him ringing. Yes. DOCTOR Z. We are surrounded. Might as well jam Linda into therapy. It's like a swimming pool. Why not? Every one else is in. Poor farm also. Even our two dogs pant for medical care, one for its sixth puppy shot and the other, next week, to be fixed. FIXED. When will we ever all get fixed.????

You need not return the Cancer seven danger signals. We don't need them. Linda, the dear, knows them by heart. She has a cold. She is upstairs reciting the seven danger signals and waiting, oh longing, to menstruate and be a woman and meanwhile please god don't let mummy die of too much of it.

I love your letters. I wish I had another joke to send you. I will send/lend the only other interesting thing, a picture that Van Gogh painted at the nut house. It's lovely. It writhes. It makes me want to stand out there with him taking my sleeping pills. Or maybe delay them for an hour or two and converse with him or be silent with him, whichever he felt like. The strange-like hairs in the skotch tape are dog hairs or dust. I haven't anaylsied them and I8m not spelling very well, am I? I keep sending you the varieties of my desk/life etc.

For the moment I seem to have lost Van Gogh in this rubble but perhaps it will pop back in a minute. So you are on Librium. That's two of the eight pills I swallow every night. Two 25, green and white types. Very nice. Are you taking round orange pills? You said something about blood pressure. Do they keep taking it? And also giving you orange pills, if so then you're also on thorazine — my favorite, get-well type drug. It took them ten years to figure out the only drug that does me any good. It is also part of my pill structure at night, but only because I might as well take everything all at once. The Thorazine is good for me. I mean it really calms me down and has more or less saved my life when it needed saving, by taking huge amounts of it more or less five times a day. It's orange anyhow, in case you've been taking orange ones. Librium is also a good calmer downer. Phil, don't look down on pills. They make a hell of a difference and are almost cleaning out the nut houses of the world. I love the story of the man with his penis saying the world. This is the truth! He is probably right! I laughed when you said that most of the patients shook too much to play poker. Did you notice me? I shake like hell. Kayo says it's all the pills, my chemical mixture, my little nightly factory. No matter why, I have distinct tremors and hate signing my name because my signature looks like I'm 89.

Glad your wife knows you love me. Nothing wrong with it anyway. I haven't told my husband. But he notices, flowers and letters. You'd like him, I think. Or nevermind, he'd like you. He doesn't like too many poets. [. . .]

Later . . . dear god . . . lost the cancer thing, lost something else but found Van Gogh . . . Where is my desk? Who took my heart? Dinner is cooking and Kayo is making Hollandaise for the broccoli and I am dressed (in same blue reading dress) for Anti-War reading. Wrong nite Anne!

                                        . . . found all notes!!!!
enc.

please find: comment of Anne Sexton
                SEXTON SPELLBINDS LISTENERS etc.
                and late, but not least, Cancer's 7 danger signals
                and VAN GOGH

I light a green cigarette. I think, Phil, of you. I am your anyhow poet. I'm not De Snod, not anyone but your anyhow, all my own and all your own . . . and it *is* a wierd abundance. Really is. Abundance the main thing, the good thing, the wished for, looked for and needed. Wierd spelled wrong is still wier weird can't spell it, forgive me. Look at me, Phil! I'm supposed to be sane. Don't worry if they say you're crazy. They said that about me and yet I was saner than all of them. I KNEW. No matter. You know. Insane or sane, you know. It's a good thing to know — no matter what they call it.

                                        i love you
                                [with a hand-drawn heart]
                                        Anne

[*To Philip Legler*]
> [*14 Black Oak Road*]
> *may 4th, 1966*
> *wednesday*

Dear Phil of the poems, the letters, of The Philip Legler Flower,

Now, I have been thinking about you for a long time — since your phone call. I've been thinking further than the phone call and seriously and wisely as I could.

Phil, that you were worried is flattering. But it isn't realistic.

Yes, we are two of a kind, the abundance stuff that runs wild, runs as wild with love as cancer. Moves in and takes over. I know. I know all about it. And you said in one letter "you're the only woman I've ever met." I told Linda (between us two) that you said that and she replied "He's wrong. There's me!" Ah, the female ego!

Seriously, Phil baby, everyone is wrong here. Your love, your abundance for me is partly sick. I can tell you this because I am the healthiest, wisest sickest human you'll meet outside the nut house (patient or doctor/nurse). The sanest thing in this world is love. And what is important is honesty.

I believe that you love me and I know how you love and yet I say that your love is too intense to be making sense for your life or mine. Okay! So I'm the only woman or the "other" or the "muse magitick" or whatever — so. So what! Yes. You are very intense and so am I. However, I am married to a very intense, practical SQUARE. He is good for me for he has complete plans on how to run each day. He is with the world. I am not of it whatsoever. You? Perhaps only your wife is of the world. And maybe you and I are otherworldly — poets, to be exact. Poets can't live for/die for/live with/breathe in nothing but themselves — they need the sensible people, the roots, the down the house world of people. You need them. I need them. We cannot exist without them.

That guy was right — only he didn't know how right. I feel in my heart that if you concentrate (as you have been doing) on your Anne Sexton campaign that you'll run off into a tornado. I mean yes we love each other — but it's a mirror — of

sorts — it's the male of the female and the female of the male.
In other words, you're me. Also I'm you. I realize that the
thought that someone else understands every motion and feeling and word is almost too much. I feel that you are ex-
periencing this with me. Be still and listen! This way leads
us both into madness. You must look homeward for sanity —
maybe not for communication. For communication I hate to
tell you where I look — for I am a very lonely person — I look
to my doctor and to Linda ... and a few friends, very few to
treasure. Phil, I'm not saying I don't love you. I'm saying that
your love for me is true and at the same time it is sick and
you're hearing this from someone who is pretty goddamn used
to being sick and told she was and knowing she is. You're
sick. You need help. Also with me, help is badly needed.

I'm not scared off by your letters. No. Your letters scare
me for you. Now, Phil, I've been hanging around the shrink's
office longer than you and I hope I've picked up a little bit of
wising up on life, driving in into it, that is. I tell you "The
Black Art" [PO] (tho written unconsciously, it's true — take
two abundances and they get weird and the children ... the
ones we love more than ourselves, the products, the exten-
sions, leave. THEY CAN'T TAKE TWO OF THEM). Neither,
in your life, can you afford to concentrate all this attention on
a girl/poet named Anne Sexton. I hope she is a good poet, and
a true person to meet. However, she isn't what you, Phil
Legler, poet and true person, need. I mean, you are sick
(which doesn't mean you don't KNOW MORE than the
nurses/doctors/wife/friends), but that you aren't operating at
your best potential. The full you isn't getting used up properly. That's why you're in the nut house. I'm not your
mother — naturally — but I lecture away and yet it isn't a
lecture, it's a worry. Worry that you'll use yourself up on me,
on loving me, protecting me, when that isn't your job. If you
love me, in passing, like the tulip that will never die, then it's
enough. You've done your job. You fill me. But don't keep
growing new Philip Legler flowers every day. Not flowers for
Sexton. Then and if you do this, that Richard Howard (is that
his name?) would be right in saying I'm poison. Christ! I
can't bear to be poison.

My self's self tells me this is wrong. The poet wants love. But not at this cost. First, foremost, Phil, work out your constant need for affection, closeness with students, or with this poet. Maybe because they aren't used up yet, or dirty with life. Maybe some poetic words like that. Oh hell. I just feel I haven't done you any favor to write needs, my needs like yours, just like yours, and to sponsor what needs to be worked on with your doctor-daddy.

Phil, I do love you. Phil, I think you need help, think you are sick. But hell, the nurse who said not to read that sick poetry is in far worse condition on account of she ain't even ALIVE. But your wife is alive. I've met her. She's alive. She was a wringlet of worry and love, all over you. Her voice, her hands, all love and need and worry. Maybe she doesn't talk our language but her language is the language of life, of living. For you I think/feel.

I know you aren't making mad proposals to me. I'm not scared of that. Hell no. It's that I'm scared for you. Scared you'll miss the point of where you are and why. Phil, take the pills and start on the road to growing. Only chance. [. . .]

About your poems. Write in there as you will, but don't send out in such a hurry. Keep them on the fire. Write more but don't make final acts on them for months. Or I wouldn't. Thorazined as you'll be and as nutty as you are, it is no time to judge. Maybe a time to write but not to judge finally, like sending out, howard moss or whoever. One poem, "Flee On Your Donkey," [LD] I wrote in 1962 in the nut house and rewrote 98765432 times until this spring, until I sent to *New Yorker* (not that they are good but that they pay), and it's coming out this week, May 7. Please buy at newsstand somewhere. Took me all those years to figure it out right. Give yourself some years. The first poem to me takes, or will, that long — I don't feel you have finished it or should have. Give that poem time. It may be getting bigger before you're done with it. Or smaller. Or less you to me. Or its own self's self. Don't hurry it. There's no hurry. It's not a horse race. [. . .]

I don't think form is constipation. But now you mention constipation I know why you couldn't finish reading my poem, "Cripples and Other Stories" [LD] ... All about it, really.

No. I don't have cancer. A D&C (Dilation and Curettage) for May 26th. Go in hospital 25th. Get home 28th. I hope that will end it. I'm fond of my womb and its life-giving characteristics. If they say it's cancer, I'll let you know right off. I promise.

I will always treasure your letter about the fight with the nurse over my *Bedlam* book. It's too much. It's great. It's a tulip! Jesus.

I love your letters, even if I can't always write myself.

[a hand-drawn heart] *Anne*

[*To Maxine Kumin*]

[*14 Black Oak Road*]
May 20, 1966

Dear Maxine,

I think I'll send this to Amsterdam where you'll be riding bikes over the canals. A lovely city. Seeing as this will take a while to get there.

... (*Time* Mag is sitting here, the vultures, reading the sketch I wrote about Sylvia for the *Tri-Quarterly* ... Mrs. Plath is having a kind of paranoid fit about their presence and so it goes) ... Charlie Newman gave *Time* permission to read the thing so what the hell. The guy is sitting here. ... Also I have the Flu, temp and a feeling of throwing up. Shit! I hate waking up in the morning and having no call to make or to answer. Your private number, on a piece of paper over my desk and on my bedside table, looks sad as I look at it sadly.

Decided that I couldn't stand that book cover [for *Live or Die*], it probably made me sick! Am pleading with HM Co. NOT to use it. Think, as I dashed in there in the rain yesterday and with a temp. and all — that I convinced them not to use, but tried, unsuccessfully I think, to get them to use Barbara [Swan]'s drawing of MAN CARRYING A MAN.

... went out to lunch with *Time* mag guy ... nothing but a boy, his first assignment and he seems awkward and scared.

Went also to dentist, weather turned suddenly hot, came

home and Joy and Linda and Joy's horse-friend (not a horse, a friend with horses . . . Molly Cameron) went swimming. I did not go in (the Flu).

I haven't even read *Is Paris Burning?* yet and soon we will have to return the copy. I imagine you have both devoured it. If you care for such things, Kayo has two others about the last days of the war. Just have no pep as must be plain from this letter. But thought you'd like my news even if I can hardly type or get up any great enthusiasm.

Love to you in Venice of the north and all of it. It's the city where I walked out on the rooftop and hung up our wash and sang "I Like Roofs" . . . and Anne Frank's city, of course.

War and Tourists
and love

After months of research, Anne and Kayo decided to take a hunting safari in Africa with the award money from the Congress for Cultural Freedom. Anne was determined to give her husband the dream of his childhood. But, close to their departure date, the impending slaughter of animals became more and more repugnant to her, as she had become virtually a vegetarian. In late July, she attempted suicide.

Nevertheless, she drew on reserves of physical and emotional strength and kept her promise to Kayo. Shortly after her release from Massachusetts General Hospital, they boarded the plane bound for London and Nairobi. For her husband the safari equaled the fantasy, but Anne found it horrible: flies, dirt, and endless blood. Still she was exultant over her gift to him; as she remarked to a friend, "I gave Kayo his dream! How many of us ever get our dreams?"

[*To Lois Ames*]

[*14 Black Oak Road*]
Aug 2 1066

Dear Lois back in Chicago,
   See date! [. . .]

I've been in a mess, Lois, from bad to wrose. Worse. I mean. Can't even type. This is first time at typewriter in over two or 3 weeks. Greater love hath no friend.

I haven't really been well. In July I tried — well, rather I took an overdose of pills and ended up in MGH being pumped out and with private nurses for 48 hours. Rather a stupid mess. Live or die, you fool, but don't mess with Mr. in-between! Still, it wasn't a serious serious attempt or I would have succeeded. Part of me is live. But I forgot about the diet from death. I went on a binge. Terrible to wake up afterwards into a little hell, strapped into bed/crib, arms tied to sides, feet tied together at the bottom of bed — lost control of all functions — literally on a cross — a little crucifixion — very sadistic nurses (and tied down for them) . . . God, Lois, one nurse was terrible, like a Faulkner preacher breathing sin and hell fire at me for such an immoral act.

Dr. Deitz was nice — I mean understanding. Have yet to really understand all I was trying to do. Now he is gone on vacation and I'm about to leave for Africa and I'm in no condition to do so but can't bring myself to let Kayo down. I just feel terrible in the body, no strength and bizarre symptoms . . . and as for the head, I know I'm crazy but knowing doesn't help. Dr. Deitz wishes I wouldn't try to go to Africa now but it's all set. Can't back out.

Don't let this letter disturb you. Remember the inner core. It's got to be there this time . . . or I've had it.

I must be nuts. Why didn't I come see you instead of killing myself? I would really prefer to visit with you. Perhaps I was punishing myself? That among other things. Perhaps I want and need my doctor to see me as sick. That and other things. The old need to die, and how it returns under any stress. An old command of my mother's. Hell. If I'd died it would have been awful in light of my forthcoming book.

I'm scared of bugs, animals, blazing sun (having upped my Thorazine so I will really burn), voices in my head. I am looking forward to falling in love with African skies. I want to see it, if only I can make it despite fears. I am all fear.

I had to tell you all this so you'd understand why the form is such a mess. I'm sorry, Lois, best I can do right now.

> *love from your all mixed up crazy friend*
> *Anne of Weston*

[*To Lois Ames*]

CAPRI, ITALY
Sept 7th, 1966

Dear Lois,

Got your letter just as we swept into Roma and came down to Capri, the island of happiness. It was wonderful to hear from you and I had thought about you often and wondered how it was going with Mrs. Plath. In your letter you told me really very little about how that went. Did she really unbend? [. . .] Say just when the phone was pulled from the root? I can see that her life is a hard one. Did your fantasy come true — that you would be able to help her face it?

I really wish that you could find a way to come visit me for a week anytime this year. We have so much talk between us that we haven't talked. It makes me feel all stoppered up, the words can't get through on the typewriter, there are too many. I have vowed solemnly not to use the long distance phone as I have done in the past and that makes it worse for our communication. How about a visit? Would it be possible?

This trip was okay. Africa, rather hunting safari, is not for me, dust, fire ball heat, thorn tree and never shade tree, blood, slaughter. Watching the animal die slowly and then be served it that night for dinner. I can't imagine living there and can't believe you would like it — but then maybe I am wrong about you. It's an angry continent, emerging, but with no rule book and great poverty and great hatred for the white man. Chicago is worse though, from what I read. But in U.S. someday the freedom will come and not through black power over white power as in Africa. Anywhere it is the feeling of hatred that gets to you, even as you said about your neighborhood. . . . Capri is the most beautiful. It is my spiritual home and like being born again. My nerves are better. I don't look forward to going home, which we do on Thursday, Sept 8th, even before you'll get this. Too many problems. I even associate home with being sick. Maybe the summer break will have changed things with my doctor. The trouble is that he is the best doctor I ever had . . . it just got too intense . . . Oh well, and Kayo and I were in Capri two years ago and yet it seems that we bore each other now. There isn't anything to say. I irritate him if I tell him what I'm thinking so I am often quiet. He adored the safari. His dream did come true and he talks about nothing else. I'm glad he had it. It's really just camping out in luxury surrounded by death, killing, unforgiving death at each turn. Capri is like a beautiful mother. The water holds you up like a float and is so clear. Capri is the mother we never had, young, beautiful, exotic, accepting and loving arms. Thank God I've been here again. Wish I could live here, with someone. My book is supposed to come out Sept 14th . . . I'll know better when I get home. I hope you like the cover, as well as the contents with which you are familiar and even helped with some lines "I'm a little buttercup in my yellow nightie" and more.

Write soon and often. Am dying to see the Sylvia article and know it will launch you.

xo Anne

Live or Die came out in the fall to mixed reviews. The dry spell of four months without a poem ended in October, as Anne began writing more love poems: "The Interrogation of the Man of Many Hearts," "That Day," "In Celebration of My Uterus," "The Nude Swim," "Song for a Red Nightgown," and "Loving the Killer." Including the three written in early June, she had completed a full quarter of *Love Poems*, a book which was to be one of her most popular with both the reviewers and the public.

[*To Robert Bly*]

> 14 Black Oak Rd.
> october 18th, 1966

Dear Bobby Bly,

What a wonderful afternoon I've just had with you and your books (*The Sea and the Honeycomb*), the spring '66 *Sixties* and the wonderful Vietnam book. I love those inked-out places and the "In Mourning." Why, this afternoon has been like a love affair. Such wondrous laughter and depth and so much talk between us (although you couldn't hear all my remarks I will give you a few). Riot! There he goes right off . . . "How like Lowell and Sexton!" (much laughter) I can still laugh even [though] your point may be well-taken. Poor me, I ain't got no Gott-natur. And maybe I don't for god's sake I think maybe I don't. Still in my opinion Arthur Miller's "ordinary salesman" not ordinary at all. He was in an EXTREME mental state and ended up killing himself. An ordinary man who killed himself. Killing oneself, sleeping with that stocking woman in Boston, lying about sales, fiddling around with a gas pipe, driving off the road (I haven't read the play for a while) and maybe more — aren't those all "Extreme mental states?" But I'm not angry. I think you are beautiful. Your magazine is full of wit and joy and love and is a wonderful experience. I think about the best lines are James Wright's "I have wasted my life." That's a great poem of his and I think highly of his work ... You know, you are right, I do think the human being is something extremely important *in itself.* I think I do. I asked myself today and said "Yah. I do." I do like passenger pigeons and blue whales ... the whales more than the pigeons (except in Venice where pigeons work on bells. Have you seen that? When one flies sometimes, especially if all the damn bells are pealing off (peeling? sp?) they all fly). But otherwise I'd say, human first, whale second, pigeon third. Also Zebras and Giraffes. I am very fond, personally, of zebras and giraffes, having just returned from Africa. Much to my horror my husband shot a zebra so unfortunately we will have a zebra skin in our "family room" which is really the room where I write, but also where everyone keeps gathering and leaving their books and stuff. Soon I will remove to the attic or build a small hut in the woods outside. Luckily giraffes are protected from hunters so I can keep on living with my love for them without suffering immediate guilt about having watched one die. My husband is an "ordinary salesman" and his case is worse (more EXTREME) than Willie Loman's because he is married to me (gray eyes). That one. Thus, instead of killing himself he goes out to kill the wild creatures of Africa and test his courage. An Elephant charged and almost killed him but the professional hunter got it (in back of the eye I believe). I tell you, Africa was better than an abortion or a cancer operation if one is looking for mutilation and butchers. However it didn't excite me. Later I washed the blood off in the Indian Ocean. And more in the Mediterranean where it is so clear and buoyant you never have the "fear of going down." Marvellous lines of Machado!

I shouldn't go on this way. The best thing about *The Sixties* is that it makes you want to start talking and it sometimes makes you want to start writing. I find that when you or Crunk or whoever is tearing something apart that I want to talk. When you offer the poem itself I want to write and I often do feel closer to life.

I don't have much to say about the Lowell attack. I feel neutral I guess. Or rather, I'd rather not say what I feel. I guess I don't feel *Union Dead* poems are melodrama. I think melodrama is more interesting. I think it's a bit stale, as you say, but I rather like "floods of objects" and I don't mind journalism either. But "a life of their own" is what is missing and gives one the feeling of a stale smoked-up room that has just been deserted by a literary cocktail party.

Oh well, I'm not much of a critic. I guess I don't know enough to be a critic. I know one thing, though, the critics (so-called) who [go] after "Lying in a Hammock" are wrong. They couldn't be real poets at all if they couldn't feel what that poem was doing. I'd rather have written that poem than any I have written.

Today is a special day for me, not only because of your gifts, not only because of the orange-yellow-bloodred trees at my window and in my woods, but because I am once again saved from cancer. Day before yesterday they were going to give me a hysterectomy but yesterday I went to some big deal specialist in Boston and I can keep it. So saved is a part of the soul of the woman who lives in me. I thought today that I would write a poem "In Celebration of My Uterus" [LP] but I haven't written it yet and, of course, you wouldn't like it (too extreme). Of course it's pretty human to want to keep it, it's even exclusively human, as you say, but I assure you I do not want to bomb foreign populations (nor kill zebras or elephants) [Letter stops at this point.]

[*To Constance Smith
The Radcliffe Institute*]

*14 Black Oak Road
November 9, 1966*

Dear Connie,

Following our conversation of last evening, I am writing to you in an official capacity to apply for a scholarship in creative writing for the year 1967–1968. More specifically, I wish to write prose.

The history of my prose writing goes back to the publication of my first short story in *New World Writing*, Number 16, in 1960. In this same collection Tillie Olsen published "Tell Me a Riddle." I saw that my own words were the words of a beginner and, much as a child learns to talk, I had only just begun. I tried to write more prose along with the poems that were coming but knew each time that the prose was inadequate. From 1961 to 1963, with the help of the Radcliffe Institute for Independent Study, I worked on poems, finished "All My Pretty Ones," started "Live or Die," and thought a lot about prose. As you know, the American Academy of Arts and Letters granted me some time in Europe in 1963–1964, and the Ford Foundation thought I could write a play in 1964 and 1965. I did write a play, not once but forty times, but it is stillborn and will be until I can find a director willing to work with me on any further rewrites.

Thus I have published three books of poems; and just at the end of my last book, the last poem dated February the Last, 1966, I started the bold and terrifying work on a novel. I worked constantly until May, when I realized that I was not writing well enough. Since then I have gone back to study [it and] found I had written three chapters and four pages into the fourth, and I started to rewrite. I want to try my hand, my heart on this foreign, mysterious, precious language. It is not easy for me to write well. Sentences come hard. But I am ready to try again. I am ready to spend four years or ten years or all years on what this novel must have.

However, I am badly in need of money; and although I have

the means to make money by public readings (my little one-night stands, my little vaudeville act), it is never enough to meet the expenses. I believe in work and am not afraid of it — I will work in a department store this Christmas if that is my only choice this year. However, the money situation will not get any better. The needs of my two children, ages 11 and 13, grow greater every year, and the only way to change the status of our income is for me to go out and do something about it. Further, a novel is a lot less "part time" than a poem. A novel eats time, and its characters refuse to do dishes and iron blouses. I have a cleaning woman once a week; I dare not fire her, for while she irons, I type. To concentrate on the enormity of a book I need her more often — further, I need a secretary now and then. One who can type, punctuate and spell. A novel seems so big, so "full time." I cannot hold it in my arms like a poem, though one may have to hold a poem in his arms for a week or even for years. Still, I am a very stubborn person and a doer of things. I *must* write this novel, and I *must* write it better than I can write. I do not aspire to merely write a novel that will be published as my first story was, so easily, but to write one that is lasting.

I do not write with facility, the pen is awkward in my hand, but I think I am ready to begin again.

Please do call me about that lunch, that "never frivolous lunch," you mentioned.

                                                        Best wishes,

The only time Anne had ever enjoyed her birthday was in 1965, when electric power failed across the northeastern seaboard. Canceling dinner at Locke-Ober's, the family had stayed home, roasted hot dogs in the fireplace, and celebrated by candlelight. In 1966 she wanted to do it the same way. Anne set out candles and turned off the lights. Then Joy went upstairs to take a bath; while she was in the tub, her candle went out and Anne ran to relight it. In the dark, she caught her heel and fell a full flight of stairs. Joy called an ambulance and Anne was taken to the hospital. Her hipbone was in fragments. "The Break" [LP], written a month later, was to recreate the experience.

[*To Lois Ames*]

[*The Newton-Wellesley Hospital*]
Sat. Nov. 19th, 1966

This is the 1st and probably only letter I'll write anyone from this joint —
Dear Lois — your ms. of Sylvia Plath is really fine! I take a certain little private pleasure in knowing I helped you get started. — Fascinating material — sick! — more about it later. —

You must be wondering why a letter by hand? — Eh? I never write by hand — it is so ugly — like my adolescence — I seldom write poems this way as you know — half the time can't read it later. And tonight this is most awkward as I'm flat on my back & WILL BE FOR A YEAR — God! On my birthday (see "Menstruation at Forty" [LD] — that day when one is *supposed* to be dead, the birth-night of the soul — Nov 9th — I tripped at the head of the gold carpeted stairs & fell & fell & fell & BROKE my hip — I can't walk for a year. Have 2 "PINS" (SCREWS really) in my hip to keep it together. Only Joy was in the house when it happened. I couldn't move — thought I'd broken my spine — worst pain of my life — am just today crawling out of the "pain machine" (I call it). I kept yelling "Jesus! Jesus!" and the nurse would shout back "Wrong name! I'm not Jesus. I'm Barbara" — I guess I get blasphemous and religious all at once when I'm pushed to the rail (& twice screwed) —

No driving my blue jewel. No walking except as a one year old, with my walker — & crutches, when I can manage them. If I step on right leg my hip will be permanently crippled ("I was an instant cripple . . . I'd known it from the start . . .") In my sleep I try to get up & walk & must be forcibly held down. What['s] wrong with me??? Must I be a cripple? Is there no other way? — Oh Lois! Lois, Lois, Lois — Will you ever come East & stay with us? I shall perish cooped up in the house for a year. Once in a while I'll have to be driven to see Dr. Deitz, Daddy — & to the bone man. [. . .]

About Sylvia — I wish you'd mentioned something about

her suicide — & you never say she was alone. Perhaps both by design? to placate Ted & Mrs. P. so you can *really* get the book. — *Your work is the work of a PRO* — I leave Newton Wellesley Hosp. on Wed. with a R.N. to help me until Dec. 20th — Please write. Lois, Lois, Lois —

XO — anne

I was cold sober — too.

After three years of silence, Brother Dennis Farrell wrote to Anne. She replied immediately to her old friend, who was no longer a monk, but it was the last letter they were ever to exchange.

[*To Brother Dennis Farrell*]

[*14 Black Oak Road*]
Dec 10th, 1966

Dear Dennis,
    Thank God you wrote to me. I've been worrying about you for years, wondering if you were alive or dead, a monk or not or where and how you were. You shouldn't have left me with this silence. Was it that last letter I wrote to you? You must excuse my letters. Often they are hasty and one must not take them as the total truth.
    I even wondered when my last book came out this fall (have you seen it? *Live or Die* is the title) if you'd ever read it and write to me once more. It had *that* poem in it, the "black but beautiful" one. Your words in my poem. [. . .]
    Tell me what you are doing. I gave a reading in Chicago last winter. We might have met, or at least spoken for a minute. But things like that can't happen if I don't know where you are.

Merry Christmas and all best,
Anne Sexton

After Christmas, Anne received an invitation from Ted Hughes to the International Poetry Festival in London. She had long wanted to meet Pablo Neruda, who was coming to the festival from Chile. When she wrote Hughes accepting his offer, she spoke frankly of her distress over a remark he had made about her poetry and Lowell's in his article on Sylvia Plath in the *Tri-Quarterly*. She attended the London Poetry Festival in July, in her wheel chair.

[*To Ted Hughes*]

14 Black Oak Rd.
Jan 20th, 1967

Dear Ted,

I assume you got my cable. I couldn't get up the energy to reply quite then ... but I was pretty sure I could come to the Festival in July and thought you ought to know. Further, my delay in answering might look like a refusal to understand your feelings about the article on Sylvia. I think I can understand what a difficult spot you were in. I knew that Cal sent you that letter as he read it to me.

I did feel a little sour about the torture cell with the daily newspaper (good writing but ... a kind of parody)))) ... Perhaps you didn't *mean* to detract from the poetry that I write or the poetry that Cal writes but you did. In this case, in Sylvia's case, I agree, it needed doing. More separation is needed. I am personally quite tired of every review etc. linking my name with Cal's — much as I respect his work, and I do. Still, my poems ARE different. Sylvia's are different too. I love her work — pure genius. And the loss of it, the terrible loss of the more she could have done! ... At any rate, I do accept your apology and thank you for it. I'm not sure what your terms "spirit" or "nature" or "society" mean ... but if *you* say so.

Cal is sick [...] and perhaps has not answered you. I'm sure he will and that if he is well he will come to the Festival in July. He simply (he said) wanted an apology; he added, at the time, that he often fought with FRIENDS and made it up subsequently. I'm sure he counted you as a friend.

I couldn't answer you personally until I had seen my surgeon (saw him today). I have a broken hip and he had said I could not walk until next November. However, there is a chance now that I might be capable of walking with a cane by this summer. He said I could come in a wheel chair. Which is what I planned to do. When I got your letter I wasn't sure if I could make it because of the hip — I would need someone to take care of me and as you know the money doesn't quite cover *my* expenses (the flight!) let alone my nurse or my husband or daughter. However, Lois Ames (she is doing that biography of Sylvia and is now on a grant to do it) tells me she will fill in and be my "caretaker" as she has work to do in London herself. She is quite nice. I think you will like her and find her easy to talk to — even better, tactful. I met her only in connection with her work on Sylvia ... but as you know, I had little to add. That poem of mine makes everyone think I knew her well, when I only knew her death well. If the poem disturbed you let me say I am sorry and apologize for it. I thought Mrs. Plath (whom I met through Lois) would hate the poem, but she doesn't.

Oh Ted, it must all be a battle for you! I do understand.

As for accommodation — Lois perhaps will find us some free digs — if not I will let you know. In the meantime you could let *me* know if everyone is staying at the same place and how much. Brown's Hotel (where I stayed last summer) is 15 dollars a day without meals. Are you fixing everyone up somewhere cheaper? Also, where (London W1 ?) is the festival being held? Brown's is in 1. I may have to use taxis with the hip. Can Neruda speak English or am I lost? I haven't talked to Tony Hecht — he is a good friend. He might be able to push me around or help me hobble. I *will* need help ... but maybe not as much as I'd feared. I fell down the stairs in November and shattered the hip bone. It is still painful and the mail is stacked up a yard high. It hurts some to sit up to type and I can't write by hand as even I can't read it ...

It looks as if I will be the only female poet at the festival (not counting Ginsberg!) ... is that so? How strange. I look drawn and haggard now, I will be no addition. I will work on a tan. Not, of course, that you asked me because I was another sex. No. That is another lump I dislike[:] "female poets lump," the "confessional poets lump," or "Lowell, Sexton, Plath lump." Your intentions were insightful and correct. Thus, be forgiven.

Oxford U.P. brings out my new book *Live or Die* this [year]. They will be delighted. I hear from Mrs. Plath that the children are blooming. I am delighted — *yrs Anne*

[*To Dorianne Goetz,*
postcard]

14 Black Oak Road
[*April 20, 1967*]

Dori! Dori! Dear! Your poem "SAFE GOODS" IS WON-
DERFUL, IS A SMALL MIRACLE. Please do not hurry. Sappho will turn in her grave. Someday you will be a great, a
lasting, a only poet. You are already as good if not better than
I am. Where you will wander one can only guess. I'm sure
you'll wander well.

I give you all my luck and some [of]
my love
Anne

My daughter loves it too. I tried to call to tell you, tell you,
tell you!

One late afternoon in May, Anne received a telegram: "Columbia
University Trustees today awarded you Pulitzer Prize in Poetry for
Live or Die. Congratulations." Soon other cables and messages
flooded in — from Nolan Miller, Ben Shaktman, John Malcolm Brin-
nin, Howard Moss, Frederick Morgan, the Governor of Massachusetts,
Hy Sobiloff, Dudley Fitts, Charles Newman, the Radcliffe Institute for
Independent Study, her college roommate, and many others. It was the
critical highpoint of her career.

Chapter V

Transformations

May 1967–December 1972

Daisy, you have been brought forth
from a stiff-necked people.
The zeal of your house
doth eat you up.
O Daisy, O Daughter of Jerusalem,
there is an enormous hunger in Zion!

from MERCY STREET

During the next five years Anne completed *Love Poems, Transformations, The Book of Folly,* and her play, retitled *Mercy Street.* Success buoyed her spirits, and she developed an aura of confidence. Therapy with Dr. Deitz supported and reassured her; her relationship with Kayo kept her stable and safe. To the joy of her friends and family, suicide ceased to be a daily threat between 1967 and 1970.

As Anne discovered new people and new ideas her life expanded. At the London Poetry Festival, she met poets she had admired for years. Returning home to her first real teaching experience, she put much of her new excitement to work. Public performances on the reading circuit still terrified her, but to compensate for her anxiety, she raised her fee to $700. The sales of her books continued to climb; she had become a genuinely popular poet.

Awards rained in, confirming her new self-confidence: an honorary Phi Beta Kappa from Harvard in 1968 and Radcliffe in 1969; a Guggenheim Fellowship in 1969; honorary Doctorates of Letters from Tufts University in 1970, Fairfield University in 1972, and Regis College in 1973.

Fan letters flooded her desk. She tried to respond to everyone — especially those writing from mental hospitals. If there was no time for a letter, she often drew a daisy on a postcard and signed her name. The memory of mental institutions never left her. She knew that any communication, any touch, was better than silence. In an attempt to conserve time, she began dictating her letters instead of typing them herself, even those of the most private nature. The appearance of her letters changed drastically — the charm of her misspellings and typos was replaced by a smooth, finished product. Anne's skill and sophistication had grown since her elopement note in 1948; twenty years later, her letters had an easy lapidary quality which sometimes masked her true feelings.

As Anne plunged into the politics of literature, demonstrating that she had as fine an acumen for business as she did for poetry, she did not hesitate to use her fame or the threat of her mental instability as a lever. Once she became fully aware of her ability to "psych into" other people, she adroitly manipulated them to do all she asked.

Her friends and family began to resist her small but taxing requests. Her husband pressed her to give up her fear of the marketplace and to shop, at least by phone, for the family groceries. Her daughters entered rebellious adolescence. Her friends were focusing on their own expanding careers and lives. On a trip to New York City in the spring of 1969, she made an appointment with Frederick Morgan. Telephoning him from a hotel two blocks away from the *Hudson Review*, she asked if he would come over and get her in a taxi — claiming that she was too frightened of the city to hail a cab herself and incapable of walking the two blocks. When Morgan refused, explaining that he was running an office, not a taxi service, she grew cool. She stopped corresponding with him and simply crossed him off her list. This pattern of demand and rejection had begun in the early 1960s with W. D. Snodgrass and grew more apparent with the years.

In late 1969, Anne underwent the trauma of changing psychiatrists again. Dr. Constance Chase, who replaced Dr. Deitz, took an unprecedented approach. She would not tolerate hysterical midnight telephone calls; she refused to accept or support Anne's weaknesses and demanded a modicum of control. Anne responded to the challenge, and made some progress in her therapy. But it was hard work. As she tried to cut down on her Thorazine and sleeping pills in an attempt to reduce her addiction, her dependence on family and friends increased.

[*To Anne Ford*
Houghton Mifflin Company
Publicity Department]

14 *Black Oak Road*
17 *May 1967*

Dear Anne,

I would like to be quoted about Sallie Bingham's book with your first sentence and not your second. "Sallie Bingham writes with precision, irony and subtle compassion," unless you'd like to add "it's a damn good book"?

Your story of Carson McCullers remains in my mind. I keep worrying about her. Anne, do you realize some day that will be me! And I won't know that my writing is lousy and sodden. In my opinion Hemingway did the right thing.

Love,
Anne

Anne had first tried her hand at teaching poetry with a small group of Harvard and Radcliffe students in 1962. Although she found it an intriguing experience, she felt she was not effective as a teacher.

In early 1967, Robert Clawson, a former English teacher at Weston High School, and Anne attended the Huntington Conference on Long Island as members of the Teachers' and Writers' Collaborative. There they met Herbert Kohl, the educator and writer. The Collaborative dedicated itself to promoting new and imaginative methods of teaching. On their return to Massachusetts, Anne and Bob convinced the Wayland High School Board to hire them as a team for the academic year 1967–1968, sponsored by a grant from the National Endowment for the Humanities. Together they set up an innovative English literature class, unprecedented in the history of the school.

[*To Herbert Kohl*]

> [*14 Black Oak Road*
> *circa spring 1967*]

Dear Herb,

I hate to try to fit words around what Bob and I would do together in a highschool class of English. How can one describe an aim? How can one be specific about "opening," "unlocking," "setting on fire" with each student? But that *is* the aim.

But you want a plan, a list of objectives. So I'll give you ours with the reminder that our objectives are flexible enough to allow for student objectives and student innovation. I feel this is as important an ideal as the ones I will list.

A group of sophomores, juniors and seniors (15 in number) of mixed ability and interest in English will gather daily in a classroom where books will be in abundance and the teacher (Bob) and the poet (me) will argue about content, meaning, life, the honesty of literature and in turn encourage all student writing as valuable communication and never give it a mark or hold it up to evaluation that would tend to kill, or block, or "clog."

Both Bob and I will keep separate journals of our lives with the students. We are going to suggest, perhaps require, the students to keep similar journals. Their feelings about us, about different books, etc. might be more interesting than our observations of them. Certainly their journals would be a value.

If we succeed the students will run the class, or at any rate should be able to call it "our class." They will learn to feel free to bring in any book that interests them. We want to find out what they feel in *their* literature and not impose *ours*. However, we will introduce *ours* and try to communicate our passions and encourage open discussion and argument. We hope this leads to their writing, their reading, and to the knowledge that books are written with honesty, despair, passion, and by real people (me, the poet), real people (them), and real people (Bob, the teacher).

When marks are required for school credit we will let them mark themselves. We will discuss their self-evaluating marks with them personally (privately) and hopefully prove that we don't care what mark they get, that we aren't in the business of evaluating them, but in the business of listening to them, reading with them, and thinking together. We are more interested in their ideas than their marks, in their openness to writing for its own sake, rather than for the "marks' " sake.

After a month or two we want to start sending them into lower grades, one through nine, to teach, to spread the word. We want them to choose the material they teach but we will give suggestions if they ask for them. We don't plan to "require" them to do this, but will try our damndest to sell them on the idea. It will be an individual problem. If they want specific "backing up" such as one of us "along" for a week or two, then they can take one of us while the other remains with the class. Later, the whole class will participate in the "feedback" of each student-teacher experience. Maybe they will want to spend three or four class periods a week with a certain grade. We'll play it by ear and try to keep our ears open. Their own teaching might be more valuable to them than our "teaching." [. . .]

As for money, we would like $3000 apiece for the year. Bob is a teacher with 7 year's experience and I am a writer with ten year's experience. It's what we need, in truth. But we don't want to ask for more than you can budget for this.

So that's it. Hastily written down for you without real or-
ganization. To unchain, to set on fire, to send forth, to set
more fires and unchain others — that's the goal. Yes, it will
be a regular credit English class, but what we hope for is far
from regular.

I thought this was going to be short but I got wordy in my
enthusiasm.

Love you all and all good luck,
Anne

[*To Claire S. Degener*]

[*14 Black Oak Road*]
21 June 1967

Dear Cindy,

It was wonderful to see you and find out you were just as
real and nice as I had expected you to be. As for me, how
could I help but be human? If you read the books, or even the
play, although the play doesn't tell that much about me, you
would know I was no Marilyn Monroe.

That nice teacher and I found a cab by talking an off-duty
cab in[to] going on-duty, but you were sweet to be concerned
and to give us that telephone number.

Both Lois and I are staying in London at the 69 Hotel; 69
Cadogan Gardens, Sloane Square. The festival will be held in
Queen Elizabeth Hall and the Purcell Room, South Bank.

Please do send me the play along with your comments on it.
I suppose I could get a reading or a production of it from the
Theater Company of Boston or maybe the Charles Playhouse
if you would like to try these avenues. I like the idea of working on the production in Boston, but I hate having it produced
here, I don't want my suburban friends clacking around about
it.

I love you, dear, and there's no bad side of Boston. There's
just a windward and leeward.

Love and kisses,

[*To Jon Stallworthy*]

14 Black Oak Road
28 June 1967

Dear Jon,

Remember me? I'm that poet from the United States that gets the lousiest reviews that Britain can hand out. You'd better give away the champagne to someone else. Tell me someone, just one person beside yourself, that likes my poetry. They've put me through a meat grinder, and I have come out weighing one quarter of a pound of hamburg. My heart and my hand is a chicken liver. Mixed imagery — very bad.

I don't know what it means to you, but finding out that I'm staying at the 69 Hotel has put me into gales of laughter. Impossible that there should be a hotel named that. What does one do in such a hotel and being the only woman at the conference? 69 Hotel! Don't they know I have a broken hip?

I hope you will meet me quickly at the Festival so that I don't become lost, and do please excuse the hysteria of this letter, but the despair over my English reviews plus my humor at the 69 Hotel have put me and my secretary into fits of madness.

Love to you,
Anne

[*To Jon Stallworthy*]

[*14 Black Oak Road*]
3 August 1967

Dear Jon,

You are simply the most. I really adore you. You're my editor and I'm proud of it. I adore being called the Nefertiti of New England. It was you that wrote that, wasn't it, although I think my reading on Sunday night was better than the reading on Thursday or so Lois tells me. I've been reading some of Fleur Adcock's poems and liking them tremendously.

The festival was very hectic. I never recovered from the plane trip and I drank too much to keep going and worse than that the broken hip was just a drag. At least I didn't follow Ted Hughes' suggestion of appearing in the wheelchair although the last night when Muggeridge introduced me as "the

lady with a stick" I felt like hitting him with it. I'm a lady
with a poem, not a stick.

I am glad I had a chance to show you some of the new
poems and that you liked some of them. The festival was a
humbling experience which is a good thing as against the
humiliating experience of my bad reviews. Do write when
you have a chance just to tell me you like me as much as I
like you.

                                                          Love,

Anne told several of her friends that she had not written a single
poem since breaking her hip. But between November of 1966 and
September of 1967, she had actually written ten new love poems: "For
My Lover, Returning to His Wife" in November; "The Break" in De-
cember; "You All Know the Story of the Other Woman" and "It Is a
Spring Afternoon" in February; "Moon Song, Woman Song,"
"Barefoot," and "The Ballad of the Lonely Masturbator" in May; "Just
Once" in June, and "The Papa and Mama Dance" in September.

[*To Philip Legler*]

                                           [*14 Black Oak Road*]
                                           Sept 6th, 1967

Dear Crazy Phil Baby dear,
    Yes. Yes. Yes. I hear. Your silence is loud. I guess you
still think "fame" has done me in. It hasn't but I guess you'll
always think so. It did do in my letter writing. Time too has
done in my letter writing. I don't write to anyone anymore.
The typewriter feels strange to my fingers, it feels difficult,
like pushing pebbles apart.
    I start teaching tomorrow and that will be daily a high
school class. I'm scared although I'm teaching it experimen-
tally along with an experienced teacher (one with a degree).
We are supposed to keep separate journals. So typewriter will
HAVE to come out of hiding. Poor typewriter with no new
poems. God, I wish I could write something. Have been
blocked for so long . . . nothing but one poem since the hip.
This has been a terrible year (not because of the hip really). I
hope this coming one won't be so difficult. It gets hard to
"keep going on." I think I have been silent because I was
down deep pretty depressed. It appears so. Appears in this

letter. Bizarre things have been happening upon me, things I can't speak to you about . . . but it is due to them that I don't write — not fame as you think.

Soon the yellow leaves will come to New England . . . ah ache and nostalgia and grief. And why? Grief comes because outdoors looks like a calendar? No, but . . .

And how are you? Your book? A job for this year? I wish (but you never comment on the wish) that you'd come to Boston to teach. Or near. Or, at least, Nearer.

Phil baby, how old are we? Are we 38 or 39? Think . . . soon it will be 40! What will we say to each other then? Or perhaps we will never say anything in person again. I mean, it doesn't look as if we have gotten together in all this time and why not, and if so how will we ever?

I can walk without a cane most of the time. I limp, but not too much.

Are you angry with me? Oh Phil, it's not the way you think it is. Not at all. I still respond to the yellow flower. I think I am the yellow flower. I bite myself and stick myself in a drink to revive.

Are you still there? Are you alright? Your silence worries me. I could bear you being angry rather than sick. Don't be sick. I'm sick enough for both of us.

Abundantly, lovingly, caringly,

[*To Anne Clarke*]

[*14 Black Oak Road*]
Sept 21, 67

Dear One,

I'm writing because I want to hear from you and this looks like ONE way of getting some mail from Hillsborough (sp wrong). We talk on the phone but that is necessarily brief and it would be good to get an envelope with some of you inside it.

I did tell you that I'm fat. The new me. It all comes from lying around drinking eggnogs and not walking. But I do walk now and most times without a cane, but I need to be the woman with girdle but I protest the discomfort and the idea and so I have just plain grown. Three sizes larger and a lot in the pot, quite a bit in the breasts and a lot in the round face. Can you imagine it, Anne? None of my clothes fit, even those that go in and out with me, seem to go out quite round in the belly. So I wear shifts and hope no one notices. I look four months pregnant. Tho I have lost about five pounds since I started teaching (nerves) and a recent gingivectomy (cut gums). I'm back on thorazine to try to calm down but I hope it doesn't make me too uncreative in the classroom. I love my students, even the very fresh ones. I'd like to stamp on the fresh ones just twice and then pick them up and hug them. It is very hard to teach with no curriculum, but so far so good or as the poet says, so good so far.

I'm supposed to be "keeping a journal" about the class and I really can't bring myself to write in the thing. I hate it. So far it's quite incoherent (that from Linda who reads it to see what in hell Momie is doing). She has pierced ears and very short skirts, first year of high school. She wants contact lenses and I don't blame her but we'll wait until her eyes stop changing. Joy seems older too, in her way, thinning out and even has a beginner bra. Egad!

How are you? How is your wonderful bathroom? How are the books you read and the things you think? Your dogs and their lives? Sarah? The weather? Your feelings? The room where we have room? As far as I'm concerned that room is still there, a little beaten down by the weather and time, but still standing and rather comfortable. Because I didn't like you leaving me with a dinner party doesn't mean I want to be kicked out permanently from the room. Sent away from the table, yes. But shoved out of the home, quite another thing. Surely the positive outweighs the negative? Surely friendship and love prevail? I ask. I feel you turned from me and only because of that stupid night. I've never given a dinner party since, or really before as a matter of fact. Two to two conversations is more my style. A lot of people confuse me.

I feel you are angry. It keeps me from relaxing in the letter. Am I crazy? (Yes I know I am, but is this feeling crazy?).

I love you,
Anne

[*To Muriel Rukeyser*]

[*14 Black Oak Road*]
November 1, 1967

Dear Wonderful Muriel,
   I still keep "The Speed of Darkness" on my desk. It glistens
here like the first washed flowers in spring when you sent it
to me. Section one goes whammy! Then flows out like an in-
fusion of blood into the body. I just want to tell you again,
beautiful Muriel, mother of everyone, how I cherish your
words as much as the memory of your good face.

Love,

[*To Zelda Wirtschafter*
Director, Teachers' and
Writers' Collaborative]

[*14 Black Oak Road*]
February 14, 1968

Dear Zelda,
   [. . .] I'm trying to get ahold of a picture of the graffiti
blackboard. I think Lila Ederman's idea of giving every kid a
piece of chalk is good. However, we didn't give it as a
homework assignment but as a class participation project.
Our kids were shy at first with the exception of a couple of
bold ones. We found one of the most interesting things was
the way they added to each other's graffiti changing its meaning. Sometimes the most sullen and refractory students became leaders of the day. One of the main things we stressed
was courage. It was called a courage day as well as a graffiti
day. I don't think people write on walls to get a wide audience but rather to declare that piece of wall their own. I think
it is the little child in us who wanted to crayon where you
weren't supposed to. The project is disturbing to conformists
who have buried that child and possibly at the same time
buried the writer in themselves. It is interesting that we see
graffiti as a private-public thing. I think maybe the white
conservative neighborhood paints over the graffitis that exist
whereas in the ghetto areas it is allowed to last. The first
thing that was written on our graffiti board was done by me

. . . something like "perhaps God does exist." This theme was never taken up in anyone else's graffiti. I'm not sure why.

I've been reading [Herbert Kohl's] *Thirty-six Children*, and it's so moving.

Best,

In May of 1968, C. K. Williams became another of Anne's favorite poets. Always ready to help new poets she found exciting, she wrote a letter in praise of his work to Houghton Mifflin, recommending that they publish him. In September they accepted his book *Lies*.

[*To C. K. Williams*]

[14 Black Oak Road]
May 15, 1968

Dear Charlie,

You are a magnificent writer. Your poems burst with originality. I like best the poem to Anne Frank and have read it over many times. I like "Saint Sex" and "Tails" and many images in other poems. I read with fascination and a deep envy. I questioned where I was going as a poet and all I haven't done. Please send me more as they come, and if there is anything I can ever do to help you get any of these published, let me know.

Have I got it right or wrong? Do you have a book out entitled *Lies*, or is this the book? If you have a book, I would love to see it.

With all best wishes,
Anne

Julie Joslyn wrote Anne from a mental hospital in 1968. She identified strongly with Anne's confessional style and needed to talk with a kindred spirit. Anne wrote back, and a small nourishing correspondence began.

[*To Julie Joslyn*]

[14 Black Oak Road
circa June 1968]

Dear Julie Joslyn,

I thought of wiring you three daffodils but I write you on yellow-sun paper instead.

The sun will come back, I promise. I don't know when . . .
but it will, it did for me. True, it hides from me now and
then and those are bad days and sometimes even months.
Still, I am much better. Your letter evokes my feelings of the
past and how well I know how it is with you!

I really did think of sending you those flowers and just this
morning, walking into my doctor's office I saw clusters of
dandelions growing on the lawn and I thought dandelions
were more sun-like. Could you find any? I think if you
would try to look at one — not even three to begin with —
just one, it might help. I have a feeling I could hand you one
and you'd look at it.

Who are the Berrtons? I mean the people who introduced
you to my poems?

Do you know my poem *"Live"* [LD]? It ends "so I say live,
because of the sun, the dream, the excitable gift." I too, am in
love with the sun. However and strangely, I take a tran-
quilizer, Thorazine, that makes me sun-allergic so that the
thing I love most is a poison. But now that summer comes
close I think I'll try not taking it.

Yes, you can go far down — but you can come back up . . .
you don't need to die down there — and I know it's hell . . .
but at least you can reach out to me and to your doctor. That
is truly hopeful. I used to say to my doctor "You're not crazy
if you can find one sane person who you can talk to."

Let me know if you find a dandelion or a daffodil.

> *Best wishes,*
> *Anne Sexton*

Harvard's Phi Beta Kappa chapter elected her an honorary member
on June 11, 1968. In a traditional ceremony in Sanders Theater, Anne
became the first woman ever to join the 187-year-old chapter. Reading
"December 17th" from "Eighteen Days Without You," [LP], she dedicated her part in the proceedings to the memory of Robert Kennedy,
who had been assassinated on June 5.

[*To Paul Brooks*]

14 Black Oak Rd.
[*circa June 1968*]

Dear Paul,

Your note is very touching. I wish that I had a lovely card to reply on. But this yellow working paper is all I have on hand, except business paper that I use for the most formal of occasions such as asking for fellowships.

Your note overwhelms me. What can one say in reply? Tell you that of course I am a witch, an enchantress of sorts and have already been worshipped and hung and in the same order. Now and then. But not very often. And in your case, I very much had the cold feet to think of reading in front of you. I may not look like a coward but I am. At any rate I am enchanted by your note and keep it by me for dark hours. There are a lot of dark hours, the hard hours.

I do suppose poetry is an oral art, as you said after the reading. However, when I am dead, it will be only the page and Houghton Mifflin have put it on the page for me. You can do no more. You gave me a cover I liked (which wasn't easy, I guess); advertisements just where I wanted and prayed for them to be but didn't dare ask after all that fuss with the cover. You may not be aware, but *The New Yorker* and *The New York Review of Books* is where I wanted ads. And where I found them. My thanks to someone and everyone. I suspect you had a part in it.

You treat me so well at Houghton Mifflin, as I said to Anne Ford, "it is better than having a lover!" Further, my books are in print. I think I am the luckiest of poets. If and when I have a next book I may have to ask for larger print as this enchantress is getting older and finds it hard to read the print at these poetry readings. See, even witches, those of us who survive worship and hanging, get old.

. . . But perhaps the work stays young! That is all that matters.

And letters like yours remind me.

Affectionately,
Anne

While Anne was teaching her class at Wayland High School, one of her students set "Ringing the Bells" [TB] to music. The idea caught her interest, and she began reading her poetry to any accompaniment her student could score. The chamber rock group "Anne Sexton and Her Kind" eventually grew out of this unique duet. Anne read "Old" [PO], "Cripples and Other Stories" [LD], "Love Song to K. Owyne" [PO], and "Man and Wife" [LD], using her voice like an instrument, accompanied by a combo of guitar, electric piano, drums, flute, and bass. With Bob Clawson as manager, the group was soon booked for their debut at a Boston nightclub, as a benefit performance for the presidential campaign of Senator Eugene McCarthy.

[*To Lois Ames
England*]

> *July 30, 1968
> Sexton-Weston
> U.S.A.*

Dear Lois-of-the-ghost-of-the-Christmas-Come,
    This will be my only letter as it is the only two cents stamp I have. And as you know — I can't get to drugstores and post-offices without aid. My secretary (aide) is away until after Labor Day ... Well nevermind that — this is to tell you that I miss you. I have been (except for three hours yesterday) so busy! I can't retell everything but a few high points (not very interesting ones, but informative) ... "Anne Sexton and her Kind" performed its first performance at Eugene's 2 in Kenmore Square. A benefit for McCarthy and no dough, but a trial run anyhoo. No one could hear us, people drank and talked, the cash register bonged, the glasses clinked, but a few people (the important ones) liked it a lot. Maxine said we'd make a fortune — tho she's aghast at my performing self — she says it's Elizabeth. Did I ever tell you about Elizabeth? She's manic-Anne and sometimes sexy-Anne. You've seen her. But perhaps didn't know her name. My father called me "a-little-bitch." I thought he meant my name was Elizabeth. Nothing to do with your dear girl, of course. Just my psychiatric history by way of Dr. Martin ... At any rate we got a PAID ($1000.00) performance for Sept. 20th at DeCordova Museum in Lincoln. A very swinging place. It was where I first heard Merwin (my first reading ever).

We went to Nantucket and it told us Islands are great, so
Kayo and I are going to Bermuda on August 19th to 29th.
Only costs $700 in all for the whole thing. Luckily I got a
good advance yesterday for *Love Poems* and it will cover it.
We are renting motor bikes, sailboats, fishing, I hope making
love, eat, swim, read. I HOPE kayo will talk to me and like
me. What a pitiful wish, really . . .
Linda, my dear one, my pal of my heart, has gone off to
camp. I miss her. Took her up Sunday and stayed for a horse
show (flies, dust — ugh — as bad as Africa) . . . I haven't written her. I love her too much to write. [. . .]
    How is ENGLAND, TED HUGHES, ASSIA, THE TOWN,
THE CITY, THE STORY?????? Tell me . . . .
            . . . . .August 2nd now . . .
I mean to ask Bob [Ames] for dinner shortly, a swim and
dinner now that things are quieting down.
    The *Look* article is not finished yet. I've seen the pics, tho,
and they aren't bad . . . from what I could tell from seeing
one-inch contacts and trying to guess which they'll use. They
may use my new poem "The Firebombers" [BF]. I've forgotten
if you like it or not. I have a feeling you didn't??? She wants
to use something new and, I think, something to show I care
about the world, the war and all that temporary crap. I do
care, but I don't think caring is the same as good writing. . . .
She is coming up August 13th to start *The Paris Review* stuff.
I wish you had TOLD ME you wanted to do that. I mean you
could have done it already!!! [. . .]
    Some t.v. man was here to do a program for NBC or CBS . . .
but he didn't make any sense. I think he is just a dreamer.
But it WAS funny. He had the idea I'd travel in a mobile unit
all across the country tracking down the U.S. poets. Can you
imagine!
    What date do you come back?
    Any chance of being here for DeCordova? I wish you could
be. Ted Hughes has a MARVELOUS poem in the *Critical
Quarterly*, "Second Bed-Time Story." If you are seeing him,
ask him to show it to you and give him my compliments and
my best wishes.
    Please write. After all I'm just hibernating in the suburbs

whereas you are getting THE STORY. Please send some brief reports to your girl

Anne of Weston
Anne

Joyce Sexton loved animals and kept a small mouse named Sassafras. Inspired by Joy's pet and the mice in the Kumin summer home in New Hampshire, Anne and Maxine began another children's book. *Joey and the Birthday Present* (McGraw-Hill, 1971) was begun on the typewriter at the edge of Anne's swimming pool. Maxine recalls, "[we] took turns banging away on it, then got very caught up in the story and continued in the study, under air conditioning, much arguing and jollying along about the dialogue . . . I do remember arguing about who first thought of the brilliant key line in *Joey!* 'And they both agreed that a birthday present cannot run away.' It seemed to fall so right that we were both sure it had occurred to us separately." For each woman these collaborations were a further celebration of their friendship.

[*To Joyce Sexton*
Warner, New Hampshire]

[*14 Black Oak Road*
circa August 1968]

Darling Joy!
How wonderfully you did in the show! Wow! Zow! Poew! Bow! Just think, a second in eqetation (sp all wrong!). You ride really well this year and we are happy to see it. It was fun to see you get those ribbons but more fun to SEE YOU. I felt we were really close even though it was a show day. I know that you made a special effort to be close and so did I and boy it was great! It made me very happy, dear Joy, and all bubbling inside. It was fun to see you eating those eggs with such energy. I hope Nana's food helps some and that you did share it with Linda. I know you did!

The lamb is funny. I like it a lot. Nice wooly coat. I like lambs.

The MOUSE. EKK I THINK IT IS PREGNANT. What did I ever do — getting you Stardust just because of that story — and because I knew you'd really like one. I knew all right. But why did we get a boy? Oh well, perhaps you can give away the baby mice. Meme says baby mice are no bigger than a fingernail. That's terribly small. Will they escape through the cage? If so we can't have them in the house!!!!!

At any rate they seem happy together, but I meant to Sas to get a pal, not a lover! Maybe it doesn't matter to Sas. After all, lovers are pals also. At any rate husbands are.

Cut your fingernails! Write us letters! Write Mrs. Alfred Sexton, Cambridge Beaches, Bermuda . . .

I love you and miss you!!!!!
MOM   XO
XO
XO
XO

Here are some stamps.
Give 2 to Linda & tell her the address.

[*To Lois Ames*
London, England]

[*14 Black Oak Road*]
August 30th, 1968

Dear Lois of London,

Yes! Yes! I am all right. . . I am fine. I am not stretched out, crucified on a hospital bed with tubes feeding me or sucking me out. I am here, in Weston, sitting at the kitchen table with an aqua table cloth, windows open on the COOL summer day, radio on my right playing opera which I usually hate but love today. I don't know why I'm so happy today. It's unexplainable. It's like being in love. I'm not (in love) but my spirits are doing well by me. I soar. Partly it's the weather and the lack of having to hide from the sun. The autumn beginning . . . the sad autumn of the yellow leaves. I feel very alive. I woke up today to a birthday (interesting mistake!) no, an anniversary present from Billie — her Grandfather's clock that chimes, etc. I just adore its little telling the hours off. From my childhood of course — a good memory. I wish you were here so that I might share my exuberance. I just now thought of calling you in London — but instead I went to my study and brought typewriter into the sun of the kitchen. My galleys arrived today — *Love Poems*. I started to look at them and then opened a bottle of Taittinger's Blanc de Blanc (Kayo gave me a case for an anniversary present). What I like about owning that case — is no one can TELL ME what is inappropriate and wrong about drinking a bottle when I'm in the mood. Since opening it I've had a lunch of hot dogs, champagne, and five pieces of cantaloupe melon. On such a day one must spoil themselves, one must rise to the occasion!!

So instead of galleys I write you this note!! It looks like a small book. It is. *Love Poems*, that is.

We have the most pristine champagne glasses. My mother's. [...]

I don't know if we'll teach. It's being fought over in committee, school. A week will tell.

The world situation is so ghastly — Chicago police!! McCarthy not even getting his *ideas* in the platform, Checoslavakia (get that spelling) ... Maybe Joe McCarthy is right (was) and Communism is a great peril. I have never thought they'd fight and take over and exterminate like Hitler. Maybe Kayo is right???? What do YOU think?

By the time you get this God knows what will have happened.

When you return we must have a long look at the Plath book — to consider what can and must be done. I'm very stubborn so it doesn't amaze me why you bother. Still, no point in screwing your whole life up when you could Lillian Ross it — or novel it, or whatever. I can't picture Ted cooperating except on his OWN terms. Can you? Really really. [...] Joy is home. Oh, it's so good. And Linda on Monday. I really miss their affection and loving ways. Maxine isn't back from New Hampshire yet. Before I went away she was feeling better. Now I don't know. Yet it's a good sign she stayed in the country this long.

I'm okay — today. I'll stay that way for a while I hope. [My doctor] comes back Tuesday, but I don't see him until Thursday. Really it's good to be away from conflict. It upsets me. He and it.

love to you Lois of London and Ireland

[*To Shannon R. Purves*
Editor, Houghton Mifflin Company]

[*14 Black Oak Road*]
September 17, 1968

Dear Mrs. Purves,

I cannot recommend C. K. Williams' manuscript strongly enough. Although I am a wordmonger of sorts, he leaves me gasping. It would be a great loss to Houghton Mifflin if you turned this down. This is strong stuff, and at his best C. K. Williams is a demon. Poems like "Saint Sex," "Three Seasons and a Gorilla," "Patience is When You Stop Waiting," "To Market," "Before This," "Don't," "Tales" and "A Day For Anne Frank" announce the coming of a new poet on the American scene. He is a master of metaphor. Better than any living American poet.

The collection does have some weak poems, maybe five or six. In places it goes a little soft. A poem like "My Wife," although pretty and positive, only hinders. As I read and re-read the manuscript, I could not possibly concern myself about whether it should be published but only about placement of poems and trimming things up a bit, cutting out the weak ones, leaving in the ones that make you gag. What is Houghton Mifflin, jelly or something? The point isn't whether the poems are negative or positive but how alive they are. Subject matter itself is not as important as the genius inherent in a great metaphor.

I'm not sure "Saint Sex" should start the book. I think I would prefer "Patience is When You Stop Waiting" or maybe "Don't." The title is marvelous. I would be glad to go over the placement and the building of the book with Mr. Williams should he care to make a trip to Boston. It's a delicate thing, the question of what to take out and what to leave in, and I think the poet should have more to say about it. In the long run, he's the one that knows. The only important thing I have to say about cutting is that we not cut the strong ones. In these so-called "unpleasant poems" he is being a Fellini of the word.

What more can I say?

Sincerely,

[*To Lois Ames*
England]

[*14 Black Oak Road*]
Sept 25th, 1968

Dear Lois are you still in England?

Bob said on the phone that you might not come home until Oct 10th. So this is just a note in case I'm not talking to you in person on the phone in a week.

DeCordova ["Her Kind" performance] was pretty good. I mean it was a little great! It had defects. The past few days all I do is argue with Bob Clawson. He can be such a prima donna. Of course I love the child in him but sometimes I hate the child in him. Trying to work things out with agents etc. It is a costly production. We have a drummer now and he costs 100 bucks; a sound man who costs the same . . . and by the time everyone gets a cut I'm working for less than I get at a reading. I made only 50 bucks from DeCordova because we hired a tape man to do a professional tape and that cost 700.

The above looks like a bad arithmetic problem. The thing was great really. All last week I had unbelievable anxiety. God! I'd wake up in the night (do you recall) and take more and more pills and Kayo tried to stop me and I said crazy things like "There is a girl on the wall" and then I'd go over and bang on the wall. Or I'd say (he tells me) "Stop writing in the ashtray." I must be slightly psychotic from the pills. I smoke during this and keep falling asleep and burning things . . . I don't know what to do. I'm in such a panic that I won't sleep that even drugged I think I'm not sleeping. Lois, I don't *think* I want to die by mistake! I feel that I'm heading for trouble. After Sunday (when we go out on somebody's boat) I'm going back on Thorazine. It's the only thing that calms me down. Right now it's noon and I'm drinking — I use booze like medication, Deitz says.

Oh well.

Have I told you I have no job? However, maybe McLean's Hospital is going to hire me for a weekly poetry workshop.

Howard Moss turned down "The Assisign" (sp!) [The Assassin," BF] but said they loved it only [William] Shawn thought maybe they couldn't print it because I USED THE SUBJECT.

I hate writing letters. I feel like an Indian sending up smoke signals or that I'm writing a telegram and leaving the most important nuances out. Since I've become a poet I am not a good letter writer. I just dash them off, knowing it's not the real thing.

This morning I had a photographer here to take a pic for my book jacket. God I was frozen. I felt like a wax dummy or a picture of a picture.

I have no poems in me. I am an empty cup.

I have discovered a new poet, Charlie Williams, in Philadelphia, and have talked H.M. Co. into publishing him. I failed with Oxford and Michael Dennis Browne. But then I've only seen one poem of his. First time H.M.Co. has ever listened to me. The poems are snaky and entwined and fearful — very unconscious — they don't tell stories as I do — quite different really. I like liking poets who aren't like me.

I am a bride but there is no groom.

Enough of this. Keep writing poems and come home soon as you can. [...]

> I miss you!

> > > *love   Anne of Weston*

[*To Howard Moss*
THE NEW YORKER]

> > > [*14 Black Oak Road*]
> > > *September 26, 1968*

Dear Howard,

Sorry you couldn't take "The Assassin" [BF], but I'm glad to hear you admired it.

The point to this letter is a query. Why does Ed Sissman get $300 for signing his contract and I get $100? What more is there to say?

> > > *With best wishes,*

In September, Henry Rago, the editor of *Poetry*, invited Anne to read at "Poetry Day" in Chicago. In spite of the then current artists' boycott of Chicago in protest against police brutality at the Democratic Convention of 1968, Anne accepted the invitation. She coupled her Chicago commitment with a promise to read at Mundelein College the night before her appearance at Poetry Day. Despite her usual adroitness, she could not soothe Rago's anger when he discovered that one of his star attractions was giving a sneak preview.

[*To James Ciletti*
English Department
Mundelein College]

[*14 Black Oak Road*]
October 23, 1968

Dear Jim,

Those telephone exchanges with Henry Rago were the worst experiences with the world of poetry that I have ever had. He was unbelievably rude to you and haughty to me. That guy must be a real sob. I keep making up fantasy telegrams to him. For instance, the night before my arrival in Chicago "Dear Henry Rago, Due to illness and rudeness, I cannot appear," "Dear Henry Rago, Due to illness and hung up phone, I will not be at poetry day." "Dear Henry Rago, Due to honesty and belief, much like an illness in Chicago, I cannot appear at poetry day as I will be at Mundelein." Or at the end of my rope, "Dear Henry Rago, Fuck you."

As you can see, I have a tendency to be flamboyant, and I try to curb this as best I can. The reason I don't do any of this is really not because Henry Rago can ever do me any good or really any harm but that I was asked to be at poetry day last spring, and it was the first commitment I had and apparently NO ONE ever takes an extra date in Chicago when they're reading at poetry day. Thus it was my own fault for making arrangements with you, and you were very kind to let me off the hook. What I can't quite see is how he could be so rude to you when you were doing him a favor. If you had said, "I will not let you out of the reading at Mundelein," I would have come and he would have hated me. Now, I will meet him at poetry day and no matter how good an actress I am, I'm afraid my hostility will show, and he will hate me anyway. *Poetry Magazine* has a long history of helping young poets. It's inconceivable to me that he could be so insensitive with you —

never mind his attitude, his mightier-than-thou, prickish attitude with me. [. . .]

If you can arrange another reading with joint colleges participating, I would be very happy. I'm sure I'll give a better reading for you than I will for *Poetry* with old sourball in the audience. The thing is, Jim, I hardly ever get angry with people. Anger is the missing ingredient in my personality, and even as I feel it now, I'm not happy with it. There seems to be nothing to do with it. Well, I'll take all my swearing and put it in little star-crossed Christmas packages and bury it under one of the black oaks in the back yard.

With all best wishes,

In the fall of 1968 Anne took on a class at McLean Hospital — a private mental institution in Belmont, Massachusetts, where a number of well-known artists had been patients. She had said in a letter to a student, "Poetry led me by the hand out of madness. I am hoping I can show others that route." Although her work there was difficult, she endured its rigors for the sake of her students. She had not left her experience with mental hospitals far behind her. Later she wrote of the class:

> my first teaching of creative writing — [1968–]1969. Very difficult due to my insufficient knowledge of handling groups and the fact that the group was constantly changing and the aides were easily mixed up with the poets. Decided more commitment on the part of the poet is needed for me to be able to teach well.

In early 1969 Anne's attitude toward teaching metamorphosed. She held a poetry workshop in her home for a group of Oberlin students during their January work-study period, organizing the class around her own ideas and goals. She was delighted with the response: "Second class ever given during a January break at Oberlin — it was a charm — I *demanded* commitment and started to learn how to put love and teaching together."

She gave the Oberlin class again the following year with the same satisfying results. Anne had found that she could pass on much of what she had learned the hard way; now it was her turn to teach students "what to leave out."

[*To Lois Ames*]

14 Black Oak Road
Tuesday, Jan 11th, 1969

Dear Lois,

This is in between (I think) calls from you. It is nine at night. I have something to say. You are so valuable. You shine out. You are a magic star. You are a body of blood made beautiful.

If I threaten you with anger you do not shut off your lips. No, you stay right there on the phone. I can not even imagine enough anger for your love. I can not even imagine enough love for your friendship. You are gentle. You do not put me in chains — even when I read your journal you do not lock the lock. We are like two apples in a wooden bowl, wishing the best for each other. We are like two eyes, hoping to see the same way (Kayo is always saying . . . "focus, Anne, your left eye is going the other way"). And it does. I don't always focus. It upsets Joy too. Linda seldom. I speak to you of eyes and yet it is friendship that I think of. Lois, we are friends! How thirsty I am for that. How you feed me. How I admire and yet, sit back and adore you for your good friendship toward me. We're "gals" together. Not quite alone. Not ever alone. Yet!!!

Death troubles me and I speak to you of it. You do not stir from friendship. You are there, listening. Sometimes I feel that I come to you out of hell and you offer me milk.

NOTHING IS TOO GOOD FOR YOU.

Lois, come back every day for I'll come back for you.

Love,
Anne

Love Poems came out on February 13, 1969. In April she won the long-coveted Guggenheim Fellowship, and used the grant to complete her play *Mercy Street.* Spending April to August on staged readings and rewrites, she traveled back and forth to the American Place Theater in New York City. Lois Ames went with her; they lived at the Algonquin Hotel in between rehearsals and writing sessions. Anne was finally to see her words on stage in the off-Broadway production in October.

[*To Wynn Handman*
Director, American Place Theater]

[14 Black Oak Road]
April 15, 1969

Dear Wynn,

Here is the beginning of the Second Act going through the remembrance scene and the first section of the show. If you can piece it all together with the other rewrites, it is the whole second act. I don't know how original or expanded this new version is. After all, one can expand forever, and to write unconsciously is not difficult for me . . . still there were things that I like that I wrote before that I have kept. I will have to see how they play. As I said on the phone, the names of the Witnesses, that is the name[s] Charity and Backbiter, are something I've held on to despite Chuck's [Charles Maryan, director of *Mercy Street*] protestations. I don't think they're ever called that in the play as you hear it, so it makes little difference at this point. They come directly from "consorting with angels," that is, "one with an ear in his hand . . . one chewing a star . . . a people apart, performing God's function." I've told Chuck that the play could start with the poem "Consorting With Angels" [LD] but he feels — and this time I think he's right — that she ought to have a healthier attitude at the beginning of the play.

I'm so pleased you like what I have done. When I come up to New York for the long week, I will bring a friend [Lois Ames] along as companion and advisor. She is also my biographer, but the reason I bring her is that New York frightens me to death. It's that old "I'm just a country girl" line again.

Last night I dreamt that I saw the play and that Daisy was too old with wrinkles and large gestures and a little drunk, and I finally said to her, "You can't be Daisy. You've had too much to drink." And today as I dictate this to my secretary I am having a whiskey and water . . . whatever it all means. Yesterday, my biographer said "who will play you?" And I said, "Daisy's not me. I never broke his Goddamn clock."

I hope you like this rewrite, too.

Best wishes,

While in New York City to work on *Mercy Street*, Anne met her match in flamboyance. Brian Sweeney, an Australian businessman, had arrived in San Francisco earlier that year, enquiring of the customs agent: "Is Anne Sexton still alive?" He made his way across the country, seeking out anyone who could lead him to "Sexton." When they finally met, a boisterous friendship bloomed. During the time she worked with the American Place Theater, Sweeney filled her room at the Algonquin with yellow roses, and pampered her with caviar and Dom Perignon suppers at La Côte Basque. He bought up her books in all the New York bookstores and then complained to her publishers that New York City had "run out of Sexton." Each time they entered a taxi, he insisted on introducing her to the cabbie, emphasizing to the driver that his cargo was precious. Although their flirtation was to remain platonic, Anne was inspired to write the love poem "Sweeney" [BF] in tribute to her friend. Over the years cables, transoceanic telephone calls, and letters passed between two high spirits who were never to meet again.

[*To Brian Sweeney,*
telegram]

May 13, 1969

WRITTEN A POEM THAT STARTS MY SWEENEY, MR. ELIOT
SEXTON

Joan Sexton, Kayo's sister, had remarried in May. Six days after the ceremony, while honeymooning, she was killed in a car accident. The news of her death came to Anne in New York, at the Algonquin Hotel.

[*To Brian Sweeney*]

14 Black Oak Road
May 16, 1969

Dearest Sweeney,

I have taken great liberty with what you say to me and what you have told me. I fear you will not like what I have done to you. I pray that you will like that *I celebrate you*!! I don't mention that life is just an overture although I know you would want me to.

I tried to call you but you had gone to Ireland. I am in despair over my sister-in-law. We were very close. Mary [Meme] is my cleaning lady. She is practically illiterate. She doesn't even know I wrote a play. No news either on whether

they'll produce it, but it's getting more religious, and I think
they will. Let me know how you like the poem.

Love,
Anne

Yes Sweeney — I miss you!

[To Linda Gray Sexton
Warner, New Hampshire]

[14 Black Oak Road]
Thuseday [sic], July 3rd, 1969

Dear Linda Pie,
  Please excuse this typewriter. I'm not too good at it.
  I'm sorry you're so sort of homesick, sweetheart, god damn
it. I used to get so homesick at camp and god damn it I remember how it feels. I'm sorry too, that I didn't write sooner.
I have been so lonely . . . too lonely to write I guess. I like
calling better because then you're right there. I know a letter
from me isn't as good as one from Kenny [Linda's boyfriend],
but I can't do a thing about that. Believe it or not you're
going to love me a lot longer than you'll love him. Even if I
say my mother was mean, I still love her and anyhow she
wasn't *that* mean. I exaggerate everything I fear.
  I had the packing taken off my teeth today. Only to have
him say the gums weren't healed and put more back on. It
has been very painful and without the packing the teeth look
awful, huge and sticking way out. The gum is way up high
and these funny looking teeth protrude forward. Gross!
  We had spaghetti two nights this week. Nana came to
dinner Sunday (cold lobster) and monday (spaghetti). Ed [Joan
Sexton's widower] is coming to Nana's for the weekend. I
don't look forward to seeing him. He simply reminds me of
the wedding and the sudden violent death. It feels like he
took her away to death. I say feels, because it is only an irra-
tional thought, a feeling, not a fact. Still, see him we will and
nothing can stop it . . . Don't worry, I'll be nice to him.
  Daddy and I think that we can't adopt Sherlock. Although
he is certainly a lovable and cuddly dog it just isn't in the
cards. I love him. One time when Joy was visiting Lorna we
sat and had coffee with Liz and Sherlock curled up in my lap.

He's so cute . . . But Penny would be too jealous. It was different with Gidget. Gidget, after all, was Penny's puppy and
you are never jealous of your own child/dog. I like Sherlock,
especially because he is a runt . . . I like runts.

Earlier this week I had a heart-to-heart talk with Judy [Ku-
min, Maxine's younger daughter]. She advising me on what
it's like to be a young girl and me telling her about possibly
you wanting to go on the pill for birth-control reasons . . .
Naturally I didn't go into the specifics of you and Kenny, but I
did value her advice. Seeing she is on the pill and is a *little*
older and wiser than you are (and yet younger and more hip
than I am), I thought she might have some wise words . . .
And she did. Today she brought in a poem she wrote to you.
It doesn't say it's to you but I guessed from the poem. It's a
good poem and I told her to send or give it to you. I think
you'll like it although you may resent the message. The main
message is that it's a trap. Nevermind me telling you what it
says. I just called Judy and she said I could send it to you . . .
She said she's worried that you'll say it's none of her business.
I said to her "Do you think she'll be angry with me for talking
about it with you?" She said "Well, we're too good friends for
her to mind too much." I hope you don't, bobolink. It's just
that I have no one to go to for advice. Hardly Daddy, who
thinks you should never go on the pill, even for cramps "You
suffered with cramps, Anne, so let her. Letting her go on the
pill is giving her a license to steal." "But Kayo," I answered,
"a relationship between a boy and a girl who are in love, no
matter what they do, is not stealing." "But a nice girl
wouldn't do that!" "Kayo, a nice girl is one who is kind to
people and loves people." "You're too god damned liberal"
                                          and so forth . . .

Linda, I think Kenny is right. The right thing, the nice
thing, the kindtoyourself thing is to wait until it will be
something special, not just fumbling on the grass or on a
couch or in a car. Wait for a bed. That won't happen for years
and I do really think it is something worth waiting for. I really think it's better to wait until you're older and readier to
handle it. But no matter what you do I'll stick by you, Linda.
As Dr. Deitz points out, girls in other cultures have married

and had babies by the time they are sixteen. But still, pie, you don't live in another culture do you!

Now I won't give another lecture about drugs but will save that for later. They worry me too.

As you can see you've been very much in my mind!!!!!! I keep having internal dialogues with you about all this. They are never arguments . . . We get along too well when we have serious talks. Usually we agree but I don't want to be too "liberal" and hurt you in any way.

I hope you like Judy's poem . . . You can send it back to me after you've read it.

The house is so empty. What will I ever do when you're both in college? or both married or both in europe for a year's study or something.

Continue to be a good CIT [counselor-in-training] dearest. I know you will gain a lot of experience and growth from this summer. Is it fun to be in a cabin with all the older girls? You might try talking over some of these things with them. Just to get their approach. Judy says if you ever want to talk things over with her she'll be glad to. Pedie is so sheltered, actually sheltered by her fat (I don't mean to be mean . . . It just occurred to me) that she isn't much help. Your friends this summer might be. I know I'm your good friend (if not your best) but I'd like you to have many and varied friends.

I ADORE YOU

XXXXXXXXXXXXXXXXXXXXXXXXXXXXXXXXXXXXXXXXXXXX
))))OOOOOOOOOOOXXXXXXXXXOOOOOOOOOXXXXXXXOOOOOOXXX
OOOOXXXXOOO

XO

[*To Linda Gray Sexton
Warner, New Hampshire*]

[14 Black Oak Road]
wed July 23rd, 1969

Dearest Pie,

It was wonderful to see you and be with you on your six-teen b - day.

I can't wait until you get home and we can talk, really talk.

I'm so worried about you ... sex, drugs, boys, cigarettes. You took a pack of Daddy's cigarettes he says. Why didn't you ASK for it instead of sneaking? I hope you don't decide to smoke but you are old enough to decide that. If you do decide to then you can buy your own cigarettes — not steal Daddy's. !!!!

I think I had trouble looking into your eyes because you seem to have grown far away. You seem to have lost the innocence I have always associated you with. Your attitude towards drugs "oh everyone is in drug trouble" for instance. Really, Linda!!! I feel very strongly and so does Daddy that you will not be allowed to go down to Ganny's again. You are just not properly chaperoned down there ... I'm sure that horrified you but it's the way we feel.

Now don't be too angry. That's all there is to that. I am worried. But I think part of it is needless. I needed to talk with you before I could go deep into your very beautiful blue eyes.

Speaking of eyes, honey, you left the little lenses box I bought you in the car along with some attachment for the radio. I'll try to remember to get daddy to bring it up on Sunday. I can't come up with him as Chuck is coming for the weekend to work on the play.

Do you like the radio? It was fun to give it to you because you wanted it so much. It will work much better at home. For god's sake don't step on it up there — or whatever. Take care.

I love you. You are closest to my heart, closer than any other human being. You are my extension. You are my prayer. You are my belief in God. For better or worse you inherit me.

You are doing a swell job up at camp and I am proud of you and happy for you. You are so busy and you do eat a lot. You look just great so the eating couldn't be hurting you any.

I've got to go and work on my play. Love you Miss Mumble Bug (new name) ...

XOXOXOXOXOX
Mom

[*To Brian Sweeney*]

[*14 Black Oak Road*]
Monday, July 28, 1969

Dear Sweeney, traveler and homebody,

Your call yesterday from Hong Kong was wonderful. I couldn't talk too openly as my director was sitting across the kitchen table from me. We worked like hell all weekend on *Mercy Street* and as I said made a trip to church ... I wish you could come to New York when they put it on ... aren't you curious to see it? Or would you like to read it — perhaps that's enough. Jean [Moulton, Anne's secretary] is away on vacation and I type this myself (usually a disaster) ... Years ago I could type a little but now I'm spoiled. But my desk is piled with mail I SHOULD be answering. Still, on this warm July afternoon you are the one my thoughts wander to.

I have spent the last two hours reading Protestant hymns. What doggerel! What tripe! It's a wonder that Christ can exist surrounded by so many foggy words. But then I've never felt he existed much for Protestants. My play ends with a hymn so I'll HAVE to find one ... The poem I wrote is almost doggerel too. I have just reread it. There are times when my genius fails, dear man, and I have no more talent than an eraser. Here it is ... maybe I can improve it later. Right now I'm exhausted from playwriting. [... She quotes from "Going Gone," BF.]

... Enuf poetry. Today's mail brings a letter from Mr. Anspach of the Algonquin Hotel saying he will give us a room for a month for five hundred dollars. It's a little more than I can afford but to hell with it — I like that Algonquin. We will arrive there on September 2nd. I hope there will be yellow roses from YOU. If not it really won't be the Algonquin at all. I'm sure without you it will appear very shabby. I plan one dinner at La Côte Basque for caviar no matter what. The play opens October 3rd.

I wish you could be there. Hell, Sweeney, you've jinxed New York City. I can't imagine the place without you!!

I tore up one letter I wrote you. Wrote it when I was drunk, or semi-drunk. Decided it was too heady, even for you. I assure you I'm cold sober right now.

That list of names. What do I do with them? Call them and ask them to take me to La Côte Basque? Can't read your handwriting well enough, if that's the case. I could use more friends in New York, even if it's only for a spaghetti dinner. That I pay for. Hell, I'm not cheap — just lonely. Lois is great but I suspect we'll need two faces.

Well, dear Sweeney, welcome home. I'll
[letter left unfinished]

[*To Brian Sweeney*]

> [*The Algonquin Hotel*
> *September 3, 1969*]

Dear Sweeney,   The rewrite finished. Today I'm a genius. I did something really fine. The room is air-conditioned (see above) thank God. The theater isn't. It's hell. 100 degrees in there. I have a fan but it isn't the same as air conditioning naturally. We walk back to save $$ and then drink in our rooms. Last night our dinner was cocoa in the room, but slept well. We had a grand lunch with lots of drinks and I'm burping Escargots right now. Haven't had time to go to ANY museum but perhaps. God, I wrote well today. God I'm happy. Sweeney, you are missed and often discussed.

> *love*
> *Anne (you are mentioned like the*
> *saints — in passing (says Lois)*

[*To Brian Sweeney*]

> [*The Algonquin Hotel*]
> *Sept 4th, 1969*

Dear Sweeney,

Just a note to tell you we are doing well. We had a reading of yesterday's rewrite and it went well. We also made a few cuts that were good. One of the actors, actresses actually, has it in for me and keeps saying "What can you expect of an author who can't spell" ten minutes later "What can you expect of a writer who can't punctuate." And she sounds serious! Oh dear. Lois just said I knocked myself too much (the conversation having drifted to how lovely my mother's handwriting was and how bad mine is.) Lois is a fine woman. Right now she is sewing a dress. Shortly she will do an interview with me for a newspaper.

love,
Anne

[*To Brian Sweeney*]

[*14 Black Oak Road*]
Saturday October 25, 1969

Dear BRIAN SWEENEY,

This is just a note from Weston. Lois and I are no longer in that big city. (I was there 2 days this week, one night for a reading, one night to see the play and on that afternoon I gave an interview to *The New York Times* ... how stupid it was, the interviewer asking "How many times have you tried to kill yourself?" ... what does that have to do with *Mercy Street.* Something perhaps because the heroine maybe kills herself in her imagination, maybe because neither Lois and I can decide which. It's all nonverbal, the killing, as she does it without saying — if you happen to look she is taking pills — but you might be looking somewhere else as other people are talking ... At one point *The New York Times* said they were only interested in doing an interview if the play was a hit. And now that the show has been opened for two weeks is it? or one? they decide to do one. At The American Place they stagger reviewers so that there is no opening-night farce. The reviewers have been coming all this week and the reviews come out this Tuesday, October 28th ... Naturally I'm on tender hooks. I confess, Sweeney dear, to wanting a few good reviews ...)

I came home from New York quite tired but exhilarated by the experience. I love theater people. Did I tell you that I had lunch with your friend — the reviewer fellow? (Forget his name). I liked him very much. You have good taste.

Lois did an interview for the book section of one of the Boston papers. I'll send you a copy but I'd like it returned. I'll mail it when Jean comes on Wednesday — also a program (which you can keep).

God, I've forgotten how to type! I tried to write a poem, the other day, but it didn't work.

Sorry I asked you for that money and after you had lost so much at the races. I sold $1,000 worth of stocks to get out of the hole. It's a bad show how broke I am. And I haven't gotten my bill from the Algonquin so I'm a little nervous in the checkbook area.

The theater was good for me. Perhaps next year I'll teach. People are good for me! If I'm not busy making *Mercy Street* into a film. That is also a possibility as well as a London and a Berlin production. Strange, Sweeney, to be sitting here at my desk with my daughter setting the table for dinner and wonder[ing] about all these seemingly big things. Perhaps I should worry about God — he's bigger than any of this. I'm glad you're straight with Him. I have yet to settle the matter. Oh, I really believe in God — it's Christ that boggles the mind. The play is about all that too.

Write!

Love, Anne

[*To Brian Sweeney*]

[*14 Black Oak Road*]
November 5, 1969

Dear, dear Sweeney,

Here are the reviews and a program. You may keep the program if you wish and a copy of William Raidy's article. As you will see, the reviews aren't too good. Then again, they are respectful. Naturally, I am disappointed, but you asked to see them, so here they are. The audiences are very attentive, and it is running an extra week because of demand. I wish you could have seen it. I still don't have a copy to send you.

I dreamt about you last night. Dreamt that you got me a reading in Australia and that I didn't even need a passport to get to you.

Love,
Anne

In 1969, Alice Smith wrote Anne from Brooklyn, New York. She too had responded to the anguish of Anne's poetry. For Anne, Alice became the quintessential fan, writing long detailed letters, sometimes daily. Anne appreciated the "gutsy woman" who bedeviled Houghton Mifflin for more Sexton books in more bookstores, and bigger and better advertisements.

[To Alice Smith]

[14 Black Oak Road]
December 3, 1969

Dear Alice,

Just a short letter to tell you I think of you often and that I love your letters and sharing your life. You are so strong. You amaze me. Not because you were once sick and, therefore, supposedly weak, but that you are an outstanding person . . . stubborn, intelligent, intuitive, perceptive and one who sees beneath the facade of other people's lives. You have a style to your life that I envy. You know how to take care of yourself. You know how to love yourself. I envy. You know how to reach out. I, too. A description of my birthday would make you wince. Of course that *New York Times* article did not help. I loved your letter to them. You told them off for me in a way I couldn't. You know, Alice, you may feel that you are lucky to have Doctor Eleanor, but I'd say she was lucky to have you.

I seem to be blocked and unable to write which is hell. I've written one poem this fall, and it stinks. I am tutoring, or rather teaching, a young Oberlin student who had a nervous breakdown this fall. He sees his psychiatrist twice a week and me once a week. His writing is improving as well as his health. I'm beginning to think more of myself as a teacher . . . at least of poetry.

I hope you have solved the problem of the heat permanently. The cold weather is settling in. If only I were writing, I wouldn't care what the weather was.

I meant that "mercy" . . . oh, you know what I meant. Among other things I meant, may you always have mercy in your life unlike Daisy. The fact that you went to the play the last night touched me very much. If I couldn't be there, at least you were. Alice, I had the feeling that Marian [Seldes, who played Daisy] was getting a little hysterial in the role to-

ward the end. I love her dearly, but it's something I always
worried about. Do you know what I mean?

Be well.

Love,

[*To Anne Clarke*]

[*14 Black Oak Road*]
Friday, Dec 26th, 1969

Dear One,

We gave Linda a record of opera arias and the voice is magnificent. A lovely woman singing always makes me think of
you. It's Puccini. The song of a beautiful woman — her soul
exposed — her voice lifting like a kite — an eternal sound.
It's all you, Annie. All and more. [. . .]

It's been a busy year for me. My play, *Mercy Street*, came
out off Broadway this October. If you get *The Times* you may
have read about it. I loved the theater people, very genuine
and loving, intuitive and down to earth, open — not boxed in.
A friend, Lois Ames (psychiatric social worker, writer) stayed
with me in New York for the two months I was there. Lois is
very funny and we had a lot of laughter and did a lot of hard
work. We came home Saturday night to Tuesday morning —
so to keep in touch with family as well as work in New York.
I kept a monk's schedule and got enough sleep — lived on
caviar which I have really acquired a taste for (what a sentence!). Anyhow Guggenheim paid the bill and now I am
stone cold broke. But it was fun. The play got so-so reviews
— some really awful ones — the ones in *The Times* were po-
lite and encouraging. Now that it is over I feel the play was a
failure actually — but maybe I'm too close to it. The audiences were packed and attentive — but I felt the leading lady
was hysterical. Anne, maybe I wrote it hysterically, I can't be
sure.

I'm blocked now. Nothing comes. A drought. No poems
. . . none, nothing. I've written one poem since June and that
one was so bad that I've lost it. Well, heaven sent — a job
teaching at Boston University starts in a week or so. I love

teaching but it scares me too. However, it will be good for me, something useful. [. . .]

Joy has a barn and a pony, out back, out back of the swimming pool . . . in the midst of the black oaks.

I don't drink martinis anymore. Jack Daniels, Canadian Club or rot-gut bourbon. Time passes . . . I smoke more and I cough more. I am size 14-16 . . . big belly . . .

Have you read *Slaughterhouse Five* by Kurt Vonnegut? And *Mother Night* by same? He is my this-year favorite. Very funny. His style is so simple.

The novel I started to write before I broke my hip is still unfinished . . . I reread it after I got back from New York and thought "so what!" and put it away. Just a woman's story, another woman's story and so what.

Kayo is well, overworked, underpaid and unfulfilled — but he is still funny. He is getting quite gray. I am too, only I get my hair tinted so you can't tell.

Well, that's all for now — I mean that's my news. So how about yours? And if not news, how about your soul? The lovely woman is singing and I think it's you, magnificent you.

My love to Sarah but most to you.

Me

With the new year came a new challenge: her appointment as Lecturer in English at Boston University. She ran a poetry workshop two hours each week, which was as special to her students as it was to her. As Suzanne Rioff wrote at the end of the first term: ". . . most of all, Mrs. Sexton has made me ultimately accept and rejoice in that irrevocable state of being — a poet. To me, this is the immeasurable achievement of a great teacher."

She continued teaching in the graduate creative writing program with George Starbuck, John Barth, and John Malcolm Brinnin until her death in 1974. She corresponded with her students outside the class, following them as they moved beyond her. Many went on to appear in magazines and to publish books. Anne had achieved her goal as a teacher: her students had learned to create without her.

[To George Starbuck]

> *[14 Black Oak Road]*
> *January 28, 1970*

Dear George,

   I hear that there is a possibility that you may be in Boston next year at BU of all places — running things. I am teaching a creative writing course there. I hope you don't fire me. I really miss having you around, dear one, and hope you will become a Bostonian once more. Arthur [Freeman] and I think it would be great if the three of us plus Maxine could duplicate that first reading we did at the Poets' Theatre just for laughs or just for tears.

   The main purpose of this letter is HELP, HELP. I am trying something different and would like to know if you think it works. I plan a whole series of poems, possibly a book if it comes to that, but I want to know if these two poems make any sense to you, and if you could pick them apart, I will buy you a drink when you get here. I'd like to explain what I'm doing in these poems, but I feel it would be wrong. I would like to know what you think I'm doing. And naturally, if you think I'm doing it well. HURRY, GEORGE BABY. I NEED YOU.

> *Love,*

   Anne had begun work on a new book of poems that winter. Inspired by Linda's constant reading of the fairy tales of the Brothers Grimm, Anne began to study her daughter's battered blue volume. Eventually she asked Linda for a list of her favorite stories and began to transform them into poems: "The Gold Key," "The Little Peasant," "Hansel and Gretel," "The Twelve Dancing Princesses." She called these modifications of the Brothers Grimm her "transformations."

[To George Starbuck]

> *[14 Black Oak Road]*
> *March 11, 1970*

Dear George,

   I send these again with two new ones thinking you may have lost the others, thinking that perhaps a second try . . . ?

Maybe they're all worthless and that's why you don't want to comment. Maybe I'm coughing down a bad cellar hole? Maybe I ain't got nottin to say? Maybe these are loose and flaccid? You said they were hard to comment on because they weren't in iambic pentameter couplets. Neither is the poem "That Day" and you liked that.

You answered Maxine about her book so fulsomely that I think in this case I'm a little jealous. True, this isn't a book, but I'd like to know what you'd think if I made it a book. At any rate, read "The Little Peasant" [TR]. It might amuse you.

I am thrilled to hear that you are coming to BU. It will be wonderful to have you so close after all these years. I hope you will see to it that I continue to be hired there. I enjoy teaching as well as needing the money. I even think I'm good at it in my kind of inarticulate half-assed manner. If you weren't so happily married, I'd have an affair with you. That's just a fact for you to put in your Univac machine.

Love,

[*To Thomas Alexander*
Cape Cod Community College]

[*14 Black Oak Road*]
May 11, 1970

Dear Mr. Alexander:

I would love to come and read my poetry and talk about it some day next year. It looks like you really have interesting lecturers, and I bet Jim Dickey set you on fire. He's quite a showman.

My fee is $1500 plus expenses. However, the expenses would be negligible, and I am willing to modify the fee somewhat because of your proximity. Let me know how this strikes you and your budget as my calendar is getting full for next year.

Sincerely,

[To Philip Legler]

[14 Black Oak Road]
May 19th, 1970

Dear Phil Baby,

I will have to burn your letter as incriminating evidence . . . but that's not the point. Your letter is full of love and I wish I could keep it. I do know you love me more than most people do. Perhaps my husband more because he had to live with me. Sometimes I think he deserves an award for putting up with me. Other times I think he's pretty lucky. Lucky because I'm quite naturally a loving, affectionate person. But then, even that can get to be a bore.

I'm sorry I put your hand in a tin box. God, I'm sorry. I didn't mean to really. You know I've never slept with anyone on a reading . . . never a one-night stand . . . never something so casual or lighthearted. I'm just not the type. I'm a pretty faithful type when you come right down to it. Sleeping with someone is almost like marrying them. It takes time and thought. If you lived in Boston or I lived where the lovely fog horns are . . . but even then I'm not sure. Just that it wasn't possible that time. I've got to be true to myself as well as to you. Further, I think I'm so busy fighting the suicide demons that I have little time for love. You saw how I go to sleep — not sleep at all. You said it [:] "death touched me." I hope to hell my present shrink can help me work this out before it's too late.

I zapped into your life and I'm so glad I did. I'll never really zap out. Put me there, friend, friend, forever.

. . . next day . . .

I've been out killing dandelions. It's a lovely spring day. I think I'll go out into [it] again. The manager (Bob) of "Her Kind" (my rock group) is coming over for lunch, or rather bringing the lunch. I will sit in the shade (thorazine makes me allergic to the sun) and he will sit in the sun. How I miss that!

I finished that fairy tale ("The Maiden Without Hands") [TR] last week and am thinking about doing Hansel and Gretel. My transformations of the Brothers Grimm are full of

food images but what could be more directly food than cooking the kids and finally the wicked lady. Smack in the oven
like a roast lamb.

Readings are accumulating for next year. I'll do few of them
I hope. Enough to pull in some dough to help out but not
enough to drain me too much. I find them very hard to do . . .
particularly those informal classes where (as they say) I can do
anything I want . . . Mostly I don't want. That's the trouble.
But you, Phil, make it easy on me and helped in every way. I
thank you. That's still the nicest Holiday Inn I ever stayed in.
And I can remember those ghost-like fog horns. I remember
too you tucking me in bed and patting my head so gently. I
don't forget! Love to you, my dear,

Annie Babe

[*To Thomas Alexander*
Cape Cod Community College]

[*14 Black Oak Road*]
May 26, 1970

Dear Mr. Alexander: Dear Director of External Affairs:

I suppose I could come for $775 although it's a little low
from my point of view. However, I have my own proposal to
make. I propose that you come up to Weston, pick me up and
drive me down to Hyannis or that someone does. Thus I will
be saved the arduous trip. I will be glad to talk informally
after the reading, but I would prefer not to meet classes.

February 10th is okay with me if you can put up with the
thought that there may be a major nor'easter that day.

It occurred to me that if you paid Jim Dickey $775 plus ex-
penses, you must have paid him at least $900, or let me put it
this way, it must have cost you $900. I would think if you
could raise it for Dickey you could raise it for Sexton, but I
hate to quibble. What do you think?

Sincerely,
Anne Sexton
Director of Internal Affairs

[To Paul Brooks]

[14 Black Oak Road]
July 17, 1970

Dear Paul,

Welcome back from Europe! You were missed. David Harris handled my problems and much to my advantage. Houghton Mifflin is certainly the most gracious publishing house in America. It is a pleasure to be connected with you in my own small way.

The honorary degree from Tufts was wonderful and further, it saved my job at Boston University where I am teaching creative writing and discovering poets and developing poets who will outlast me. In a few years their manuscripts will be coming in to Houghton Mifflin. It is kind of like believing in God to see the young ones lift up the banner.

You will find on your desk a long involved letter from a fan of mine, Miss Alice Smith. She came to the party. I have kind of taken her under my wing. She's a spunky old gal (and extremely intelligent) and she has been promoting my books in every bookstore in New York City for five or six years. I would say that many of my sales can be attributed to her zeal. She lives in Brooklyn on welfare, has been very seriously ill for the last year, and six years ago she had spent four years in a state mental hospital. My books, she tells me, contributed to her coming to terms with life and getting well. This is not an uncommon experience for me and, of course, I get hundreds of letters like her first one, but for some reason I took her on.

She has made me very aware of the lack of advertisements for my book. Perhaps this can be remedied in the future. I sell well, to be sure, but think of how well I would sell with an ad in *The Village Voice* and a large ad in the Sunday *New York Times*. Doubleday did James Dickey a full-page ad for his poems in the Sunday *Times*. Naturally, I was jealous. Your advertising manager stated to Alice Smith that ads don't sell books. That's a hell of an attitude for an advertising manager to have! He doesn't even believe in his own work. I find that strange. It would seem to me that it might be time to write a NEW ad telling the public that all my books are in print and that they're selling damn well. *Love Poems,* in this short time and as you undoubtedly know, has sold over 14,000 copies. Well, Paul, I don't mean to be a whining author begging for advertisements and becoming a fool, but I did think I ought to let you know how I felt about this. Maybe the advertising manager doesn't care if my books sell, but I know you do, and I know you will fight for me if it's within reason.

I'm working away on a new book. There was an article in the *Globe* about it as I spilled the beans on my secret. I would send you the *Globe* article except that I think the poems will present themselves better than the news media could. It's something quite strange and different, and I'm having an awfully good time.

With love,

[*To Tillie Olsen*]

[*14 Black Oak Road*]
July 21, 1970

Dear Tillie,

I haven't meant to keep you waiting, and I imagine you had given up on me, but I didn't know how to answer your letter. I am glad that there were some things in *Love Poems* that you liked. I understand you could not write to me when you were busy with your own work. At that crest time one must hoard their own fullness. And the fact that you did not write later can be understood. I am a terrible correspondent myself and have slighted people — people whom I love — without meaning to. And over-sight can be so easily forgiven. I do not usually harbor grudges.

I was so shocked those many years ago when you said that I shallowized Maxine's book that I could have not possibly written you a letter of anger — it was like a knife in the back. No, Tillie, I never understood what you meant. If you would ever care to tell me, I would surely listen and listen hard. It wouldn't matter to me if I didn't love and respect you, but I do, and it still matters. One of Maxine's favorite writers is John Cheever. Maybe *he* shallowized her book. Her new book is about a black and white relationship (no influence by me).

Maybe you will like that better. Even if you can't explain the shallowizing to *me,* please know that I am your devoted reader and wish you all the best in your life and in your work.

Anne

In June, Anne wrote to Cindy Degener, who was now placing her poems, and suggested that she send "The Little Peasant" to *Playboy* for its Ribald Classics series.

[*To Claire S. Degener*]

[*14 Black Oak Road*]
August 18, 1970

Dear Cindy, — maker of the popular culture whoopee

I am pleased with the luck you've had in placing my poems. I'm not sure I approve and God knows what Houghton Mifflin will think when it comes time to publish the book. It worries me a little to be published in *Playboy.* They exploit women, and now I've got a hand in it. As you say, I'm "in," but I was never conscious of being out. Still, what the hell. I'd feel a lot worse if they'd turned them down.

Dickey at *Esquire* is my enemy as you know. He is a truly disgusting man although I like some of his work. He seems to like me but not my work.

It is good, Cindy, to know that what I am doing has worth. I have confidence in it myself, but it is nice to know I'm not alone.

Audience Magazine, as you probably know, is interested in seeing some transformations. They will pay $1000 for two of them or maybe one of them, depending on the length. I've been working on one all summer. Since about June 15th to August 14th. Sometimes it's hard to write a poem. As soon as *The New Yorker,* by the end of September, I think, turns them down, I will have two new ones for you.

Other matters. You did notice, I hope, the revised royalty statement from Houghton Mifflin. I improved things by over $700. I noticed that you took 10% commission on that. Last I heard you were taking 5% commission on *Love Poems.* It's probably not that important ... a matter of $20 probably, but you might make note of it for the future as *Love Poems* is

selling pretty well for a book of poems. I am having lunch
with Paul Brooks this Friday. Perhaps there will be more
news by next week. I will have to tell him I'm part of the US
heritage.

You're wonderful, Cindy. *Love and kisses,*

[*To Alice Smith*]

[*14 Black Oak Road*]
August 19, 1970

Dear Alice,

Here are two poems. "Sleeping Beauty" [TR] took me from
July 5th to August 17th . . . a long block was in process. It
was a difficult poem for me as you might imagine and seems
now to deal with one of the themes of *Mercy Street.* As many
times as I saw that play, I never worked it out. I guess
therapy is the place for it, not the stage.

Other matters. We [Her Kind] gave a concert July 24th at U
of Mass. and I wish you could have been there. It was sensa-
tional. We had the world's best sound system provided by the
University, and it was held outdoors to about 2,000 people. It
was a very warm night and just the right atmosphere. We
didn't have Mark [Levinson]'s hysterics to put up with, and it
was a great relief. Our new bass player is a black fellow
named Hank [Hankinson]. When not playing, he is a barten-
der at the Harvard Club. His playing is not as good as Mark's
but he will do. He sings a song that Steve [Rizzo] wrote to
one of my poems. Steve used to sing it but it just didn't
sound professional. Hank has a nice voice and it was a beautiful moment so unlike Emmanuel Church fraught with ten-
sions and dissent and sound problems. I wish we could save
the money to buy our own sound system and maybe we will.

Other matters. This summer I've been seeing Dr. Chase
three times a week and working at a high pitch. Everything
was going fine until a week ago last Monday when I woke up
feeling very strange. Matters got worse and I went in to see
her. I could hardly talk. About the only thing I could say was
"I'm on a trip." Everything had strange colors and sounds
were either very loud or very far away. She should never have

let me leave that office in that condition. Driving home I became convinced that Maxine was dead and headed for Joan Smith's house (my former nurse and Maxine's very good friend). I tried to tell Joan some of my confusion. She called Maxine who is in New Hampshire, and I talked with Maxine but was convinced it was a tape recording. I remember that I cried when I talked with her. At any rate then Joan drove home with me and meanwhile Maxine had called Dr. Chase. When I got home Dr. Chase called me. It's hard to remember much from then on. I remember that Dr. Chase said "you're out of your tree but I don't think you need to be hospitalized." Out of your tree meaning crazy. I thought she then said "at any rate, you're not going to kill yourself," but she says that I said that. She told me to take two thorazine which certainly wouldn't have done much, certainly didn't. Joan came in and I took two thorazine and two noludar. Kayo was home suddenly and he was going to drive Joan home. I told him I might take my pills and go to sleep. He left with Joan and I took 17 noludar. Maxine called after I'd taken them and I told her what I had done. I don't remember if I thought she was dead then or not. She had convinced me to call Dr. Chase and tell her what I had done and the last thing I said to her was I can't see to dial the phone. I don't remember saying that but that's what Max says I said. Max screamed on the phone and got Joy's attention. Max told Joy what I had done and Joy called Dr. Chase. Poor Joy. How could I have left her with that. Dr. Chase called my mother-in-law and then Kayo came home. According to Kayo I was stiff by then. He called the internist who said to bring me into Mass. General which Kayo driving, my mother-in-law holding me in the back seat they did. They got stuck in a traffic jam on Storrow Drive and they could hear my breathing get shallower and shallower. At any rate they made it. I got pumped out and put in intensive care and came to the next day. I was in the hospital for two days and then home. Dr. Chase has taken all my pills away from me and put me on much higher doses of thorazine which she doles out and three cloralhydrate to sleep. It took me a while to adjust, but I find I'm sleeping quite well. I'm taking six to eight hundred thorazine a day. I still feel quite weak and I'm

still terrified by what happened, but at least I survived. I
blame myself for all that happened but Dr. Chase is trying to
help me work that out. She refers to it as an attack. I wonder
what it was. I guess it was an attack, but it certainly was a
strange one. I can only remember thinking I was crazy and
that I'd have to kill myself. At any rate it's over. I've told
you the facts coldly and clinically almost because I couldn't
bear to tell them with feeling. Hell is too wide to describe.

I'm glad that you're to go to Chicago. I think it's a fine
idea. Yes, Alice, you can go home again. Well, I've got to get
on to other things, Alice. Sorry to tell you this whole sad,
grisly story but it didn't seem to me I could keep it from you.

Love as always,

In August, she sent "The White Snake," "Godfather Death," "The
Little Peasant," "Hansel and Gretel," "Iron Hans," and "Rapunzel" to
Paul Brooks. Houghton Mifflin did not take well to the dark ribaldry of
her book, and told her so in no uncertain terms. Undaunted by subtle
pressure from Houghton Mifflin not to publish her book, Anne hinted
that she might take her work elsewhere. Ultimately, *Transformations*
was to sell more hard-bound copies than any other Sexton book.

[*To Paul Brooks*]

[*14 Black Oak Road*]
August 25, 1970

Dear Paul,
I want to thank you so much for the fine lunch and charming company. I got caught up and you got caught up or at
least as best as one can do in a lunch time. I was pleased to
see how many copies I had sold of *Love Poems*. It is strange
as we both remarked that it took a sudden leap forward.
Maybe it was Alice Smith buying them throughout Manhattan
and Brooklyn!

I enclose a sampling of my transformations. "The Little
Peasant"[TR] was sold to *Playboy* and "Hansel and Gretel"
[TR] and "Snow White" [TR] were sold to *Cosmopolitan*. It is
a little odd to send you a book in progress, and I have no idea
what Cindy Degener would say to it, but I think it's good to

let you know what is in the works and the direction I'm moving in.

Did I hear you correctly? Did you tell me that Doubleday gave James Dickey a $25,000 advance? That seems preposterous. At any rate it's what I told my husband when I got home. It raised his opinion of poets. He's always saying to me "if only you'd write a sexy novel." If I did hear you correctly, then it is no wonder they gave him a full-page ad in the Sunday *Times* trying somehow to get their money back. Maybe it impresses me unduly as right now I am having financial problems and within a year I have a daughter to send to college. $25,000 is just enough to put a child through college. Well, enough of money. My job is to write.

I await your reaction to these poems. I think about twenty of them will make a book. I have written eleven.

With love,

[*To Claire S. Degener*]

14 Black Oak Road
September 22, 1970

Dear Cindy,

Here are four new ones. I think they are better than the ones you've seen before, or at least I think "Rapunzel" [TR] and "Sleeping Beauty" [TR] are two of my best. These have been turned down by *The New Yorker*, and I have three more there at the moment. As we mentioned on the phone, I would like to try Bob Manning at *The Atlantic* and then your man at *Harper's* although I believe that John Hollander is the poetry editor at *Harper's*. Come to think of it I'm not even sure these are poems. I think they are artifacts.

By now you have probably seen the first issue of *Audience* and I'd be interested in your opinion of it as I am on the board of advisors. They would like to see more, and if you like the magazine and with due consideration for the fact that they pay $1,000, we might send them some of these after they have been turned down elsewhere. How about Richard Howard at *The New American Review*? I don't think he's too warm to my former stuff, but I think he might like this. At any rate he is not my enemy like James Dickey.

Sorry to have called you at home but Paul Brooks' letter distressed me. It is quite true, Cindy, that many of my former fans are going to be disappointed that these poems do not hover on the brink of insanity or, to be more accurate, intensity. I plan to write Paul a letter. God knows what I'll say, but I surely intend to publish these poems, and I'd like them well-illustrated — a real zap of a production even if they aren't the old Sexton style. One always makes a mistake projecting into the future. I think I would like to do a book of very surreal, unconscious poems called *The Book of Folly.* After that I would like to do a very Sexton, intense, personal perhaps religious in places book called *The Death Notebooks* and in between I do plan to look at *Mercy Street* and change a few things and decide with you whether it should be published. I would say what I am doing now is the opposite of *Mercy Street,* my confessional melodrama. That's just to keep you up with my plans. God knows if they'll be fruitful.

Thank you for standing by me in my hour of need. It is surely that when one's editor goes sour.

Love,
Anne

P.S. Both *Atlantic & Harper's* have seen the "Transformations" you *now* have. So keep those aside.
P.P.S. Don't send "The Gold Key" [TR] to *anyone* — it is too prefatory & doesn't stand on its own.

XO
Anne

[*To Paul Brooks*]

[*14 Black Oak Road*]
October 14, 1970

Dear Paul,

I wanted to let some time elapse before I answered you so that I could think carefully about what you had to say. I've written seventeen "Transformations." My goal was twenty, but I may have to make do with seventeen. Seventeen would be a nice book anyway, but I will wait a couple of months and see what comes. I am in the process of typing up the manuscript to submit to you.

But back to your comments. I realize that the "Transformations" are a departure from my usual style. I would say that they lack the intensity and perhaps some of the confessional force of my previous work. I wrote them because I had to . . . because I wanted to . . . because it made me happy. I would want to publish them for the same reason. I would like my readers to see this side of me, and it is not in every case the lighter side. Some of the poems are grim. In fact I don't know how to typify them except to agree that I have made them very contemporary. It would further be a lie to say that they weren't about me, because they are just as much about me as my other poetry.

I look at my work in stages, and each new book is a kind of growth and reaching outward and as always backward. Perhaps the critics will be unhappy with this book and some of my readers maybe will not like it either. I feel I will gain new readers and critics who have always disliked my work (and too true, the critics are not always kind to me) may come around. I have found the people I've shown them to apathetic in some cases and wildly excited in others. It often depends on their own feelings about Grimms' fairy tales. You mentioned showing them to an outside reader. I think so much depends on who that reader is. I even think an introduction would be nice if we could talk someone like John Updike into doing it . . . or someone like him. Maybe I'll have to write my own, but I am not very good at that sort of thing. I'd like them illustrated . . . woodcuts perhaps, or line drawings. A real zap of a production. I wonder how Houghton Mifflin can give me that if you are apathetic about the book? As for outside readers, what about X. J. Kennedy? He's in the English Department at Tufts and a poet himself. He gave me a very good review for *Love Poems* and pointed out the humor in the book. He might be a good one to ask.

Now that I've almost finished *Transformations* I see it as part of my life's work . . . a kind of dalliance on the way.

After this, and I have already begun, I would like to do a book of very surreal, unconscious poems called *The Book of Folly*. At the same time I plan to start another book called *The Death Notebooks* where the poems will be very Sexton . . . intense, personal, perhaps religious in places. I will work on the *Death Notebooks* until I die. It's strange being a writer. You see your life not only in terms of kids being in college, braces, grandchildren, but in terms of what you write and how imminent death is and how one writes to forestall being blotted out. If I were to heed your warnings about *Transformations* and see my life work with that book omitted, I would be very sad. It would be a mistake. Perhaps it has even been a mistake not to publish *Mercy Street*. I plan to look at that in the future. One thing for sure . . . with *Transformations* I got as far away from *Mercy Street*, that confessional melodrama, as possible. I know it's dangerous to project into the future as I just have, but I thought it would give you a feeling of where I'm headed and where the *Transformations* fit in.

All this is rather heavy, but do let me know what you think. Cindy Degener suggests that I let another publisher publish *Transformations* and that I then come back to you with the rest of my books. I was not too keen on that idea but perhaps . . . it depends on what you want.

Love,

[*To Anne Clarke*]

[*14 Black Oak Road*]
November 17, 1970

I have so much to say to you, Annie, that I'll never get to it except by saying it in installments. When two friends are as close as we were and then let all those years go by without writing, it is impossible to catch up, and I don't think I'll even make the effort. The reason you didn't get a reply five days after your letter came was that I felt I must be in perfect zestful, ongoing order to write to you.

To hell with that. This is just me on a Tuesday morning paying you a little visit. What we need are two weeks to-

gether. The kids ask for you, ask when you'll be coming to
Boston. Kayo too. And last winter, Mary [Meme]. I second
them all. Come.

I am teaching at BU, creative writing. I started last January.
It was great fun last year. One class, meeting two hours a
week and then every other week I met with the students privately. As someone pointed out to me, "no wonder you're so
happy teaching. It's like having a love affair." And it was.
They loved each other. They loved me. I loved them. Unfortunately, this year there seems to be a lot of anger in the
class, a lot of destructiveness. They seem out to get each
other, and I'm not sure how to handle it. I told them "this
isn't an encounter group. For one thing, I'd charge more for an
encounter group." And more. I talked about loving and they
seemed to be more gentle for about two times and now they're
back to cutting each other down at every turn. Oh well, the
money helps and there are some good moments. This year it's
kind of like having a love affair with a rhinoceros.

I've been having some sort of trouble with my heart. I don't
know the name of it, but it's rapid heart beat, and at the same
time I have blackouts. I don't mean I pass out. I mean everything goes black. I had one about a month ago on the Mass.
Pike doing 65. I get no warning or maybe a ten-second warning of the heart pounding so I drove in blackness for one mile
and the gods were looking after me. I haven't driven since
then which is very difficult. I like to choose my dependen-
cies. My internist put me on Quinidine for the heart but
finally told me the blackouts were of psychogenic origin. God
damn it, that made me depressed, so I went to another internist and he said it was entirely possible that when the heart
became so rapid it couldn't get oxygen up to the brain and,
thus, the blackouts. He also persuaded me to cut down drastically on the cigarettes. Apparently cigarettes are very bad for
this condition. For the past two weeks on only fifteen cigarettes a day as opposed to three packs a day, I have not had a
blackout. I was having them at least every day, sometimes
seventeen a morning, so we'll see. All of the tests were negative. No petit mal. No low blood sugar. No thyroid. No
heart block from Thorazine. So it's up in the air really. The

next thing we'll try is digitalis, the new internist says. Otherwise I am in fine health. Fit as a fiddle. BUT I WANT TO DRIVE AGAIN. And I will. I've had these blackouts and this heart condition for four years, but I always thought it was psychological. I attributed it to anxiety and took seven 50 mg. Librium. You can imagine. I know you can just picture it.

The heart emotional is just fine. It would be nice to be making a run for it to use your words to Maxine, and maybe I will some day again.

My new poems are a strange sort of thing. I am submitting the book this week. The title is *Transformations* and the subtitle inside the book will read "Transformations From the Brothers Grimm." They are kind of a dark, dark laughter. They are very modern, sometimes fall into cuteness. Well, I can't describe them. I see that I have seven copies here, so I think I'll send them. They aren't unfortunately the best ones or the most moving, but they'll give you an idea. There is one that I don't have a copy of that mentions Ypsilanti and Ann Arbor. It is a rather lovely one, and I hope you will like it. Not that Grimm had ever heard of Ypsilanti, but he's there whether he knows it or not. I have just sent a full set of these, my last set, to Kurt Vonnegut, asking him if he'd be interested in writing an introduction. I think he would be wonderful, but of course, he'll probably turn me down. I met him this fall, and he's a nice guy, but what he'll think of me sending the book and asking him to join up, I don't know. I think I would like woodcuts, too. I think it lends itself to that. I sold "The Little Peasant" [TR] to *Playboy* of all places. I'll be very interested to [hear] your reaction to these. A lot of people who really like my work don't like these. But I think it's about time I showed some signs of a sense of humor.

Kayo got fired from his job. It was obvious that was going to happen. Last January they cut his salary in half. The wool business is awful. Within twenty-four hours, however, another fellow who was in the wool business took him in as a partner. There are only the two of them, and they are managing to make ends meet. He's much happier on his own, and I don't have to feel so guilty about being happy. For years I've been married to a gray man, a martyr whose only happiness was Africa. Now he sees a challenge in his present position almost as great as shooting an elephant. He's out there all by himself, and he's got to make it. He had to invest some money, but we borrowed on insurance, sold stocks, and I was proud to give him $5,000 from my earnings. Often when he comes home he is manic and enthusiastic. It's so wonderful. He is still rigid and politically repulsive. Last year he had a sign in his car that said "Register Communists, Not Firearms." I didn't say much, but I was ashamed. Then he put an American flag sticker on the car. Oh well, with this new job he has a new car, and there are no flags or signs as yet.

Linda is seeing a psychiatrist, supposedly to get over her closeness to me. She is succeeding in doing that. I adore her and we fight often. She has a car of her own, a used Mustang, and we are trying to give her some freedom or independence. She wants to go to Radcliffe or Tufts or Simmons or Wells. I'd like to see her at Tufts. They gave me an honorary degree [Doctorate] of letters last year. So now I'm like you. Just call me Doctor Sexton. Can you imagine that? Linda has a steady boyfriend at the moment. She is still a virgin I think. At any rate she's on the birth control pill for cramps. Joy is a woman fifteen years old. She has huge boobs and she is tiny, just five feet. We call her our Italian mama. She eats spaghetti for breakfast.

Are you reading the profile on Erik Erikson in *The New Yorker*? God, it's fascinating. I'd love to be analyzed by him, but I suppose everyone who reads the profile feels the same way. I'd like him to put the finger of greatness on me. Did you read Joan Didion's book *Play It As It Lays*? It certainly makes Southern California sound as awful as I thought it was. Maxine is reading *Sexual Politics* and then will lend it to me.

Glad that you woke up in 1970 and started gabbing to me. Jesus, I'm sorry to hear about the three dentists. That root canal man sounds ghastly. My opinion of a periodontist is "I'd rather not be there" if you please. All that blood. God! How I hate that.

So many songs remind me of you. You are indeed my musical lovely one. Just for instance, "The Girl From Ipanima" (sp?). Just think about that for a minute. The winter descends here, a few yellow leaves hang on.

Love,

[*To Kurt Vonnegut, Jr.*]

[*14 Black Oak Road*]
November 17, 1970

Dear Kurt,

I meant to write you a postcard before your dentist appointment, but I was away at the time I should have sent it. Sorry. Your graph for "Cinderella" [TR] is right over my desk.

The enclosed manuscript is of my new book of poems. I've taken Grimms' Fairy Tales and "Transformed" them into something all of my own. The better books of fairy tales have introductions telling the value of these old fables. I feel my *Transformations* needs an introduction telling of the value of my (one could say) rape of them. Maybe that's an incorrect phrase. I do something very modern to them (have you ever tried to describe your own work? I find I am tongue-tied). They are small, funny and horrifying. Without quite meaning to I have joined the black humorists. I don't know if you know my other work, but humor was never a very prominent feature ... terror, deformity, madness and torture were my bag. But this little universe of Grimm is not that far away. I think they end up being as wholly personal as my most intimate poems, in a different language, a different rhythm, but coming strangely, for all their story sound, from as deep a place. To get to the point. I am submitting the book to my publishers this week. I have already discussed with them that I would like an introduction. Is there any chance you would be willing to write it? Naturally you would be paid for doing this. I'm sure you have plenty of money now so that won't be much inducement ... only if you're in the mood. I was talking with Dan Wakefield two days ago and asking him if he thought you would consider the project. He seemed to feel you were between things, saying things like "fuck books," so I am rushing this off to you in hopes of catching you at the right moment.

The first poem is an introductory one and doesn't give the flavor or have the zest of the others, so I'd skip it to begin with. Perhaps "Snow White," "The Little Peasant," "Iron Hans," "Rapunzel," "Hansel and Gretel," "Briar Rose" could give you a feeling of the project. "Cinderella," unfortunately, is not very good despite the aura of your graph.

Sending you this seems like a rather forward move on my part, but I thought I'd give it a try. I enclose a self-addressed stamped envelope in which you can whisk these back to me if you're so inclined. Many thanks.

Best wishes,

[*To Brian Sweeney*]

[*14 Black Oak Road*]
November 24, 1970

Dear, dear Sweeney,

I liked your effusive letter. Perhaps you should call me more often. It was wonderful to talk to you and Happy Birthday. We are born four days apart . . . only on different years. Of course I will need you more in my fifties. As a matter of fact, I think I shall save you for my fifties. But you'd better be around.

The overseas phone is not too trustworthy. The book of poems that I shall work on all my life is entitled *The Death Notebooks.* The one I shall work on until it's finished is *The Book of Folly.* I have just written a new one for the *Notebooks* which is enclosed. It may be part of a series. I haven't quite decided. Just so you can get a feeling for it, I enclose one from *The Book of Folly.* I like it when you know what's going on with me.

You are so right about my fear of death. I think I have embraced it only because I feared it so. By the way I embraced it this August only to come out alive. I hate it. I love it.

Yes, it is time to think about Christ again. I keep putting it off. If he is the God/man, I would feel a hell of a lot better. If there is a God, Sweeney, how do you explain him swallowing all those people up in Pakistan? Of course there's a God, but what kind is he? Is he our kind? [...]

You have a wonderful voice yourself. I suggest you buy 100 copies of *Poetry Australia.* I suggest that because I know how much you like to give things away, and before you know it the magazine will be out of print. I love you.

[*To Ted Hughes*]

[*14 Black Oak Road*]
November 24, 1970

Dear Ted,

Just a word to you, dear Ted, to tell you I think the *Crow* poems are brilliant. They go further than anything you've done. They go into that unknown land where spirits live — crow spirits. I hear a book is forthcoming, and I can't wait to own it.

I have been hearing for a year that you were coming to the USA, but you do not appear. When and if you do, let's be sure to get together. We have an extra bed if you feel like a little home life.

With best wishes,

[*To C. K. Williams*]

[*14 Black Oak Road*]
December 8, 1970

Dear Charlie,

I Am the Bitter Name is not a good book. It is a great book. I think of you as the last guru singing your poems to God. They are so associative they delight and evoke. I can't pretend to understand them any more than I understand my dreams, but the aura of gentleness and sorrow for man pervades. I like the title and yet they are not bitter poems. As far as titles go, in sixty to seventy percent of the poems I personally see no connection between the poem and its title. Not so with something as easy as "My Shopping Trip" but so with a poem like "Creams," but I feel this is my flaw not yours. The progression of the book, that is, the order of the poems, seems good to me with the exception of "In The Heart of The Beast." I am sure you have been roundly praised for that poem, but I found myself disappointed by it. It was as though the whole book said it about mankind forever with its wars and cruelties. It's the first time you don't forgive the murderer. It's the first time your anger really showed. I'm sure you wouldn't consider omitting it and perhaps that is for the best, making you less guru and more human, but I wouldn't put it right at the end because it isn't like your other poems. I think you ought to end on something that says the same thing in the C. K. Williams style, even "The Sting" would do or perhaps there are others that would be better.

At any rate, the book is a solid one and lacks the somewhat uneven quality of your first book. It is more religious in tone and my envy knoweth no bounds.

I'm awfully glad you're not calling the book "Bad Mouth." It couldn't suit it. I'm going to hold on to this copy for as long as you'll let me, to share with friends and to reread. Thank you for returning my *Transformations* so promptly and hope to see you in February.

Love,

Still uneasy about publishing *Transformations,* Houghton Mifflin asked Anne if she would mind if they solicited an outside reader's opinion. Taking the initiative herself, Anne wrote the distinguished poet Stanley Kunitz, asking him to read the book and comment upon it. He did not disappoint her.

[*To Stanley Kunitz*]

> [*14 Black Oak Road*]
> *December 23, 1970*

Dear Stanley,

What a great guy you are to read my book not only once but three times! You can't know how much your words mean to me. I'm drawn, of course, particularly to that first paragraph with its bug-eyed Jonahs. I had hoped you would like it, but I

hadn't let myself hope you'd be wild about it . . . even with
your qualifications.

I wish now that I could have shown it to you as I was writing it, for your most important suggestion (switching the prologues and making them epilogues) could have been done
then, but somehow not now. After tearing open the envelope
and reading your letter seven times, I sat down for an afternoon and reread the poems in light of that suggestion. With
about four of them it was a stroke of genius. With about five
of them it's so-so. With eight of them it destroys. The poems
seem to grow out of the prologue to, as it were, take root in
them and come forth from them. I appreciate what you mean
when you say that they tell the story in advance, or rather
what it means to me. I see that as kind of a necessary flaw.
Damn it all. If only last January I had thought or dared to
send you the early poems. But you see, if you hadn't liked
them at that writing and most tentative stage, it might have
stopped me . . . cut me off. I consulted with Maxine about
your suggestions, and she agrees that it's too bad I couldn't
have brought you in sooner. Maybe I should put it I just don't
have the "strength."

But let me tell you exactly how much your praise means to
me. I showed this book to my editors at Houghton Mifflin,
and they felt it was not up to my other work and that the critics would hate it and that my fans would hate it. They
suggested I get an outside reader . . . or rather they get an outside reader. I didn't tell them and I didn't tell you, but you
were my secret outside reader. You were the kind of person I
was writing for. I had a secret suspicion you were fond of
Grimms' Fairy Tales. Need I say that I adore them? At any
rate, you liked the poems. May I have your permission to
show your letter to Houghton Mifflin? They have already accepted the book (this happened yesterday) without the so-
called outside reader. But I would like to have them have
more confidence in it. How would you feel if they wanted to
quote a line of your letter? I think they may want to for an
ad, but I know this was a personal letter from you to me, and
I won't let them quote from it unless you feel right about it. I

don't think I'd dare ask you if you hadn't said "let the praise stand." My question is more exact. May I stand up your praise like a toy soldier? May I wind it up and let it march into my editor's office? May I press it with an iron and fold it into an ad? The most important thing for me is that you said it and meant it — that was my first reaction. My second reaction is needy, but then, we poets are always needy.

I didn't find your criticism harsh or supercilious. It was very much to the point, and I thank you for taking the time from your own work for me. It strikes me funny that you say it is my sacred confession to be confessional. I don't see *Transformations* as confessional but perhaps it is indeed. At one time I hated being called confessional and denied it, but mea culpa. Now I say that I'm the *only* confessional poet. No matter how hard you work at it, your own voice shows through.

It's exciting about your book coming out in March. I can't wait to see it. That will be an event of note. By the way, your letter is so well-written. You can't touch anything without turning it into an angel.

Love,

[*To Paul Brooks*]

[*14 Black Oak Road*]
December 30, 1970

Dear Paul,

I am so happy that Houghton Mifflin is taking *Transformations*. It would break my heart to leave Houghton Mifflin even for one book.

I gave some thought to your doubts and after I typed up the manuscript for Houghton Mifflin I sent a copy to Stanley Kunitz. He is the judge for the Yale Younger [Poets] Series, a Pulitzer Prize winner and one of our most respected men of letters. I don't know him very well. Just well enough to ask him to take a look. He has some reservations. He wanted my prologues to be epilogues . . . something that clearly doesn't work . . . at least I thought about it, and I couldn't make it work. Here, however, is the first paragraph of his letter:

I must tell you that I was wary of your MS because I expected not to like it. The brothers Grimm are so much a
part of me that I really didn't want to see their tales re-
capitulated, modernized, diluted. Now that I have read
Transformations more than once — three times, to be
exact — I know how wrong I was not to put more trust in
you. You have swallowed the tales alive and carried them
in the belly of your imagination until you were ready to
disgorge them like a whole brotherhood of bug-eyed
Jonahs. What a wild, astonishing, blood-curdling book you
have written!

I've written to ask him if he will let me quote his letter. He
just may not, but one can hope.
I hope your work goes well.

Love,

[*To Stanley Kunitz*]

[*14 Black Oak Road*]
January 20, 1971

Dear Stanley,
Thank you so much for your letter. Sorry you had the flu
and the holiday depression, but more than that I'm awfully
sorry you had to go to the hospital and have the repair job.
That can be hell. Kayo has gone through similar problems,
and I'm rapidly approaching.
I have shown your letter, or rather an excerpt from your letter, to my publishers, and they are delighted. Now I hope
they'll really get behind this book and promote it. Naturally,
what I quoted to them was your first paragraph which I will
repeat to you in case you don't keep carbons. [Quotation from
preceding letter follows.]
A bit of a coward, what, not to have included your "almost
written" but then you did say "let the praise stand." What
they can take from that paragraph I'm not sure, but "bug-eyed
Jonahs" and "blood-curdling book" sound awfully good to me.
Believe me, the bloody effort that you mention, the work
and the sweat preceded my sending them to you. If I could
have sent them right after I wrote them, not a first draft

perhaps but a second or third or fourth or fifth, but it didn't work out that way. I'm a little scared of you, Stanley, and like to show you my more finished work. I adore you, you know. By "scared" I mean respect.

The "blazing hurry" is that I'm so God damned sure I'm going to die soon. I know it's silly, but it's a conviction. At any rate, here I am very much alive, writing at full tilt — some trapeze acts and even a hand at prose — dark tales but not confessional. Take care and be good to yourself.

Best wishes,

The preface, blurbs, and illustrations for *Transformations* kept Anne busy all winter. As a collaborator she enlisted Barbara Swan, whose art she had admired since their days together at the Radcliffe Institute. A detail from Barbara's sepia, *Gothic Heads* had appeared on the book jacket for *Live or Die*.

As Anne and Barbara read and reread *Transformations* a series of seventeen ribald grotesqueries formed, and the Swan drawings became an integral part of the book.

Anne continued her experiments with prose, working on two short stories: "The Letting Down of the Hair," and "The Buffoon." These pieces were eventually to be part of *The Book of Folly*, which she began in earnest in early 1971.

[*To Stanley Kunitz*]

[*14 Black Oak Road*]
February 17, 1971

Dear Stanley,

I have special knowledge about daisies. They last and last as both you and I will. They are my favorite flower. There is something innocent and vulnerable about them as if they thanked you for admiring them.

I am sorry that you had a rough time but am glad to hear that you are on the mend.

Thank you for that sentence about *Transformations*. I read it every day to bring my spirits up, and I'm sure the publishers will put it to good use, and it has indeed quieted their qualms about the worth of this new work.

It's strange that you say I'm "too tough" for my "blazing

hurry" (that sentence makes no sense, but you know what I mean). People are always telling me I'm tough. Maybe because I've survived so much. Inside I feel like cooked broccoli, and I don't mean the stalks which should be crisp and tasty. I mean the heads that fall apart when you cut them. The only time I'm tough in my own mind is when I'm seized by a poem and then determined to conquer it and let it live its own peculiar life. All my toughness goes into my writing. All an effort, really, to not sound like a sap. Oh well, I'm just going on. Don't feel in any hurry to answer this. Do so at your most leisure.

> *With best wishes and fond regards,*
> *Anne the Broccoli*

In June, a strange and painful query appeared in the daily mail. A young woman wrote that her mother had shown her "The Sun" and "The Fortress" in a 1962 *New Yorker* and claimed that she'd written the poems under a pseudonym. Struggling with the desire to believe her dead mother's story, but aware of Anne's inimitable style, Anne Gallagher wrote to learn the truth.

[*To Anne Gallagher*]

> [*14 Black Oak Road*]
> *June 23, 1971*

Dear Anne Gallagher,
I am awfully sorry to have to tell you that I did write the poems "The Sun" [LD] and "The Fortress" [PO], and I did publish them in *The New Yorker.* I am sure that your mother liked these poems and perhaps felt they were so meaningful to her that she had almost written them. It can happen that way. I wish I could tell you otherwise, but of course you want the truth.

> *Sincerely yours,*

In the autumn of 1971, Colgate University offered her the Crawshaw Chair in Literature for the spring semester. They were willing to pay her handsomely to teach one course in poetry writing and another on her own poetry. Although this meant commuting weekly to Syracuse from Boston, she accepted.

As a guest professor at Colgate University, Anne gained additional power which she did not hesitate to use. She waged a campaign to be appointed a professor at Boston University, and she won.

[*To George Starbuck*]

[*14 Black Oak Road*]
September 8, 1971

Dear George,

Here is a copy of my résumé newly brought up-to-date. May I point out it includes two Honorary Phi Beta Kappa awards, three Honorary Doctor of Letters Degrees, a professor at Colgate with a chair yet. As I said to you at lunch, a professor at Colgate shouldn't have to be a lecturer at BU. What do I want? MORE! I'd like more bucks once the freeze is off.

That was a good lunch, but next time I say Joseph's with or without Elizabeth Bishop.

Love,

[*To Morton Berman, Chairman,*
Department of English
Boston University]

[*14 Black Oak Road*]
November 17, 1971

Dear Mort,

Just a reminder from a happy member of your department. I will be going to Colgate the spring term to hold a chair (Crawshaw Professor of Literature). I will be teaching from February to the first of May, and I am being paid $13,000. I will be teaching a creative writing course and another course that the department chairman calls "Anne on Anne." There is a lot of work to be done on the latter, but I'm finding it challenging and even an original concept.

I would like to have more feeling of permanence with BU. If not tenure, then some form of written agreement that would not leave me up in the air about the forthcoming year. Not only do I enjoy the work, but I desperately need the money. I know I am a good teacher, and this year is my best class of all.

My students are getting things published in small magazines and two of them have had acceptances from *The New Yorker* as well as one acceptance from *The Sewanee Review.*

BU's writing department is becoming the best in the country, and it is exciting to be a part of it. Colgate will be an adventure, and I hope to return to you more vital and somehow stronger.

So there is money to think about and some sort of permanence to think about. I know you are harried but perhaps you will find time for this, too.

With best wishes,

[*To Brian Sweeny,*
telegram]

February 1, 1972

ON NEW YEARS GOD REMEMBERS YOU STOP SO DO I

ANNE SEXTON

[*To Julie Joslyn*]

14 Black Oak Road
February 1, 1972

Dear Julie,

Sorry to have been so long in answering. I have been in a supermarket of work and there just hasn't been time to be in touch with the people that mean a lot.

I do hope you are writing prose. It is a kind of opening up. In my forthcoming book, *The Book of Folly,* to be published February, 1972, I have three pieces of prose. In one of them I used part of a letter you sent me. Of course I don't use your name and your privacy is indeed respected, and I hope it will please you as it does me. A piece of your life put into mine. The story is called "The Letting Down of the Hair" [BF] and will appear in the March *Atlantic.* It's really about the life of a poet and what it's like to have people like your poetry but not know you really. The letter is changed. You might not recognize it, but I wanted you to know that you are part of my life as a poet. As well as a human being.

The thorazine is just a drag, but my shrink won't let me off it, so what the hell can I do? I've been on mellaril, too. I don't mind it except for the sun. I say to myself, why must I hide from the thing I love the most? I went off it a year ago and got sick. But my shrink says I won't ALWAYS be on it.

Yes, for me death is always very close. Life is fragile, but then I'm a very apprehensive person and in one of my poems I describe my husband as "as straight as a redwood." And it sounds as though Josh is the same for you. That is good.

I like your poems — both. "A Futile Experiment" I would take out the word "damn." Otherwise it's perfect.

Do let me hear from you and take care.

All best,
Anne

In June, Anne went into the Newton-Wellesley Hospital for an operation: removal of the steel screws which had held her broken hip, and repair of her bladder. She spoke on the phone with Lois Ames, who also underwent surgery that day at Massachusetts General Hospital. They shared a sense of fury at their impotence in the face of pain, hospital authoritarianism, and carelessness. Anne turned her agony to good use by beginning the "Fury" poems. The Furies of "Sunsets," "Sundays," "Cooks," "Cocks," "Bones," and "Overshoes" were only a few from the series that was to go into *The Death Notebooks*.

[*To Charles Newman*]

[*14 Black Oak Road*]
June 20, 1972

Dear Charlie:

Forgive, forgive that I never answered your letter from Budapest. Forgive, forgive, forgive that I never sent my condolences over the death of your wife. I was broken for you, Charlie, but I was quiet, thinking that perhaps the letters just ate into you all the more.

Now to business. I am fully aware that a year ago your *Tri-Quarterly* was full all the way through 1973. What is it now, Charlie, '75? You see, I have this long poem, and after I got it back from *The New Yorker*, I thought to myself, "Anne, this is a major poem. It goes places you've never been. You want it in the most important magazine in the country. Doesn't that mean the *Tri-Quarterly?"* I don't mind waiting two or three years to get it in a right place. So what do you say Charlie, my dear, to taking a reading of "O Ye Tongues"? I don't intend to publish it in book form except posthumously from my book, *The Death Notebooks.* If it appealed, you could have a few shorter pieces from that too.

Hope all this fits into your schedule, busy as it is.

Love,

[*To Ben Shaktman*]

[*14 Black Oak Road*]
August 3, 1972

Dear, dear Ben:

It was good to get your warm letter, but I was sorry that you couldn't think up some theater project for *Transformations.* I don't know why I expect to get so much mileage out of one little book.

As for writing a new Daisy — only if you were working in Boston, could I manage it. I don't work well in New York. A hotel room is not conducive to rewriting for me. I work well from my own desk here in Weston, but I disliked trying to rewrite in that squalid little room at the Algonquin under pressure. I *do* love the theater, but in truth for the short time I worked with you it was far more productive than anything I did with Chuck.

I worked two years on that play and hold nothing in my hand but dust. I know. I could print it, but I don't even like it well enough for that. It bores me. Walter Kerr was gracious. Clive Barnes was gracious, but I can't get out of my head Daisy throwing herself all over the stage. One thing I've learned, not to be quite [so] hysterical. At any rate, madness is not hysteria. It can be very quiet, but it wasn't so directed.

Enough of these machinations and musings. Maybe, indeed, I will write another play. I have been writing so madly that I haven't had a chance to think of it. But there will come a lull eventually perhaps. At any rate, let us keep in touch, so that if I do write a play or start a play, I can let you know.

I'm glad you are writing and selling. You speak of my daughters and the birch trees, and I tell you, Ben, they are lovely. Should you come to Boston, I will meet you for lunch or a drink (and not throw up), or make the monk's bedroom ready for you.

With love,

In the summer of 1972, Kayo incorporated a new element into his wool business: mail-order crewel and needlework. He named this new addition "The Needleworker" and began spending long hours on the design of its first color catalogue. Once again, Anne turned her creative ingenuity to a task other than poetry, and began to write catalogue copy with Kayo. All through the heat of August they composed catchy blurbs, loudly arguing over what was best. Kayo complained that Anne's copy was "too artsy" and that it wouldn't appeal to a general public. Anne replied, "But Kayo, you've got to be imaginative!" Although Anne often made light of her part in the project, she was pleased that her craft was helpful to her husband in such a concrete manner. Soon the entire family began to think in terms of advertising jingles, and there was constant good-natured joking over Anne and Kayo's arguments. She said in a letter to Dan Masterson in August: "Kayo and I have been working on this new business every night. I've only been in the pool twice even in this terrible heat. When I'm not working with Kayo, I've been writing myself."

[*To Joy Sexton*]

[*14 Black Oak Road
circa August 4, 1972*]

Darling Joy
we're here to say
we're glad it is
your birthday!
We think it's sweet
that you were sixteen.
But now you'll really
be a queen.
At seventeen you can drive.
We hope there's someone left alive!
At seventeen you can stay out
later

than a mater (mom)
sometimes.
or a pater. (dad)
You'll still have to mind
and not be fresh. Be kind
and you'll be okay in every way.
You'll have to study even more.
We hope it's fun and not a bore.
Hot Line will keep you hopping.
And, Joy, there'll just be no stopping
the things you can do when you're seventeen.
It's no longer dress up. Dress like a queen.
Feed the cats. Feed the horse!
Well it could be wourse.
Drive the car. Buy the gass.
In that short skirt you'll never pass!
Introduce the right way. Be nice.
And we promise not to be ice.
We promise to love and the whole bit.
We love you. You are our kit-
ten, and we are smitten,
with Joy at Seventeen!
Blue Eyes! Big butt. A queen!

love from Muggy
love from Thorpe

[*To Anthony and Helen Hecht*]

14 Black Oak Road
August 29, 1972

Dear Tony and Helen:

Hooray for Evan Alexander! I heartily congratulate you, and please tickle the dear baby's feet for me.

I was sorry not to see more of you that night at the Y. [Anne and Anthony Hecht had read at the YMHA in New York City that year.] I was feeling so goddamned lousy, and there were so many people afterwards, that I turned around once, and you were gone. Did you know, Tony, that that is the largest crowd they have gotten at the Y with the exception of Neruda? I think we must be a good team. Let's do it again.

My *Transformations* book is getting ghastly reviews in England, which they end with comments such as, "God bless America." I doubt O.U.P. will do my next book, which is coming out in the U.S. on my birthday, November 9, the *Book of Folly*.

Kayo is starting a new business — mail-order needlework kits. I write the ads and the catalog, but not very well.

I taught at Colgate last year and will be at Boston University for the next five years. But the writing goes well — fluidly, that is.

Please write. I'd like more news, and even to see a new poem would be a pleasure.

x o
Anne

[*To Rosalyn Tureck*]

[*14 Black Oak Road*]
October 4, 1972
Dear Rosalyn:

Just a note lest we lose touch. In haste let me say that I listened to your record with devoted attention and supreme happiness, as well as writing to it, but I do believe that great works of art can inspire. I loved the way you phrased it, "Bach understood a great deal about God, creation, and death, but less about life."

And so it is with me. I wonder if the artist ever lives his life — he is so busy recreating it. To work is to live. To create is to live. To perform (for me) is essentially false. Only as I write do I realize myself. I don't know what that does to "life".

I hope your concert tour goes well and that all good things come to you.

With best wishes,

In November, Olwyn Hughes — the literary agent for Sylvia Plath's estate — wrote Anne in distress. Concerned about the impending publication of a book of poems by Robin Morgan which included derogatory remarks about her brother, Ted, she entreated Anne to do anything she could to stop the book's publication.

[*To Olwyn Hughes*]

[*14 Black Oak Road*]
November 1, 1972

Dear Olwyn Hughes:
I'm so glad that you liked the poem and that you'd like to publish it. I'm not clear what "early next year" means. Do you mean February of '73 or September of '73?

I'm glad that Ted liked it. I respect his judgment more than anyone's. Tell him I send my love. Tell him there's nothing I can do about Robin Morgan. I called Fran McCullough as soon as I got your letter, and she said the books had already been shipped to the stores. You were right. The poem is vile, and the only reason Random House is publishing it is because anything about Sylvia is news. It is terribly written. It is not art. Anyone who knows anything about poetry will discount it. It's a personal attack on Ted, and my heart goes out to him.

I think a libel action is a terrible idea. It would only give further publicity to ugliness. But frankly, I don't think anyone will take it the least bit seriously. At least I hope not. I don't think anyone will come ringing Ted's doorbell. In a way it is too terrible to be in the public eye. But as Ted once told me, praise begets abuse. At the same time, I am fully aware that this [is] personal abuse, not literary.

I will do all I can to discount this Robin Morgan on this side of the Atlantic, but it is too late to stop her from publishing.

Let me know about the date of publication for Rainbow Press, and give my love to Ted.

Sincerely,

In November, Anne accepted a position on the Pulitzer Prize poetry jury. She was excited by the prospect of judging the prize she had won herself only five years before. Louis Simpson and William Alfred were her fellow jurors, and before they finished, they had read nearly eighty books of poetry.

On her birthday, November 9, Houghton Mifflin gave a party at 2 Park Street, celebrating the publication of *The Book of Folly*. Subsequent reviews were disappointing. In England, Chatto and Windus replaced Oxford University Press as her publisher.

New interpretations of her poetry always intrigued Anne, and when Conrad Susa approached her with his ideas for converting *Transformations* into an opera she was ecstatic. On May 5, 1973, the Minnesota Opera Company opened its production of *Transformations*, with Anne in the audience. She adored it. She made another trip to Minnesota to hear the opera, and eventually bought herself an expensive tape recorder so that she could listen to the performance at home. Daughters, neighbors, and friends listened with her, note by note. It was the realization of a dream to hear her words become song.

[*To Conrad Susa*]

[*14 Black Oak Road*]
November 29, 1972

Dear Conrad:

I'm so glad that you got my new book, and more than that, happy that you like it. You write a damn good letter for a music man.

I so enjoyed meeting you, and let me thank you for that afternoon at Joseph's. I was fascinated with your ideas and plans for the opera (dare I call it that?).

I hope the arrangements are settled. I spoke with my agent and told her some of your plans (the Andrews Sisters, the Mills Brothers).

You have all my warm feelings as you compose. May you be giddy, and may the ice hold you no matter how many gold bricks you wear on your back.

Best,

[*To George Starbuck*]

[*14 Black Oak Road*]
December 3 or 4 or something, 1972

Dear dear George,

[. . .] Query: If John Barth doesn't come back next year and you pay his replacement four grand per course more than I am getting I'm going to wonder if a woman's fist shouldn't be painted on my classroom door. !!! Even if John Barth stays at his same salary I'm going to wonder. I know it is a desperate time of money at B.U. but if a man gets it then why doesn't a woman. Need I list my qualifications as a writer, teacher etc? If I'm important I want to be paid importantly.

Enough. I hope you like the poem. That's all I meant to talk about in this letter and then my mind just kept right on — as in the poem itself.

Love,

Chapter VI

To Tear Down the Stars

January 1973–October 1974

That does not keep me from having a terrible need of — shall I say the word — religion. Then I go out at night to paint the stars.

Vincent Van Gogh

The town does not exist
except where one black-haired tree slips
up like a drowned woman into the hot sky.
The town is silent. The night boils with eleven stars.
Oh starry starry night! This is how
I want to die.

It moves. They are all alive.
Even the moon bulges in its orange irons
to push children, like a god, from its eye.
The old unseen serpent swallows up the stars.
Oh starry starry night! This is how
I want to die:

into that rushing beast of the night,
sucked up by that great dragon, to split
from my life with no flag,
no belly,
no cry.

"The Starry Night"
from ALL MY PRETTY ONES

In February of 1973 Anne asked Kayo for a divorce. During their twenty-four years together, she had occasionally threatened him with the possibility of a separation, and now, against the advice of her psychiatrist and many of her friends, she began legal proceedings. Kayo contested the divorce until its bitter end in November, convinced that Anne was acting precipitously, continually questioning whether she knew what she was doing.

Having left Kayo in their home at 14 Black Oak Road, Anne spent seven weeks drifting from friend to friend, sharing her grief. At first, it was exciting to be a house guest, the center of attention, the dramatically estranged wife. But soon the sympathy waned. When the court awarded her temporary custody of both children and the house, she gratefully returned home. Terrified of being alone, she immediately advertised for a live-in couple who would rent a few rooms and serve as companions.

The summer months passed slowly. Anne tried to forget her separation through a premature love affair. She taught a summer class by the pool, had two teeth pulled, and wrote very little. In August, just before Joy's eighteenth birthday, Joy signed Anne into McLean Hospital.

In the fall, Linda returned for her junior year at Harvard and Joy began her first semester at boarding school in Maine. Unable to sustain the complicated relationship, Anne's first set of boarders departed. The house was empty. She thought often of Kayo, especially as the divorce date neared; he had protected her, supported her, waited for her. Even as she approached her divorce hearing, scheduled for November 5, she talked of marrying him again. Relying more heavily on her friends now, she insisted they fill the emptiness he had left behind. She asked them to humor her, to care for her like a child.

Her friends grew angry and frustrated with her midnight suicide threats, her inability to go to the dentist alone, enter a store alone, mail a letter alone. She required constant service and care, and those closest to her began to set limits in self-protection. Anne saw these limits as unreasonable fences erected by those she loved — the ultimate desertion.

She began cultivating new friends who would do all she asked, and punished those of long standing with silence. If they failed to give her what she wanted, she simply turned to someone else. No one was indispensable.

The gradual dissolution of her deepest relationships is mirrored in her letters of the early 1970s. Maxine Kumin, Lois Ames, Anne Clarke, Brian Sweeney, and Linda and Joy all gradually retreated from her life. Her files contain few exuberant letters to Snodgrass, Miller, Hecht, Morgan, Newman, Stallworthy, Shaktman. Instead she concentrated on her fans — short glassy notes which revealed little of herself. In letters to those she had known for years, a cheerfully glib tone replaced her earlier openness.

As her friends provided less and less support, she turned to God for comfort. During the spring and summer months of 1974, she read xeroxed weekly sermons from a church in Dedham, becoming friends with the curate, Patricia Handloss. Religion suddenly became quite important, but she answered defensively when questioned about her new-found faith. She had succeeded in creating her own private God — perhaps He would never leave her.

Anne had always been a romantic. With divorce she finally obtained the freedom to examine fully the other side of the fence. She was convinced that, as a divorcée, she would be overwhelmed by the attentions of many men. After all, they had been writing her love letters for years, despite her marriage. But what she found in her new state was neither rich nor strange, but instead remarkably disappointing. Eligible men were scarce for a forty-five year old woman; in desperation she finally sent her name to a computer dating service. Still, she was lonely. One afternoon in September of 1974, she confided to Linda that she had made a mistake. Divorce had not given her that dream man; it had only made her acutely aware of what she had lost.

Anne turned increasingly to her work — often writing all day long and forgetting to eat. Her class at Boston University became a kind of family. Between June of 1972 and October 1974, she had written three new books: *The Death Notebooks*, *The Awful Rowing Toward God*, and *45 Mercy Street*. Her methods of revision had altered drastically: often she wrote two or three poems in a few hours. On the file folder of first drafts for *The Awful Rowing Toward God* in the Boston University archive, she noted that "these poems were started 1/10th/73 and finished 1/30th/73 (with two days out for despair, and three days out in a mental hospital). I explain this so you will understand they are raw, unworked poems, all first drafts, written in a frenzy of despair and hope. To get out the *meaning* was the primary thing — while I had it, while the muse was with me. I apologize for the inadequate words. As I said in one of the poems, 'I fly like an eagle, but with the wings of a wren.' (1/31/73)"

The published poems in *The Awful Rowing Toward God* differ little from those first early drafts. The days of spending months over a single stanza were gone. Often her poetic instincts and natural ear allowed her to produce spontaneous poems that needed little revision; but many more awkward mistakes also slipped through into print. An unfinished tone crept in among the polished words. Her imagery became wilder, her lines more prosaic.

With this vast outpouring, she wrote against death; she seems to have been preparing instinctively for a final silence. Her late poetry, while not as carefully crafted as her early work, is an outstanding document of the evolution of her thought and emotion in these last two years.

Her life rapidly spiraled inward. She gave fewer readings, saw fewer friends, used fewer worksheets — blotting out all but the essentials.

[*To J. Steinbeisser*]

[*14 Black Oak Road*]
January 10, 1973

Dear Ms. Steinbeisser:

Mercy Street is not available to anyone. I consider it, among other things, a failure of nerve, and there really is nothing in it that is not in my poetry.

I do not intend to ever publish it, and I do not wish anyone to read it, even talk about it in a Ph.D. thesis. I do not know the subject of your thesis, whether it be contemporary plays or my work. If it is my work, I would be happy to send you a copy of a forthcoming book of poems.

I have not written any other plays, nor do I intend to. To write for the theater is like writing on an elf's wing. He flies away and is lost to you forever.

With all best wishes,

[*To Claire S. Degener*]

[*14 Black Oak Road*]
January 11, 1973

Dear Cindy,

Here is the new manuscript [*The Death Notebooks*]. I want your reaction, so please let me know, although I am *myself* sure that here and there in this book is the beginning of a "new life".

As of yesterday I started a new book, entitled *The Life Notebooks* [later retitled *45 Mercy Street*], which indeed [it] could be called, because with the clear realization of death, one gets (as dear, old *Time* magazine says) less concerned with getting the house-cleaning done. Both you and I, it seems, are questioning life, as perhaps millions of people are, our own lives especially.

Herewith some of my questions, some of my answers. I hope it is well written, but that seems extraneous. I ought to be able to know how to write by now, and it seems to me at this point I ought to know how to live. That is, I ought to be able to dig a trench in my soul and find something there.

To business! Dick McAdoo and I have agreed that this book will come out in the winter of 1974. That seems right to me.

Love,

P.S. Cindy and Dick, I want to be an important poet more than I want to be a popular one. Only God knows if the two go together.

[*To George Starbuck*]

[*14 Black Oak Road*]
January 27, 1973

Dear George:

Here is some ammunition. It seems ridiculous to me, but if under arts and humanities for the *Ladies' Home Journal* Woman of the Year Award there are only two writers mentioned, Joyce Carol Oates, whom you are fighting to get and will pay what I deserve, and me, it seems to me worth your attention. You *have* been taking advantage of the fact that I live in Boston, that I am a good kid, etc.

Does Boston University want to be written about in my biography as undervaluing me in the way that the universities undervalued Theodore Roethke? I do not want this money — and money is what I am talking about — for the fall of 197[4]. I want it for the fall of 197[3].

Aside from the fact that I am "a name", I am a great teacher. I do not mean to sound immodest, but I do know that *I will* the best out of my students. I will it with love and craft and knowledge of what makes a great poem. That may not be important to you, but it is important to me to teach well because it is important to my soul. If you do not believe *me*, gather my students into Mort's office and ask *them*.

I do dislike being a trouble maker, and because of this, I have only mumbled my discontent. Now I shout it. If I do not get a response within two weeks from you or Mort, I will send this letter to the Dean and the President.

I have been loyal to B.U. and will continue to be. My loyalty was shown when Hunter College offered me $18,000 for one class this spring semester, and you said you couldn't let me go. I understood why and I stuck with you.

I am very well aware of B.U.'s financial difficulties, but I am just as famous as John Barth or Joyce Carol Oates, and there is something criminal going on at B.U. if this is ignored.

With love,

[*To Claire S. Degener*]

[*14 Black Oak Road*]
March 7, 1973

Dear Cindy:

I am living nowhere. I am getting a divorce. Don't try to call. I'll call you when I can.

This gentleman [Yorifumi Yaguchi] I have corresponded with before. I think he would be a good translator, but I have no idea. I'd only like it handled legally. As far as I'm concerned, there could be twenty Japanese translations, and it wouldn't be enough for me.

As I told Mr. Evans of your office (dear man) I want to get

translated all over the damn world, somehow. I hope he is
working on it.

Love and kisses,

Out of the loneliness following her decision for a divorce, Anne
Sexton wrote to the woman who had been the Harvey housekeeper
since Anne's birth. "Meme," as Anne's children had affectionately
nicknamed her, had been a family member for over forty-five years.
Straightening, polishing, and scolding, she was a silent mother to all
those she loved. At a barren moment in her life, Anne reached back to
the gruff eighty-year-old woman who embodied the very essence of her
childhood.

[*To Mary LaCrosse*]

[14 Black Oak Road]
April 19, 1973

Dear, dear Me-me:
     I know that words are hard between us sometimes, and
there are some that have been piling up in my head these last
few weeks that I must speak to you in this personal way. We
go back a long time together. You are my link with Ralph
Harvey and Mary Gray Harvey and Anna Dingley: in other
words, a link with the past — the childhood. Although I have
sisters, as you know, we are not close.
     I've not spoken to Jane for nine years, although I have tried
to call her, and once in a while Blanche calls, but it is like I
was talking to a stranger almost — fond of her though I am.
     The feeling I have for you is a continuous one from the
littlest child that I was. I remember you and Fred too — don't
forget I remember Fred very well, and he was very dear, but
mostly Mary [. . .], of whom my mother would write in her
diary, which I still have, "Mary has been here today, and the
house looks altogether different; the house looks like magic
had made it clean." I share my mother's feeling about you,
only more so, because you were part of my childhood, my
young motherhood, and my adulthood.
     So many things you do for me, so many small things, and
each one I notice and don't always thank you, but I always
notice. Last night I crawled in between clean sheets and

thought, "Thank you Me-me." And there are many things — the flowers you arrange, the seasons you observe, the way you make a room look after you leave it, the pure artistry of the way you cut bushes and little things and water plants and love dogs, which are as much yours as mine.

Now, I know it has been a terrible ripping, the divorce of Kayo and Anne, and it has hurt you a great deal, for you are very fond of Kayo, and who wouldn't be? He is a great man, Mary. I can only say I could not stay married to him any longer and stay alive, and it is very hard for me still to be without him, and harder on him even more perhaps. I do not wish to go into the gruesome details, and I know they say "till death do us part," but there are many kinds of death, and our marriage had multiple ones.

I remember you when I was nine or ten at Oxbow Road, bringing up a coke to me when I was sick, and you were the only one who came all day, even though I was a terribly un- disciplined girl and very messy and even worse than Joy. And inside of me is still that same girl although I try to be more adult, and I am indeed supporting myself somehow by my teaching and my writing. [. . .]

Back to us, Mary. What it means to me that you are still here is that my life is not completely broken, that Mary Gray Harvey and Ralph Churchill Harvey are not quite dead, that not all the beauty of my life has gone out of it, and I want to thank you very much for sticking by me.

I couldn't say these words to you in any way aloud because you would have been embarrassed, and I would have cried. But in a certain way, you are something more special to me than anyone else I have.

Love,

[. . .]

The Wizard's Tears, a children's book published by McGraw-Hill in 1975, was a lighthearted venture in collaboration with Maxine Kumin. Anne invented the cure for the chicken pox and the chocolate cake breakfast.

Readers of all ages felt at home in Anne's study, where the knotty pine shelves were filled with thousands of books, and whenever a daughter, a student, or a friend wanted new reading material, they had only to ask. Joyce Carol Oates's novels were some of her favorite lending books, never safely perched on a shelf for very long.

[*To Joyce Carol Oates*]

[*14 Black Oak Road*]
June 4, 1973

Dear Joyce Carol Oates:

What a wonder the United States Post Office is when it brings forth a letter from one whom I admire so much and read avidly. [. . .]

I don't know quite how I can point out the differences between you and me. You write of heartbreak so well, crunching, terrifying things, and yet are not nervous yourself. You investigate, but perhaps not yourself but something that is so deeply lodged within you like a gall stone that no one has discovered, and you know it not. Of course, when one thinks of the experience or of my own experiences so similar, one could call it just good, old-fashioned drama, but I like my drama to be between a few intimate people, not up on some damn stage being stared at. Of course, one must not avoid unpleasant events. I would say they come to me weekly like a strange tide, but they are usually personal, not public.

Yes, it is my nature to be apprehensive almost constantly, and my hunger for love is as immense as your eating people in *Wonderland.* When I feel the antithesis, I do not know how to get enjoyment out of it, although it is part of life, and as a writer I should enjoy being in touch with agony. I think it is true that I have been given a dramatic role in that I am popularly known as the crazy poet, something I avoid acting out in front of people. And after all, it is my fault. I did write about it thoroughly, explored it so I made my own costume, so to speak, and at each reading I must step into it, although it no longer fits, and I do everything within my power to act perfectly normal and charming and win them over.

Of course, the words come from a communal level of consciousness. As I often say to my students, (I, too, teach at Boston University), don't worry about being original. You will do it quite naturally, but beyond that, it's all one large poem, parts and parts being written by each poet.

I have a feeling from reading your many articles, letters in the New York Times, columns — not especially from reading your creative work — that you have the ability to rush right in, and yet at a remove, something impersonal, as you say. As for your creative work, to speak of the art, the guts leak out and tear at the reader on every level.

I try, I try, I try to gravitate towards the positive emotions, and there *are* many God-given experiences and people. Yet there is a motor in me that keeps vibrating, sucking up the room, and at the same time embracing the people who are in it.

I wish I could borrow some of your surface, your ease, your composure. Please stay just as prolific. To hell with the critics who complain about it. What do they know? For happiness is picking up a new book of yours.

Fondly,

In early 1973 Anne gave a reading in Cleveland, Ohio. She later felt it was such a traumatic experience that she wrote "The Freak Show," detailing each real and imagined horror — from specific commentary on her heartless hosts to generalizations about antagonistic, predatory audiences:

> What's in it for the poet? Money, applause, adulation, someone to hear how the poems sound coming out of the poet's mouth, an audience. Don't kid yourself. You write for an audience ... You are the actor, the clown, the oddball. Some people come to see what you look like, what you have on, what your voice sounds like. Some people secretly hope that your voice will tremble (that gives an extra kick), some people hope you will do something audacious — in other words (and I admit to my greatest fears) that you vomit on the stage or go blind, hysterically blind, or actually blind.

After "The Freak Show" was published in *The American Poetry Review* in 1973, Anne received a furious letter from one of the members of the Cleveland audience, Diane Friebert. Friebert felt that Sexton had mistaken a hall of loving fans for an army of hungry vultures. Anne filed Friebert's letter under "Hate Mail" and then wrote her back.

[*To Diane Vreuls Friebert*]

[*14 Black Oak Road*]
July 20, 1973

Dear Diane:

Jesus, your letter dug deep. I read and reread. It digs and digs. You were the one I read to — or at least the other one aside from Janet Beeler — you and your husband. I do not think the reading itself was bad, and I hope that it gave something to you despite my terrible despair due to its strange beginning.

I want you. I need you. There are few of you. Although you mention many, there are still few. For those I would climb a rope ladder or even crawl on the stage on hands and knees and as I said in my column, "read my God-damned heart out." Of course, you do not come as executioners, but for some reason I am terribly afraid, and I could go on about that in detail, but for those few who did come to hear my living voice I say, "God is holding me."

I did not cut myself off from the positive vibes, although you seem to think I did. It's just that a large fear like a crab was gripping me. As for making money, that really isn't the point. The crab has never even met a dollar bill.

I did not feel cynicism, not really, and as for "hardboiled contempt", that was far from my thoughts. I was like a stick of butter that had come out of the refrigerator and felt itself melting.

I am, very plainly speaking, sorry that I hurt you. "La-de-da" is making fun of myself, is calling attention to the absurdity of the poet reaching for God or the past or the present or whatever.

I could go on for pages, but I won't. I just ask you to forgive me for seeing blindly.

Sincerely,

In September of 1973, after her parents' separation, Joy Sexton had entered a private boarding school in Maine. She wrote letters full of anguish for a home which would never be resurrected. Anne comforted her with answers which resound with the sincerity and warmth found in so much of her earlier correspondence.

[*To Joyce Sexton*]

[*14 Black Oak Road*
circa September 1973]

My darling:

Be strong. Know you are deeply loved by your mother and that it is even a strange thing to be a mother seeing we are only just human beings who live together in our own ways.

Know that I pray for you and your happiness and that I am with you, with you, with you, whenever you DO need me, wherever, whenever. I hope it will help, being at Gould and that you can get away, somehow, from the turmoil, at home and some of the turmoil within you. If — or whenever you wish to call or write or whatever, your muggy is here to listen, or try to listen to any grief or sorrow or even, god bless us all, joyousness that will occur.

My love is with you like a pillow (if and when you need or reach out for it) always, always, always.

Mom

[hand-drawn daisy]

[*To May Swenson*]

[*14 Black Oak Road*]
September 19, 1973

Dear May,

Sorry to hear you've not been well this summer. I do hope this letter reaches you in bare fact and also finds you of stout heart and good health.

I have a favor to ask — one of these terrible grovelling favors that poets ask of one another. Would it be possible for you to recommend me for a Guggenheim? I am three-quarters of the way through a divorce and very broke and have a Christly need for some foreign land and some space to work in. If you would like, please feel free to call me collect (it is so much easier than writing a letter). My numbers are unpublished, unlisted [. . .]

All best wishes for your work and all that can give pleasure or even soothe.

Best wishes,

Only nine months after her separation from Kayo, another crisis erupted. Anne began having serious difficulties with Dr. Chase. While discussing her divorce settlement with her doctor, she inadvertently revealed the truth about her financial status. Dr. Chase, who had adjusted her rates to accommodate what she believed to be Anne's "restricted finances," felt duped and raised her fee accordingly. When Dr. Chase asked Anne to accept realities she did not wish to see, Anne insisted that the doctor had lost her professional objectivity and was confusing her own needs with those of her patient. Anne's powerful and demanding personality made it difficult for any psychiatrist to remain totally objective.

At a time in her life when so many other elements were cut adrift, dissolving, or shattering in her hands, the rupturing of this mainstay was too much. During the fall and early winter of 1973, Anne spent much time hospitalized in the Human Resources Institute in Brookline. Her overwhelming bitterness toward Dr. Chase in the spring of 1974 made termination of the therapy inevitable. After several consultations with a noted psychoanalyst, Anne was referred to a psychiatric social worker, Irene Rosenberg. But the improvement in her condition was slight.

She distorted situations increasingly, often so casually, so skillfully, that she managed to convince those around her, and perhaps even herself, that she was seeing clearly. Although she was earning a substantial living yearly in royalties, readings, and teaching fees, she became obsessed with money and complained bitterly that she was in debt. In letters, she wrote of financial obligations she had not actually incurred, and she repeatedly told friends that she had assumed responsibility for her children's education and support, which was, in fact, paid for by others.

Yet Anne spent money more lavishly than ever on restaurants, wines, clothes. She had succeeded in liberating herself from Thorazine with the assistance of Dr. Chase, but her drinking was escalating sharply, and her friends and family slowly began to admit that she had become alcoholic. She grew harder and harder to live with.

[*To Donald Hall*]

14 Black Oak Road
December 12, 1973

Dear Don,

Humblest sorries. Dear Christ I called the moment my psychiatrist handed out her edict. I've just been too Christly busy — either readings or my class or hospitals. Dear God, only one poem since July and that not finished. I must remember that I am a poet — at least I must remember it now and then and I must get working on a book written (forgive me all poets and critics — indeed the poet and critic in me) in two and a half weeks last January just prior to leaving my husband. After all OF COURSE it needs to be totally rewritten or at least partly because inspiration ain't all — at least for an entire book. [. . .]

I am fed up with a lot of things: the terrible financial responsibility that I alone face with two rather adult daughters — but costly in their schooling which necessitates more readings than I would care to give and may necessitate me going from a part time professor at Boston University to a full time (of course I don't teach English — I am lucky, just a small, ten to thirteen, creative writing class who become my allies, mostly, and I pretend that I am doing some good and I know they feed me too. But there's just so much *time* and if one feels committed, as I do, to writing SOMETHING — for good or bad — then one must absolutely discard anything that is too interruptive or costly emotionally.

I know when I meet you and your dear wife (whose poetry I greatly admire in APR) that it will not be costly at all! It will be fine and right. I hope you're not so angry with my cancellation that you do not share this view — we who finally spoke to each other over your beautiful poem "Gold" must keep on with what might be precious friendship.

Love as ever,

[*To Kathleen Spivack*]

> [*14 Black Oak Road*]
> *January 10, 1974*

Dear Kathy,

All is rush or pain or shit or glory. I think my life is becoming like the Perils of Pauline. It is exaggerating itself. New book [*The Death Notebooks*] comes out February 21st (paper as well as cloth). I'd love to see you when one of us isn't too busy.

> *Love,*

[*To Michael Benedikt*]

> [*14 Black Oak Road*]
> *January 10, 1974*

Dear Michael Benedikt,

Hooray for your creeping. May it soon be jumping and leaping (excuse the rhyme, the meaning being of the only importance). I will certainly send you some poems for P.R. [*Paris Review*]. (Thank God they've got someone good editing it.) I hope you hang around with it for a while because I haven't sent a thing out for almost a year. Much, much work that needs reworking. And why hurry, Anne, I say to myself. They'll shoot you down anyway for being over prolific as I have a new book coming out February 21st.

Because of an old hip injury, it is not within my capabilities to drive to Hampshire College. I can last at the car for about an hour at the very best. Number one problem. Number two problem is the dough. I am certainly not James Dickey who now that he's a movie star is charging $3,500, but I have somehow crept up into the high numbers for reading which is usually $1,500 but I could try to negotiate it downward if you could possibly gather close to that amount.

At any rate, do let me hear from you. Hampshire is very exciting from what I hear, but I'm sure it is *more* exciting now that Michael Benedikt is there.

> *All best,*

Houghton Mifflin brought out *The Death Notebooks* in February of 1974. The reviews were uniformly poor, but Anne was not surprised; she had become inured to the critics' response to her work.

[*To Claire S. Degener*]

[*14 Black Oak Road*]
February 7, 1974

Dear Cindy,

Herewith a copy to send on to H-M Company of the new book [*The Awful Rowing Toward God*]. It's a bit "odd" but after all, *I* didn't do it, the typewriter did it.

I would very much like your opinion of the book as you send it quickly onward to Dick McAdoo and his cohorts.

The stories will come to you, but this somehow took precedence being at last finished after a year of discarding, rewriting, etc., the book that was written in two and one half weeks prior to leaving my husband.

Another book [*45 Mercy Street*] slowly being filled, but I feel it must be quite delayed because part of it is too personal to publish for some time. ("Jesus", Cindy thinks, "What in the hell is this Sexton woman doing?" Answer: "She don' quite know!")

I am fully aware *The Death Notebooks* will get bad reviews even if they were the Song of Solomon. It's the time for me to be cut down in this poetry world.

Love to you and beauteous
secretary,

The Harvard Literary Club wrote Anne in February, inviting her to read at Sanders Theater. She accepted the engagement eagerly: it was the final coup for the girl who had never gone to college. She invited everyone she knew, including Dr. Florence Ehrhardt, her first psychiatrist.

[*To Florence Ehrhardt*]

[*14 Black Oak Road*]
February 20, 1974

Dear Dr. Ehrhardt,

I'm not doing awfully well, but I am trying, very, very hard, and you were a great help to me. We go back a long time you and I, and I feel a very honest, not really "transference" love for you and will continue. You are one of those remarkable people that one finds seldom in life.

I don't know if it would interest you to hear me read, but if it should, I am reading at 8 o'clock at Sanders Theatre, Harvard University, March 7th, Thursday night.

With best wishes,

[*To Joyce Sexton*]

[*14 Black Oak Road*]
February 21, 1974

Dearest Joyball with a tiny bit of jellybean cheeks, I hope my phone call last night was of some help, and I cannot tell you, my dear daisy giver, what it meant to me for you to share your pain and terror and feeling of being cooped up like an animal with me. You must know that I understand only too well. Here I sit at forty-five and have known and often know the very feelings you poured out to me, so what can I say but that MUGGY UNDERSTANDS. She knows where you're at, without you telling me I've known where you're at but have felt helpless because you did not want to speak of it to me but to run, run, run — and that too I understand.

The thing is, honey, I'm afraid those feelings go with you no matter what your environment or what cage you look upon at the moment. You do *need* certain limits, rules, despite that fact that you are 18 and in many, many ways a grown woman and want to burst forth upon the world and be free, free as if you were flying your own airplane or skiing the perfect mountain, or galloping on the most beautiful autumn day on the most beautiful horse, etc., etc. I do know how you *want* to be FREE, and can only say like an old philosopher and suf-

ferer that I am[,] that freedom[,] that freedom[,] comes from
within and with it comes many responsibilities and restrictions that YOU must set for yourself. In this life there is no
exact thing like freedom, not even in love[,] for it carries with
it the necessity to meet the loved one's needs which ideally is
simple and natural and joyful. (What I mean is there is not
one damn thing wrong with love, but I think one has to get
their own animal out of their own cage and not look for either
an animal keeper or an unlocker. I am sure that life can have
a good enough rhythm for even someone as sensitive as you in
time. Loneliness is a terrible thing and to be alone *with*
people can be pretty horrible. To keep a closed mouth, as you
say, as you are locked in the set of stocks is indeed horrible.
If you feel like opening your mouth — then do! And if you
want to ever again open it to me, I would be as honored and
touched as I was yesterday when I received your heartfelt, suffering letter. It means a great deal to me, more than I can put
in words, for I have felt quite alone lately and the fame, the
poetry seem to make little difference.

You say I called at just the right moment as though a message, an invisible message had been sent that you were in
trouble, and I can only say that your letter came as if YOU
had been sent an invisible message that you needed me and
that gave me a sense of meaning to my life that had absolutely melted.

If you would like over vacation or over the summer, we can
discuss further alternatives to Gould and consult with Daddy,
etc. And perhaps your dear Dr. Schoen, although I am pretty
broke, I don't think it would hurt you and I could manage to
pay for you to see her a little — if you have the courage. I feel
she ought to see this letter but will do nothing behind your
back.

You do know that "home" becomes quickly a kind of jail
and your resentment against ANY restrictions makes it hard
on both of us — I guess you feel guilty about being angry, to
no end, of course, in its own way it hurts me although I know
it is perfectly normal and natural. And the gas situation is so
terrible, and I imagine finding jobs is next to impossible unless the Want Advertiser comes through (which I doubt) and

there will have to be a hard look for a job. Even the house cleaning jobs are getting scarce. But we'll put our heads together and think of SOMETHING. I hope you are still looking through the camera's eye. I was indeed amazed by your pictures, extremely original, almost with Xray eyes.

I'm glad you liked *The Death Notebooks*. I am glad you read it. I don't think Linda has. She is too busy. I guess we are all busy, but one does make time for the really important things in life. I treasure your letter more than any I have ever gotten. I love you.

Your daisy lady,
Muggy

P.S. Check enclosed. Hope it will help.

Anne was disgusted with the publicity the Harvard group had arranged; a 5″ × 9″ handbill with the title of *The Death Notebooks* misspelled. Terrified that no one would come, she put together and paid for her own advertising campaign: spot radio announcements, items in suburban newspapers and a full-page photo layout inserted into the Harvard *Crimson* and the Boston *Phoenix* the day before the reading. When she arrived at Sanders Theater that evening, she found a standing-room-only audience awaiting her.

[*To Jeffrey Lant*
Harvard University]

[*14 Black Oak Road*]
February 25, 1974

Dear Jeffrey Lant,

Thank you for your letter. It is hard to read your handwriting, but mine is undecipherable. I thought you might be interested in this flyer (if one could call such professional work by that name) which will be inserted into *The Crimson*, the *Phoenix* as well as distributed to various colleges and universities around and about. I thought your handbill was very nice, but when one calls that "promotion" I think you can see that this that was done in twenty-four hours and paid for by me is somewhat more effective although it all remains to be seen at Sanders Theatre. It is a new experience for me. Except for the very beginning of my career in 1959 to read for the "honor" and then to promote myself at my own expense, but perhaps that's the way it goes and one can learn something from it.

It is nice, I think, for Harvard that I will be taped. (I have never been at any university where this did not happen and thought it a matter of course for it gives the university a wider use of what happens for an hour.)

I do believe you spoke to Dr. Loring Conant or perhaps his wife and said something to the effect that I didn't have confidence in your promotion. I feel that is quite true, although I cast no aspersions upon you yourself — it is just that when one is *used* to doing something like this, one knows *how*. But all life is learning and with the agony, or should I say trauma, of how to put something together. I leave to you a few things to put together: (1) A table beside the podium. (2) A glass of water (not a pitcher, please). (3) An ashtray. (4) Dealing with Houghton Mifflin about the table, etc. for setting up for the sale of the books (if there be any sale). (5) An adequate sound system — and I do really mean adequate — I prefer a mike that bends if it is available. I am practical enough to understand feedback and know that fire engines and jets are unavoidable, but otherwise wish to remind you I am only a voice not a string quartet and would like the best possible and findable sound system that surely Harvard has. (6) I guess you know by now that Dan Wakefield is introducing me. I've forgotten whether he attended Harvard or graduated from Harvard, but he was a Nieman Fellow and will, I think, speak well of me, although, of course, despite a few novels on the best seller list no one will know who in hell he is. I decided *that* didn't matter — enough had gone wrong already.

Let us hope that the reading will go well and all foreboding will reverse instantly as Sanders Theatre and I merge.

With all best wishes,

Paul Brooks had been Anne's editor for eleven years when he decided to retire as Houghton Mifflin's editor-in-chief in December of 1970. Although Anne did spend some interim time working with Arabel Porter, eventually Richard McAdoo took over the editing of her manuscripts.

[*To Richard B. McAdoo*]

[*14 Black Oak Road*]
February 25, 1974

Dear Dick,

Thank you so much for your call on my publication date. I fear I sounded a bit drunk on the phone — but those things do happen. I suppose in certain ways I'm cracking up, but don't let anyone know, because until the poems crack, it's all okay. I thought you might be interested in my "advertisement for myself" done by a brilliant ad agency [Impact Advertising, Inc.] — actually a couple [Robert Clawson and Betsy Duval] who are friends of mine and got this done within actually twenty-four hours. I know it's the picture you hate, but I cannot help but feel it is "more interesting — more provocative" than the one all of you picked. This will be spread throughout the Boston area in the cheapest way possible, but it is a hell of a lot better than Harvard's very mediocre Xeroxed printed announcement of my appearance. At any rate, I thought you would be interested to peek at it and perhaps pass it on for whatever appeal it might have. A long time ago I recommended to you a Robert Clawson as an editor. It was even before we had met. Yet he was the master of this ad along with his superior, brilliant wife and their cohorts. Things are not going too well for their business. It seems as though Houghton Mifflin is missing out on two very perceptive, ingenious, quick witted individuals. I would go on about them if you would like me to at a later date.

I am very pleased with *The New York Times* ad and *The*

New York Review of Books and *The New Yorker* and do hope
the books sells well for you and that you are not too disappointed by bad reviews which are due at this point in my
career.

Hope you find time to read the new manuscript and further
hope you like it.

Love,

[*To Florence Ehrhardt*]

[*14 Black Oak Road*]
April 1, 1974

Dear Dr. Ehrhardt,

How perfectly gracious and loving your note to me [follow-
ing the Sanders Reading] was. The story wondrous for the
child in all of us and your words wondrous for the child/
woman/poet, reader I have become. As for being an actress, it
worries me a bit. I have a certain guilt about the ham in me,
but then if it puts the poem across, I suppose that's *all* that
matters. Yes, I am accustomed to ovations but not from first
Mama-therapist. *That* ovation is extremely precious. When
slowly gaining success I used to say, "if only there were
someone to be proud of me." Your letter fits the bill. I'm
pleased that you thought I looked well — I do endeavor to look
as pretty as possible as some sort of proof that poets aren't
all that queer. With many thanks for your generous letter.

Affectionately yours,

[*To Brian Sweeney*]

[*14 Black Oak Road*]
April 1, 1974

Dear Sweeney;

How nice to be "evocative one". I ought to have more of
your letters that go wild as I think they are good for me.

I too like Dylan Thomas, and anyone who says he was shal-
low is crazy and ought to be immediately locked up or at least
have a muffler put on their mouth.

Of course I have wonderful eyes! And so do you, but then

you're quite aware of it. Yes, indeed it has been five years — I
had not realized it was that long. Yes, last year you insulted
me. When I told you the news of my divorce, your response
was that unfortunately you were not getting one — or something to that effect. What an insult! What a cruelty when I
who have thought of you as a good friend am suddenly put in
the position of lusting after you. Believe me, Sweeney, there
are plenty of men around here. End of discussion . . . It would
be nice to see you once more, but then I just met an Australian fellow who says it's a 27-hour flight. I wouldn't fly 27
hours if Apollo were to greet me at the end of the trip — or
Adam. This Aussie I met is separated from his wife and reminds me crazily of you although he is a bit younger. I suppose he reminds me of you because of the accent and a certain
zest and the fact that he buys my books by the fifties and
hundreds.

At any rate, dear Sweeney, there are so many here who have
heard of you and want to meet you, and there is this here poet
who hopes in the future that could bring us together.

Love,

In the spring she again tried her hand at prose. "The Bat," "The
Vampire," and "The Ghost" were all horror tales of chilling caliber,
but she was unable to interest a publisher.

[*To Claire S. Degener*]

14 Black Oak Road
April 18, 1974

Dear Cindy and Joan [Brandt],

Well, so Chatto and Windus want to drop "O Ye Tongues"
[DN]. This displeases me. I am even sorry I let them drop the
stories from *The Book of Folly*. I don't give a damn about the
"Praying on a 707" [DN]. I always thought the poem stunk
anyway. If you would tell Dennis Enright that I would be glad
to trade "Faustus and I" [DN], which I also don't think too
highly of, although there are those who do. If perhaps he
could write me a letter explaining *why* my last prayer (or
whatever in hell it is) must drop out of Britain, it might help.

So the money advance is not so hot, but then I think those British are pretty cheap anyway and, after all, my major market is the U.S.A.

I am awfully sad about the *New Yorker* — It would have been better if they loathed them than that they almost took them and fought over what was most interesting or the better of the three. Of course, it is pleasant to think the *New Yorker* is so regretful, but I do think "The Bat" is so far superior that they wouldn't have much trouble choosing.

Whither next!

> *Love you,*
> *Anne*

P.S. Still with the palms closed over the happiness of Cindy's recovery.

[hand-drawn daisy]

[*To George Starbuck*]

> [*14 Black Oak Road*]
> *April 18, 1974*

Dear George,

Pursuant to our conversation about my position changing from "part-time professor" to "full-time professor", I am writing a more or less official letter. (You do know how *difficult* it is for me to write anything that is in any way official.)

On with it! I would very much like to teach a second class either to a mixed group of graduates or undergraduates;;;or if we have a great mass of graduates, I would be more than willing to teach two classes of dem guys. At any rate the undergraduate level is not unappealing to me for, as I have outlined to you, I have been busy this year developing a new methodology for bringing the fresh image forth[,] the concept unusual[,] and I have developed what could be called various "tricks". Of course it depends on the students, each being an individual with different needs and potentials. However I have seen it work on the most unlikely student and I would like to give it a certain terminology thusly:

> Creative Writing of Poetry
> Raising of the Unconscious

This is a rather fancy title and yet quite accurate for the

type of work I have been trying to do. That does not mean one forgets form and plot and what makes a good line, and how to end — It means that I have ceased to say words like "cliché", "there is no news in that", but to instead try to show them a method for bringing up strange juxtapositions and of course, I could go on and on about the various methods I have tried.

I could add that I am very fond of my students — even the difficult ones and they are THERE. However, I feel very fed by this kind of teaching and I don't think it is an ego feeding; I think it is an attempt to give back what a few teachers and the Muse have given me.

A few months ago I spoke with President Silber and said I thought I was his only "part-time professor" and his reply was adamant. "You can be *full-time* any time you want to be". I want to be! (Of course at the same salary; but that goes without saying) and I do hope you can find room for me to teach that second course within the department.

All best,
Professor Anne Sexton

[*To Brian Sweeney*]

14 Black Oak Road
April 25, 1974

Dear Sweeney,

I do not know Suzanne Blake's paper in *The National Times*. Is it a good one or a hatchet job? Thank you for sending me clippings that I would never see otherwise — how interesting that Tennessee Williams has ever read me, much less wanting to call his autobiography, *Flee, Flee This Sad Hotel*.

As for me — you asked how I am, and I'd say that I'm writing pretty consistently and dating pretty consistently — but there is no one special.

So sorry about King Nixon. He is our anathema but perhaps, only perhaps, will be thrown out.

Love to you, Sweeney,
Anne

P.S. In truth I'm a little sad.

[To D. J. Enright
Chatto & Windus Ltd.
London, England]

14 Black Oak Road
May 16, 1974

Dear D. J. Enright,
I want to thank you so much for explaining the necessity for cutting *The Death Notebooks*. I am sorry not to be more of a commercial venture for you but what will be will be. Strangely enough in the States I am a rather commercial venture for Houghton Mifflin.

If "O Ye Tongues" [DN] must go, then let's just plain unhook it from the book — most especially if it makes (along with "Praying on a 707" [DN]) the 64-page limit. I feel grateful that I have the Chatto & Windus imprint and can most certainly "bear" with your requirements at this point in time when poetry sales have sunk to such an untimely low. By all means schedule it for next year's program.

May I add that I am an admirer of your own work and hope that such a plight does not exist when you publish it.

With all best wishes,

In the year before she died, Anne began a friendship by letter and telephone with the poet and novelist Erica Jong. They met only twice. The second time was the summer of 1974 when Anne journeyed to New York City to make a record for Caedmon, *Anne Sexton Reads Her Poetry*.

[To Erica Jong
(first handwritten page missing)]

[14 Black Oak Road
June 1974]

There! That's better. You probably can't read a word of that terrible scribble. I haven't written anyone by hand for about ten years — but I wanted the imprint, the touch.

Well, at any rate we met at a reading and it can't be helped. I only want to say . . . that isn't the real me, the woman of the

poems, the woman of the kitchen, the woman of the private
(but published) hungers. Perhaps you knew that? Perhaps I
didn't seem like a goddamn show off at all.

No matter. I hope we can meet and talk privately. I never
get down to New York (if I can help it) but do you ever come
to Boston? Or rather would you come to Boston — I'd love to
have you come out here to Weston and we could sit over beer
or martinis or whatever (tea too if you prefer) and talk and
talk. If you like we could put you up for the night. (Do you
remember when you were little and were making or trying to
make a new friend and you say "can you come over to play?")
That's what I'm trying to say only I'm using up more words.

I loved your first book. I, further, love your second book.
You tell it true. (I just read it yesterday.) I'll make up some
comment for the publishers but right now I want to assure
you that it's the goods and you must take heart and have the
courage! You have some of Neruda's power, some of mine or
Plath's or whoever. Don't dwell on the book's reception. The
point is to get on with it — you have a life's work ahead of
you — no point in dallying around waiting for approval. We
all want it. I know, but the point is to reach out honestly —
that's the whole point . . . I keep feeling that there isn't one
poem being written by any one of us — or a book or anything
like that. The whole life of us writers, the whole product I
guess I mean, is the one long poem — a community effort if
you will. It's all the same poem. It doesn't belong to any one
writer — it's God's poem perhaps. Or God's people's poem.
You have the gift — and with it comes responsibility — you
mustn't neglect or be mean to that gift — you must let it do
its work. It has more rights than the ego that wants approval.
When you come here (I hope you'll come here) I'll show you
something Ted Hughes wrote me about "reviews". I have it
over my desk. It's pretty damn good and helps one take heart.
But *my* point is — if you can feel you are in touch with experience, if you've (so to speak) stuck your finger into experience and have got it right and can put it down so that others
(even other experience tellers) can comprehend their own lives
better, can crawl in closer to the truth of it, then you must get
on with it! And keep right on. The awful blocks — and I've

had them — must be undone[,] for the listener awaits. The listener (reader) waits trembling on the sore hole of his own abyss and he needs you!

Enough. Christ, I sound like a preacher. I've never even thought this out before. But here I sit in my kitchen with the winter sun coming in through the window. The sugar bowl, fat sugar, squatting in front of me and beside me, pasted up on the refrigerator is someone's letter. It says (in only one line) "Thank you, Anne Sexton, for the poetry of your life".

Erica Jong, thank you for the poetry of your life.

with love from my kitchen to your kitchen,

[*To Claire S. Degener*]

[*14 Black Oak Road*]
June 27, 1974

Dear Cindy and Joan,

This note is primarily a business one but, Cindy, it was good to have that conversation about far more important matters such as what is the Meaning of Life; Men, Women and Children; One's destiny, fulfillment and onward to the universal unconscious. Not being a philosopher I feel the best I can come up with is a poem or a story where philosophy might be found without my awareness of its presence — after all, I am only a mere writer of poems and a few stories and a bad play. One does what one can.

ENOUGH!

Re: "The Bat (To Remember, To Remember)"

I in my innocence but with a certain instinct think this could interest a really fine movie director and be made into a damn good movie by the right script writer, director, actors, etc. and there could be dough in it as well (it is hard to forget money *all* the time when one is scratching in the dirt for a treasure chest.) [. . .]

The major thrust of these remarks is that I hate to think of the three stories sleeping somewhere in your offices, and if you do not have the energy to market them I will have to summon up my own.

Re: The Awful Rowing Toward God

(1) I have sold "Riding the Elevator Into the Sky" [AR] to *The New Yorker*, "Rowing" [AR], "The Children", and "Courage" [AR] to *Mundus Artium*, and "The Sickness Unto Death" [AR] to a small English magazine *Contrasts*.

(2) Do you wish to market the remaining ones to, for instance, *Mademoiselle* and its ilk — *Vogue*? *Harper's Bazaar*? *Cosmopolitan* (ugh) and places like that. Do not bother with *Esquire* because my arch enemy James Dickey would vomit on the manuscript if he were in any way forced to publish it.

(3) I am happy to market them myself and wish to rather get on with it for certain places that don't pay but have an immense circulation and can deal with the editors, etc. well.

Re: Present Work.

I actually have finished another book but am glad to have the time to reform the poems, rewrite and delete. I have it in mind to call it *45 Mercy Street* and see no reason why I can't. Do you? I absolutely cannot call it *The Life Notebooks* because I think I have yet to write that book. So much for the unwritten.

End of business letter. Hope I have not bored you to death. And just to add to the ghastliness of it all, I think I need a reply in writing or I'll never remember all your answers.

                                                    Love, love, love,

[*To Linda Gray Sexton*]

                                                    [*14 Black Oak Road*]
                                                    July 3, 1974

July 3rd — looking forward to that WONDEROUOUS [*sic*] DATE, July 21st when first child, a wonder of a daughter came bursting forth into the world. (In other words happy birthday, in other words, my God! That Linda Gray, that Linda Pie, that stringbean has become that surprising age 21!!!!!!!!!! TWENTY ONE! WOW! ZAP! YIKES! ZOOM! POW!

What does a mere mother do upon such an occasion? Aside

from two pairs of very pretty panties (we Sextons always seem to find ours in rags and tatters it would seem.) Well, my darling in her age of ages, what I can I offer up to the gods in thanks for such a woman as you have become, true fighter, true to trust your instinct for right and wrong, a hard worker who can't even afford ketchup in her first apartment/work on her own?

I would tear down a star and put it into a smart jewelry box if I could. I would seal up love in a long thin bottle so that you could sip it whenever it was needed if I could. Instead I, who am lost in stores, and have further lost the Caedmon catalogue, give you bucks. I worked hard for them and I'm sure you realize what kind of work that is —

It would be nice to start them in your OWN saving account to withdraw at will for ketchup by the case or a diamond if it's your present wish, or any damn thing that Linda Gray Sexton who is twenty-one years old might want to do with it, them, dem bucks. I wish they were six million bucks — even more I wish they were stars that would buy you the world. But mothers can't give the world (nor fathers, nor even husbands, lovers or children) — the world sometimes just happens to us, or if we begin with more wisdom than your muggy had, we might help ourselves happen to the world. I feel that wisdom in you and I offer a prayer to it and to its growth.

Dearest pie, today nominated and legally named my literary executor (because I know you know the value, the potential of what I've tried in my small way to write, not only in financial potential for your future income, but maybe, just maybe — the spirit of the poems will go on past both of us, and one or two will be remembered in one hundred years ... And maybe not.)

You and Joy always said, while growing up, "Well, if I had a normal mother ... !" meaning the apron and the cookies and none of this typewriting stuff that was shocking the hell out of friends' mothers ... But I say to myself, better I was mucking around looking for truth, etc ... and after all we did have many "night-night time has come for Linda Gray" and "Goodnight moon" to read and "Melancholy baby" for your tears.

Forgive. Muggy gets sentimental at the thought of Linda pie, little girl, baby, growing and now grown (in a sense although we never stop growing and learning and most learning comes from the hard knocks). Could you possibly keep the amount of this million bucks titled stars to yourself? It is between you and me although the love with which it's given could be plain to a perceptive observer . .
KETCHUP   DIAMONDS   RECORDS   BOOKS?   Who knows, only Linda.

In happy moods, Anne filled the house with the sound of Ella Fitzgerald and danced from room to room. She loved every note, every phrase, every soft croon. When she heard that Ella and Count Basie were giving a concert on Cape Cod she was determined to go, and convinced the *Boston Globe* to sponsor her review of the performance. The *Globe* provided Anne and a friend with tickets and hotel lodgings, free of charge.

[*To Robert Taylor*]

> [*14 Black Oak Road*]
> *July 22, 1974*

Dear Mr. Taylor,
Here is my review of the Ella Fitzgerald–Count Basie concert. I hope you like it. The emphasis is all on Ella because that's where I wanted it to be. When we spoke on the phone, you said I had 1200 words, and I have counted them faithfully and could easily write five more but thought you might need the space.
I enclose the hotel bill for me and my secretary. I hope it is not too steep. Because of the amount I did not feel it would be fair to charge you mileage for the drive.
If you do like this rather unorthodox review, then I hope there will be another occasion to repeat the effort.

> *Sincerely yours,*

[*To Erica Jong*]

[*14 Black Oak Road*]
July 31, 1974

Dearest Erica,

So glad that your dinner party liked me, and of course I do remember saying, "Keep your fuck zipped up until I ask for it!" and I am glad it was of some use. It was wonderful to see more of you, and I'm sure all our lives we'll keep in touch because there is a bond — one of those special ones, and I feel very close to you although our meetings and communications have not been many. There is a vulnerability we share — the warmth, the hunger.

Glad that you could get to know Cindy, and I would take her advice if she steers you toward Sterling and don't worry, they'll do *well* by you. As a matter of fact, they'll probably both be in on it.

I am sad to hear that you and Allan had marital crisis, and I hope the "try again" will work. It is more hell than you could imagine to be on the loose and "dating" is obnoxious. And the men are all what I call "fraidy cats" and it makes it even worse if you're some sort of famous woman because it makes them more afraid or else more enticed and is based on a false assumption. There are many times when I wish I had not left my husband or that at least I had left him for *somebody*, and although that would have engendered guilt on my part, it might be easier than this madness. You are right when you say that women have transcended so much and that men have not. I can only acquiesce numbly when you say you feel "such a deep hunger in myself". My brain waves keep telling me that this is simply disgusting and debasing, but there it is, and I am sunk into a mire this past week of utter despair.

Enough! Your Whitman poem is really fine and makes me feel guilty for the assorted poems I send because gloom *is* cheap, yet one writes what one must. And Oh, God, I would so much rather write for joy and affirmation and have done so only to sink now into this morass.

The enclosed poems come from a 1976 (probably) publication entitled *45 Mercy Street* which is kind of a jumble of a book but does deal with my divorce and a deep love affair that ended in disaster [. . .]

I hope the film *Fear of Flying* is going well, and I can't wait for the next novel that answers the questions the novel poses.

Take care, dear one — dear, dear friend.

Love,

[. . .]

[*To Nolan Miller*]

14 Black Oak Road
[*August 7, 1974*]

Dearest Nolan,

Hosannas for hearing from you. My news is many new books and I'll enclose a biographical data sheet just to let you see the progression of things like becoming a full professor at Boston University and three honorary degrees, etc.

I have just gotten a divorce. The most unfortunate part of it is that I did not divorce him for anyone else. But so it goes. Glad to hear of your fine time in the decent city of London.

Mark Strand is no more "bonded" to *The New Yorker* than I am. It only means they get first look at everything.

Quickly, quickly I am sending you two new poems from a forthcoming book (February 1975) entitled *The Awful Rowing Toward God*, and please forgive the condition of the submitted two poems, but in order to expedite this, I must send you one that is xeroxed.

Love to you, dear Nolan, and welcome back to the beheading
of our King [*President Nixon*],

Rise and Steven Axelrod of the University of Southern California visited Anne in the summer of 1974. Later, they wrote asking significant questions about the evolution of Anne's work, and sent an article they had written.

[*To Rise and Steven Axelrod*]

14 Black Oak Road
September 10, 1974

Dear Rise and Steven,

I so enjoyed reading your article on my work as well as the other review and poem — the poem by the way gets my compliments and admiration. I found your article very insightful although perhaps in places hopeful where I am merely ignorant. How does a poet in 1974 admit they have not read Blake and thus the parallels are perhaps only Jungian. I do think there is somewhere a "visionary mode" in my work, but I'm usually unaware of it until it comes to me. I have read Christopher Smart, at least *Jubilate Agno* and that surely did influence "O Ye Tongues" [DN] but I feel that having never attended college, I am way behind in the important reading I should be doing.

Steve, I don't mind my work being called "confessional" yet I can see why Snodgrass can easily be "domestic". In Lowell's class he did speak of Snodgrass, W. C. Williams, but the Williams and Pound that you quote to me I'm not to this day familiar with [.] Although I've tried a bit at the *Cantos*, I found myself becoming bored. Of course I do know Elizabeth Bishop and Emily Dickinson. I do not know how I feel about such an old poem as "Live" in *Live or Die*. The poems stand for the moment they are written and make no promises to the future events and consciousness and raising of the unconscious as happens as one goes forward and does not look backward for an answer in an old poem. I guess of all my old poems "The Truth the Dead Know" [PO] and the two last stanzas of "The Touch" [LP] have the most meaning for me to this day although that is just a passing thought, and I could change my mind in five minutes.

It was so nice to meet both of you, and I wish we could have had longer and certainly if I am in LA, I will let you know. And of course if you are here, I hope you can find more time to share with me.

All best wishes,

Epilogue

Anne's death was not unexpected. All those close to her had known that one day she would choose to commit suicide. At home in Weston on Friday, October 4, 1974, she took herself quickly and quietly.

Only the day before she had returned from a successful reading at Goucher College in Maryland, where the audience had given her an extended standing ovation. The academic year had just begun at Boston University and her students welcomed her home at the airport instead of meeting her in their weekly Thursday class. At Black Oak Road, housekeeping arrangements looked promising: a new young couple had moved into the basement apartment.

The weather that Friday was particularly invigorating — the "black" oaks and swamp maples were turning color. Anne shared lunch with Maxine Kumin in Newton, and proofread the galley sheets for *The Awful Rowing Toward God* with her as they had done with her previous books. She had planned an evening out with one of the men she was currently seeing. But despite these signs of renewal and strength, she returned home to her death with no dramatics, no warning, no telephone calls.

Of all those who unconsciously prepared for her death, perhaps Anne herself was the most thorough. By July 1974 she had finished putting her house in order, asking particular friends which of her possessions they would like as remembrances, and offering to write holographs of their favorite poems. She had selected a biographer and prepared the Boston University archive of her manuscripts and letters. After much thought, she had appointed her literary executor, and drawn up a will with specific instructions for her funeral. In the last few years she had repeatedly told family members and friends that she wanted a palindrome from the side of an Irish barn carved on her gravestone. The words RATS LIVE ON NO EVIL STAR gave her a peculiar kind of hope.

She was acutely aware of how her death would affect others. In a letter written in April 1969 to her daughter Linda, she attempted to comfort and to hold, anticipating the day when touch would be impossible.

Wed — 2:45 P.M.

Dear Linda,

I am in the middle of a flight to St. Louis to give a reading. I was reading a *New Yorker* story that made me think of my mother and all alone in the seat I whispered to her "I know, Mother, I know." (Found a pen!) And I thought of you — someday flying somewhere all alone and me dead perhaps and you wishing to speak to me.

And I want to speak back. (Linda, maybe it won't be flying, maybe it will be at your *own* kitchen table drinking tea some afternoon when you are 40. *Anytime.*) — I want to say back.

1st I love you.

2. You *never* let me down.

3. I know. I was there once. I *too*, was 40 and with a dead mother who I needed still. [. . .]

This is my message to the 40-year-old Linda. No matter what happens you were always my bobolink, my special Linda Gray. Life is not easy. It is awfully lonely. *I* know that. Now you too know it — wherever you are, Linda, talking to me. But I've had a good life — I wrote unhappy — but I lived to the hilt. You too, Linda — Live to the HILT! To the top. I love you, 40-year-old Linda, and I love what you do, what you find, what you are! — Be your own woman. Belong to those you love. Talk to my poems, and talk to your heart — I'm in both: if you need me. I lied, Linda. I did love my mother and she loved me. She never held me but I miss her, so that I have to deny I ever loved her — or she me! Silly Anne! So there!

XOXOXO
Mom

Index

Linda Gray Sexton is the author of the novels *Rituals, Mirror Images, Points of Light,* and *Private Acts* as well as a book of nonfiction, *Between Two Worlds: Young Women in Crisis.* A graduate of Harvard University, she is Anne Sexton's elder daughter and has served as literary executor of her mother's estate since 1974. She lives in California with her husband and their two sons. **Lois Ames**, one of Anne Sexton's closest friends, is a graduate of Smith College and the University of Chicago. A lecturer on the faculty of Harvard University Medical School, she also maintains a private practice in psychotherapy and lives in Sudbury, Massachusetts.